Greeks without Greece

Faced with discrimination in Turkey, the Greeks of Istanbul and Imbros overwhelmingly left the country of their birth in the years c.1940–1980 to resettle in Greece, where they received something of a lukewarm reception from the government and segments of the population. This book explores the myriad ways in which the expatriated Greeks of Turkey daily understand their contemporary difficulties through the lens of historical experience, and reimagine the past according to present concerns and conceptions. It demonstrates how the Greeks of Turkey draw upon the particularities of their own local heritages in order simultaneously to establish their legitimacy as residents of Greece and maintain a sense of their distinctiveness vis-à-vis other Greeks; and how expatriate memory activists respond to their persecution in Turkey and their marginalisation in Greece by creating linkages between their experiences and both Greek national history and the histories of other persecuted communities. *Greeks without Greece* shows that in a broad spectrum of different domains – from commemorative ceremonies and the minutiae of citizenship to everyday expressions of national identity and stereotypes about others – the past is a realm of active and varied use capable of sustaining multiple and changeable identities, memories, and meanings.

Dr Huw Halstead is a research fellow at the University of St Andrews. He was previously the Macmillan-Rodewald Postdoctoral Student at the British School at Athens (2018), an associate lecturer in the Department of History and a member of the Institute for the Public Understanding of the Past (IPUP) at the University of York (2017–2018), and the postdoctoral research fellow in history at the Humanities Research Centre, University of York (2016–2017). His research focuses on displacement, memory, and public history with a particular emphasis on the Mediterranean world. He is director of the pedagogic project *Personalising History*, which uses oral history to develop educational resources to teach about the Holocaust in secondary education.

Routledge Studies in Modern European History

Italy Before Italy
Institutions, Conflicts and Political Hopes in the Italian States, 1815–1860
Marco Soresina

Ethnic Cleansing during the Cold War
The Forgotten 1989 Expulsion of Bulgaria's Turks
Tomasz Kamusella

The Peace Discourses in Europe, 1900–1945
Alberto Castelli

Israel's Path to Europe
The Negotiations for a Preferential Agreement, 1957–1975
Gadi Heimann and Lior Herman

Liberalism in Pre-revolutionary Russia
State, Nation, Empire
Susanna Rabow-Edling

Bringing Cold War Democracy to West Berlin
A Shared German-American Project, 1940–1972
Scott H. Krause

Greeks without Greece
Homelands, Belonging, and Memory amongst the Expatriated Greeks of Turkey
Huw Halstead

The Mediterranean Double-Cross System, 1941–1945
Brett E. Lintott

For more information about this series, please visit: www.routledge.com/history/series/SE0246

Greeks without Greece
Homelands, Belonging, and Memory amongst the Expatriated Greeks of Turkey

Huw Halstead

LONDON AND NEW YORK

First published 2019
by Routledge
2 Park Square, Milton Park, Abingdon, Oxon OX14 4RN

and by Routledge
711 Third Avenue, New York, NY 10017

Routledge is an imprint of the Taylor & Francis Group, an informa business

© 2019 Huw Halstead

The right of Huw Halstead to be identified as author of this work has been asserted by him in accordance with sections 77 and 78 of the Copyright, Designs and Patents Act 1988.

All rights reserved. No part of this book may be reprinted or reproduced or utilised in any form or by any electronic, mechanical, or other means, now known or hereafter invented, including photocopying and recording, or in any information storage or retrieval system, without permission in writing from the publishers.

Trademark notice: Product or corporate names may be trademarks or registered trademarks, and are used only for identification and explanation without intent to infringe.

British Library Cataloguing in Publication Data
A catalogue record for this book is available from the British Library

Library of Congress Cataloging in Publication Data
A catalog record has been requested for this book

ISBN: 978-0-8153-7290-5 (hbk)
ISBN: 978-1-351-24471-8 (ebk)

Typeset in Times New Roman
by Swales & Willis Ltd, Exeter, Devon, UK

In memory of Giorgos Isaakidis, who first introduced me to the Greeks of Istanbul.

Contents

List of figures x
List of tables xi
Acknowledgements xii

PART I
Introduction 1

Introduction 3

Greeks without Greece: overview 4
Terminology 6
Methodology and sources 8
Structure of the book 13

1 The Greeks of Turkey 17

Istanbul 17
Imbros 26
Greece 30

PART II
Local homelands and national belonging 43

2 *Patrída* as a local metaphor 45

Patrída *as a local metaphor 47*
Through the looking glass: continuity, invention, imposition 49
The 'usable past': the everyday life of national identity 52

3 More than simply Hellenic: belonging and inclusive particularity 59

The Greeks of Turkey: a diaspora community? 59
The Helleno–Romaic dilemma 62

'The Romiós *is one thing and the Hellene is another'* 65
Inclusive particularity (1): Polítes *and Byzantium* 69
Inclusive particularity (2): Imvriótes *and Ancient Athens* 73
Expatriate protoselves 80
Conclusions 83

4 Without barbarians: Turks and *Elladítes* 87

Ethnicity as an 'interpretive prism' 88
Good Turk, bad Turks 91
Nominal and experiential Turks 97
Privileged knowledge (1): the 'bad Turks' 100
Privileged knowledge (2): the 'good Turk' 105
Conclusions 109

PART III
National and transnational histories 115

5 Everyday multidirectional memory 117

Holocaust memory 118
Mediated memory 122
An everyday history of multidirectional memory 124

6 'The Third Fall': commemorations and national history 134

'The 300 who stayed': thinking analogically 134
Commemorating the 1955 Istanbul Riots 138
Commemorating the 1453 Fall of Constantinople 140
1453 and 1821 144
1453 and 1955 148
Transcending the national paradigm: the Federation of
  Constantinopolitans 151
Conclusions 155

7 '*Kristallnacht* in Constantinople': parallel and analogous histories 164

Parallel histories: Armenians and Kurds 164
Analogous histories: Jews and Nazis 169
Asymmetric histories: the Western Thracian minority 173
From 'pogrom' to 'genocide': classifying the persecution
  of the Greeks of Turkey 175
Transcultural memory in personal testimony 178
Transnational nationalism? 182
Conclusions 187

PART IV
Homelands new and old   195

8 Welcome to Gökçeada: the Greek return to Imbros   197

Between 'New Imbros' and 'Old Imbros' 200
Confronting 'the real Imbros': challenges and prospects 207
'Native tourists': belonging in the Imvrian return 210
'When you return to your patrída*': the second generation 217*
Conclusions 223

Conclusions   229

Inclusive particularity 229
The past as a critical mirror 232
Excavating and backfilling the past 233
Everyday multidirectionality 235

Appendix: Tables   238

Table 1 – List of interviewees: Polítes	239
Table 2 – List of interviewees: Imvriótes	242
Table 3 – List of interviewees: second generation	246
Table 4 – Decline in Greek-speaking/Orthodox Christian populations of Istanbul and Imbros	247

Glossary	249
References	250
Index	251

Figures

1	Decline in Greek-speaking/Orthodox Christian population of Istanbul, 1927–2000s	24
2	Decline in Greek-speaking/Orthodox Christian population of Imbros, 1927–2000s	29
3	The Constantinopolitan Society in *Kallithéa* (Athens), 2017	31
4	The Constantinopolitan Cultural Centre in *Ampelókipoi* (Athens), 2017	32
5	*Imvriótes* gathered together in the café of the Imvrian Association, 2017	33
6	The sign for the *Paipalóessa* café in the Imvrian Association, 2017	77
7	Leonidas Koumakis, author of *The Miracle* (see Chapter 7), lays a wreath at the Tomb of the Unknown Soldier on the anniversary of the Fall of Constantinople, 2004	142
8	Speeches at the statue of Constantine Palaiologos in Metropolitan Square, 2013	143
9	Members of the Constantinopolitan associations, holding flags bearing the double-headed eagle of Byzantium, observe the wreath-laying ceremony at the Tomb of the Unknown Soldier, 2004	143
10	*The Annihilation of the Constantinopolitans*, 1979. Poster produced by the Constantinopolitan Society	145
11	'Open the gate. I'm a European!' Cartoon by Zavikos from *O Polítis* November 1997	168
12	Cartoon by Nikos Koilos from *Imvros* May 1985	200
13	Panoramic view of *Schoinoúdi* (Imbros), 2013	205
14	Photographs by Giorgos Xeinos and Vaso Xeinou from *Imvros* October–November 1987	206
15	Looking back along the path in *Agrídia* (Imbros) walked by Kostas and the author in August 2013	212

Tables

1 List of interviewees: *Polítes* 239
2 List of interviewees: *Imvriótes* 242
3 List of interviewees: second-generation 246
4 Decline in Greek-speaking/Orthodox Christian populations
  of Istanbul and Imbros 247

Acknowledgements

First and foremost, I am greatly indebted to my interviewees, who responded thoughtfully and patiently to my questions, were exceptionally welcoming and hospitable, and served me endless cups of the best tea in Greece. The guarantee of anonymity prevents me from thanking them individually by name. Without their enthusiasm and good humour, this book would never have been written.

I am particularly grateful to my guides in Greece for their tireless efforts in helping me locate people to interview and material to read. Giorgos Isaakidis kindly took me under his wing in Athens, providing crucial first introductions to his fellow *Polítes*, and continuously vouching for me as I sought further contacts across the city and beyond. Even though Giorgos and I did not always agree on methodology or historical interpretation (he sometimes jokingly suggested that I was working for MI6!), he continued unfailingly to support my research throughout the project. I also owe a debt of gratitude to my self-appointed research assistant in Thessaloniki, Sofia Livarda, without whom my fieldwork there might never have got off the ground. Stelios Poulados was likewise instrumental in arranging my research with the *Imvriótes* – day after day helping me, in his words, to 'fish' for interviewees in the café of the Imvrian Association – as were Makis Kampouropoulos and Meni Triantafyllou, especially in making my trip to Imbros so productive and enjoyable. Yiannis Stangidis and Lefteris Tsorakis were exceptional guides in Central Macedonia and Western Thrace respectively. The assistance and guidance of Paris Asanakis, Kostas Christoforidis, and Nikos Ouzounoglou were also essential to the successful completion of my research. For hosting my research activities, providing access to archives and libraries, and generous gifts of literature and other source material, I am thankful to the Constantinopolitan Society, the Ecumenical Federation of Constantinopolitans, Ekdóseis Tsoukátou, the Imvrian Association, the Tenedian Society, and the Union of Constantinopolitans of Northern Greece.

My fieldwork in Greece and elsewhere was made possible by the hospitality, generosity, and counsel of Efthimis Ainalis, Pitsa Ainali, Antonis Asanakis, Katerina Asanaki, Periklis Chrysafakoglou, Vassilis Dalkavoukis, Angelos Gkotsinas, Ali Huseyinoglu, Despina Isaakidou, Eleni Konidari, Nancy Krahtopoulou, Alexandra Livarda, Tasos Livardas, Dimitra Papafotiou, Christina Tsoraki-Chan, Eleni Tsoraki, Tasoula Tzelepi, Tasos Tzevelekidis, Vaso Tzevelekidi, Duska Urem-Kostou, Nikos Valasiadis, Rena Veropoulidou, Fani Zafeiri, Thanasis Zafeiris, and

Acknowledgements xiii

the staff at the British School at Athens, the Centre for Asia Minor Studies, and the Historical Archive of Refugee Hellenism.

My research has greatly benefited from the advice, expertise, and insightful observations of Geoff Cubitt, whom I have been most fortunate to have as my mentor over the last ten years. For stimulating discussion and critical comment on my research, I also thank Graeme Callister, Jennie England, Sarah Goldsmith, Joanna de Groot, Paul Halstead, Glynis Jones, Sharon Macdonald, Shane O'Rourke, Sebastian Owen, Asa Roast, Andrew Stead, Corrine Vibert, Tom Wright, and all of my colleagues and friends in the Department of History and in the Humanities Research Centre at the University of York. Valasia Isaakidou, Paul Halstead, Sam Hardy, and Hasan Munusoglu provided invaluable advice on translation (any errors, naturally, are my own). My acquisition of the Greek language was greatly facilitated in the early stages by Nancy Krahtopoulou's encouragement to communicate in 'Grenglish' (pronounced 'Gringlish') and to use Greek as a means of clandestinely expressing my opinions at football matches in the UK.

The research on which this book is based was made possible by the generous support of the Arts and Humanities Research Council, the Humanities Research Centre (University of York), and the James Jarvis Fund. Some of the material used in Chapter 3 has been published in the article H. Halstead, 'Heirs to Byzantium: Identity and the Helleno-Romaic Dichotomy amongst the Istanbul Greek Migrant Community in Greece', *Byzantine and Modern Greek Studies* 38, no. 2 (2014): 265–84. Copyright The Centre for Byzantine, Ottoman and Modern Greek Studies, University of Birmingham 2014. This material is reprinted with permission of Cambridge University Press. Parts of Chapter 7 have been published in the article H. Halstead, '"Ask the Assyrians, Armenians, Kurds": Transcultural Memory and Nationalism in Greek Historical Narratives about Greek-Turkish Relationships', *History & Memory* 30, no. 2 (2018): 3–39. Copyright Indiana University Press. Reprinted with permission. The photograph in Figure 5 was taken by Stelios Poulados, and is reprinted with his permission. Copyright Stelios Poulados. Figures 7, 9, and 10 derive from the archive of the Constantinopolitan Society and are reprinted with the permission of the Constantinopolitan Society. Copyright Constantinopolitan Society. Quotations from unpublished material from the archive of the Constantinopolitan Society are used with the permission of the Constantinopolitan Society. Copyright Constantinopolitan Society. The text from Leonidas Koumakis' *The Miracle: A True Story* (Athens, 1996) quoted in Chapter 7 is reprinted with the permission of Leonidas Koumakis. Copyright Leonidas Koumakis. Figure 11 is reprinted with the permission of the publisher Ekdóseis Tsoukátou. Copyright Ekdóseis Tsoukátou. Figures 12 and 14 are reprinted with the permission of the Imvrian Association. Copyright Imvrian Association. I am grateful to all copyright holders for kindly granting permission for material to be reprinted in this book.

Finally, I want to express my gratitude to my parents, Paul Halstead and Glynis Jones, for their continual support, and for first introducing me to modern Greece; and to Corrine Vibert for her relentless positivity (only she would describe five hours waiting in a sweltering Greek bus station because I got the timetable wrong as 'a really fun time').

Part I
Introduction

Introduction

In a scene from Tasos Boulmetis' *Polítiki Kouzína* – a film set against the backdrop of the deportation of Greek citizens from Istanbul in 1964 – protagonist Fanis recalls how his parents' bickering over trivial day-to-day matters would always descend into debates about important historical events and figures. So, for instance, during a typical family meal in Istanbul in 1959, the Byzantine past is drawn into a household dispute over food, after a young Fanis clandestinely mixes cinnamon into his mother's meatballs. Although she initially protests her innocence, Fanis' mother ultimately finds herself justifying the use of the spice by implying that Constantine Palaiologos, the last emperor of Byzantium, was known to be in the habit of having his meat prepared with cinnamon. Fanis' father – consuming the meatballs – reacts with incredulity to these claims, demanding to know the source of his wife's information. Unmoved by her response that proof can be found in the history books, Fanis' father maintains that as a graduate of the Phanar Greek Orthodox College – a prestigious school in Istanbul – he would most certainly have been informed if Palaiologos ate his meat with cinnamon (Boulmetis 2003)!

In this scene, the most mundane everyday discourse is steeped in the archetypes of the distant past, culinary decisions justified through reference to the dietary habits of a figure who inhabited the city 500 years previously. I am concerned in this book with such 'past presencing', a term I adopt from the anthropologist Sharon Macdonald (2013). Past presencing refers to 'the empirical phenomenon of how people variously experience, understand and produce the past in the present' (Macdonald 2013:52). This is not merely a question of how contemporaries might talk about the past, nor how particular aspects of the past might endure unchanging in the present, but rather concerns the 'interplay of pasts and presents' through which individuals, consciously or otherwise, simultaneously interpret contemporary situations in view of historical experience and reimagine the past according to present concerns and conceptions (Macdonald 2013:55, 216; see also Cubitt 2007:17). More specifically, I am interested in how the Greeks of Istanbul and the island Imbros/Gökçeada – who were pressurised into leaving the country of their birth and subsequently resettled in a somewhat ambivalent 'national homeland' (Greece) – appeal to and rework the past in the present as they attempt to establish belonging in their new place of residence, make sense of their recent historical experiences, and communicate these understandings to others.

Greeks without Greece: overview

Greeks without Greece speaks primarily to four interdisciplinary fields – diaspora studies, migration studies, memory studies, and nationalism studies – that have in recent decades shared two common and overlapping analytical concerns: 1) interrogating the relationships between the local, the national, and the global in a world of flows; and 2) challenging a 'methodological nationalism' allegedly bequeathed to the discipline by earlier scholars.[1] Transnationalism, globalisation, glocalisation, and cosmopolitanism have arisen as key concepts in each field, and researchers have been preoccupied equally with how a 'national gaze' (Beck and Sznaider 2006:11) or 'ethnic lens' (Glick Schiller, Çağlar, and Guldbrandsen 2006) might have distorted previous work, and the extent to which localities and nation-states have been transformed in the interconnected modern world.

Scholarship on diaspora has witnessed debates over the concept of an 'epochal shift' in contemporary history from 'the age of the nation-state to the age of diaspora' (Brubaker 2005:8), and exhibited concern that previous work was constrained by simplistic and unidirectional understandings of migration rooted in the logic of the nation-state and dichotomous conceptualisations of 'home' and 'host' (see Chapter 3). Research on transnational migration flows has prompted a comparable critique of methodological nationalism in migration studies. In an influential paper in 2002, Andreas Wimmer and Nina Glick Schiller characterised methodological nationalism as 'the assumption that the nation/state/society is the natural social and political form of the modern world', and described how this nation-centred lens contributes to the perception of immigrants 'as potential security risks, as culturally others, as socially marginal and as an exception to the rule of territorial confinement' (2002:302, 311). For them, the turn towards transnational understandings of migration in the late 1990s and early 2000s did not mark a new, more mobile historical epoch so much as the beginnings of a move away from an analytical approach governed by methodological nationalism (Wimmer and Glick Schiller 2002:322–323). Scholars of nationalism have similarly extensively debated whether globalisation has weakened or strengthened national identity, reaching sometimes radically opposing conclusions (Ariely 2012:461). There has also been a renewed interest in the ways in which 'ordinary people' experience national identity on local levels, leading some commentators to question the assumed salience of the nation in everyday life, and to criticise earlier work for taking supposedly coherent and tangible national or ethnic groups as the starting points for their analyses (see Chapter 2). More recently, there has likewise been intensive discussion within the field of memory studies as to the impact of globalisation and mass media on the power and coherence of national memory cultures, coupled with a growing dissatisfaction with earlier scholarship for allegedly taking for granted that the nation is the sole or principal mnemonic community commanding people's allegiance and orientating their memories (see Chapter 5).

The Greeks of Istanbul and Imbros are particularly appropriate communities through which to develop and reflect upon these research agendas. They have typically been studied either through the lens of ethnicity and nationalism as a community with a relatively unambiguous national or ethnic identity (Alexandris 1980; Alexandris 1992; Alexandris 2004; Vryonis 2005), or as a community that transcends or represents an exception to national distinctions or categories (Babül 2004; Babül 2006a; Babül 2006b; Örs 2006). I maintain that neither perspective takes full measure of the heterogeneity or complexity of national belonging and national identity, nor of the ways in which the latter is adaptable to particular individuals in different local contexts. The Greeks of Istanbul and Imbros were exempted from a compulsory exchange of population between Greece and Turkey in 1923 (see Chapter 1), but, faced with discrimination on the basis of their ethnic and religious identity, overwhelmingly left their birthplaces in Turkey during the period c.1940–1980 and resettled in what many regarded as their 'national homeland': Greece. Here they received something of a lukewarm reception, both from a government that saw them as abandoning historic Greek territories, and from segments of the population who viewed them with suspicion due to their Turkish birthplace (see Chapter 1). This is a history that is both inherently transnational, and intimately connected to nationalism and national identity in both Greece and Turkey; a displacement that could be – and often is – characterised both as 'exile' and 'return'; and, by consequence, a story that is told by its protagonists in a variety of ways and not infrequently with considerable ambivalence. It is – in the words of one expatriate from Istanbul, known in this book as Maria – about 'a group of people who essentially have two homelands and none'.[2]

Greeks without Greece explores how the expatriated Greeks of Istanbul and Imbros process their experiences of persecution in Turkey and respond to the challenges to their legitimacy as residents of Greece. I document the processes through which they draw upon the particularities of their own local heritages in order to simultaneously establish their authenticity as Greeks and differentiate themselves from the inhabitants of the Greek state. I describe how national belonging can be sought through what I call 'inclusive particularity'; that is, the pursuit of *inclusion* within an imagined national community (Anderson 1983) by emphasising *local distinctiveness* rather than – or as well as – *national sameness*. In doing so, I seek to formulate a conception of national identity that allows for its heterogeneity and malleability in distinctive local contexts, and that declines to be beguiled by its surface impression of homogeneity and unity, but that nonetheless accounts for its durability, its persistence even in a world of flows, and its capacity to sustain claims of national commonality. To borrow terms from Daniel Chernilo, if academic literature has tended to naturalise nationalism, the solution is to 'pay more rather than less attention to the nation-state itself' (2011:112), and in this way to unveil its complexities, contingencies, and contradictions rather than asserting its simplicity, coherence, or irrelevance.

As I discuss in Chapter 1, the Greeks of Istanbul and Imbros commonly express a profound disappointment with the level of support they received from the Greek state, both whilst they were living in Turkey and after their arrival in Greece, and a sense of dismay at the lack of general awareness amongst the Greek populace about their community and its experiences in Turkey. The book therefore also focuses on the efforts of expatriate memory activists to combat this diplomatic and historical marginalisation and raise awareness of their persecution and expatriation in domestic and international forums. I investigate the different ways in which these individuals – through publications, speeches, and commemorative activities – seek to articulate a compelling and intelligible historical narrative of their experiences in Turkey, and, in order to do so, adopt and adapt archetypes both from Greek national history and the mnemonic repertoires of other non-Greek groups. I analyse these discourses in light of the recent 'transcultural turn' in memory studies. I emphasise, first, that national memories are also transnational and multidirectional (Rothberg 2009), in that they frequently involve reaching back-and-forth across national, cultural, historical, and spatial boundaries (even if many of these are boundaries that nationalist historiography seeks to render invisible). Secondly, I demonstrate that even narratives that explicitly cross contemporary national or cultural borders can nevertheless lead narrators to national(ist) conclusions, and, in this way, strengthen some national distinctions and enmities even as others are called into question.

The efforts of scholars to overturn a perceived methodological nationalism in their respective fields have led to a growing sensitivity to discourses, memories, and identities that transcend or blur the borders and boundaries between nation-states, and that obey a 'both/and' rather than an 'either/or' logic (Beck and Sznaider 2006:14). These interventions have arisen not only from a need to question the implicit centrality of the nation in some scholarly analyses, but also from an important and laudable desire to see beyond the exclusion, marginalisation, and violence that have so often accompanied nationalist projects. In *Greeks without Greece*, I seek to further this attention to the mobility and malleability of belonging, identity, and memory in the modern world, but to do so whilst evading the conceptual pitfall that sees fluidity, complexity, and multiplicity as existing only *outside* the national paradigm, and, as a result, is not able satisfactorily to account for the continuing prevalence of nationalism, nor the diversity of its local permutations.

Terminology

I collectively refer to the Greeks of Istanbul and Imbros as 'the Greeks of Turkey', by which I mean those Orthodox Christians who were exempted from the 1923 Greek–Turkish population exchange, distinguished from the 'refugees' i.e. those Orthodox Christian residents of the Ottoman Empire who were exchanged in 1923.[3] I refer to the Greeks of Istanbul as *Polítes* – singular *Polítis* (m.) or *Polítissa* (f.) – a contraction of *Konstantinoupolítes* ('Constantinopolitans'), and use the English adjective 'Constantinopolitan'. My informants – in common with most contemporary Greek speakers – generally refer to the city as *Konstantinoúpoli* or simply *Póli* (I translate both as 'Constantinople'). I call the Greeks of Imbros/Gökçeada *Imvriótes* – singular *Imvriótis* (m.) or *Imvriótissa* (f.) – and deploy the adjective Imvrian.[4] The island Imbros (*Ímvros* in Greek, *İmroz* in Turkish), was officially renamed Gökçeada in 1970, but is still called Imbros/*Ímvros* by its (former) Greek inhabitants, and I follow this convention. This terminology reflects my informants' own terminological choices, and is not intended to pass comment in any way on the political sovereignty of Istanbul or Imbros/Gökçeada. Members of both communities also call themselves *Romioí* – i.e. Orthodox Christians or the descendants of the Eastern Roman Empire – and/or *Éllines*. Although both words are sometimes translated, particularly in non-academic work, as 'Greeks', distinguishing between the two terms is important for my purposes (see Chapter 3). I translate *Éllinas* (m.), *Ellinída* (f.), *Éllines* (pl.), *ellinismós* (noun), and *ellinikós* (adj.) as Hellene/Hellene/Hellenes/Hellenism/Hellenic, and preserve *Romiós* (m.), *Romiá* (f.), *Romioí* (pl.), and *romiosýni* (noun) in the original Greek, as no appropriate translation exists (although I use the adjective 'Romaic'). I reserve the English word 'Greek' and its derivatives for when it is not profitable (or possible) to distinguish between the Hellenic and the Romaic. When distinguishing themselves from other Greeks, my interviewees frequently (and sometimes interchangeably) deploy the terms *Elladítes* (meaning 'Greeks of Greece', i.e., loosely speaking, those born in the Greek state) and *dópioi Éllines* ('native Greeks', i.e., strictly speaking, *Elladítes* of non-refugee origin, but sometimes used by informants to refer more generally to all *Elladítes*; literally, 'people of this place' (Cowan 1997:153)). I use the terms '*Elladítes*' (singular *Elladítis* (m.) and *Elladítissa* (f.)) and 'Greeks of Greece' interchangeably to mean 'Greeks born in the Greek state'. I do so in order to convey the distinction drawn by interviewees between themselves and the Greeks they encountered when they arrived in Greece, though it should be noted that this terminology masks significant internal diversity within Greece. I reserve 'native Greeks' to refer to residents of the Greek state of non-refugee origin.

As a collective noun to refer to those *Polítes* and *Imvriótes* who left Turkey after 1923 (the vast majority of both communities), I have settled upon 'expatriates'. This term is far from perfect, but has been chosen as a compromise that best reflects the diverse experiences of the Greeks of Turkey. Within the community, there is significant uncertainty over how they should categorise themselves, and different individuals present their emigration from Turkey in different ways. Interviewees generally (though not exclusively) avoid the label 'refugee'. With the exception of those expelled as Greek citizens in 1964 (who commonly call themselves 'expellees'), they were not *forcibly* removed from Turkey. At any rate, in Greek discourse the term 'the refugees' is typically used to refer specifically to those who left Turkey as part of the 1923 compulsory population exchange with Greece. The umbrella term 'forced migrants' would be inappropriate for similar reasons, whilst 'exile' has connotations of politically motivated displacement. Nevertheless, the majority of my informants feel that they were compelled to leave Turkey by factors beyond their control, and accordingly generally eschew the term 'migrant', lest it be interpreted that they relocated to Greece for economic reasons. Community organisations founded by the Greeks of Turkey in Greece have used the terms *ekdiochthéntes* (literally: 'those who have been driven out') and *ekpatristhéntes* ('those who have been expatriated'), and when publishing material in English typically prefer variations upon 'the expatriated Greek community of Istanbul' (Ouzounoglou 2014). This terminology presents problems of its own, partly as its etymology (from the Latin *ex-* ('out') and *patria* ('fatherland')) implies a rather unidirectional and static understanding of homeland somewhat inappropriate to the Greeks of Turkey (see Chapter 3), and partly because in British usage 'expat' is commonly taken to mean an individual living abroad by choice, often for the purposes of work or retirement. Taken more literally, however, to mean 'those living outside their country of birth', the term 'expatriates' has the distinct advantage of covering the diverse range of reasons given by the Greeks of Turkey for their emigration, from those who were forcibly expelled as Greek citizens to those (few, amongst my informants) who left for personal or economic reasons.

Methodology and sources

In this book, I draw first and foremost on oral testimonies, primarily produced during fieldwork in Greece between 2011 and 2015.[5] I was first introduced to oral history by my father, the archaeologist Paul Halstead, who often took me along as he conducted ethnographic fieldwork with agricultural communities in the Mediterranean. He has always felt that these encounters are most productive when they are approached in an open, fluid, and relatively informal manner, so much so that in a monograph based on his findings he keeps the word 'interview' at arm's-length:

> Informants did not sign 'informed consent' forms. Some, whom I had known for decades, would have treated any such request with disbelief. Others I met for the first time when I 'interviewed' (i.e., talked with) them, and any invitation to sign a printed form would have ended our acquaintance before it began. A few were illiterate, some had failed eyesight, and several died before I thought of writing about what they told me. Informants often provided greatest insight when they strayed from the preplanned questions that a consent form would have covered.
>
> (P. Halstead 2014:ix)

My approach is similar. I avoided a rigid pre-determined questionnaire that would have risked unnecessarily imposing my own pre-conceived ideas and narrative structure upon my informants' narratives (P. Halstead 2014:6–7; Portelli 1991:xi, 54; Thompson 1981:294). I began all my interviews by soliciting a 'life history', usually with the statement 'tell me about your life', in order to see what topics and themes my informants' narratives would gravitate towards without external guidance. As I have discussed elsewhere, many of my interviewees' life histories either emphasise particular incidents of violent intercommunal strife whilst eliding benign aspects of daily life, or stress harmonious everyday coexistence whilst skipping over intercommunal flashpoints, reflecting divergent contemporary understandings of self and belonging (H. Halstead 2014).[6]

It is, nevertheless, impossible to remove the social presence of the interviewer from the interview context – even if he/she says very little – as testimony is always delivered with an audience in mind (Portelli 1991:54–55; Portelli 1997:9–10; Thompson 1978:139–140, 157; Tonkin 1992:2, 54). In Alessandro Portelli's terms, 'informants tell [researchers] what they believe they want to be told and thus reveal who they think the researcher is' (1991:54). Indeed, it was apparent that some of my interviewees had assumed that my research would focus on a particular topic or period, and selected the material for their initial narrative accordingly. At a meeting of the Union of Constantinopolitans of Northern Greece, for instance, I was introduced as 'a young man who is writing a thesis about the Istanbul Riots', though all I had myself said is that I wanted to write about the memories of the Greeks of Istanbul. After the meeting, I was approached by Ioanna, who immediately launched into a narrative about her life in Istanbul and migration to Greece structured around her experiences during the riots in 1955, delivered at a frenetic pace with liberal back-and-forth between the traumatic experiences of the past and her contemporary nostalgia for the city of her birth (Ioanna 21/11/2011). When we met for an in-depth interview at a later date in the more relaxed setting of her home, the narrative velocity (Portelli 1991:49) of her life history was notably changed, and her account was furnished with details that were absent in our original encounter (Ioanna 23/11/2011). As this example demonstrates, the content and form of a life history are significantly influenced by the particular context of its capture, as well as narrative genres/archetypes and prior rehearsals typically unavailable to the researcher (Bertaux-Wiame 1982:193; Leydesdorff *et al.* 1999:15; Portelli 1991:61; Schrager 1998:284; Tonkin 1990:34; Tonkin 1992:57). My social presence as a British researcher (and therefore always partly an outsider) speaking Greek (and therefore in some sense an insider) doubtless also played a role in shaping interviewees' narratives, though not necessarily in a consistent way. Some interviewees may have felt more comfortable passing negative comment about both Turkey and Greece to a foreign ethnographer, or conversely that they should conceal 'culturally intimate' (Herzfeld 1997) details from an outsider; speaking Greek may have given me access to this culturally intimate space but also inclined some interlocutors to assume that I would adopt a particular stance on Greek–Turkish conflict; and on at least one (though I think rare) occasion an interviewee surreptitiously sought reassurance from one of my contacts that I was not an agent of the Turkish state.

It is, therefore, important to recognise that oral histories are inherently subjective and protean; 'partial truths', in James Clifford's terms (1986:6–7). Yet if it is this subjectivity that has commonly been highlighted by the discipline's detractors, it is also its most productive analytical asset (Portelli 1991:ix, 26; Thompson 1978:160; Tonkin 1992:8; Yow 1994:25). Selective emphasis, omission, inconsistency, and even demonstrable historical error in oral accounts can themselves generate important observations about the meaning that individuals derive from historical events; as Portelli has stressed, '"wrong" statements are still psychologically "true"' and may tell us 'less about *events* than about their *meaning*' (1991:15, 50–51). Accordingly, rather than subscribing to a 'positivistic fetish of noninterference', Portelli urges oral historians to recognise that 'the changes that our presence [as interviewers] may cause' may be 'some of the most important results of our field work' (Portelli 1991:43–44). From this perspective, the 'inter/view' is a 'mutual sighting' between researcher and informant, and a respectfully challenging and dissenting interviewer employing a dialogic approach is more likely to gain access to a nuanced personal narrative that dissents from formal or official discourse (Portelli 1991:31; Portelli 1997:12).

For these reasons, after giving my interviewees the opportunity to offer a life history for as long as they wished, I followed up with a more fluid dialogue in which I allowed informants to explore and question my perspectives as well as *vice versa*. On occasion, I posed purposefully leading questions in order to see how interviewees would react to my perceived assumptions, or introduced loaded terminology such as 'identity' or 'nation' to explore how they would respond to these categories. Sensitive, however, to the danger – as J. Paul Goode and David R. Stroup put it – that 'those who go looking for ethnic behaviour will assuredly find it' (2015:13), I began the dialogic portion of my interviews with more open-ended questions, adopting a 'wait-and-listen approach' (Fox and Miller-Idriss 2008:556–557) to see what discursive frameworks my informants would choose for themselves. This often required a degree of orchestrated naivety, such that the interviewee, 'in an effort to teach or inform the interviewer' (Goode and Stroup 2015:13), might reveal information that would otherwise have seemed too 'obvious' to them, or explain and deconstruct familiar categories or narratives for the researcher's benefit. Having waited and listened, I also proceeded to ask questions and to probe topics that might achieve what Jon Fox has recently called 'breaching the nation' – that is, making its subtle or taken-for-granted influence explicit – by exposing its 'spatial, temporal, and political edges' (Fox 2017:41). This included, for instance, exploring border crossings (first visits to Greece, return trips to Turkey, conversations with Greek and Turkish officials at border posts); encounters with 'others' (whether Turks or other Greeks) and representatives of national authority (e.g. when renewing work/residence permits at the 'Aliens' Bureau' (*Tmíma Allodapón*); and moments of heightened popular nationalism and/or political upheaval (such as the Greek financial crisis, Greek and Turkish national holidays, or episodes of Greek–Turkish bilateral tension or reconciliation). Often these dialogues elicited some consternation and prompted 'nationally inflected repair work' (Fox 2017:33, 41–42) as interviewees came face-to-face with memories that seemed to run contrary to the rhythms of national history or of the life history hitherto expressed, and in the process revealed some of the slippery internal workings of nationhood.

Oral histories, following Portelli, are typically 'told with the present in mind', and are marked by extensive 'narrative shuttlework' between past and present or 'the use of history as a repertory of examples' (Portelli 1991:65). Such multitemporality (Macdonald 2013:54–56) makes oral history an ideal methodology with which to explore past presencing, or how the past impinges upon the present (and *vice versa*) and what it means to people in their contemporary lives. It does not follow, of course, that we should unthinkingly equate discourses solicited in the course of an oral history interview with the ways in which people talk about the past on a day-to-day basis. Interviewees may feel freer or more constrained when discussing a particular topic in an interview context than they would with their peers in quotidian interactions, or may simply have recourse to categories that do not serve as salient frameworks in their everyday lives (Fox and Miller-Idriss 2008:555). Accordingly, I supplement the findings of my oral histories with information drawn from participant observation – for instance, by attending expatriate social and cultural events, and by joining the seasonal return of the Greeks to Imbros (see Chapter 8) – as well as conducting interviews in diverse social settings and, in some cases, with multiple participants, in order to observe how changing discursive contexts might influence individuals' narratives.

Nevertheless, I want to emphasise that whilst oral histories may not be able to tell us anything about the *salience* of particular categories or discourses in everyday life, it would be a mistake to assume that their content is somehow created *ex nihilo* at that particular moment in time. Oral histories are not the same as everyday discourse, but they do commonly draw on narratives that have been acquired, developed, and tested in the course of everyday life. As Samuel Schrager has argued:

> [T]he oral historian is an intervener in a process that is already highly developed [. . .] In any such performance there is new and unique creation [in which] the oral historian has a participatory role. But here, as in most circumstances of storytelling, most of what is told has been said before in a related form [. . .] An account's previous tellings give it validity apart from the moment of the interview. If it belongs to the teller's repertoire of narrative, it is grounded in his or her life and in the social world in which that life is lived.
>
> (1998:284–285)

In what follows, I take care not to interpret oral testimonies as a static representation of how people would talk about the past in any context, but nor do I treat informants' responses to the discursive challenges occasioned by the oral history interview as necessarily alien to those emerging in response to the challenges of everyday life. I seek to understand oral histories within their discursive context without disregarding their potential to tell us something about the capacities people have for organising past and present more generally.

I conducted 107 oral history interviews with 49 *Polítes* and 58 *Imvriótes*, of whom 17 (5 *Polítes*, 12 *Imvriótes*) were from the second generation born outside Turkey. These two communities were selected for analysis not only because of their simultaneously distinctive and overlapping histories, but also because of the interesting opportunity for comparison between an urban and a rural population (see particularly Chapter 3). I reference these interviews in the text in the format '*pseudonym* dd/mm/yyyy' (pseudonyms are employed as many interviewees requested anonymity, principally out of concern that something they said might create difficulties for them on any future journeys to Turkey). Biographical details of the interviewees can be found in Tables 1–3 in the Appendix. I also conducted interviews with

Giorgos Isaakidis of the Constantinopolitan Society and Nikos Ouzounoglou of the Ecumenical Federation of Constantinopolitans about the work of their respective organisations: both consented to be referred to by name. Interviewees were located, variously, via expatriate community organisations (both through formal introductions and by providing a venue for meeting community members); by asking interviewees to introduce me to friends and relatives; through mutual acquaintances or chance encounters; and by approaching shopkeepers whose establishments boasted likely sounding names. Interviewees were given free rein to select the interview setting, and whilst some chose to conduct interviews in private so that their narrative would not be disturbed, others preferred to be interviewed in public places, sometimes involving friends or passers-by in the discussion.

Additionally, I make use of interviews with 47 expatriates conducted and published by Turkish researchers for a project undertaken as part of Istanbul's tenure as the European Capital of Culture 2010 that was 'designed to find out the nostalgic aspects of Istanbul as pronounced by its former dwellers [. . .] and their reasons for departure' (Turan *et al.* 2010:243). The interviews were primarily conducted in Turkish and in Athens or Thessaloniki, and were presented alongside biographical information and personal photographs, though the interviewers' voices have been silenced in the transcripts such that it is not possible to determine what questions were asked. I also take into consideration 50 testimonies from witnesses to the 1955 Istanbul Riots collected and published by Ekdóseis Tsoukátou (1999), the publisher of the expatriate newspaper *O Politis* (see below). These testimonies were mostly solicited by *O Politis* and sent in by witnesses – sometimes anonymously, sometimes not – although the volume also includes testimonies from the archive of the Constantinopolitan Society, and two testimonies adapted from Leonidas Koumakis' semi-autobiographical novel *The Miracle* (1996; see Chapter 7).

I integrate these personal testimonies with a range of other written sources drawn from the archives of the expatriate organisations, including institutional correspondence, press releases, publicity materials, and, in particular, the two most prominent expatriate newspapers: the Constantinopolitan *O Politis* ('The Citizen' or 'The Constantinopolitan') and the Imvrian *Imvriaki Ichó* ('Imvrian Echo'), which was renamed *Imvros* in 1975. *O Politis* was founded in 1967 by members of the Association of Hellenic Citizens Expelled from Turkey, although as it emphasised in its inaugural issue it was to cater not just to those Greeks forcibly expelled from Turkey in 1964 but to the entire expatriate Constantinopolitan community (*O Politis* 1967). Since then, the paper has been in continuous monthly publication, dealing particularly with issues relating to the Greeks of Turkey and broader Greek–Turkish relations, as well as domestic developments in both Greece and Turkey. According to a source at Ekdóseis Tsoukátou, in 2012 the newspaper had 4000 subscribers; the majority of these were resident in Greece, followed by subscribers living in Turkey. *Imvriaki Ichó* was first printed in 1971 by the Imvrian Association in Athens with the intention of filling the gap left by the discontinuation of two Imvrian journals (*Imvriaki Ichó* 1971). The newspaper is published monthly, bimonthly, or occasionally tri-monthly. It is first and foremost a community publication and organ of the Imvrian Association, but also deals with issues affecting Greece and Turkey more generally.

Structure of the book

Greeks without Greece is divided into four parts. Part I concludes in the chapter that follows, in which I sketch out the recent history of the Greeks of Istanbul and Imbros in Turkey and in Greece. Parts II and III are each made up of three chapters, and both parts begin with theoretical chapters (Chapter 2 and Chapter 5) establishing the scholarly context and conceptual direction of the two chapters that follow. In Part II, I focus on the representation of self and others by the Greeks of Turkey, and what these can tell us about the relationship between the locality and the nation. Chapter 2 proposes parallels between the historian Alon Confino's work on the *Heimat* idea in German nation building and the Greek concept of *patrída* ('homeland'), both of which can interchangeably refer to an abstract national homeland and a familiar local one. My discussion not only repudiates an analytical opposition between the locality and the nation, but also demonstrates how the two might be mutually reinforcing. I develop this idea in Chapter 3, exploring how the expatriated Greeks of Istanbul and Imbros mobilise the particularities of their origins to develop a distinctive Greek identity. I further this discussion of identity and belonging in Chapter 4 by considering the variable ways in which members of the expatriated community depict two 'others' in their personal testimonies: Turks and *Elladítes* (or Greeks of Greece).

In Part III, I turn my attention to expatriate memory activism and the construction of historical narratives about the Greeks of Turkey. This section adds an explicitly transnational dimension to the analysis, as it explores not only the connections between expatriate commemoration and Greek national history, but also how these relate to broader regional and global histories of violence and to international human rights discourse. Accordingly, I begin in Chapter 5 by discussing the recent 'transcultural turn' in memory studies, and I argue that this literature would benefit from paying closer attention to the local and everyday aspects of memories on the move. Chapter 6 then investigates how expatriate organisations create linkages between local experience and national history, focusing in particular on the commemorative activities organised by two organisations founded by expatriated Greeks from Istanbul for the anniversaries of the 1955 Istanbul Riots and the 1453 Fall of Constantinople. In Chapter 7, I examine the ways in which the Greeks of Turkey draw parallels between their own experiences and those of other persecuted communities, namely the Armenians, the Jews, and the Kurds.

Finally, Part IV moves on to more recent developments, by exploring the Greek return to Turkey and the transmission of memory and identity to the younger foreign-born second generation. In Chapter 8, I focus on the growing seasonal, semi-permanent, and permanent return of Greeks to Imbros, which has precipitated a struggle not only to tackle the practical obstacles involved in the re-establishment of a Greek community on the island, but also to confront a multitude of daily challenges to the returnees' sense of belonging in a locality greatly transformed by changes to its demographics, its built environment, and its touristic status. The possibility of returning to a locality with (at least in the summers) an active Greek community somewhat sets the *Imvriótes* apart from the Greeks of Istanbul, and has had a noticeable impact upon the Imvrian returnees' sense of self and belonging, the relationship of the community to Greece and Greek national history, and the identity of the second generation that increasingly visits the island in the summers alongside their parents.

Notes

1 For general discussion of the notion that methodological nationalism is a recurrent problem in social theory see, for instance, Beck and Sznaider (2006); Chernilo (2008); Chernilo (2011); Wimmer and Glick Schiller (2002).
2 In the original Greek, this is '*mía merída anthrópon pou ousiastiká eímaste me dúo patrídes kai chorís patrída*'.
3 The Greeks of Tenedos – neighbouring island to Imbros – were also exempted from the 1923 exchange, but are not dealt with in detail in this book.
4 *Imvriótes* is the slightly more informal term typically preferred by the Imvrian Association and most of my interviewees. Greek and Imvrian writers also commonly refer to the Greeks of Imbros as *Imvrioi*. For clarity and consistency, I translate *Imvrioi* (and its singular equivalents) as *Imvriótes* (and its singular equivalents) throughout.
5 There is something of a gender imbalance in my sample (71% male, 29% female), which can be accounted for in large part by the fact that, particularly amongst older age groups, men were more likely to frequent community organisations, cafés, and other public meeting places than their female counterparts, making it more difficult to make contact with potential female interviewees. As I sought to address this imbalance during my fieldwork, however, I also sometimes ran into difficulties due to the perception seemingly held by some potential informants that speaking about history (or at least the kinds of history it was often assumed that I was interested in) and talking to a foreign ethnographer were characteristically 'masculine' activities. On one particular occasion, for instance, I had arranged by telephone to meet a female informant, only to arrive at the meeting and find that her husband (with whom I had never spoken) had come in her stead.
6 It was sometimes suggested to me, by both interviewees and colleagues, that I might find clear patterns in narrative emphasis (for example, that those expelled from Turkey as Greek citizens, or those with personal memories of the 1940s and 1950s, would express particularly resentful and strife-laden narratives). In practice, however, both antagonistic and harmonious accounts were offered to me by individuals with broadly comparable biographies (and not infrequently by the same individuals), and different constructions of the past came to the fore in different narrative, social, and temporal contexts. For examples see H. Halstead (2012:70–71, 94–99); H. Halstead (2014).

References

(Items marked * are in the Greek language.)

Alexandris, A. (1980). Imbros and Tenedos: a study of Turkish attitudes toward two ethnic Greek island communities since 1923. *Journal of the Hellenic Diaspora*, 7(1), 5–31.

Alexandris, A. (1992). *The Greek minority of Istanbul and Greek–Turkish relations, 1918–1974*. Athens: Centre for Asia Minor Studies.

Alexandris, A. (2004). Religion or ethnicity: the identity issue of the minorities in Greece and Turkey. In R. Hirschon (Ed.). *Crossing the Aegean: an appraisal of the 1923 compulsory population exchange between Greece and Turkey*. New York: Berghahn Books, 117–132.

Anderson, B. (1983). *Imagined communities: reflections on the origin and spread of nationalism*. London: Verso.

Ariely, G. (2012). Globalisation and the decline of national identity? An exploration across sixty-three countries. *Nations and Nationalism*, 18(3), 461–482.

Babül, E. (2004). Belonging to Imbros: citizenship and sovereignty in the Turkish Republic. Paper presented at the conference *Nationalism, Society and Culture in Post-Ottoman South East Europe*. 29–30 May 2004. St Peter's College, Oxford. Available at: www.academia.edu/6707095/Belonging_to_Imbros_Citizenship_and_Sovereignty_in_the_Turkish_Republic [Accessed on 17 April 2016].

Babül, E. (2006a). Claiming a place through memories of belonging: politics of recognition on the island of Imbros. *New Perspectives on Turkey*, 34, 47–65.

Babül, E. (2006b). Home or away? On the connotations of homeland imaginaries in Imbros. *Thamyris/Intersecting: Place, Sex and Race*, 13(1), 43–53.

Beck, U. and Sznaider, N. (2006). Unpacking cosmopolitanism for the social sciences: a research agenda. *The British Journal of Sociology*, 57(1), 1–23.

Bertaux-Wiame, I. (1982). The life history approach to the study of internal migration: how women and men came to Paris between the wars. In P. Thompson and N. Burchardt (Eds). *Our common history: the transformation of Europe*. Atlantic Highlands: Humanities Press, 186–200.

Boulmetis, T. (Director). (2003). *Politiki kouzína*. [Film]. Athens: Village Roadshow Productions Hellas SA.

Brubaker, R. (2005). The 'diaspora' diaspora. *Ethnic and Racial Studies*, 28(1), 1–19.

Chernilo, D. (2008). *A social theory of the nation-state: the political forms of modernity beyond methodological nationalism*. London; New York: Routledge.

Chernilo, D. (2011). The critique of methodological nationalism. *Thesis Eleven*, 106(1), 98–117.

Clifford, J. (1986). Introduction: partial truths. In J. Clifford and G. E. Marcus (Eds). *Writing culture: the poetics and politics of ethnography*. Berkeley, CA; London: University of California Press, 1–26.

Cowan, J. K. (1997). Idioms of belonging: polyglot articulations of local identity in a Greek Macedonian town. In P. A. Mackridge and E. Yannakakis (Eds.). *Ourselves and others: the development of a Greek Macedonian cultural identity since 1912*. Oxford: Berg, 153–171.

Cubitt, G. (2007). *History and memory*. Manchester: Manchester University Press.

Ekdóseis Tsoukátou. (1999). Septemvrianá *1955: The 'Kristallnacht' of the Hellenism of Constantinople*. Athens: Ekdóseis Tsoukátou.*

Fox, J. E. (2017). The edges of the nation: a research agenda for uncovering the taken-for-granted foundations of everyday nationhood. *Nations and Nationalism*, 23(1), 26–47.

Fox, J. E. and Miller-Idriss, C. (2008). Everyday nationhood. *Ethnicities*, 8(4), 536–563.

Glick Schiller, N., Çağlar, A., and Guldbrandsen, T. (2006). Beyond the ethnic lens: locality, globality, and born-again incorporation. *American Ethnologist*, 33(4), 612–633.

Goode, J. P. and Stroup, D. R. (2015). Everyday nationalism: constructivism for the masses. *Social Science Quarterly*, 96(3), 717–739.

Halstead, H. (2012). *Heirs to Byzantium: multidirectional narrative and identity amongst the Istanbul-Greek migrant community in Greece.* Unpublished: University of York. MA by research.

Halstead, H. (2014). Harmony and strife in memories of Greek–Turkish intercommunal relationships in Istanbul and Cyprus. *Journal of Modern Greek Studies*, 32(2), 393–415.

Halstead, P. (2014). *Two oxen ahead: pre-mechanized farming in the Mediterranean.* Chichester: John Wiley & Sons.

Herzfeld, M. (1997). *Cultural intimacy: social poetics in the nation-state.* New York: Routledge.

Imvriakí Ichó. (1971). The 'Imvrian Echo', and its targets, October 1971.*

Koumakis, L. (1996). *The miracle: a true story.* Translated from the Greek by P. Tsekouras. Athens.

Leydesdorff, S., Dawson, G., Burchardt, N., and Ashplant, T. G. (1999). Introduction: trauma and life stories. In K. L. Rogers, S. Leydesdorff, and G. Dawson (Eds.). *Trauma and life stories: international perspectives.* London; New York: Routledge, 1–26.

Macdonald, S. (2013). *Memorylands: heritage and identity in Europe today.* London; New York: Routledge.

O Polítis. (1967). Appeal to our friends the readers, June 1967.*

Örs, İ. R. (2006). Beyond the Greek and Turkish dichotomy: the *Rum Polites* of Istanbul and Athens. *South European Society and Politics*, 11(1), 79–94.

Ouzounoglou, N. (2014). Skype interview with author. Athens/York, 16 May 2014.*

Portelli, A. (1991). *The death of Luigi Trastulli and other stories: form and meaning in oral history.* Albany: State University of New York Press.

Portelli, A. (1997). *The battle of Valle Giulia: oral history and the art of dialogue.* Madison: University of Wisconsin Press.

Rothberg, M. (2009). *Multidirectional memory: remembering the Holocaust in the age of decolonization.* Stanford: Stanford University Press.

Schrager, S. (1998). What is social in oral history? In R. Perks, (Ed.). *The oral history reader.* London; New York: Routledge, 284–299.

Thompson, P. (1978). *The voice of the past: oral history.* Oxford; New York: Oxford University Press.

Thompson, P. R. (1981). Life histories and the analysis of social change. In D. Bertaux (Ed.). *Biography and society: the life history approach in the social sciences.* Beverley Hills: SAGE Publications, 289–306.

Tonkin, E. (1990). History and the myth of realism. In P. R. Thompson and R. Samuel (Eds). *The myths we live by.* London; New York: Routledge, 25–35.

Tonkin, E. (1992). *Narrating our pasts: the social construction of oral history.* Cambridge: Cambridge University Press.

Turan, Ç., Pekin, M., and Güvenç, S. (2010). *Constantinople/Istanbul, my nostalgia: refugee narratives and the nostalgia of the* Romioí *of Constantinople/Istanbul.* Istanbul: Lozan Mübadilleri Vakfı. [In Greek and Turkish].

Vryonis, S. (2005). *The mechanism of catastrophe: the Turkish pogrom of September 6–7, 1955, and the destruction of the Greek community of Istanbul.* New York: Greekworks.

Wimmer, A. and Glick Schiller, N. (2002). Methodological nationalism and beyond: nation–state building, migration and the social sciences. *Global networks*, 2(4), 301–334.

Yow, V. R. (1994). *Recording oral history: a practical guide for social scientists.* Thousand Oaks: SAGE Publications.

1 The Greeks of Turkey

After the dust from the 1923 Greek–Turkish population exchange had settled, there were over 100,000 Greeks living in Turkey; by the turn of the twenty-first century, only a few thousand remained. Most had left for the Greek cities of Athens and Thessaloniki, where they encountered a culture and lifestyle often somewhat removed from what they had imagined whilst living in Turkey, and a reception rather different from that which they had been expecting. In this chapter, I seek to give the reader an introduction to this history and to provide context for the narratives and memories analysed in later chapters.

Istanbul

Ottoman census data give figures of 152,741 Orthodox Christians in Istanbul in 1885 and 176,442 in 1906 (not including Greek citizens resident in the city; Vryonis 2005:7). This population peaked at around the time of the First World War, when there were, according to upper estimates, over 300,000 Orthodox Christians living in Istanbul and its environs, forming a significant part of the city's entrepreneurial bourgeoisie and skilled working class (Alexandris 1992:31–32, 51, 96, 108; Örs 2006:83; Vryonis 2005:10, 14). Their position, however, was brought into question in the aftermath of the 1919–1922 Greek–Turkish War, which, following an initially successful but ultimately disastrous Greek military campaign in Asia Minor, was brought to an end by the signing of the Treaty of Lausanne in July 1923. By this time, a large proportion of the Ottoman Empire's Orthodox Christian population had been displaced, fleeing to Greece and elsewhere ahead of the advancing Turkish troops after the collapse of the Greek forces. In light of this post-war demographic chaos, the Convention Concerning the Exchange of Greek and Turkish Populations was drawn up, envisaging a compulsory exchange of populations between Greece and Turkey. The defining characteristic for the exchange was religion: Muslims resident in Greece were to be expelled to Turkey, and Orthodox Christians living in Turkey were to be expelled to Greece.

Turkey pushed for the inclusion in the exchange of the Greeks of Istanbul – who had been comparatively unaffected by the conflict as Istanbul had been under Allied occupation – to which Greece was strongly opposed (Alexandris 1992:84–93; Oran 2004:99). Ultimately, it was agreed that the Orthodox Christians of Istanbul, as well as those resident on the islands of Imbros and Tenedos (see below), would be exempted from the population exchange, along with the Muslims of Western Thrace in Greece who would act as a counterweight. As Turkey was pushing for proportionality in terms of these exempted minorities, it was agreed that only those Orthodox Christians settled in Istanbul prefecture before 30 October 1918 – called *établis* – would be exempted, as a result of which some 38,000 *Polítes* became subject to the exchange (Alexandris 1992:96; Oran 2004:100). Additionally, Turkey blocked the return of around 40,000 Orthodox Christians who had left Istanbul in 1922 in fear of an impending Turkish takeover of the city, and expelled around 1500 Greeks (along with their dependents) who had served with the British administration during Allied occupation (Alexandris 1992:82, 101–102). Accordingly, between 1920 and 1924, some 60,000 Greek citizens resident in Istanbul, 40,000 non-exchangeable Orthodox Christians who had left before the signing of the treaty, 38,000 individuals established after 1918, and 20,000 Orthodox Christians from Istanbul's suburbs left the city (Alexandris 1992:104). Around 100–110,000 Orthodox Christians thus remained in Istanbul in the post-Lausanne period, of whom two thirds, who had been Ottoman subjects, were given Turkish citizenship, whilst one third, Greek citizens who had been established in the city before 30 October 1918, retained Greek citizenship (Alexandris 2004:118; Hirschon 2004:8). These Greek citizens were not necessarily less indigenous to Turkey than their counterparts who held Turkish citizenship: many had never set foot on Greek soil, and held Greek citizenship purely because their forebears had come from former Ottoman territories that became part of the Greek state after Greek independence (Alexandris 1992:281).

Section three of the Treaty of Lausanne granted the Greek minority of Istanbul the right to the free exercise of religion and the free use of any language in public or in private, as well as the right to establish and operate (at their own expense) charitable, religious, educational or social institutions (Treaty of Lausanne 1923: articles 38–40). Turkey undertook to extend the same rights to non-Muslims as Muslims and to treat all inhabitants equally before the law (Treaty of Lausanne 1923: articles 38–39). The treaty also stipulated that, in any town or region with a significant non-Muslim population, provisions should be in place to allow educational instruction in primary schools to take place in the minority's own language, although Turkey retained the right to make the Turkish language also compulsory in those minority schools (Treaty of Lausanne 1923: article 41). In addition to these safeguards, the Greeks of Turkey were also (in theory) protected by article 88 of the 1924 Turkish Constitution, which provided for the complete equality of all citizens regardless of race or religion (Özkirimli and Sofos 2008:165). Although in principle the legal position of non-Muslims was thus improved relative to what it had been in the Ottoman Empire, in practice the role of non-Muslims in Turkish public life declined after 1923 (Özkirimli and Sofos 2008:165). Although non-Muslims could be Turkish *citizens*, the perception remained that they could not be *Turks*, which was a serious impediment to their realisation of equal status (Alexandris 1992:139; Güven 2009:170; Özkirimli and Sofos 2008:165). For instance, with the enactment of the 1926 Civil Servant Law, non-Muslims were effectively barred from civil service, as the law required civil servants to be *Turkish* rather than simply Turkish citizens (Özkirimli and Sofos 2008:165).

The fortunes of the *Polítes* fluctuated in the course of the twentieth century. In the tense post-war environment of the 1920s, there were various transgressions of the terms of the Treaty of Lausanne regarding minorities by both Greece and Turkey (Alexandris 1992:105–142; Oran 2004:102). In the 1930s, a period of Greek–Turkish rapprochement under Eleftherios Venizelos and Mustafa Kemal heralded improvements for the Greeks of Turkey: in October 1930, the Convention of Establishment, Commerce and Navigation was signed, which reiterated the right of those *Polítes* with Greek citizenship to remain in Turkey, and in 1933 Turkey permitted the foundation of a community organisation bearing an ethnic appellation in the form of the Hellenic Union of Istanbul, although only Greek citizens were allowed to be members (Alexandris 1992:177–180; Alexandris 2004:118). Nevertheless, some restrictive measures affecting the minority were also implemented in the 1930s. In June 1932, law 2007 banned foreign nationals from over 30 professions, precipitating the emigration of a number of Greek citizens (anywhere from 5000–13,000, according to estimates) (Alexandris 1992:185, 191; Ecumenical Federation of Constantinopolitans 2014; Ecumenical Federation of Constantinopolitans 2015a:6; Ekdóseis Tsoukátou 2004:11; Güven 2009:168; Özkirimli and Sofos 2008:165–166; Sarioglou 2012a:108; Turan *et al.* 2010:245; Vryonis 2005:33). In 1934, the Surname Law was passed, which required all Turkish citizens to take a surname, and banned surnames denoting, amongst other things, nationality (Alexandris 1992:183). The 1930s also saw the launch of the 'Citizen, speak Turkish!' campaign, in which pressure was put on minorities to adopt the Turkish language (Alexandris 1992: 140, 183; Güven 2009:171; Özkirimli and Sofos 2008:167).

During the Second World War, in which Turkey remained neutral and Greece fell to Axis occupation, the *Polítes* came under renewed pressure. In 1941, Turkey mobilised non-Muslims between the ages of 18 and 45 into labour battalions to construct roads and buildings in Anatolia; they faced harsh conditions and many lost their lives before the battalions were disbanded in 1942 (Alexandris 1992:214; Constantinopolitan Society 2009:15; Güven 2009:205–208; Turan *et al.* 2010:246; Vryonis 2005:33). Creating vacancies for Muslim Turks in Istanbul's urban workforce, and controlling a potential fifth column in the case of Turkish participation in the war, were, in Dilek Güven's view, amongst the primary motivations that lay behind the mobilisation (2009:208). In late 1942, Turkey adopted the *Varlık Vergisi* or 'wealth tax', which disproportionately targeted non-Muslims with harsh and often unpayable duties that in some cases exceeded the total value of debtors' estates (Alexandris 1992:215–219; Güven 2009:216–218; Özkirimli and Sofos 2008:169). In Istanbul, 87% of the taxpayers were from the non-Muslim population (Güven 2009:215). Debtors were required to pay the tax within 15 days, or within 30 days with interest, and non-payers had their property confiscated and/or were deported to forced labour camps (Alexandris 1992:221–222; Güven 2009:216; Özkirimli and Sofos 2008:170; Turan *et al.* 2010:246; Vryonis 2005:34–35). According to the Constantinopolitan Society and the Ecumenical

Federation of Constantinopolitans (on which, see below), 21 debtors lost their lives in these labour camps (Constantinopolitan Society 2009:15; Ecumenical Federation of Constantinopolitans 2015a:8). Under international pressure, the tax was abolished in March 1944, non-payers were released, and the outstanding sums were written off (Güven 2009:225; Özkirimli and Sofos 2008:170). Although the ostensible purpose of the tax was to tackle inflation, many commentators – both Greek and Turkish – have argued that the intent of the law was to wrest control of commerce from the non-Muslim minorities (Alexandris 1992:211, 215–219; Güven 2009:12, 209; Oran 2004:113; Özkirimli and Sofos 2008:169).

In the post-war period, mutual fears of Soviet expansion led to more cordial Greek–Turkish relationships (Alexandris 1992:234–237). Both Turkey and Greece were concerned by Russian attempts to undermine the ecumenical character of the Orthodox Christian Patriarchate in Istanbul, leading to some Turkish concessions towards the Patriarch and his Greek flock (Alexandris 1992:237–243). Patriarch Athenagoras I – elected in 1948 – reciprocated by taking measures to improve relationships with the Turkish authorities, for instance flying the Turkish flag outside the Patriarchate on Sundays (Alexandris 1992:246–247). In 1954, an agreement between Greece and Turkey set the number of Greek citizens allowed to teach in minority schools in Turkey, and reciprocally the number of Turkish citizens teaching in minority schools in Western Thrace, as well as permitting each country to supply the minority schools in the other with textbooks (Alexandris 1992:249). Tensions over Cyprus, however, and the rise of the Greek Cypriot guerrilla movement EOKA – whose goal was to achieve independence from the British Empire and union with Greece – disrupted this period of reconciliation (Alexandris 1992:253). Segments of the Turkish press accused Greek Orthodox archbishops of raising money to fund the Greek Cypriots, and lambasted the Patriarch for maintaining neutrality (Alexandris 1992:253–254). Popular opinion was also inflamed by the activity of the 'Cyprus is Turkish' Association, which had links with the ruling Democratic Party (Özkirimli and Sofos 2008:171).

The 6–7 September 1955 Istanbul Riots, known in Greek as the *Septemvrianá*, occurred against the backdrop of these tensions,[1] and are generally agreed to have been organised (or at the very least sanctioned and encouraged) by the Turkish state (Alexandris 2004:119; Campbell and Sherrard 1968:256–257; Güven 2008:9–15; Güven 2009:14–15; Oran 2004:113; Vryonis 2005:97–99; de Zayas 2007:137–138).[2] The riots were ostensibly triggered by an attack on the birthplace of Kemal in Thessaloniki on the night of 5 September, although later investigations revealed that the explosion that occurred near the house in question was caused by a bomb planted by an agent of the Turkish intelligence services (Güven 2009:137–138; Oran 2004:113; Özkirimli and Sofos 2008:171; Vryonis 2005:94–95). The bombing was reported on Turkish state radio and in the Turkish newspaper *İstanbul Ekspres* the following day, and on the evening of 6 September a crowd of demonstrators gathered in Taksim Square, primarily made up of students, workers, members of the 'Cyprus is Turkish' Association, and residents of nearby villages (Alexandris 1992:257; Güven 2009:31, 332; Özkirimli and

Sofos 2008:171; Vryonis 2005:72). Organised groups of rioters proceeded to target non-Muslim property, which according to scholars and eyewitnesses was identified by lists that were in the possession of group leaders as well as through information given by some of the neighbours of those targeted, and had also, in some cases, been marked in advance (Güven 2009:32–36; Özkirimli and Sofos 2008:171; Petros 26/11/2011; Vryonis 2005:104). With a few exceptions (see Güven 2009:43 and below), the police did not intervene to prevent the riots, and some even participated (Güven 2009:40–41).

The rioters attacked, looted, and in some cases set fire to houses, businesses, places of worship, and schools belonging to Istanbul's non-Muslim populations. Estimates as to the damage caused by the riots vary, but taken together indicate that between 1000 and 4000 homes, between 1000 and 4000 shops, some 70 to 80 places of worship, 20 to 30 minority schools, and thousands of other buildings were attacked (Alexandris 1992:259; Clogg 1992:153; Constantinopolitan Society 2009:17; Güven 2009:63–64; Özkirimli and Sofos 2008:171; Vryonis 2005:551). The majority of these belonged to the Greek community (80% of homes and 59% of shops, according to figures given by Güven), though the property of Armenians, Jews, and some Muslims was also damaged (Güven 2009:65–66). Contemporary reports from the British and American embassies based on hospital attendance indicated that 60 women were raped, although as Güven emphasised significant underreporting is highly probable (2009:74), and many Greek sources give higher estimates of 200 to 300 rapes (Alexandris 1992:257–258; Alexandris 2012:138; Constantinopolitan Society 2009:17; Ecumenical Federation of Constantinopolitans 2012:2; Ecumenical Federation of Constantinopolitans 2015a:20; Vryonis 2005:220, 224). Estimates as to the number of deaths vary considerably, with most sources providing a figure of between 15 and 37 fatalities.[3] The rioting also spread to some of the Princes' Islands, a chain of small islands off the coast of Istanbul in the Sea of Marmara.[4] Speros Vryonis has described how rioters were ferried across from Istanbul, allegedly supported by elements of the islands' Turkish population, to attack non-Muslim property on the islands of *Chálki* and *Prínkipos*, although on *Prótos* and possibly *Antigóni* the local Turkish authorities refused to allow the rioters to disembark (2005:182). Information from my own interviewees confirms that incidents occurred on *Prínkipos* (Evangelos 08/05/2013; Maria 09/05/2013) and *Chálki* (Dimitris 30/11/2011) but not on *Prótos* (Nikolaos 30/01/2012), and suggests that *Antigóni* was spared thanks to the actions of a local Turkish policeman (Evangelos 08/05/2013; Kyriakos 03/02/2012; Sotiris 08/02/2012).

Vryonis lamented that representatives of many groups within Turkish society participated in the riots, and that whilst some 'Muslim secularists (and Turkish communists)' came to the aid of non-Muslims this was 'very limited in extent' (2005:76, 531). A number of my informants did indeed report that they saw friends and neighbours participating in the rioting or directing the crowd to Greek properties, or alleged that their neighbours first protected the Greeks in their own neighbourhood before travelling to another part of Istanbul to join in the rioting there (for instance, Apostolis 03/02/2012; Michalis 29/01/2012; Marios

29/01/2012; Milena 30/11/2011; Rita 21/11/2011; see also Güven 2009:47–48). Nevertheless, there are reasons to qualify Vryonis' somewhat pessimistic assessment. Although frequently absent from published accounts of the *Septemvrianá*, many oral testimonies contain stories of Muslim Turkish friends and neighbours providing support or protection to the Greeks (see also Örs 2006:83 and Chapter 4), either by offering cryptic warnings (mentioned, for instance, by Alexandros 11/03/2014; Fotis 01/02/2012; Gerasimos 06/02/2012; Michalis 29/01/2012), advising them to turn on their lights and hang out a Turkish flag in order to mislead the rioters (Fotis 01/02/2012; Panagiotis 24/11/2011),[5] opening their houses to provide shelter (Andreas 11/02/2012; Antonis 10/08/2013; Stavros 29/11/2011), diverting the rioters by telling them that there were no Greeks in the area (Mimis 13/08/2013; Rita 21/11/2011), guarding streets or multi-storey apartment blocks and preventing the crowd from entering (Andreas 11/02/2012; Petros 26/11/2011; Tasos 13/03/2014), or personally intervening to prevent acts of violence (Alexandra 22/07/2011; see also examples in Güven 2009:45–48).

The *Septemvrianá* has become the centrepiece of the *Polítes*' narratives of persecution in the Turkish Republic (see Chapter 6), and is commonly directly associated with the expatriation of the community. Vryonis, for example, wrote that the events of 1955 'destroyed the Greek community of Istanbul in a matter of some nine hours' (2005:27). Certainly, the psychological ramifications of the attack were severe, leaving many *Polítes* with a profound sense of insecurity and despondency as regards the future of the community in Turkey, and several interviewees recalled that fears of a repetition of 1955 were playing on their minds when they did leave the country some years later. Nevertheless, the scale of Greek emigration from Turkey was at this stage comparatively minor. According to the Ecumenical Federation of Constantinopolitans, only around 10% of the community left the country in the immediate wake of the *Septemvrianá* (2014).

In the remainder of the 1950s, the *Polítes* were faced with further difficulties and discrimination. According to the Constantinopolitan Society, in the late 1950s the Greek community was targeted by a propaganda campaign pressurising Muslim Turks not to shop at Greek-run businesses, in which leaflets were distributed with slogans such as: 'this shop belongs to an infidel. Prefer the shop next door, it belongs to a Turk' (2009:17). At around the same time, the 'Citizen, speak Turkish!' campaign of the 1930s was reignited (Constantinopolitan Society 2009:17; Sarioglou 2012b:197). In April 1958, the Hellenic Union was shut down after a court ruled that it was engaged in anti-Turkish activities, and some of its members – including the father of my interviewee Konstantinos – were expelled from Turkey (Alexandris 1992:272; Konstantinos 05/02/2012). After the London and Zürich agreements established an independent Cyprus, Greek–Turkish bilateral relations improved, and had it not been for the military coup in Turkey in 1960 a renewed friendship agreement might have been concluded (Alexandris 1992:275–276). Nevertheless, these improved diplomatic relationships heralded a better period for the minority between 1959 and 1964 (Alexandris 1992:277).

In early 1964, however, as tensions once again flared in Cyprus, there were renewed problems in Istanbul. In March 1964, purportedly in retaliation for the murder of several Turkish Cypriots in Cyprus at Christmas in 1963 (Oran 2004:104), Turkey unilaterally denounced the 1930 Convention of Establishment, Commerce and Navigation, and began to expel from Turkey those *Polítes* with Greek citizenship (Alexandris 1992:280–281). According to Alexis Alexandris, expellees were forced to sign a declaration by which they admitted to committing currency offences, being members of the banned Hellenic Union, and financing Greek Cypriot guerrilla fighters, and agreed to leave Turkey of their own accord (1992:284). The names of those who were to be expelled were published in the Turkish press, their assets were frozen and their property confiscated, and they were compelled to leave Turkey with little notice, taking only minimal possessions and small amounts of money (22 dollars and one/two suitcase(s) weighing around 40 kg, according to Alexandris, Güven, and Vryonis) (Alexandris 1992:284; Constantinopolitan Society 2009:21; Ekdóseis Tsoukátou 2004:18–21; Güven 2009:287–288; Mills 2005:447; Turan *et al.* 2010:248; Vryonis 2005:562). In addition to those expelled in this manner as 'enemies of the state', other Greek citizens were forced to leave after 16 September 1964 when their work permits expired and were not renewed, and by 1967 almost all Greek citizens had been removed from Turkey (Alexandris 1992:284; Alexandris 2004:119; Ekdóseis Tsoukátou 2004:21; Lazaros 10/05/2013). Between 10,000 and 13,000 Greek citizens were expelled in total, and they were followed out of the country by an estimated 30–40,000 Turkish citizens (different members of the same family often held different citizenships, such that an entire family might decide to leave Turkey after one individual was expelled) (Alexandris 1992:284–286; Alexandris 2004:119; Mills 2005:447; Oran 2004:104; Turan *et al.* 2010:248; Vryonis 2005:565). In purely numerical terms, the expulsions of 1964 were thus by far the most damaging single blow for the *Polítes* (Güven 2009:286–287).

Many interviewees also reported that during the 1960s they were pressurised not to speak Greek in public, and noted the appearance of graffiti or notices on Greek establishments with variations on the theme: 'every cent that you give to the infidel becomes a bullet which kills our brothers in Cyprus' (also documented by the Ecumenical Federation of Constantinopolitans 2014). In 1971, the Patriarchate's ability to train clergy in Turkey was impeded when the theological seminary on *Chálki* was closed by the Turkish authorities, which had potentially serious ramifications as only those holding Turkish citizenship were eligible for the office of Patriarch (Alexandris 2004:121; Oran 2004:106). After the conflict on Cyprus in 1974, there was a further substantial exodus of Greeks from Turkey (Alexandris 1992:294; Turan *et al.* 2010:248). Informants reported an increasingly difficult and fearful atmosphere in this period, in which they were once again afraid to speak Greek in public, and worried that an incident like the *Septemvrianá* might occur again. In accordance with the history described above, the Greek population of Istanbul declined drastically in the course of the twentieth century (see Figure 1): by 1975 less than 10,000 Greeks remained, and by the late 1990s there were only some 2,500 year-round Greek residents (Alexandris 2004:119; Turan *et al.* 2010:243).

24 Introduction

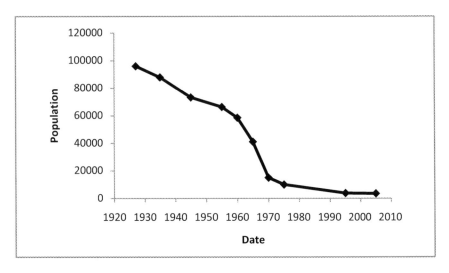

Figure 1 Decline in Greek-speaking/Orthodox Christian population of Istanbul, 1927–2000s.

The data on which this graph is based come from a variety of sources, which are detailed in Table 4 in the Appendix. Clear population figures are difficult to establish, due in large part to variation in who is being counted (e.g. Orthodox Christians or Greek-speakers, residents of Istanbul city or the wider Istanbul province, Turkish and Greek citizens or just Turkish citizens). Nevertheless, an overall trend of decline is clear, with a particularly dramatic exodus after the 1964 expulsion of Greek citizens. Where there is a date range for population figures, or a range for the population number, the median point is used. Where two different population figures are available for the same date the mean of the two is used.

In terms of quotidian intercommunal relationships between the non-Muslim minorities and the Muslim Turkish majority, personal testimonies paint a varied picture (see Chapter 4). In their life histories, many of my interviewees placed emphasis either on harmonious everyday interaction between Greeks, Armenians, Jews, and Turks, or on intercommunal antagonism, distance, and strife (Halstead 2014:399–405). Several informants articulated both narratives, either when remembering different periods of time or different neighbourhoods within Istanbul, or in shifting discursive contexts within the interview (Halstead 2014:408–411). Oral accounts commonly suggest that majority–minority relationships were tenser in central Istanbul and more harmonious in the suburbs or on the Princes' Islands. Generally speaking, male *Polítes* had a greater degree of contact with Muslim Turks than their female counterparts, due to sharing places of work and completing military service together. Mixed marriages were very rare, although not entirely unheard of (Tunç and Ferentinou 2012:910), and many *Polítes*, in particular women, recalled that their parents vehemently discouraged them from forming romantic relationships with Turks. The post-1950s generation of *Polítes* showed greater signs of integration into Turkish society and culture than their parents, largely due to the increased prominence of the Turkish language and culture in the minority schools, as a result of which relationships between Greeks and Turks, particularly in commerce, were on the increase in the 1950s and 1960s (Alexandris 1992:297). Many *Polítes* attended Turkish universities and joined Turkish sports clubs and athletic associations, with talented *Polítes* even representing Turkey internationally, and a handful served as members of the Turkish Parliament (Alexandris 1992:250–251). The standard of Turkish spoken by members of the Greek minority varied, primarily depending upon their degree of interaction with Turks and length of time spent in the education system, but most from the post-1950s generation were fluent (Alexandris 1992:297), and although at home and amongst themselves most spoke Greek rather than Turkish there were a few individuals who spoke only Turkish.

In accordance with the Treaty of Lausanne, the *Polítes* were predominantly educated in Greek minority schools, in which the classes took place roughly half in Greek and half in Turkish. Due to the 1954 agreement between the two countries, the minority schools were supplied with textbooks from Greece, although a number of informants recalled that certain pages relating to Greek national history had been cut out (Alexandros 11/03/2014; Fotis 01/02/2012; Kostas 07/06/2013; Kyriakos 03/02/2012). There were no minority secondary schools on the Princes' Islands, and residents either had to relocate to Istanbul during the school term, or commute daily by boat (Lazaros 10/05/2013). Alongside the minority schools, the Orthodox Church was a focal point of Greek community life in Istanbul, 'the place where you met your friends, the first flirtations' (Fotis 01/02/2012). The *Polítes* were generally not involved in party politics, with a few exceptions, and tended not to have strong political leanings to either the left or the right (Apostolis 03/02/2012; Evangelos 08/05/2013; Gerasimos 06/02/2012; Marios 29/01/2012; Spyros 02/12/2011; for exceptions see Halstead 2012:103–114). Men who held Turkish citizenship were required to perform national service in the Turkish military. Some interviewees gave a positive account of their national service, insisting that their Muslim Turkish comrades protected them from discrimination (see also Turan *et al.* 2010:260), though others – particularly those who served during moments of heightened Greek–Turkish tension – felt persecuted, or even feared for their lives.

The Greeks of Istanbul ranged across the socio-economic spectrum, and some were wealthy merchants and bankers, but most were middle-class professionals/traders/employees (e.g. architects/doctors/lawyers/shopkeepers) or skilled workers/craftsmen (Alexandris 1992:185, 250; Bouzi 2002:216 and passim; Chatziioannou and Kamouzis 2013:122; Vryonis 2005:20). This is reflected in the composition of my interviewees and their families, who were primarily shop owners/employees, professionals, or skilled craftsmen. Some were better off than others (for instance, some interviewees' families rented accommodation, whilst others owned their homes, and sometimes owned/rented an additional summer property in the suburbs or on the Princes' Islands), but generally most emphasised that their economic situation in Turkey was better than that of the average resident of Greece. Frequently, where economically viable, Constantinopolitan women did not work outside the home after marriage, a tradition which has continued for some couples in Greece (Nikolaos 30/01/2012; Sofia 11/02/2012; Spyros 02/12/2011).

Imbros

Imbros/Gökçeada is an island in the Aegean Sea, in the Çanakkale Province of Turkey. It became part of the Ottoman Empire shortly after the Fall of Constantinople, yet at the end of the nineteenth century its population was overwhelmingly Greek-speaking and Orthodox Christian: according to the Ottoman census of 1893, only 99 Muslims were resident on Imbros to 9357 Orthodox Christians (Alexandris 1980:6). In 1912, an expanding Greek state took control of the island following the First Balkan War. Although the island should have reverted to Ottoman control after the Treaty of Athens in 1913, due to the outbreak of the First World War the island remained in Greek hands for ten years, and Greek authority over the island was confirmed in the 1920 Treaty of Sèvres (Tsimouris 2008:12; Xeinos 2011:60–61).[6] Following the 1919–1922 Greek–Turkish War, Imbros – along with its neighbouring island Tenedos – was ceded to the Turkish Republic by the Treaty of Lausanne. The Orthodox Christians of Imbros and Tenedos, like those of Istanbul, were exempted from the population exchange between the two countries. Under article 14 of the treaty, the two islands were to 'enjoy a special administrative organisation composed of local elements' (Treaty of Lausanne 1923: article 14), thus, in theory, gaining a significant degree of local self-rule of a sort not applied to the minority in Istanbul (Alexandris 1980:5–13; Xeinos 2011:62–63).

In practice, however, article 14 was never implemented, and the Turkish authorities took over direct administrative control of the island (Alexandris 1980:16–17; Xeinos 2011:63). Around 1500 *Imvriótes* who were abroad when the treaty was signed were declared *personae non-gratae* and not permitted to return (Xeinos 2011:63). In 1927, Turkey published the law 1151 dealing with the 'special administrative organisation' of Imbros and Tenedos, which put an end to the idea of administrative self-control and brought the islands under central Turkish authority (Alexandris 1980:20–23; Babül 2004:4–5; Tsimouris 2008:59–66). Furthermore, the 1927 law provided that all education on Imbros was to be Turkish, secular, and public, precluding Greek language education in minority schools (Babül 2004:5; Constantinopolitan Society 2009:13; Helsinki Watch 1992:14, 28; Tsimouris 2008:130–131). Greek–Turkish rapprochement in the 1930s brought some improvements for the islanders – they were, for instance, permitted to elect a local Greek mayor – although during the Second World War some *Imvriótes* were caught up in the forced labour battalions and the discriminatory wealth tax (Alexandris 1980:23; Xeinos 2011:66). In 1946 the Turkish administration attempted (largely unsuccessfully) to settle Muslim Turks from the Black Sea on the island, in what Elif Babül has classified as the first attempts at Turkification on Imbros (Babül 2004:5; Babül 2006b:46; Xeinos 2011:66–67).

With renewed Greek–Turkish rapprochement in the 1950s, the law 5713 was passed in 1951, abolishing the educational provisions laid out in the 1927 law, and thus permitting minority schools teaching half in Greek and half in Turkish to open in 1952 (Alexandris 1980:24; Babül 2004:5; Xeinos 2011:67–68). This marked the beginning of something of a golden age for the Greek minority on Imbros, which was accompanied by improvements in the island's infrastructure alongside economic and touristic growth (Alexandris 1980:24; Tsimouris 2008:50). Greek–Turkish tensions over Cyprus in the early 1960s, however, heralded a disastrous decade for the *Imvriótes*, known locally simply as 'the events'. In 1964, the prohibition of Greek language education was reinstated, minority school buildings and equipment were confiscated by the state, and henceforth classes took place only in Turkish (Christoforidis 1993:66; Imvrian Association 2002:14; Tsimouris 2008:134). As the island's population was still overwhelmingly Greek-speaking, most of the Imvrian children spoke little or no Turkish, which made their education on Imbros highly problematic. As Voula – a child of primary school age in 1964 – recalled:

> In my third year of primary school, the Greek language was abolished. The school operated as normal, and I studied in Turkish for one year. I forgot Greek, and nor did I speak Turkish. We had a Turkish teacher then, who, the poor thing, struggled to get us to understand [. . .] One time, he was explaining and explaining something, he wanted to tell us something, and we looked at him blankly. In the end he drew it for us on the blackboard, he tried to explain it to us using hand gestures, and eventually he became frustrated and he went and banged his head on the blackboard, the poor man!
>
> (12/08/2013)

In addition to these practical difficulties, Imvrian parents overwhelmingly felt that their children should learn Greek and not grow up speaking only Turkish (*Imvriakí Ichó* 1974). Characteristic is the recollection of Mirela that after the Greek language was abolished in the schools her youngest son 'started to speak to us in Turkish. It was then that we were driven mad and decided to leave' (10/05/2013). Indeed, it was largely as a result of the school closures that a Greek exodus from the island began (Tsimouris 2008:134). Initially, many children were sent to Istanbul to be educated in the Greek minority schools there, which required either the entire family to uproot to the city, or the children to move without their parents, staying variously with relatives, with strangers, or even in orphanages (Pavlos 29/05/2013; Tsimouris 2008:134). Decamping to Istanbul involved a major cultural shock for the islanders, who were accustomed to a rural lifestyle and often felt overwhelmed in their new urban environment. Moreover, intercommunal tensions were often running high in Istanbul in the 1960s and 1970s (see above), and the Imvrian children had to adapt to a more tense and controlled environment than that prevailing in the Greek villages on Imbros. Pavlos, who went to live with an aunt in Constantinople at the age of six in order to attend primary school, described the experience as an 'unbelievable change. From being a child of five years who is left to do what he wants [on Imbros], to be taken to school by the hand, to be protected [you became] a prisoner [in Istanbul]. Literally a prisoner' (29/05/2013). Many families and children made the move to Istanbul in the hope that the situation with the Greek-language education on Imbros would be temporary, and that they would be able to return to the island. Ultimately, however, the majority were forced to migrate again, either to Greece or elsewhere, whilst others left for Greece directly from Imbros in their search for a Greek-language education.

At around the same time, the Turkish authorities began to expropriate farming land on the island (ultimately amounting to around 90% of cultivatable land, according to Greek sources) (Imvrian Association no date-b; Tsimouris 2001:2–3; Tsimouris 2008:120; Xeinos 2011:71), and militarise the island, which in turn led to restrictions on entrance (Babül 2004:5; Tsimouris 2008:120; Xeinos 2011:70). Many interviewees reported that they were left with only mountainous, largely uncultivable land, and that the recompense they were issued by the authorities amounted to a small fraction of the value of the expropriated land. These expropriations were particularly damaging as the *Imvriótes* were predominantly agriculturalists (Asanakis 2017:130–131; Tsimouris 2008:296). Between 1965 and 1966, Greek olive groves near the village of *Schoinoúdi* were expropriated for the establishment of 'open prisons' for serious offenders brought from the Turkish mainland. These free-roaming prisoners committed various acts of vandalism, theft, assault, and even murder (Alexandris 1980:25–26; Babül 2004:5; Tsimouris 2008:120, 145; Xeinos 2011:70–71). Meanwhile, from as early as 1966 and particularly during the early 1970s, the Turkish authorities began in earnest to settle Anatolian Turks and Kurds on the island (many themselves from nationalised lands), significantly altering the demographic composition (Tsimouris 2008:121–122; Xeinos 2011:71; on these settlers, see Babül 2004:13–16).

These measures intensified the exodus of the *Imvriótes*, who declined in number from 5487 in 1960 to 2571 in 1970; in the same period, the Muslim population rose from 289 to 4020 (Imvrian Association 2002:14). The *Imvriótes* mostly migrated to large Greek cities, although some also settled elsewhere, particularly Australia, America, and Europe (Xeinos 2011:73). This was due in no small part to the obstructive stance of the Greek government in issuing visas to the *Imvriótes* for entry to Greece, which was seemingly an attempt to preserve the Greek minority on the island (Tsimouris 2008:271). Many islanders worked around this obstacle by entering Greece via other European countries where the local Greek embassies were unaware of the visa embargo, which sometimes resulted in convoluted and costly detours across the continent (Tsimouris 2008:82; Xeinos 2011:71–72). Others left Imbros illegally by boat to neighbouring islands (Tsimouris 2008:256). In 1970, the island was officially renamed Gökçeada, completing the symbolic transition from the 'Greek' island of Imbros to the 'Turkish' island of Gökçeada (Babül 2006a:52; Babül 2006b:46). As in Istanbul, the conflict on Cyprus in 1974 caused the situation on Imbros to deteriorate further, and during the 1970s and 1980s there were further expropriations, assaults, and murders (Constantinopolitan Society 2009:23, 25; Imvrian Association no date-b; Tsimouris 2008:146). By 1985 only 496 Orthodox Christians remained on the island to 7114 Muslims, and by 2000 there were around 200 Orthodox Christians and 8000 Muslims, an almost complete reversal of the 1923 demographic situation (Imvrian Association 2002:14; Babül 2006a:50; see Figure 2).

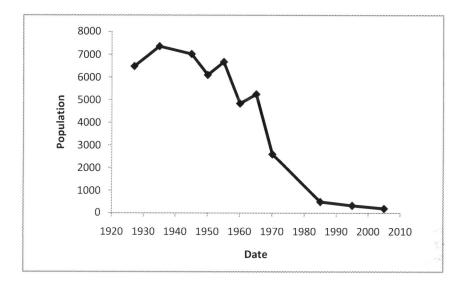

Figure 2 Decline in Greek-speaking/Orthodox Christian population of Imbros, 1927–2000s.

The data on which this graph is based come from a variety of sources, which are detailed in Table 4 in the Appendix. Establishing consistent population data is problematic. As well as the issue of whether religion or language is being used to identify the minority population (see Figure 1), there is inconsistency in the available data as to whether the population of Imbros alone is being counted or the whole Çanakkale province (including Tenedos). This accounts, in particular, for some of the erratic behaviour in the graph for the 1950s and 1960s. Nevertheless, as for Istanbul, the overall trend is apparent, and a rapid Greek population decline in the 1960s and 1970s reflects the devastating impact on the Imvriótes of the abolition of Greek language education, the expropriation of farming land, and the establishment of the open prisons. Where there is a date range for population figures the median point is used. Where different population figures are available for the same date from two sources the mean of the two is used. In cases where different population figures are available from the same source, the mean of the two is taken (before averaging with any other sources).

Before 'the events' Imbros had seven principal settlements. The biggest was the capital, known locally as *Panagía Baloméni*, where most of the island's few Turkish residents were located. The remaining six settlements were villages. Of these, *Schoinoúdi* was the biggest and, due to its proximity to the open prisons and the confiscated lands, experienced one of the fastest and most dramatic drops in population in the 1960s. This sprawling settlement – which according to many *Imvriótes* was until 1964 the biggest village in Turkey (Xeinos 1998:201) – was joined by the mountainous *Agrídia*, the picturesque *Ágios Theódoros*, the seaside village of *Kástro*, the northeastern *Glyký*, and *Evlámpio*, close to the capital. After 1970, five new settlements – *Eşelek, Şahinkaya köyü, Şirinköy, Uğurlu köyü*, and *Yeni Bademli köyü* – were created for the Turkish and Kurdish settlers, who have also taken up residence in large numbers in *Panagía* (now *Çınarlı*), *Evlámpio* (*Yenimahalle*), and *Kástro* (*Kaleköy*), as well as in smaller numbers in *Ágios Theódoros* (*Zeytinli köyü*), *Glyký* (*Bademli köyü*), and *Schoinoúdi* (*Dereköy*); at the time of my visit to the island in 2013 (see Chapter 8), no Turks (or Kurds) had settled in *Agrídia* (*Tepeköy*).

Oral accounts, particularly from older *Imvriótes*, tend to paint a picture of life on the island prior to 'the events' as one of hard work and poverty but also autonomy and simplicity. Informants stressed that the islanders produced most of the food they consumed, importing only a few items such as salt, sugar, coffee, cigarettes, or *rakı*. Imbros did not have electricity until 1970, nor piped water in the houses in earlier years, and communication with the outside world was often difficult. Winters could be harsh, as residents – particularly in the more mountainous villages – were often cut off by snow, and families had to ensure that their larders were well-stocked for the winter months. Although Imbros is an island, only the residents of the seaside village of *Kástro* had a close connection with the sea, and most *Imvriótes* were farmers rather than fishermen (in contrast to Tenedos where fishing was an important part of the economy) (Tsimouris 2008:296). The island's numerous churches and chapels were a focal point for the community; as Kostas put it, 'the church was not just a religious place, but a place of ethnic expression, where we could all gather together to show that we are Hellenes, that we are something different' (07/06/2013). In common with the Greeks of Istanbul, *Imvriótes* who held Turkish citizenship performed national service in the Turkish army. As there were few Turkish residents on Imbros prior to the settlements in the 1970s, many *Imvriótes* – in contrast to the *Polítes* – only had the opportunity to interact with Turks when dealing with the island's authorities, serving in the Turkish army, travelling to the Turkish mainland (for instance for medical care), or when they relocated to Istanbul.

Greece

Most of the Greeks of Istanbul and Imbros settled in Greece, principally in the urban centres of Athens and Thessaloniki. In Athens, many settled in the seaside neighbourhood of *Palaió Fáliro*, claiming that it reminded them of the Bosporus or the Princes' Islands, as well as in the adjacent former refugee neighbourhoods *Néa Smýrni* and *Kallithéa*. They established numerous community organisations in their new places of settlement, which serve both as social and cultural associations and as pressure groups. The oldest of these is the Constantinopolitan Society, established in January 1928 by Constantinopolitan refugees who came to Greece as a result of the Greek–Turkish War and the population exchange. Based in *Kallithéa* in Athens, its founding purpose was to address the particular problems faced by *Polítes* in Greece as well as to preserve Constantinopolitan culture and traditions (Constantinopolitan Society 2008:3). When expatriated *Polítes* began to arrive in Greece in growing numbers after 1955, many chose to join the Constantinopolitan Society. During the 1970s, these expatriates rose to prominence within the Society's organisational structure, and the Society became increasingly active in publicising the persecution of Turkey's Greek minority, organising seminars, protests, exhibitions, and awareness-raising anniversary memorials (Constantinopolitan Society 2008:14; Isaakidis 2014; see Chapter 6). The Society has worked towards the resolution of issues such as uncertainty over pensions and national service obligations in Greece, as well as the long-standing struggle over the acquisition of Greek citizenship (see below) (Constantinopolitan Society 2008:15).

Whilst some expatriates joined the existing Constantinopolitan Society, others felt that there was a need for an organisation that more immediately differentiated between the different circumstances faced by the 1923 refugees and the post-1923 expatriates, and accordingly in 1963 founded the New Circle of Constantinopolitans (Constantinopolitan Union no date-b).[7] The Association of Hellenic Citizens Expelled from Turkey was founded at around the same time, in order to deal specifically with the problems faced by those Greek citizens forcibly removed from Turkey in 1964, and saw itself as the natural successor to the dissolved Hellenic Union (see above) (Constantinopolitan Union no date-c). Since 1981, these two organisations have together constituted the Constantinopolitan Union, based at the Constantinopolitan Cultural Centre in the *Ampelókipoi* neighbourhood of Athens (Constantinopolitan Union no date-a). As well as lobbying domestic and international institutions on issues pertaining to the expatriate community, both the Constantinopolitan Union and the Constantinopolitan Society pursue social, cultural, and philanthropic activities, including supporting research and running seminars about Constantinopolitan and Byzantine history; offering lessons (e.g. in the Turkish language); and operating extensive libraries. There are also several expatriate associations outside Athens, such as the Union of Constantinopolitans of Northern Greece based in Thessaloniki, as well as many smaller organisations catering for more specific communities, such as former residents of the Princes' Islands, or the alumni of particular schools in Istanbul.

Figure 3 The Constantinopolitan Society in *Kallithéa* (Athens), 2017.

Both the Greek flag (centre) and yellow flags bearing the double-headed eagle of Byzantium (left and right) are flying. Photograph by the author.

Figure 4 The Constantinopolitan Cultural Centre in *Ampelókipoi* (Athens), 2017. Note the double-headed eagle of Byzantium. Photograph by the author.

After two abortive attempts in the 1970s and 1980s to create an umbrella organisation that would unite and provide a communal voice for the entire expatriate community, in 2006 the Ecumenical Federation of Constantinopolitans (henceforth referred to as the Federation of Constantinopolitans) was founded by 25 Constantinopolitan associations in Greece and abroad (Ecumenical Federation of Constantinopolitans 2008:7; Ouzounoglou 2014). Its stated aims were to unify the efforts of the expatriated *Polítes* and strengthen their ties with the community that remained in Istanbul, in order to study and raise awareness both domestically and internationally of the difficulties faced by the Greeks of Istanbul, Imbros, and Tenedos, provide support for the Ecumenical Patriarchate, and promote measures for ensuring the preservation of a Greek community in Turkey (Ecumenical Federation of Constantinopolitans 2009). The Constantinopolitan Society, the New Circle of Constantinopolitans, and the Association of Hellenic Citizens Expelled from Turkey are all members of the Federation, although there have been significant differences of opinion between the board of the Constantinopolitan Society and that of the Federation, particularly as regards the latter's decision to pursue direct dialogue with Turkey (see Chapter 6). The stance of the Constantinopolitan Society towards Turkey and Greek–Turkish relationships is sometimes seen by others in the expatriate community as too robust, whilst in turn representatives of the Constantinopolitan Society sometimes complain that other expatriates are unduly conciliatory or too nostalgic in their attitudes towards Turkey.

There are, additionally, several Imvrian organisations, both in Greece and elsewhere, the largest of which is the Imvrian Association founded in Athens in 1945 (Tsimouris 2008:251–255, 263). Following a hiatus of almost a decade after 1947, the Imvrian Association began to operate again in 1956, and its principal aims were, first, to unite and to provide support for those *Imvriótes* living in Greece and, secondly, to support the community remaining on the island (Imvrian Association no date-a; *Imvros* 1995). In 1999 the Imvrian Association relocated to new multi-storey premises in *Néa Smýrni*, funded by expatriate donations as well as state aid (Tsimouris 2008:267), which with its attached café serves as a social hub for the expatriated islanders. The Imvrian Association also organises historical and cultural events including theatrical, musical, and dance performances, activities for younger-generation *Imvriótes*, and Turkish language lessons (Imvrian Association no date-a; Tsimouris 2008:268). It is instrumental in supporting and advocating for the seasonal and permanent return to the island (see Chapter 8), and like its Constantinopolitan counterparts attempts to raise awareness of the persecution the islanders faced through petitions to domestic and international bodies, and by publishing books and the newspaper *Imvros* (Tsimouris 2008:267). As Giorgos Tsimouris has observed, the Imvrian Association – particularly in recent decades as their return movement gathered momentum – has commonly carefully avoided aligning itself with extreme nationalist positions, and is strong in its criticism not only of Turkish policy but also Greek indifference towards the Greeks of Imbros (2008:278).

Figure 5 *Imvriótes* gathered together in the café of the Imvrian Association, 2017.
Photograph by Stelios Poulados. Copyright Stelios Poulados. Reproduced with permission.

Events organised by the Constantinopolitan and Imvrian associations at which I have been present have typically been very well attended. Nevertheless, it should be noted that those expatriates who are actively involved in the associations' activist endeavours are a minority amongst the expatriate population at large, and, moreover, many expatriates – including several of my interviewees – have had no significant involvement with any association. As in Turkey, many expatriates remain aloof from party politics in Greece (though it was frequently suggested to me that *Polítes* tend towards the centre–right), and interviewees often expressed disinterest in Greek politics and bemusement at the depth of political partisanship in their new place of residence. This is reflected in a disinclination in many of their testimonies to propose political explanations for social phenomena, or to structure their narratives in relation to major political developments in Greece such as the fall of the military dictatorship in 1974 (for exceptions, see Halstead 2012:103–114). It was also very common for interviewees to report that, despite having been regular churchgoers whilst living in Turkey, in Greece they attend church comparatively infrequently or not at all. Reasons often cited include the fact that the church is no longer the primary central meeting place for conversing with other Greeks as it had been in Turkey, but also the suggestion that the ceremonies and liturgies are less authentic in churches in Greece, and that there is a lack of respect amongst the Greeks of Greece for the church and religion (see also Chapter 4); according to Dimitris' pithy analysis, the approach taken in Greece is: "Christ is risen, let's leave!" (30/11/2011).

The vast majority of my interviewees speak Greek amongst themselves, though many throw in occasional Turkish phrases, or sometimes switch to Turkish when they do not want *Elladítes* to understand them. Some *Polítes* – particularly, according to many interviewees, older residents of the *Palaió Fáliro* neighbourhood of Athens – are known to converse extensively in Turkish (see also Alexandris 1992:297), much to the chagrin of some other members of the expatriate community (*O Polítis* 1994). Indeed, there are many in the community who actively avoid speaking Turkish, or find that doing so provokes traumatic memories. Loukas, for instance, though a fluent and regular Turkish speaker, finds that it troubles him to speak Turkish to his son, because he cannot shake the feeling that 'Turkish is the language of the "other"' (03/07/2013). So whilst the Turkish language might represent an intimate code for some people in certain contexts, it is also frequently a source of anxiety and internal conflict.

Emigration to Greece represented both an escape from fear and harassment and a traumatic and daunting uprooting, and accordingly is recounted in different ways by different individuals in different contexts (see Chapter 3 and Halstead 2014). On the one hand, the expatriates had moved from a country where it was sometimes dangerous to speak Greek in the streets to one where Greek was ubiquitous, and from a country where they were a religious minority to one that overwhelmingly shared their Orthodox Christian religion. On the other hand, many had lost much or all of their financial and material wealth, and their early years in Greece were often difficult. Many interviewees recalled that they or their parents had to work several different jobs in order to make ends meet, commonly taking on lower-paid and less prestigious/skilled employment than that which they had undertaken in Turkey. Migration to Greece also represented something of a culture shock for many informants, particularly as the country and its inhabitants often failed to conform to images they had formed whilst living in Turkey. Despite being of the same religion and (for the most part) speaking the same language, the expatriates were distinguishable from the Greeks of Greece by their accent and idiom as well as certain differences of culture and mentality (see Chapter 4). Particularly for those who had resided in cosmopolitan Istanbul, first impressions of Greek cities were commonly that they were 'like villages' and their inhabitants 'villagers' (see also Chapter 3 and Örs 2006). As Sotiris put it, describing his arrival in Athens from Istanbul in 1970:

> I was born and grew up in an urban environment, where all of the ethnic groups were city-dwellers. Here in Greece, then, the urbanisation of Athens was still underway. And I laughed at the state of the new Athenian, who was still a villager, he wasn't an urbanite [. . .] If it was possible they would even have fowl on their balconies! Unthinkable things for someone who has grown up in a city.
>
> (08/02/2012)

It is important to note in this context that the post-1945 population of Greece – despite a veneer of homogeneity, particularly in terms of language and religion – was itself diverse, comprising Greek refugees from the Ottoman Empire and their descendants (with distinctive cultures and traditions) as well as '*dópioi*' or 'native' Greeks settled in the country before 1923. My interviewees sometimes (though not always) expressed a stronger affinity with Greeks of refugee origin (especially those deriving from the cosmopolitan cities on the Asia Minor coast) than with the native Greeks.

When the Orthodox Christian refugees arrived in Greece in the aftermath of the Greek–Turkish War, they received a sometimes ambivalent, sometimes hostile welcome from the native Greeks, who saw the refugees 'as somehow less Greek than themselves' (Karakasidou 1997:147), questioned their claims to Hellenic identity by deriding them as 'seeds of the Turks' (Hirschon 2004:19), and distinguished themselves as *dópioi*, i.e. 'natives'. The expatriated Greeks of Istanbul and Imbros sometimes encountered comparable antipathy from segments of the Greek population.[8] They found that many *Elladítes* knew little about their communities or the reasons why they had left Turkey, and that they viewed the new arrivals with suspicion. Interviewees recalled that their Hellenic and Orthodox Christian credentials were called into question: 'did you have churches?' 'Did you learn Greek?' 'Were you baptized?' A great many reported that sections of the Greek-born population referred to them as 'Turks' or derided them, like the refugees before them, as 'seeds of the Turks'. Michalis and Thanasis both remembered that the Greeks of Athens would direct customers to their shops by sending them to 'the Turk', whilst Michalis' daughter Theodora was one of several informants to recall that as a child she got into a fight with a classmate who called her 'little

Turkish girl' (Michalis 29/01/2012; Thanasis 06/02/2012; Theodora 19/04/2012). During the Cyprus crisis in 1974, the Greek-born neighbours of Lefteris' mother started to treat her with suspicion, falling into silence and muttering 'look out, the Turk is passing' when she was walking down the road (Lefteris 12/05/2013). Sometimes, the expatriates' birthplace was betrayed in unexpected ways: Fotis related how a bank worker pegged him as a Turk after noticing that his signature, designed when he was 18 and still living in Turkey, was written in Turkish; whilst Andreas remembered causing consternation in a café amongst his new Greek-born workmates when he ordered tea rather than the coffee favoured by most Greeks (Fotis 01/02/2012; Andreas 11/02/2012).[9]

Many informants also expressed profound disappointment with their treatment by the Greek state. Chief amongst their grievances was the issue of citizenship. The Greek state is notoriously reluctant to issue citizenship to foreign-born people (Hirschon 1999:169). Amongst foreign-born migrants, a distinction is commonly made between those who are *omogeneís* – i.e. of Greek descent – and those who are *allogeneís* – of non-Greek descent – with the latter category particularly unlikely to be awarded citizenship (Christopoulos 2009:1–16). Although the expatriated Greeks of Turkey would be forgiven for assuming they fell into the former category – especially in the context of irredentist nationalistic rhetoric that made them 'unredeemed Greeks' – most were denied Greek citizenship for years or even decades.[10] In the meantime, the expatriates were required periodically to attend the Aliens' Bureau in order to renew work and residence permits. Lack of Greek citizenship brought a variety of practical problems, including difficulties in purchasing property, acquiring financial loans, working in the public sector, or voting in elections. Some expatriates lost their Turkish citizenship (most commonly because they had failed to report for their military service) and became stateless persons. Some purposefully renounced their Turkish citizenship as a symbolic act; in Ioanna's terms, '[we wanted to] erase everything that was Turkish [. . .] we didn't want to have links' (23/11/2011). Others were afraid to make return visits to Turkey on their Turkish passports, lest they be detained to fulfil outstanding national service. As well as these practical considerations, the denial of Greek citizenship to the expatriates provoked sentiments of rejection – particularly amongst those who had felt that Greece was their national homeland – as well as exacerbating popular suspicion about their ethnicity. Interviewees commonly encountered confusion and even hostility when they presented their Turkish identity papers in banks or public offices. Pavlos, for example, recalled an incident in which an official at the Aliens' Bureau turned to him and said, 'and how do I know that you are not a Turk?' (Pavlos 29/05/2013).

Ultimately, principally through action taken by the expatriate organisations, most expatriates who wanted to obtain Greek citizenship were able to do so from the early 1980s onwards. Most interviewees also felt that by the turn of the century, at least, popular suspicion towards the expatriate community had largely dissipated, and several informants pointed to the 2003 release and subsequent popularity of the film *Polítiki Kouzína*, with its sympathetic portrayal of the plight of the *Polítes*, as a moment of catharsis in this regard. For many, however, their treatment in the first few decades of their settlement in Greece was a source of profound disillusionment, and it is common to hear expatriates offer variations of the lament: 'in Turkey we were the Greeks, and in Greece we were the Turks'.

Notes

1 Although the *Septemvrianá* has often been interpreted as closely connected with escalating Greek–Turkish tensions over the future of Cyprus (Calotychos 2003:188; Clogg 1992:153), several scholars have emphasised that the riots are better understood within a broader history of national homogenisation in Turkey (Güven 2009:13, 16, 263–264, 338; Güven 2015:45; Özkirimli and Sofos 2008:172), a perspective frequently reiterated by the Ecumenical Federation of Constantinopolitans (2013; 2015a:5, 30; 2015b).
2 Detailed discussion of the degree of involvement of various state (and other) institutions in the Istanbul Riots can be found in Güven (2009) and Vryonis (2005).
3 In the immediate aftermath of the riots, British and American diplomats asserted that one Greek lost his life (Vryonis 2005:212), whilst the Turkish press gave a figure of 11 (Güven 2009:75). A 1992 Helsinki Watch report claimed that 15 Greeks lost their lives (1992:8), the same number reported by Turkish author Rıdvan Akar (cited in Turan *et al.* 2010:247). A 2009 Constantinopolitan Society report stated that there were 'no less than 17 deaths' (2009:17), whilst in 2012 the Ecumenical Federation of Constantinopolitans reported in excess of 30 deaths (2012:2) and in a 2015 presentation gave a figure of 37 (2015a:20). Vryonis has made the most systematic attempt to establish the number of deaths, noting that the available sources are problematic (partly due to confusion over the identification of certain victims, and partly due to the absence of official statistics), compiling a list of 37 potential fatalities in an appendix, and ultimately concluding that at least 30 Greeks were killed (2005:213, 581).
4 There were also a smaller number of incidents in İzmir, and demonstrations in Ankara (Güven 2009:333).
5 Panagiotis remembered an Armenian woman married to a Turkish policeman who lived opposite them shouting across to his mother, 'hang a Turkish flag out of the window!' In the ensuing panic, his mother's red dress was hung out of the window instead of the flag, prompting the neighbour to once again shout across, 'no, not a red dress! A red flag! The Turkish flag!' (Panagiotis 24/11/2011).
6 For detailed discussion of this period from a Greek perspective, see Gryntakis (1995:43–77) and Sifounakis (2017).
7 Although such differences of opinion may have been of crucial significance to some, several informants suggested that geographical proximity and happenstance in terms of one's acquaintances and relatives were often decisive in determining whether *Polítes* became affiliated with one association or the other.
8 Again, some (though not all) interviewees felt that they were treated better by Greek refugees or those of refugee descent than by the native Greeks.
9 Until fairly recently, tea in Greece was generally reserved for the sick.
10 The only exception was those Turkish citizens who were the sons and daughters of *Polítes* who held Greek citizenship, and a handful of Turkish citizens who acquired citizenship through personal connections (Isaakidis 2014).

References

(Items marked * are in the Greek language.)

Alexandris, A. (1980). Imbros and Tenedos: a study of Turkish attitudes toward two ethnic Greek island communities since 1923. *Journal of the Hellenic Diaspora*, 7(1), 5–31.

Alexandris, A. (1992). *The Greek minority of Istanbul and Greek–Turkish relations, 1918–1974*. Athens: Centre for Asia Minor Studies.

Alexandris, A. (2004). Religion or ethnicity: the identity issue of the minorities in Greece and Turkey. In R. Hirschon (Ed.). *Crossing the Aegean: an appraisal of the 1923 compulsory population exchange between Greece and Turkey*. New York: Berghahn Books, 117–132.

Alexandris, A. (2012). The minority question (1954–55). In E. Sarioglou and K. Sarioglou (Eds). *Fifty years on from the Septemvrianá. Constantinople: before – then – after*. Athens: Ellinikó Ídryma Istorikó Meletón, 133–144.*

Asanakis, A. (2017). *Panagía Imvriótissa of Salamis: its history*. Athens.*

Babül, E. (2004). Belonging to Imbros: citizenship and sovereignty in the Turkish Republic. Paper presented at the conference *Nationalism, Society and Culture in Post-Ottoman South East Europe*. 29–30 May 2004. St Peter's College, Oxford. Available at: www.academia.edu/6707095/Belonging_to_Imbros_Citizenship_and_Sovereignty_in_the_Turkish_Republic [Accessed on 17 April 2016].

Babül, E. (2006a). Claiming a place through memories of belonging: politics of recognition on the island of Imbros. *New Perspectives on Turkey*, 34, 47–65.

Babül, E. (2006b). Home or away? On the connotations of homeland imaginaries in Imbros. *Thamyris/Intersecting: Place, Sex and Race*, 13(1), 43–53.

Bouzi, S. (2002). *The Hellenism of Constantinople*. Athens: Elliniká Grámmata.*

Calotychos, V. (2003). *Modern Greece: a cultural poetics*. Oxford: Berg.

Campbell, J. and Sherrard, P. (1968). *Modern Greece*. London: Ernest Benn.

Chatziioannou, M. and Kamouzis, D. (2013). From a multiethnic empire to two national states: the economic activities of the Greek Orthodox population of Istanbul, ca. 1870–1939. In D. Reuschke, M. Salzbrunn, and K. Schönhärl (Eds), *The economies of urban diversity: Ruhr area and Istanbul*. New York; Houndmills, Basingstoke: Palgrave Macmillan, 117–143.

Christoforidis, K. (1993). Imbros seventy years on from Lausanne. In *Imvrian two-day conference: Imbros today. Problems, prospects*. Athens: Imvrian Association, 61–71.*

Christopoulos, D. (2009). *Country report: Greece*. Florence: EUDO Citizenship Observatory.

Clogg, R. (1992). *A concise history of Greece*. Cambridge; New York: Cambridge University Press.

Constantinopolitan Society. (2008). *Constantinopolitan Society: 1928–2008 80 years of contribution*. Athens: Constantinopolitan Society.*

Constantinopolitan Society. (2009). *The violations of the human rights of the Greek minority in Turkey: atrocities and persecutions 1923–2009*. Athens: Constantinopolitan Society.

Constantinopolitan Union. (no date-a). *Who we are*. Available at: www.enokon.gr/poioi-eimaste [Accessed on 7 January 2016].*

Constantinopolitan Union. (no date-b). *The New Circle of Constantinopolitans*. Available at: www.enokon.gr/poioi-eimaste/neos-kyklos [Accessed on 7 January 2016].*

Constantinopolitan Union. (no date-c). *Association of Hellenic Citizens Expelled from Turkey*. Available at: www.enokon.gr/poioi-eimaste/somateio-apelathenton [Accessed on 7 January 2016].*

Ecumenical Federation of Constantinopolitans. (2008). *Proceedings of international conference: Septemvriana 6–7/9/1955 an act of annihilation of the Greek community of Istanbul*. 13 September 2008. Athens. Available at: www.conpolis.eu/

Septemvriana/2008/Πρακτικά%20Συνεδρίου%20Σεπτεμβριανών%20ΟΙ.ΟΜ.ΚΩ%20 2008.pdf [Accessed on 15 May 2014].
Ecumenical Federation of Constantinopolitans. (2009). *The 54th anniversary of the Septemvrianá 6–7/9/1955*. Conference proceedings. Available at: www.conpolis.eu/Septemvriana/2009/Πρακτικά%20Συνεδρίου%20Σεπτεμβριανών%20ΟΙ.ΟΜ.ΚW%20 2009.pdf [Accessed on 15 May 2014].*
Ecumenical Federation of Constantinopolitans. (2012). *The Greek Orthodox minority of Turkey: history of human rights violations and the need of remedy and reparations*. PowerPoint presentation, May 2012. Available at: www.conpolis.eu/uploadedNews/Human%20rights%20of%20the%20Greek%20Orthodox%20minority%20of%20Turkey-May%202012b.pdf [Accessed on 15 May 2014].
Ecumenical Federation of Constantinopolitans. (2013). *The petitions that have been submitted to the Turkish Government for restitution and remedy of the mass scale violations of human rights against the Greek-Orthodox community of Constantinople*. PowerPoint presentation at the Ecumenical Federation of Constantinopolitans event for the 58th anniversary of the *Septemvrianá*, 7 September 2013. Available at: www.conpolis.eu/uploadedNews/Presentation%20%207.9.2013.pdf [Accessed on 15 May 2014].*
Ecumenical Federation of Constantinopolitans. (2014). *16 March 1964: the banishment of the Greek community of Istanbul through deportations and expatriation*. PowerPoint presentation, February 2014. Available at: www.conpolis.eu/uploadedNews/16%20 Mart%201964-Eng.pdf [Accessed on 15 May 2014].
Ecumenical Federation of Constantinopolitans. (2015a). *60 years on from the 6–7 September 1955: the organised attack by the Turkish state with the aim of the annihilation of the Hellenism of Constantinople*. PowerPoint presentation at the Ecumenical Federation of Constantinopolitans event for the 60th anniversary of the *Septemvrianá*, September 2015. Available at: www.conpolis.eu/uploadedNews/H%20Tragiki%20 Epeteios.3.pdf [Accessed on 15 May 2014].*
Ecumenical Federation of Constantinopolitans. (2015b). *60 years on from the pogrom of 6–7 September 1955 against the Greek-Orthodox community of Istanbul: time for remedy and reparation for the survival of the community*. PowerPoint presentation to the European Parliament, 12 October 2015. Available at: www.conpolis.eu/upload edNews/European%20Parliament%20-%20Monday%2012%20October%202015.pdf [Accessed on 15 May 2014].
Ekdóseis Tsoukátou (2004). *'You will never forget the place where you were born...': The expulsions of 1964. Testimonies of Greeks of Constantinople*. Athens: Ekdóseis Tsoukátou.*
Gryntakis, G. (1995). *Imbros and Tenedos: two forgotten Greek islands (1910–1930)*. Athens: Imvrian Association.*
Güven, D. (2008). The 'deep' state, the *Septemvrianá* and democracy in Modern Turkey. In Ecumenical Federation of Constantinopolitans. *Proceedings of international conference*: Septemvrianá *6–7/9/1955 an act of annihilation of the Greek community of Istanbul*. 13 September 2008. Athens, 9–15.*
Güven, D. (2009). *Nationalism, social changes and minorities: the episodes against the non-Muslims of Turkey (6/7 September 1955)*. Translated from the German by S. Avgerinou. Athens: Estía.
Güven, D. (2015). 55 years later. In *The* Septemvrianá: *the persecution of the Hellenes of Constantinople*. Special issue of *Kathimeriní*, 10 September 2015, 45–46.*

Halstead, H. (2012). *Heirs to Byzantium: multidirectional narrative and identity amongst the Istanbul–Greek migrant community in Greece*. Unpublished: University of York. MA by research.

Halstead, H. (2014). Harmony and strife in memories of Greek–Turkish intercommunal relationships in Istanbul and Cyprus. *Journal of Modern Greek Studies*, 32(2), 393–415.

Helsinki Watch. (1992). *Denying human rights and ethnic identity: the Greeks of Turkey*. New York; Washington; Los Angeles; London: Human Rights Watch.

Hirschon, R. (1999). Identity and the Greek state: some conceptual issues and paradoxes. In R. Clogg, (Ed.). *The Greek diaspora in the twentieth century*. New York: St. Martin's Press, 158–180.

Hirschon, R. (2004). 'Unmixing peoples' in the Aegean region. In R. Hirschon, (Ed.). *Crossing the Aegean: an appraisal of the 1923 compulsory population exchange between Greece and Turkey*. New York; Oxford: Berghahn Books, 3–12.

Imvriakí Ichó. (1974). It's time, September–October 1974.*

Imvrian Association (2002). *The Imvrian question in the Greek Parliament*. Athens: Imvrian Association.*

Imvrian Association. (no date-a). *Imvrian Association*. Available at: www.imvrosisland.org/sillogos.php [Accessed on 7 January 2016].*

Imvrian Association. (no date-b). *Calendar of important events*. Available at: www.imvrosisland.org/imvros.php?subid=15&catid=1 [Accessed on 12 December 2015].*

Imvros. (1995). 'Imvrian Association' 1945–1995: '50 years of contribution and activity', September–October–November 1995.*

Isaakidis, G. (2014). Interview with author. Athens, 22 March 2014.*

Karakasidou, A. (1997). *Fields of wheat, hills of blood: passages to nationhood in Greek Macedonia, 1870–1990*. Chicago, IL: University of Chicago Press.

Mills, A. (2005). Narratives in city landscapes: cultural identity in Istanbul. *Geographical Review*, 95(3), 441–462.

O Polítis. (1994). The loss of memory, September 1994.*

Oran, B. (2004). The story of those who stayed: lessons from articles 1 and 2 of the 1923 convention. In R. Hirschon, (Ed.). *Crossing the Aegean: an appraisal of the 1923 compulsory population exchange between Greece and Turkey*. New York: Berghahn Books, 97–115.

Örs, İ. R. (2006). Beyond the Greek and Turkish dichotomy: the *Rum Polites* of Istanbul and Athens. *South European Society and Politics*, 11(1), 79–94.

Ouzounoglou, N. (2014). Skype interview with author. Athens/York, 16 May 2014.*

Özkirimli, U. and Sofos, S. A. (2008). *Tormented by history: nationalism in Greece and Turkey*. London: Hurst.

Sarioglou, E. (2012a). '... And afterwards it became what dreams become, flames and blood...'. In E. Sarioglou and K. Sarioglou (Eds.). *Fifty years on from the Septemvrianá. Constantinople: before – then – after*. Athens: Ellinikó Ídryma Istorikó Meletón, 107–110.*

Sarioglou, E. (2012b). The Greek minority of Constantinople after the *Septemvrianá*. In E. Sarioglou and K. Sarioglou (Eds). *Fifty years on from the Septemvrianá. Constantinople: before – then – after*. Athens: Ellinikó Ídryma Istorikó Meletón, 193–199.*

Sifounakis, N. (2017). Imbros-Tenedos: from the Treaty of Lausanne to the dramatic contraction of Hellenism. Athens: Ekdotikós Organismós Liváni.*

Treaty of Lausanne. (1923). 24 July 1923. Available at: www.mfa.gov.tr/lausanne-peace-treaty.en.mfa [Accessed on 7 January 2016].

Tsimouris, G. (2001). Reconstructing 'home' among the 'enemy': the Greeks of Gökseada (Imvros) after Lausanne. *Balkanologie*, 5 (1–2).

Tsimouris, G. (2008). *Imvrioi*. Athens: Elliniká Grámmata.*

Tunç, A. and Ferentinou, A. (2012). Identities in-between: the impact of satellite broadcasting on Greek Orthodox minority (Rum Polites) women's perception of their identities in Turkey. *Ethnic and Racial Studies*, 35(5), 906–923.

Turan, Ç., Pekin, M., and Güvenç, S. (2010). *Constantinople/Istanbul, my nostalgia: refugee narratives and the nostalgia of the* Romioí *of Constantinople/Istanbul*. Istanbul: Lozan Mübadilleri Vakfı. [In Greek and Turkish].

Vryonis, S. (2005). *The mechanism of catastrophe: the Turkish pogrom of September 6–7, 1955, and the destruction of the Greek community of Istanbul*. New York: Greekworks.

Xeinos, G. (1998). *Schoinoúdi*, its *Chálakas* and its *Piátsa*. In *The settlements of Imbros: symposium proceedings*. Thessaloniki: Etairía Melétis Ímvrou kai Tenédou.*

Xeinos, G. (2011). *Imbros and Tenedos: parallel histories*. Athens: Etaireía Melétis tis Kath' Imás Anatolís.*

de Zayas, A. (2007). The Istanbul pogrom of 6–7 September 1955 in the light of international law. *Genocide Studies and Prevention*, 2(2), 137–154.

Part II
Local homelands and national belonging

2 *Patrída* as a local metaphor

Over the past decade or so, there has been renewed interest in the everyday reception and articulation of nationhood by 'ordinary people', i.e. non-elites (Antonsich 2016; Brubaker *et al.* 2006; Edensor 2006; Fox 2017; Fox and Jones 2013; Fox and Miller-Idriss 2008a; Fox and Miller-Idriss 2008b; Goode and Stroup 2015; Hearn 2007; Miller-Idriss and Rothenberg 2012; Piwoni 2015; Skey 2009; Todd 2015). This built on earlier discussions that had attempted to address a perceived imbalance in favour of elite or top-down perspectives in the classic literature on nationalism, typically associated in particular with Ernest Gellner, Benedict Anderson, and Anthony Smith (Billig 1995; Brubaker 2004; Cohen 1996; Confino 1993; Edensor 2002; Eriksen 1993; Herzfeld 1997; Mavratsas 1999; Sutton 1998; Thompson 2001).

Some of the earliest contributions to this literature were made by anthropologists. In 1993, for instance, Thomas Hyland Eriksen advocated an analytical distinction between 'formal nationalism' – associated with the state, the written word, and mass media – and 'informal nationalism' – expressed through civil society, speech, and face-to-face communication (1993:2, 19). Writing in 1996, Anthony Cohen similarly urged scholars to discriminate between the aims of nationalist elites and the 'personal nationalism' created when people 'refract nationhood through their own personal experience and aspirations' (1996:804, 807–808). The study of informal nationalism was taken in an important new direction by social psychologist Michael Billig in 1995, who placed emphasis on what he called 'banal nationalism'. Billig focused not on explicit expressions of nationalism found in public ceremonies or at moments of national crisis, but on the ubiquitous, unconscious, and mundane 'reminders of nationhood' embedded in everyday life; on the 'unwaved flag' rather than the 'waved flag' (1995:8–9, 39–43, 50–51, 58–59). In 2002, Tim Edensor – in part building on Billig's account – similarly argued that national identity is typically 'mundane' rather than 'remarkable', consisting of a 'national habitus' comprising practical everyday knowledge, embodied habits, and everyday routines (Edensor 2002:vi, 12, 92–96; see also Edensor 2006:531–539). In contrast to Billig, however, Edensor placed greater emphasis on the heterogeneity and dynamism of national identity, stressing that the national habitus is constantly challenged and reworked by everyday performance (Edensor 2002:29, 33, 100–102, 188; although cf. Billig 2009:347–348).

More recent scholarship has confirmed this dynamic nature of nationhood whilst also calling into question its salience as a component of everyday life. In a study of ethnicity in the Transylvanian town Cluj, Rogers Brubaker and colleagues – unlike Billig and Edensor – emphasised the *weakness* and *intermittency* rather than pervasiveness of nationhood in day-to-day life (Brubaker *et al.* 2006:5–6, 11, 168, 191, 206–208, 219, 237–238, 363). Drawing on Brubaker's earlier criticism of 'groupism' – that is, 'the tendency to take discreet, bounded groups as basic constituents of social life' (Brubaker 2004:8) – they conceptualised ethnicity as something one *does* or *becomes* rather than *has* or *is*, something that *happens* in specific contexts rather than *exists* generally (Brubaker *et al.* 2006:208–209). For them, conceiving of ethnicity not as an entity but as 'a way of seeing, a way of talking, a way of acting' would allow us to challenge 'over-ethnicized interpretations' and avoid uncritically equating 'the *political* centrality of nationalist rhetoric with the *experiential* centrality of nationness in the lives of ordinary people' (Brubaker *et al.* 2006:167, 207, 263). In recent years, analysts – including Fox, one of Brubaker's co-authors – have been drawing on these earlier interventions in an effort to fine-tune a methodology for studying everyday nationhood that would focus attention on 'ordinary people as active producers – and not just passive consumers – of national discourse' (Fox and Miller-Idriss 2008a:539, 555–556; see also Fox 2017; Fox and Jones 2013; Goode and Stroup 2015; Miller-Idriss and Rothenberg 2012; Piwoni 2015; Skey 2009; and cf. Smith 2008).

In Part II of this book, I aim to contribute to this research by exploring what nationhood means to my interviewees, and what they *do* with national identity and national stereotypes in their oral testimonies. In particular, I am concerned with examining the interface between nationalist rhetoric and local, individual concerns and meanings. I begin in this chapter by surveying influential studies of Greek nationalism and national identity through the lens of everyday nationhood. I demonstrate that there is a strong body of work that has treated ordinary Greeks as active producers of nationalism rather than simply its passive consumers. At the same time, I seek to demonstrate how the historian Alon Confino's characterisation of the nation as a 'local metaphor' can provide a useful framework for describing the relationship between 'ordinary people' and nationalist discourse.

It is important to note at this juncture that there is in (non-academic) modern Greek no comparable distinction between 'ethnic' and 'national', both of which are covered by the term *ethnikós* (Deltsou 2000:31; Herzfeld 1997:41–42). Furthermore, Greek *ethnikótita* ('ethnicity' or 'nationality') cannot be equated with the possession of Greek citizenship or loyalty to the Greek state (Millas 2008), and there is a clearer distinction than in English between the *éthnos* (nation) and the state (*krátos*) (Just 1989:72). In Anastasia Karakasidou's terms, 'the nation of the Hellenes is a conceptual entity entirely distinct from the citizens of Greece' such that 'many Greeks today are forceful critics of the state and those who work for it, while at the same time they are equally impassioned defenders of the nation' (1997b:26; see also Herzfeld 1997). When translating from the Greek, I endeavour to infer from the context which of the English words 'ethnic' or 'national' (or 'ethnicity' or 'nationality') would best convey the narrator's meaning (though I preserve *éthnos* in the original Greek). Whilst this involves an element of subjective interpretation, it is preferable to the wholesale adoption of one of the English terms over the other, which would result in some misleading translations.

Patrída as a local metaphor

In a comparative discussion of nation-building and national identity in Germany and India, Confino and Ajay Skaria criticised existing scholarship for conceiving of the relationship between the local and the national according to a 'logic of transcendence' that treated the locality as an essentially passive entity that is moulded and transcended by the nation and nationalist elites (2002:8–9). According to this logic of transcendence, the local is not itself 'a shaper of nationalism' but rather 'a repository of national belonging created elsewhere' (Confino and Skaria 2002:9). Confino and Skaria argued that such approaches sidelined another kind of local, one which they dubbed the 'other local', a space where the nation is subordinated to, and draws meaning from, the local, as well as *vice versa* (2002:9–12). This local is not exhausted, sublated, or transcended by nationalism, but rather 'continues to live, in the era of nationhood, not so much outside the national but beyond and alongside it' (Confino and Skaria 2002:10). It is this 'other local' in Greek nationhood with which I am concerned here.

The notion of the 'other local' drew on Confino's earlier criticism of scholarship on nationalism for its 'failure to encompass the malleability of nationhood' (1993:43). He explored how people use the nation as a 'local metaphor' in order to 'devise a common denominator between the intimate, immediate and real local place and the distant and abstract national world' (Confino 1993:44). Confino developed this argument through a discussion of the *Heimat* movement in Germany. This word lacks a direct equivalent in English, but is often loosely translated as 'homeland', and 'denotes one's emotional attachment to a territory conceived as home, be it a small locality or large, abstract homeland' (Confino 2014:64). The *Heimat* movement rose to prominence in the 1880s, and found expression principally in local and regional *Heimat* associations, *Heimatkunde* (*Heimat* studies) on the school curriculum, *Heimat* museums, and *Heimat* publications (Confino 1993:50–51). These initiatives sought to represent the specificity of local communities and histories, but also simultaneously to integrate these into a 'national whole', thereby making the German nation meaningful to local people by 'endow[ing] the abstract nation [with] the tangibility of local experience' (Confino 1993:60–62). The *Heimat* idea thus represented belonging, but was taxonomically malleable, 'an interchangeable representation of the local, the regional and the national community' (Confino 1993:50). Even though a 'thousand Heimats dotted Germany, each claiming uniqueness and particularity', when brought together 'the Heimats informed the ideal of a single, transcendent nationality' (Confino 1993:62). In other words, belonging to a national collectivity in Germany was largely constructed through attachment to one's local area: '[a]rmed with hometown patriotism, every locality wrote its own *Heimat* history, emphasising its own historical importance and inheritance' (Confino 1993:55) and 'publiciz[ing] [its] singularity in national and local history' (Confino 2014:65).

We can draw certain instructive parallels between the importance of the *Heimat* idea in German nation-building, and the significance of the Greek notion of *patrída* in Greek nationalism, a term that we might also translate as 'homeland'.[1] Writing in 1910, the folklorist John Lawson observed that if a Greek 'be asked what is his nation land (*patrida*), his answer will be, not Greece nor any of the larger divisions of it, but the particular town or hamlet in which he happened to be born' (quoted in Peckham 2001:62). In this sense, *patrída* and the sense of belonging it evoked were firmly rooted in the locality. Yet in Greece as in Germany, 'the logic of nation-state formation harmonized extraordinarily well with the persistence of localist ideologies' (Herzfeld 1997:74). As Robert Peckham identified, the construction of Greek national identity was 'closely bound up with the celebration of local, regional identities', expressed through literature, folklore, and local historical and topographical studies (2001:67–68). German *Heimatkunde* inspired a *patridografía* (*patrída* studies) movement in Greece in the 1880s, in which 'the "local" homeland or *patrída* was emphasized as an essential cultural and historical constituent of the national space' (Peckham 2001:76). In line with this movement, school curricula in Greece 'increasingly focused on students' acquaintance with the localities before moving outwards to engage with other larger geographical categories' (Peckham 2001:76), thereby endowing the nation, to use Confino's terms, with a sense of 'coziness' by making use of 'personal, recognisable experiences, which were immediately familiar and capable of being projected onto larger entities' (Confino 1993:70). In this way, *patrída*, like *Heimat*, came simultaneously to represent the locality and the nation, such that, for instance, amongst the Greek refugees from the Ottoman Empire, *patrída* could refer both 'to a physical homeland, from which people were obliged to emigrate' and 'embody the notion of a national collectivity and refer to a national homeland' (Karakasidou 1997b:150–151). Each Greek can envisage the national *patrída* through the lens of their own local *patrída*, and feel belonging to an abstract national collectivity grounded in belonging to a tangible local community. The national *patrída* thus draws its appeal and durability from its ambiguity and malleability.

Understanding *patrída* as a local metaphor for national attachment helps us to avoid a logic of transcendence that juxtaposes local and national identity and sees the former as subordinate to the latter (Confino and Skaria 2002:9), and instead to perceive how Greeks can be 'at one and the same time, say, local and national' (Confino 1997:1399). Michael Herzfeld tells a story of a Cretan man who was moved to tears when relating an incident in 1866 in which a group of Cretans surrounded by Turks in a monastery killed themselves rather than submitting to their opponents. Herzfeld posed the question:

Is he, at that moment, celebrating kin, local, Cretan, or Greek identity? Only a literalist would insist that we should choose only one level of identification, for his performance resonates at all of them. Yet this adumbration of concentric loyalties runs counter to the exclusivism of nation-state ideology. While the old man might wish to identify with the national ideal, his message is always potentially subversive, because it raises the possibility that one of the less inclusive levels of solidarity might eventually prevail and command a more immediate attachment.

(1997:81–82)

As this anecdote demonstrates, a national identification does not necessarily preclude attachment to other identities (Confino 1993:44). But there is more to it than that. Herzfeld has also written about Cretan sheep thieves who find justification for their defiance of Greek law by portraying their 'exploits as emblematic of Cretan daring and of the Greeks' unquenchable love of independence' (Herzfeld 1987:45), the latter a cornerstone of Greek nationalist narratives of resistance to the Turks. In this sense, local dissent from national authority can still represent idealised national values (Herzfeld 1997; see below). Cretan sheep thieves can see themselves as *quintessentially* national precisely *because* of their local, Cretan particularities, even if these are in direct defiance of national authority. Put differently, we are dealing not simply with the capacity for an individual to be both national (Greek) and local (Cretan), but with the two as overlapping realms such that national identity is made tangible through local particularity, whilst local particularity takes on broader significance through national abstraction (Confino and Skaria 2002:11). This is the 'other local' where the locality and the nation are mutually reinforcing rather than locked in an antagonistic contest in which one must trump the other. I develop these observations in greater detail in the next chapter, but first I consider how Greek national identity, notwithstanding its surface simplicity and near universal acceptance in Greece (Just 1989:71), is premised upon the incorporation (and not just the silencing) of local particularities and complexities.

Through the looking glass: continuity, invention, imposition

A key debate in the literature on modern Greece – as in scholarship on nationalism generally – has been whether modern Greek identity should be conceptualised in terms of awakening (the nationalist and primordialist position), invention (Hobsbawm 1983) and imagination (Anderson 1983) connected with modernisation, or structural and symbolic continuity (the ethnosymbolist perspective; see, for instance, Smith 2008). Greek nationalist scholars, in Karakasidou's words, have often tended to 'imply that a Greek nation, apparently impervious to change, has survived since ancient times as a vestibule of high culture in the path to civilisation, both for the world in general and for the Balkans in particular' (1997b:15). To cite an example pertinent to the present study, the Greek American historian Vryonis, introducing his account of the *Septemvrianá*, declared:

> Along with the Jews, Egyptians, and Italians, the Greeks possess one of the longest, most continuous, and most extensively recorded histories in the Mediterranean basin. Because of this unbroken chronological presence – as well as the role of the ancient element of this history in the formation of Western civilization and Byzantium's contribution to the formation of the civilization of much of Eastern Europe – the Greeks are extremely sensitive to their historical presence as a people.
>
> (2005:1–2)

A desire to demonstrate commonality between the ancient and the modern Greeks has been a feature both of domestic nationalist discourse and that of many foreign admirers. The history textbooks used in Greek schools, for instance, have often strived to demonstrate cultural and territorial continuity from prehistory via ancient history to the present day, sometimes blurring 'empirical archaeological facts and mythology' in the process (Hamilakis 2003:45, 48, 50, 54–55), whilst numerous non-Greek classicists and folklorists have scoured the Greek countryside for the vestiges of ancient Greek civilisation, such that the contemporary Greeks became 'nothing more than a blank screen on which we can project our romantic fantasies of ancient Greek life' (Danforth 1984:53, 64).

Karakasidou characterised such nationalist historical narratives as 'looking-glass histories' that 'search backwards over the hills and valleys of historical events to trace the inexorable route of a given (or "chosen") population to the destiny of their national enlightenment and liberation' (1997b:17). Through the looking-glass, scholars may fail to recognise the constructed nature of self and other (Karakasidou 1997b:18). The inappropriateness of this national looking-glass is exacerbated by the fact that, before the nineteenth century, what are today national identities were often occupational or religious identities: Greeks were called 'Greeks' because they were merchants, or Bulgarians called 'Bulgarians' because they were peasants (Cowan 1997:156; Danforth 1995:59; Mackridge 2009:56), whilst for non-Ottomans, 'Greek' meant Orthodox Christian of the Ottoman Empire, in much the same way as 'Latin' meant Catholic (Mackridge 2009:47).

In response to these looking-glass histories, several researchers have highlighted the processes of construction and contestation involved in the proliferation of Greek national identity in Macedonia before, during, and after Greek acquisition of territory in the region in 1913. Loring Danforth – in his study of the emergence of a Macedonian national identity and its conflict with Greek nationalism – argued that nation-building in Macedonia involved the imposition of national identities on previously-existing and comparatively fluid ethnic, linguistic, and religious distinctions (1995:57, 61). Under the Ottoman Empire, Macedonia was host to Greek-speaking and Slavic-speaking Orthodox Christians, Turkish-speaking and Albanian-speaking Muslims, and smaller numbers of Vlachs, Jews, and gypsies, many of whom had no clearly defined national consciousness (Danforth 1993:3; Mackridge and Yannakakis 1997:5). In the late nineteenth and early twentieth centuries, Greek, Bulgarian, and Serbian nationalist movements competed for the allegiance of these populations (Danforth 1995:58). Danforth described how Greece, after its territorial acquisitions in 1913, pursued an assimilationist agenda in an effort to 'Hellenise' the inhabitants of southern Macedonia, particularly targeting Slavic-speaking Christians by changing Slavic toponyms and clamping down on the use of the Slavic language (1993:4; 1995:69–70). This Hellenisation process, comparatively successful amongst the Greek and Albanian-speaking Orthodox Christians and the Vlachs, encountered significant resistance amongst the Slavic-speaking population, some of whom, in Danforth's terms, 'came to identify themselves in a national sense as Macedonians, not as Greeks' (1995:71). By the mid-twentieth century, therefore, comparatively fluid nineteenth-century ethnic identities had been 'transformed into sharply polarized and mutually exclusive national identities' (Danforth 1995:73).

Karakasidou offered an equally forceful critique of national(ist) histories based on research in a central Macedonian village in Greece in the 1990s, which, according to informal local histories, had in the late Ottoman period been peopled by Slavic-speaking agriculturalists, Greek-speaking merchants, Turkish-speaking landowners, and others (Karakasidou 1997b:10). She argued that the apparently 'primordial sentiments' that bound contemporary villagers together as 'descendants of ancient Hellenes' were 'a constructed tradition' that was 'not so much a matter of choice or primordial attachment as it was a result of historical contingency' (Karakasidou 1997b:74). According to Karakasidou, Greek nation-builders transformed 'the population of a diverse ethnic tapestry into Greek nationals' thereby imposing 'a homogeneity on the Macedonian region and its inhabitants' (1997b:25, 94). As a result, 'the boundaries that people once crossed with relative ease were tightened, reified, or closed', as Greek national identity and history were written over pre-existing 'localized memories of personal experience' (Karakasidou 1997b:21, 235). Karakasidou, in common with Danforth, stressed that for some Macedonian inhabitants the acquisition of a Hellenic identity 'was gentle, even profitable' (Karakasidou 1997b:227). Equally, she emphasised that the spread of Greek national identity was not simply the 'result of a heavy-handed acculturation campaign directed by national elites', but was also a 'dialectical product of the interaction of state and local interests' (Karakasidou 1997b:188). Nevertheless, she concluded that nation-building in Macedonia – especially for those who had already formed an allegiance to an alternative ethnic or national identity – was 'nasty, brutish, and short' (Karakasidou 1997b:72, 227).

Danforth and Karakasidou shared an admirable desire, in Karakasidou's words, to challenge 'the charade of modern chauvinism' and 'make an effort at dismantling boundaries rather than raising them' (Danforth 1997:668–669; Danforth 2003:212; Karakasidou 1997b:82). I do not contest their portrayals of the ways in which Greek nation-builders attempted to proliferate Greek national identity in Macedonia, nor of the frequently (and often severely) damaging implications of these attempts for particular local populations. In terms of understanding the complexities of national belonging *after* these initial processes of nation-building, however, and the range of ways (beyond antagonism) in which national identity might relate to local particularities, both studies are for our purposes somewhat limited by a logic of transcendence. Danforth contrasted the pre-national ethnic identities of the nineteenth century with the national identities imposed by elites in the twentieth century, and viewed the latter as transcending or sublating the former. Karakasidou, similarly, saw national identity as existing in an antagonistic, one-way, and ultimately destructive relationship with local identities, pre-national heterogeneity replaced by national homogeneity. Although she showed awareness of how nation-building functioned by incorporating local discourse, for instance considering how local village myths of ancestral descent from Alexander the Great linked 'the locale to the nation of the Hellenes' (Karakasidou 1997b:32, 36), the locality in her study remains 'only the context for the national idea' (Confino and Skaria 2002:8), and the 'other local' that continues to exist alongside the nation, adapting and reshaping its contours in the course of everyday life, is left unexplored. Simultaneously, by placing emphasis on the homogenising impact of Greek nation-building in the region, both authors discounted the possibility that Greek identity today might mean different things to different people in diverse local settings (although cf. Karakasidou 1997a:99). In this sense, they risked assuming that identity can only be fluid and multifaceted insofar as individuals have access to distinctive ethnic or linguistic heritages, in the process downplaying the performative plasticity of national identity itself. When Karakasidou argued that the nation-building process in northern Greece

> has been enormously successful. Most of the inhabitants today, regardless of their ethnic background and how their ancestors might have defined themselves 100 or even 50 years ago, conceive of themselves now as nothing less than Greek.
>
> (1993:5)

she was almost certainly right. But it is also probable that many would conceive of themselves as *more than simply Greek*: to feel, for instance, that they are Greek Macedonian, and that this is different from being, say, Greek Peloponnesian, or that they are 'native Greeks' and that this is different from being of refugee descent; and perhaps, moreover, that it is this local particularity that makes them *particularly* Greek (see Chapter 3). This is not mere pedantry, nor an attempt to deny the role of coercion and imposition in the proliferation of national identities. Rather, it is to suggest that we cannot understand the contemporary success and appeal of nationalism by focusing on its homogenising effect alone, to the exclusion of how its unifying potential is partly premised on the ways in which it accommodates and, even, is driven by local heterogeneity.

The 'usable past': the everyday life of national identity

As K. S. Brown and Yannis Hamilakis observed, '[m]any accounts of the construction of Greek national identity construct a picture of a monolithic, imposing, and overarching political and ideological structure (the nation-state) which

Patrída *as a local metaphor* 53

dominates the lives, bodies, and minds of its citizens' (2003:6). To a greater or lesser degree, this is the impression created by the studies considered in the previous section. Brown and Hamilakis argued for an alternative perspective, one which would recognise Greek nationalism as a 'complex and internally fragmented phenomenon' (2003:8); as Hamilakis put it, 'the national "usable past" is a matter of constant (and often successful) negotiation in people's everyday lives' (Hamilakis 2003:61). In this section, I present the work of several scholars who have paid attention to this 'usable past', and suggest that these better equip us to avoid the logic of transcendence and uncover the different ways in which nationhood becomes meaningful in people's lives.

In his study of tradition and modernity on the Aegean island of Kalymnos, David Sutton sought to demonstrate that an awareness of the past looms large in everyday experience, and, in turn, that it is through such everyday experience that references to history become meaningful (1998:207). For Sutton, studies of nationalism had focused disproportionately on uncovering and debunking 'invented traditions' and exploring top-down constructions of the past, rather than considering how nationalist movements 'often achieve their appeal by accommodating themselves to local-level discourses, and by mobilizing already existing cultural ideas' (1998:6, 174). Indeed, connections between the local and the national were a feature of Sutton's fieldwork on Kalymnos. Residents of Kalymnos (Kalymnians) frequently used local kinship metaphors to explain national politics – referring, for example, to neighbouring countries as 'bad neighbours' – and, *vice versa*, deployed metaphors derived from national politics to explain local situations – as when one Kalymnian woman compared her dictatorial father to the Turkish invasion of Cyprus (Sutton 1998:124). Through such examples, Sutton was able to demonstrate that national history is a resource that people on Kalymnos actively deploy to make sense of the day-to-day present, a 'usable past' (Hamilakis 2003:61) that is not simply imposed by nationalist elites but is 'grounded in everyday human activity' (Sutton 1998:10). Moreover, he showed that national history is, in turn, interpreted and made meaningful through local experience, thereby 'anchoring the imagined community in daily practice' (Sutton 1998:123). In this way, Sutton drew attention to the interpenetration of national and local experience in everyday discourse, confirming that the durability and pervasiveness of nationalism is premised in part on the mutual accommodation of the nation and the locality rather than simply the transcendence of the latter by the former. To borrow terms from Confino and Skaria, Kalymnians 'imagined nationhood as a form of localness, while [in turn] the immediate local world imparted on the abstract national one a sense of physicality, everydayness, and authenticity' (2002:11).

Fellow anthropologist Herzfeld expressed similar scepticism about top-down approaches to the study of nationalism, which he argued not only disregard the impact that ordinary people have 'on the form of their local nationalism', but also gloss over the fact that 'national identity comprises a generous measure of embarrassment together with all of the idealized virtues' (1997:6). As a corrective to such approaches, Herzfeld proposed the concept of 'cultural intimacy' (1997:13–14). According to this theory, an intimate knowledge of national imperfection, which is kept hidden from outsiders, is commonly acknowledged in informal everyday discourse, and provides the basis for internal solidarity between co-nationals (Herzfeld 1997:3). For Herzfeld, studying this cultural intimacy allows us to see beyond the 'deceptively transparent surface' of the nation and to recognise that '[t]here is no single "national view"' except that presented externally in an effort to hide an intimate knowledge of imperfection (1997:2, 171). His argument is not only that such imperfection is kept hidden from national outsiders, but that 'it is paradoxically the insubordinate values and practices that make patriotism attractive from day-to-day' (Herzfeld 1997:169), as in the case of the Cretan sheep thieves (see above) who evoke national ideals of resistance and independence as justification for contravening the authority of the Greek state (Herzfeld 1987:45–46). As Herzfeld put it, people can be 'fiercely patriotic and just as fiercely rebellious at one and the same time' (1997:55).

Herzfeld's study of cultural intimacy flags the disjuncture between the idealised fixity of nationalist discourse and the imperfect contours of nationhood in everyday life. He argued that nationalism's apparently 'semantically stable terminology' belies a quotidian plasticity: as objects of intimacy, national identities and ideologies can in the course of day-to-day life be reshaped and experience significant changes in meaning without disrupting their external appearance of rigidity and simplicity (Herzfeld 1997:30, 42–43). This has significant implications for how we interpret people's usages of ethnic or national signifiers. In Herzfeld's terms, '[f]ixity of form does not necessarily entail a corresponding fixity of meanings and intentions' (1997:22). He gave the example of the term 'Vlach', which in Greek discourse could refer to a member of the pastoralist Koutsovlach community, to a northern Greek shepherd more generally, or figuratively to a country bumpkin. For most Greeks, the context in which the term is used would be sufficient for them to ascertain what meaning was intended (Herzfeld 1997:44). Herzfeld referred to these identity labels as 'ethnic shifters', whose 'semantic fixity' allows people to treat them as 'existential absolutes' whilst also permitting 'a surprising amount of semantic slippage' (1997:45, 51).

The plasticity of ethnic and national labels has also been explored by Jane Cowan and K. S. Brown, in their introduction to a collection of essays on identity in Macedonia. They were critical of the 'endlessly reiterated metaphors of *macédoines*, mosaics and cheese boards' that scholars used to characterise identity and difference in the region (Cowan and Brown 2000:9). By the logic of such metaphors, Cowan and Brown suggested, conflict in Macedonia is seen as a product of the essential differences between its various inhabitants, and each of its groups is treated as a distinctive component of an ethnic fruit salad, 'maintaining their separate but juxtaposed identities or flavours' (2000:3). Thus even as scholars 'tirelessly declared' the self-evidently constructed nature of nations and national identities, they nevertheless reinforced a perception of ethnic groups 'as discreet and irreducible "billiard balls" in collision' (Cowan and Brown 2000:3).

Consequently, the variability and contingency of identity labels are 'rendered invisible', setting up '"odd equivalences" such that Albanians are considered to be the same whether in the Republic of Macedonia or Kosovo, whilst Macedonians in Greece are the same as Macedonians in Bulgaria' (Cowan and Brown 2000:13). The ways in which individuals respond to national categories and their 'differing orientations to a "shared" identity' are, in the process, given comparatively little thought (Cowan and Brown 2000:13). In contradistinction to such approaches, Cowan and Brown sought to 'emphasise the contingent and context-specific ways in which identity and difference are expressed, or eschewed' (2000:3). Like Brubaker *et al.* (see above), they stressed that ethnicity is 'not always and everywhere an equally salient rubric for organising individual lives, biographies and social relations' (Cowan and Brown 2000:15). They offered the term 'inflections' as an alternative metaphor for identity in the region, one which would reject 'a notion of the signifier as singular and univocal', and instead capture how 'a single word is altered by the particularities of enunciation – tone, colour, voice, emotion – within particular contexts, enabling a rich variability in connotation and, ultimately, denotation' (Cowan and Brown 2000:20). By exploring the inflections of ethnic identities, Cowan and Brown, like Herzfeld, took 'the meaning of a word to inhere not in the word itself, but in its enunciation within particular performative contexts' (Cowan and Brown 2000:20).

The discussion pursued in this chapter allows us to elaborate a conceptual framework for describing how ordinary people experience and construct national attachment through the particularities of their own local experiences. If the terminological stability of ethnic and national categories provides an illusion of fixity and commonality that facilitates large-scale solidarity between co-nationals, at the same time the capacity of identity labels to produce variable semantic inflections in everyday performative contexts allows for considerable flexibility in terms of what it *means* for an individual to be 'Greek' at any given moment. In fact, because idioms of national belonging and national virtue are so readily subordinated to local particularity (Sutton 1998), 'being Greek' is often given substance through the familiar local world rather than the abstract national one. Nationalism is intimately malleable, and therefore comforting and recognisable, but is simultaneously formally static, thereby providing a common denominator that draws together individuals otherwise separated by 'real social and political differences' (Confino 1997:1399–1400). In this sense, national identities are semantically neither fixed nor free-floating, but 'hollow' in that they have 'quanta of available empty space that can be loaded with additional properties: more virtues, more glories, more blame' (Theodossopoulos 2006:3). They do not *lack* content, but rather have no firmly *fixed* content beyond their surface form, and can thus be differently configured and reconfigured in order 'to allow new sets of meaning to dwell in their available hollowness' without severely or irreparably disrupting the illusion of national unity (Theodossopoulos 2006:18, 23). In the next chapter, I pursue this discussion by exploring how the Greeks of Turkey developed their sense of self and belonging as residents of the Greek state after emigration from Turkey.

Note

1 It is not my intention to equate these two terms, which have distinct etymologies and histories, but rather to suggest certain commonalities as regards the relationship between the local and the national in Greek and German nationalism. I translate *patrída* as 'homeland', although, for etymological exactitude, it could also be translated as 'fatherland', which, as Danforth observed, would make the common expression *mitéra patrída* ('mother fatherland') something of a mixed metaphor (1995:82).

References

(Items marked * are in the Greek language.)

Anderson, B. (1983). *Imagined communities: reflections on the origin and spread of nationalism*. London: Verso.

Antonsich, M. (2016). The 'everyday' of banal nationalism: ordinary people's views on Italy and Italian. *Political Geography*, 54, 32–42.

Billig, M. (1995). *Banal nationalism*. London; Thousand Oaks: SAGE Publications.

Billig, M. (2009). Reflecting on a critical engagement with banal nationalism – reply to Skey. *The Sociological Review*, 57(2), 347–352.

Brown, K. S. and Hamilakis, Y. (2003). The cupboard of the yesterdays? Critical perspectives on the usable past. In K. S. Brown and Y. Hamilakis (Eds.). *The usable past: Greek metahistories*. Lanham: Lexington Books, 1–19.

Brubaker, R. (2004). *Ethnicity without groups*. Cambridge: Harvard University Press.

Brubaker, R., Feischmidt, M., Fox, J., and Grancea, L. (2006). *Nationalist politics and everyday ethnicity in a Transylvanian town*. Princeton, NJ: Princeton University Press.

Cohen, A. P. (1996). Personal nationalism: a Scottish view of some rites, rights, and wrongs. *American Ethnologist*, 23(4), 802–815.

Confino, A. (1993). The nation as a local metaphor: Heimat, national memory and the German Empire, 1871–1918. *History & Memory*, 5(1), 42–86.

Confino, A. (1997). Collective memory and cultural history: problems of method. *The American Historical Review*, 102(5), 1386–1403.

Confino, A. (2014). *A world without Jews: the Nazi imagination from persecution to genocide*. New Haven; London: Yale University Press.

Confino, A. and Skaria, A. (2002). The local life of nationhood. *National Identities*, 4(1), 7–24.

Cowan, J. K. (1997). Idioms of belonging: polyglot articulations of local identity in a Greek Macedonian town. In P. A. Mackridge and E. Yannakakis (Eds.). *Ourselves and others: the development of a Greek Macedonian cultural identity since 1912*. Oxford: Berg, 153–171.

Cowan, J. K. and Brown, K. S. (2000). Introduction: Macedonian inflections. In J. K. Cowan (Ed.). *Macedonia: the politics of identity and difference*. London: Pluto Press, 1–27.

Danforth, L. M. (1984). The ideological context of the search for continuities in Greek culture. *Journal of Modern Greek Studies*, 2(1), 53–85.

Danforth, L. M. (1993). Claims to Macedonian identity: the Macedonian question and the breakup of Yugoslavia. *Anthropology Today*, 9(4), 3–10.

Danforth, L. M. (1995). *The Macedonian conflict: ethnic nationalism in a transnational world*. Princeton, NJ: Princeton University Press.

Danforth, L. M. (1997). Tolerance, nationalism, and human rights in Macedonia. *American Ethnologist*, 24(3), 668–669.

Danforth, L. M. (2003). Afterword. In K. S. Brown and Y. Hamilakis, (Eds.). *The usable past: Greek metahistories*. Lanham: Lexington Books, 211–221.

Deltsou, E. (2000). 'Tourists', 'Russian–Pontics', and 'native Greeks': identity politics in a village in northern Greece. *Anthropological Journal of European Cultures*, 9(2), 31–51.

Edensor, T. (2002). *National identity, popular culture and everyday life*. Oxford: Berg.

Edensor, T. (2006). Reconsidering national temporalities: institutional times, everyday routines, serial spaces and synchronicities. *European Journal of Social Theory*, 9(4), 525–545.

Eriksen, T. H. (1993). Formal and informal nationalism. *Ethnic and Racial Studies*, 16(1), 1–25.

Fox, J. E. (2017). The edges of the nation: a research agenda for uncovering the taken-for-granted foundations of everyday nationhood. *Nations and Nationalism*, 23(1), 26–47.

Fox, J. E. and Jones, D. (2013). Migration, everyday life and the ethnicity bias. *Ethnicities*, 13(4), 385–400.

Fox, J. E. and Miller-Idriss, C. (2008a). Everyday nationhood. *Ethnicities*, 8(4), 536–563.

Fox, J. E. and Miller-Idriss, C. (2008b). The here and now of everyday nationhood. *Ethnicities*, 8(4), 573–576.

Goode, J. P. and Stroup, D. R. (2015). Everyday nationalism: constructivism for the masses. *Social Science Quarterly*, 96(3), 717–739.

Hamilakis, Y. (2003). 'Learn history!' Antiquity, national narrative, and history in Greek educational textbooks. In K. S. Brown and Y. Hamilakis, (Eds.). *The usable past: Greek metahistories*. Lanham: Lexington Books, 39–67.

Hearn, J. (2007). National identity: banal, personal and embedded. *Nations and Nationalism*, 13(4), 657–674.

Herzfeld, M. (1987). *Anthropology through the looking-glass: critical ethnography in the margins of Europe*. Cambridge; New York: Cambridge University Press.

Herzfeld, M. (1997). *Cultural intimacy: social poetics in the nation-state*. New York: Routledge.

Hobsbawm, E. J. (1983). Introduction: inventing traditions. In E. J. Hobsbawm and T. O. Ranger, (Eds.). *The invention of tradition*. Cambridge; New York: Cambridge University Press, 1–14.

Just, R. (1989). Triumph of the ethnos. In E. Tonkin, M. McDonald, and M. Chapman (Eds.). *History and ethnicity*. London; New York: Routledge, 71–88.

Karakasidou, A. (1993). Politicizing culture: negating ethnic identity in Greek Macedonia. *Journal of Modern Greek Studies*, 11(1), 1–28.

Karakasidou, A. (1997a). Women of the family, women of the nation: national enculturation among Slav-speakers in north-west Greece. In P. Mackridge and E. Yannakakis (Eds.). *Ourselves and others: the development of a Greek Macedonian cultural identity since 1912*. Oxford: Berg, 91–109.

Karakasidou, A. (1997b). *Fields of wheat, hills of blood: passages to nationhood in Greek Macedonia, 1870–1990*. Chicago, IL: University of Chicago Press.

Mackridge, P. (2009). *Language and national identity in Greece, 1766–1976*. Oxford; New York: Oxford University Press.

Mackridge, P. A. and Yannakakis, E. (1997). Introduction. In P. Mackridge and E. Yannakakis (Eds.). *Ourselves and others: the development of a Greek Macedonian cultural identity since 1912*. Oxford: Berg, 1–22.

Mavratsas, C. V. (1999). National identity and consciousness in everyday life: towards a sociology of knowledge of Greek–Cypriot nationalism. *Nations and Nationalism*, 5(1), 91–104.

Millas, H. (2008). History writing among the Greeks and Turks: imagining the self and the other. In S. Berger and C. Lorenz, (Eds.). *The contested nation: ethnicity, class, religion and gender in national histories*. Basingstoke; New York: Palgrave Macmillan. Available at: www.herkulmillas.com/en/hm-articles/76-on-historiography/439-history-writing-among-the-greeks-and-turks-imagining-the-self-and-the-other-.html [Accessed on 17 April 2016].

Miller-Idriss, C. and Rothenberg, B. (2012). Ambivalence, pride and shame: conceptualisations of German nationhood. *Nations and Nationalism*, 18(1), 132–155.

Peckham, R. S. (2001). *National histories, natural states: nationalism and the politics of place in Greece*. London; New York: I.B. Tauris.

Piwoni, E. (2015). Claiming the nation for the people: the dynamics of representation in German public discourse about immigrant integration. *Nations and Nationalism*, 21(1), 83–101.

Skey, M. (2009). The national in everyday life: a critical engagement with Michael Billig's thesis of *Banal Nationalism*. *The Sociological Review*, 57(2), 331–346.

Smith, A. (2008). The limits of everyday nationhood. *Ethnicities*, 8(4), 563–573.

Sutton, D. (1998). *Memories cast in stone: the relevance of the past in everyday life*. Oxford; New York: Berg.

Theodossopoulos, D. (2006). Introduction: the 'Turks' in the imagination of the 'Greeks'. *South European Society and Politics*, 11(1), 1–32.

Thompson, A. (2001). Nations, national identities and human agency: putting people back into nations. *The Sociological Review*, 49(1), 18–32.

Todd, J. (2015). Partitioned identities? Everyday national distinctions in Northern Ireland and the Irish state. *Nations and Nationalism*, 21(1), 21–42.

Vryonis, S. (2005). *The mechanism of catastrophe: the Turkish pogrom of September 6–7, 1955, and the destruction of the Greek community of Istanbul*. New York: Greekworks.

3 More than simply Hellenic

Belonging and inclusive particularity

In 1924, Orthodox Christian refugees newly settled in the Greek city Volos established a football team called 'Athletic Club: Refugees of Volos' (Giossos 2008:56). In order to reflect the distinctive origins of its founders, the team played in yellow and black – colours associated with the Byzantine Empire – and bore the double-headed eagle of Byzantium as its emblem (Giossos 2008:56). By the end of 1926, however, in the face of derision from opposition fans who labelled the team's players and supporters 'seeds of the Turks', the club changed its name to 'Athletic Club "*Níkī*" of Volos', adopting the emblem of the Greek goddess Nike that had previously been used by the Smyrna-based club Panionios, and changing their team colours to the blue and white of the Greek flag (Giossos 2008:56–58). According to the official club website, these changes were made to provide a 'confirmation of the Greekness of the people of Asia Minor' (anon. 2017; see also Giossos 2008:58). In this example, a group of displaced people sought to establish inclusion in a new location by emphasising sameness over distinctiveness, replacing the yellow and black of Byzantium with the blue and white of Greece. In what follows, however, I want to demonstrate that this is not the only strategy available to a displaced community attempting to establish belonging in a 'national homeland'. My interviewees, faced with similar suspicion from the *Elladítes* or Greeks of Greece, often respond by foregrounding rather than masking the distinctiveness of their origins, and by suggesting that this distinctiveness makes them more rather than less Hellenic.

The Greeks of Turkey: a diaspora community?

The Greeks of Turkey have sometimes been referred to as a diaspora community (noted by Örs 2006:91). But what exactly makes a community diasporic? As Brubaker observed, different definitions and conceptual usages of the term abound, to the extent that one might refer to a '"diaspora" diaspora – a dispersion of the meanings of the term in semantic, conceptual and disciplinary space' (2005:1). In the words of Ulrike Meinhof and Anna Triandafyllidou, diaspora in a 'narrow sense carries connotations of alienation, displacement, nostalgia and with it a wish to return to a "motherland"' (2006:200; see, for instance, Connor 1986;

Safran 1991). Yet, if diaspora, following Walker Connor, thus refers to 'that segment of a people living outside the homeland' (1986:16), it is unclear whether the Greeks of Turkey were a diaspora community whilst living in Turkey and were thus *re*patriated to a Greek 'motherland', or whether they only became diasporic when they were *ex*patriated from Istanbul and Imbros. On the one hand, many informants recalled possessing an emotional attachment to Greece whilst living in Turkey – some would walk past the Greek embassy in Istanbul so as to be able to see the Greek flag, or collect soil on visits to Greece to take back to Turkey – and saw Greece as a national *patrída* that would protect them, or in which they might seek refuge from persecution.[1] As Gerasimos, who came to Greece as a teenager in 1964, put it to me:

> Of course [we saw Greece as a *patrída*], because we are Hellenes, we speak Greek. We are Christians, and we were in a country where everyone was Muslim, and was hostile towards us. So, yes, we saw it as a *patrída*, a place where you would like to live.
> (06/02/2012)

At the same time, however, Greece was for many an alien place, and numerous informants stressed that they never had any intention to cross the Aegean until circumstances forced them to think otherwise. As the newspaper *Imvriakí Ichó* wrote in its inaugural issue:

> In its narrowest sense *patrída* begins from the home, our village, it broadens and it is called Imbros. Away from its shores, from its narrow horizons the meaning of the word *patrís* begins to be lost for us. Away from Imbros what is our *patrída*? Where do we belong?
> (*Imvriakí Ichó* 1971)

Furthermore, many expatriates were profoundly disappointed with the reception they received in Greece when they arrived (see Chapters 2 and 4): as Vasilis lamented, 'we saw Greece as a mother *patrída*, but unfortunately Greece did not accept us as her children' (12/08/2013); or, as a relative of Fani more colourfully put it, 'we did not return to our mother *patrída*; it was rather a *step*mother *patrída*' (Fani 07/06/2013). This led many interviewees to express a feeling of disconnection from Greece as a physical place and alienation from the land on which they now lived. In the words of Thanasis, a resident of Istanbul from his birth in 1953 until emigration in 1971:

> Here 90% of Hellenes have the tendency to buy plots of land. I will never buy a plot of land. I bought a house; I bought a car; I bought a shop; I established a business; I'll buy a second shop: [but] I'll never buy a piece of earth. That means I am a refugee: I do not have the culture of the land.
> (06/02/2012)

From this perspective, as İlay Romain Örs has written, emigration from Istanbul and Imbros was an act not of 'return' but of 'expatriation', and the Greeks of Turkey could be seen as 'a Greek diaspora community *inside* Greece' whose 'only homeland' is Istanbul or Imbros (2006:91).

Yet, whilst this represents an accurate description of the discursive positions taken up by some of my interviewees (see below), it fails in three ways to capture the multiplicity of belonging commonly in evidence in expatriate narratives. First, it disregards those who feel that they have two homelands, that they belong both in the *patrída* of their birth and in the Greek national *patrída*: individuals like Panagiotis – born in Istanbul in 1946 and a resident of Greece since 1963 – who has decided to acquire dual Greek and Turkish citizenship because he has 'two *patrídes*' and wants to feel like a 'free citizen' in both (24/11/2011; for the full story see Halstead 2014:276–277).

Second, it ignores the possibility that a particular place might be invoked as a *patrída* in a certain context for 'strategic' purposes. In the pages of the newspaper *Imvros*, for instance, it is particularly common for writers to refer to Imbros as their only *patrída* – and to characterise their presence in Greece as an exile in foreign lands – when they are encouraging their compatriots to direct their energies towards the preservation of a Greek community on the island (see Chapter 8). Conversely, they tend to invoke Greece as their 'true *patrída*' (*Imvros* 1980) when advocating for support from the Greek state or protesting about the treatment of the expatriates as 'aliens' (for example, in terms of the state's disinclination to issue Greek citizenship).

Third, and perhaps most importantly, it does not take account of the (somewhat obscure) distinction between the abstract concept of the national *patrída* and the physical territory of the Greek state (Karakasidou 1997:26). During our interview, Aris initially characterised Greece as his *patrída*, commenting that every group has a place to which they return in times of need, but, when asked if he felt that he was returning home when he migrated to Greece, he responded, 'no, [it was] like I was going to a foreign place' (23/05/2013). For him, Greece is a *patrída* in an abstract and collective way, but not a home in a tangible and individual sense, a diachronic historical homeland rather than a contemporary physical one. In Artemis Leontis' terms, a place becomes a homeland not when it is *inhabited* but when it is *mapped* with history and meaning (1995:3). From this point of view, an individual might feel alienation from the physical territory of the Greek state but simultaneously feel attachment to the abstract Greek homeland, the latter constructed and sustained through attachment to their own local *patrída* (see Chapter 2, and below). Or, alternatively, they might feel a sense of belonging both to their old *patrída* in Istanbul or Imbros and to their new home in Greece, the two localities made proximate by the encompassing abstraction of the Greek national *patrída*. In this sense, the Greeks of Turkey complicate 'the very ideas of "home" and "host"' (Cohen 1997:127) by adhering to a more ambivalent sense of belonging that need not be precisely or singularly 'located' in one place or another.

Definitions of diaspora, however, have moved beyond the home/host dichotomy to focus on the centrality of 'boundary-maintenance' and, increasingly, 'boundary-erosion' (Brubaker 2005:6). For the Greeks of Turkey, boundary-maintenance – that is 'the preservation of a distinctive identity vis-à-vis a host society' (Brubaker 2005:6) – has certainly been a feature of their experiences, both in Turkey, where they attempted to preserve a distinctive identity as Greek-speaking Christians in a predominantly Turkish-speaking Muslim country, and in Greece, where many distinguish themselves from the Greeks of Greece by emphasising cultural and historical differences (see below and Chapter 4). Boundary-erosion has in particular been emphasised by scholars who see the dynamics of diaspora as antithetical to those of nationalism. Andreas Huyssen, for instance, argued that whilst national memory 'presents itself as natural, authentic, coherent and homogenous', diasporic memory 'in its traditional sense is by definition cut-off, hybrid, displaced, split' (2006:85). The expatriated Greeks of Istanbul and Imbros have often been written about in comparable terms, as communities that transcend nationalism and national distinctions (Babül 2004; Babül 2006a; Babül 2006b; Örs 2006; see below). Certainly, the expressions of expatriate identity that I examine in this and the following chapter undermine dichotomous and essentialist concepts of self and other, and disrupt the 'deceptively transparent surface' of national identity (Herzfeld 1997:2). I share, however, Brubaker's scepticism about a 'conceptual antithesis between nation-state and diaspora' (2005:10). In a sense, such approaches constitute an extension of the logic of transcendence (see Chapter 2), as they imply that complex or hybrid identities can flourish only by *transcending* national categories, thereby disregarding the possibility of hybridity existing *within* national categories. As Brubaker observed, whilst '[s]ophisticated discussions are sensitive to the heterogeneity of diasporas [. . .] they are not always as sensitive to the heterogeneity of nation-states' (2005:10).

In this chapter, I aim to lay bare the heterogeneity of national identity that would be rendered invisible in an antithesis between the locality and the nation or the nation and the diaspora. I explore how the expatriated Greeks of Turkey express their sense of self and belonging in Greece through the adaptation of two historical legacies: Romaic Byzantium and Ancient Hellenism. I demonstrate that the expatriates commonly deploy the particularity of their local heritages *both* to differentiate themselves from the Greeks of Greece *and* to affirm the authenticity of their Hellenic credentials. Responding to the perception of some *Elladítes* that their Turkish birthplace makes their ethnicity suspect, my interviewees commonly emphasise the specificity of their origins in Istanbul and Imbros in order to suggest that they are *particularly* Greek; 'Greeker', even, than the Greeks of Greece. Such narratives of *inclusive particularity* suggest that claims to national belonging may be premised on the accentuation of local heterogeneity as well as the assertion of national commonality.

The Helleno–Romaic dilemma

Patrick Leigh Fermor wrote that 'inside every Greek dwell two figures in opposition [. . .] the *Romios* and the Hellene' (1983:106). He outlined 64 parallel characteristics that distinguish the Romaic figure from the Hellenic one: the *Romiós* is concrete and tangible, whilst the Hellene is an abstract ideal; the former worships the Byzantine Empire and the dome of the Hagia Sophia in Istanbul, whilst the latter adores Ancient Greece and the Parthenon; nevertheless, they share the practice of 'settling the world's problems over endless cups of Turkish coffee' (Fermor 1983:107–113). The terms Hellene and *Romiós*, sometimes interchangeable, sometimes oppositional, have experienced fluctuating fortunes through the ages. Although the Ancient Greeks saw themselves as Hellenes in the sense that they were different from 'barbarians', prior to the establishment of the Kingdom of Greece in 1832 there was no strictly defined 'Greece' or 'Greeks' (Just 1989:73). The term *Romioí*, meanwhile, probably originated from the Ancient Greek for 'Romans' (Mackridge 2009:51), and indeed the Byzantines called themselves *Romaíoi*, i.e. the inheritors of the Roman Empire (Just 1989:74; Mackridge 2009:48). In the Byzantine period, the label *Romioí* became closely associated with Orthodox Christianity, whilst the term Hellene was commonly equated with paganism and Ancient Greece, although it did not disappear from contemporary usage altogether (Herzfeld 1986:6; Heurtley *et al.* 1965:36; Mackridge 2009:48–49). The Ottoman Empire took up this terminology, classifying its Orthodox Christian subjects as *Rum*, just as the Turkish Republic would categorise its Greek minority after 1923.

In the build-up to the 1821 Greek Revolution, however, Greek intellectuals – inspired by Western narratives of Classical Greek glory – began to call themselves Hellenes, even though the peasantry who would fight the revolution against the Ottoman Empire continued to self-identify as *Romioí*, that is as Orthodox Christians, and fought less for the glory of Pericles than for freedom from their Muslim rulers (Herzfeld 1986:31; Herzfeld 1997:176; Just 1989:83; Özkirimli and Sofos 2008:25). As Herzfeld has discussed, Greek nation-building thus involved two competing visions of Greece and Greek identity: the Hellenic thesis and the Romaic thesis. The Hellenic thesis was 'an outward-directed conformity to international expectations' and evoked 'ancient pagan glories', whilst the Romaic thesis was 'an inward-looking self-critical collective appraisal' that identified with the more recent Byzantine past (Herzfeld 1986:20–23). If the Hellenic was the ideal oriented towards modern Europe, the Romaic represented the familiar, simultaneously the comfort of Orthodox Christianity and the stigma of oriental taint (Herzfeld 1986:20–23; see also Özkirimli and Sofos 2008:21–23). This contest was played out in debates over the Greek national language (Mackridge 2009:18) and a 'cartographic anxiety' over Greece's territorial boundaries (Peckham 2001:40), as well as through folklore, literature, and historiography (Herzfeld 1986; Leontis 1995). Ultimately, it was the Hellenic thesis that became dominant, and the citizens of the new Greek state, in Peter Mackridge's words, 'were born again as Hellenes, having realized, as it seemed to them, who they truly were' (2009:55; see also Just 1989:83).

Yet, if this foundling Hellenic identity looked forward to modern Europe and backwards to Classical Greece, its claims to historical continuity had to deal with a gap of some 15 centuries in the Byzantine and Ottoman periods

(Özkirimli and Sofos 2008:22, 83, 100). This situation was exacerbated both by the scholarship of Austrian historian Jakob Philipp Fallmerayer – who rejected the notion of modern Greek descent from Ancient Greece, claiming that the modern Greeks were derived from Slavic and Albanian populations of the late Byzantine era – and by the fact that Byzantine Christianity meant more to most of the Kingdom's population than the legacy of Ancient Greece (Just 1989:85; Millas 2008; Özkirimli and Sofos 2008:83). A solution was found by revisionist Greek intellectuals in the mid-nineteenth century, most famously the historians Konstantinos Paparrigopoulos and Spyridon Zambelios, and the folklorist Nikolaos Politis (Mackridge 2012:34; Özkirimli and Sofos 2008:83–88). Building on Zambelios' conception of a 'Helleno–Christian' Byzantine period that achieved the fusion of ethnicity and religion, Paparrigopoulos reintegrated Byzantium into Greek national history by characterising the Empire as Greek, such that Greeks today are taught about their Byzantine heritage as an established historical fact (Mackridge 2012:34; Millas 2008; Özkirimli and Sofos 2008:84; Tzanelli 2006:42). So whilst it was the Hellenic thesis that emerged triumphant from Greek nation-building, its consolidation required the accommodation of aspects of the Romaic legacy (Özkirimli and Sofos 2008:101). As Mackridge observed, it is important here to distinguish between two different conceptions of this Byzantine past: Byzantium as *Empire* and Byzantium as *Christianity* (2012:38). Whilst dreams of resurrecting the former may have died in the wake of Greek military defeat in Asia Minor in 1922, it is arguable that the latter – on quotidian and informal levels, at least – still resonates more strongly with the residents of modern Greece than does the legacy of Classical Hellenism (Mackridge 2012:38–39).

Although all residents of the Kingdom of Greece thus became Hellenes in the eyes of the Greek state, a Romaic sense of self persisted on local and informal levels, both amongst the native Greeks (even, to an extent, into the present day) and amongst the 'unredeemed' Greeks of the Ottoman Empire, who were still officially called *Rum* (Herzfeld 1997:176; Holden 1972:29). Indeed, the Greeks of Turkey often use the term *Romioí* to distinguish those Greeks born in Turkey from the Hellenes of the Greek state: as Stefanos recalled, when a man came to visit his family from Thessaloniki, 'we called him "the Hellene" [. . .] we separated him in some way from us' (01/12/2011). Sometimes, slightly more specifically, '*Romioí*' is used to refer to those Greeks of Turkey who possessed Turkish citizenship and 'Hellenes' to those with Greek citizenship, regardless of birthplace (mirroring the official Turkish distinction between *Rum* and *Yunan*). Accordingly, when Savvas – formerly a Turkish citizen – recalled his first return to Imbros after his acquisition of Greek citizenship, he described himself as returning 'as a Hellene now' (14/08/2013). Interviewees also sometimes distinguished Greeks born in Greece (and occasionally Greek citizens born in Turkey) as *Elladítes* (singular: *Elladítis* (m.) or *Elladítissa* (f.)), i.e. 'Greeks of Greece', thereby preserving a more ecumenical meaning for the word Hellene. As Tasos put it, 'the *Elladítis* is the Hellene who was born in Greece; the *Romiós* is the Hellene who was born and grew up in Constantinople' (13/03/2014).

'The *Romiós* is one thing and the Hellene is another'

For the expatriated Greeks of Turkey, the Helleno–Romaic dilemma is a matter of ongoing debate. In a characteristic opinion piece in *O Polítis* in 1988, one expatriate writer expressed disappointment at having recently heard an acquaintance say 'we are *Romioí*. The *Romiós* is one thing and the Hellene is another' (*O Polítis* 1988). He countered that the term *Romiós* – once preferred by the Byzantines due to the association between Hellenism and idolatry, and later by the Ottomans to prevent the rise of national sentiment amongst Orthodox Christians – was in essence a synonym for 'Hellene' that had 'completed its historical role' (*O Polítis* 1988). He concluded:

> There is no longer any reason for us to call ourselves *Romioí* as the correct definition of 'Hellene' has been historically restored. And of course we are all proud that we are the descendants of Ancient Greece that has given so much to civilisation.
>
> (*O Polítis* 1988)

The divergent positions on expatriate identity represented in this article concern both diachronic questions of history and ancestry and synchronic issues of belonging and commonality: should the Greeks of Turkey be distinguished from the Greeks of Greece and the Hellenic legacy, or should they see themselves as the siblings of the former and the descendants of the latter, separated only by happenstance of history and politics?

These wider questions are commonly reflected in my interviewees' oral history testimonies. Some informants used these two terms interchangeably, and when challenged argued that they are essentially synonymous. Others maintained a fairly narrow distinction based on citizenship or place of birth, or treated Hellene as an ethnic label and *Romiós* as a religious one. Several interviewees, however, placed emphasis on one identity to the exclusion of the other, explicitly choosing between the Hellenic and the Romaic legacies. On the one hand, those whose life histories stressed a sense of alienation and exile in Greece, and a longing to return to their *patrída* in Turkey, often presented a Romaic self. Vangelis – born in Istanbul in 1934 and a resident of Greece since 1980 – expressed profound regret about leaving Istanbul and a longing to return, stressing that he was well integrated into Turkish society and had only emigrated to fulfil his wife's desire to leave. He was exceptionally disillusioned with life in Greece, complaining that the Greeks of Greece 'didn't want me, they teased me', and dismissing Greece as a 'degenerate, barbaric land' (Vangelis 03/02/2012). When we first met, he initially described his community as Hellenes, before immediately correcting himself:

> You want to know how the Hellenes lived – not Hellenes, *Romioí*, right? There are no Hellenes in Constantinople. They baptised us as Hellenes. We don't have any connection with them.
>
> (Vangelis 03/02/2012)

He proceeded to disassociate the *Romioí* from the Ancient Greeks, and was critical of the decision of Greek nation-builders to call themselves Hellenes:

> Look, the Hellenes finished 2000 years ago. Afterwards came the Byzantine Empire [...] The Eastern Roman Empire. The *Romiós* is a Roman [...] Because the *éthnos* of the *Romioí*, of the Romans, was the first *éthnos* to rise up within the Ottoman Empire, enthusiastic foreigners called them Hellenes. That was a big mistake, because afterwards, as Hellenes, they began to lose their identity. The identity of the *Romiós* is that which it was within the Ottoman Empire: the Christian Ottoman [...] After [18]21, the Ottoman became a Turk and the *Romiós* became a Hellene [...] Suddenly [Greek revolutionary leader Giorgos] Karaiskakis and co. stand up and claim to be the descendants of Socrates. Such things cannot happen; you cannot erase 1000 years of history and then suddenly go back further [...] I adore Byzantium, or that which they call Byzantium [...] If you read and you know the books, they speak of the Eastern Roman Empire, and that is what it is. I am a *Romiós*. The '*Rum*' is correct. I'm not a Hellene, I'm a *Rum, Romiós*, Roman.
> (Vangelis 03/02/2012; see also Halstead 2014:272–273)

Vangelis' rejection of Hellenic identity, which he saw as a corruption of a more authentic Romaic identity, reflects his deep-seated disenchantment with life in Greece.[2] By re-centring Greek history on Byzantium and disregarding the ancient Hellenic legacy, he emphasised his feeling of being in exile away from his true home in Istanbul. Ilias, who was born on Imbros in 1923, was similarly embittered with his experiences in Greece after his arrival in 1965, concluding his life history as follows:

> I came to Greece. I sold my business because the Turks took our schools [...] They didn't tell us to leave, [but] they took our schools, they also took our buildings. What could you do? So we came here to this place. This place is lovely. God gave it everything: sun, sea; but he gave it immoral people [...] I go about my business with my Turkish identity card. I also have a Hellenic one. Look what I have done to it.
> (21/05/2013)

At this point, Ilias produced his Greek identity card, across the front of which he had scrawled *ÓHI* ('NO') in black marker pen. He explained:

Ilias: 'No.' It means, 'I do not want you'.
Halstead: I do not understand. Who wrote 'no' on the card?
Ilias: I did. I only got it in order to go to the bank. It is my identity card that I acquired here [in Greece], and I use it only to go to the bank. I do not want anything else.
Halstead: Tell us exactly why you wrote 'no' here.
Ilias: I do not want it. I am a Turkish citizen.
(21/05/2013)

Like Vangelis, Ilias juxtaposed his disappointment with Greek society with positive memories of Turkish society, and accordingly (unlike most of my Imvrian informants, see below) preferred to present a Romaic self:

Ilias: I have good relations with Turkey, relationships that I work to create. Over here, they tell lies. They have robbed me five times. Five.[3] I say to them, 'I am a *Romiós*. I am not a Hellene.' [. . .]
Halstead: [In a later phase of the interview] You told me that you would describe yourself as a *Romiós* not a Hellene –
Ilias: Look, as a *Romiós*, Orthodox Christian. I wanted to be a Hellene, but a proper Hellene. Not that kind. Not that kind of Hellene. I do not want to be that kind [. . .] It is a shame: the place is nice, but the Hellenes are immoral.
Halstead: So when you go abroad, what do you normally say? That you are a Hellene, or –
Ilias: No, Turk. Turkish citizen, Turkish citizen.

(21/05/2013)

Ilias expressed his disillusionment with the Greek state by defacing his Greek identity card, and presenting himself – wherever possible – as a Turkish citizen rather than a Greek citizen. His experiences in Greece had, he felt, tainted the very idea of Hellenic identity, and accordingly he preferred to characterise himself as a *Romiós*. Vangelis too saw the politics of citizenship as an opportunity symbolically to reject Hellenic identity, electing to reclaim his Turkish citizenship in the early 2000s after becoming fed up with what he called the 'Hellenic reality' (Vangelis 03/02/2012; see also Halstead 2014:276).[4] For individuals like Vangelis and Ilias, rejecting Hellenic identity and adopting a Romaic self-presentation was a means of distancing themselves from the Greek state and its inhabitants, affirming a sense of alienation in Greece and belonging in Istanbul/Imbros.

Informants, on the other hand, who presented their emigration from Turkey as an escape from persecution to the safety of Greece, often preferred to place special emphasis upon their Hellenic credentials. Gerasimos – who left Istanbul at the age of 15 when his father, a Greek citizen, was expelled in 1964 – contrasted a feeling of freedom in Greece with one of fear in Turkey, and portrayed Greece as a national *patrída* to which – as Hellenes – they would naturally want to come (see above). He persistently referred to the *Polítes* as Hellenes throughout his life-history narrative, and when I specifically asked how he conceived of his identity, he replied 'Hellene, without any qualification' (Gerasimos 06/02/2012). This self-designation mirrors and provides credence to his broader life history. As he described it, he was persecuted in Istanbul because he was a Hellene, and then welcomed in Greece as a Hellene. He expressed no particular objection to the application of the label *Romioí* to the Greeks of Turkey, but ventured that it was simply a broader term used to describe Hellenes living outside Greece, and did not see it as in any way distinct from Hellenic identity (Gerasimos 06/02/2012; see also Halstead

2014:271). The fact that Gerasimos' father was a Greek citizen may perhaps contribute to his preference for a Hellenic identity, but it is significant that many other interviewees whose families were Turkish citizens expressed comparable narratives. Thekla – who was born in Istanbul in 1950 to Greek Cappadocian parents with Turkish citizenship, and relocated to Greece in the late 1970s – similarly evoked an atmosphere of perpetual fear in Istanbul, and suggested that it was the allure of freedom and equality that drew her family to Greece (21/08/2012). Asked to describe herself, she replied: 'a Hellene of Cappadocia, born in Constantinople to Cappadocian parents, of Hellenic descent. But I never hesitate to say I'm a Hellene. In my life I have never thought of my identity as anything but Hellenic' (Thekla 21/08/2012). When I asked her if she would call herself a *Romiá*, she replied:

> I might say it, as a *Romiós* [sic] of Constantinople, but the *Romiós* of Constantinople is still a Hellene. Many use that '*Rum*' to cut the Hellenism of Constantinople from its roots. It is a trap [. . .] I've noticed *Polítes* who – *Romioí*, er, that is to say Hellenes of Constantinople who say, 'I am not a Hellene, I am a *Romiós*'. 'A descendant', he says, 'of the Roman Empire'. That is an error that was created over the years, and it is like – how can I explain it? – a disavowal of the Greek state that was indifferent towards them. Because, truly, it was indifferent towards us [. . .] As long as we lived there, we did not feel the mother hugging its child, to put it metaphorically [. . . For that reason some *Polítes*] renounce their Hellenic descent and say, 'we are *Romioí*' [. . .] It is certainly true that our culture is different from the *Elladítes*, but that does not stop us from all being Hellenes. It has become a bit political, to disrupt the cohesion of Hellenism.
>
> (Thekla 21/08/2012; see also Halstead 2014:272)

Thekla's objection is not to the use of the term *per se* – in the extract above, she herself defaulted to calling her community *Romioí* and, because of the context, was obliged to correct herself – but rather the particular performative inflection put on the term by some of her fellow expatriates. Thekla was afraid that the use of the term *Romioí* by some *Polítes* carries an implication that she and her community are somehow separate from Greece and the roots of Hellenism (which, as we saw above, was precisely the rationale behind Vangelis' preference for a Romaic identity).

Several interviewees shared Thekla's concerns, telling me that they avoid the term *Romiós* as they see it as a method used by the Turkish authorities to separate the Greeks of Turkey from the Greeks of Greece. Evangelos – who was born on the island of *Prínkipos* in the Princes' Islands in 1945, and came to Greece 20 years later – categorised himself as 'a Hellene of Constantinople', and when I put it to him that some *Polítes* call themselves *Romioí* he opined:

> The [term] *Romiós* is in some ways bastardised. The Turks did not want to call us Hellenes, so they called us *Rum*. Just like here our people do not refer

to them [the Turks/Muslims of Western Thrace, presumably] as Turks, they call them Muslims, even though they are Turks.

(08/05/2013)[5]

Marios – who was born in Istanbul in 1941, left for Greece in 1966, and also described himself as a 'Hellene' – gave a similar response to the same question:

> The word *Romiós* is a misunderstanding. I don't ever use it. It might be a correct phrase, but because the Turks use it – I mean, *Romioí* are [for the Turks] only those in Constantinople and in Cyprus. Those that are here [in Greece], they call *Yunan*. To separate them, and maybe to split them up. So I don't use the word *Romiós* at all. I say, 'Hellene', always.
>
> (29/01/2012)

In attempting to ensure that the Greeks of Turkey are not fragmented from the Greek national body, and to indicate a sense of belonging and legitimacy in Greece, these narrators stressed a Hellenic identity and avoided Romaic distinctions.

Inclusive particularity (1): *Polítes* and Byzantium

In the above examples, interviewees appear to take up antithetical perspectives on the Helleno–Romaic dilemma, stressing one identity over another and attempting to maintain terminological consistency throughout their narrative. These terminological choices, however, seem to be primarily geared towards the articulation of a particular message for consumption by the interviewer: either that 'we are Hellenes and therefore belong in Greece' or that 'we are *Romioí* and have nothing to do with Greece'. It is not, necessarily, to be assumed that these informants would strictly adhere to their chosen label in everyday discourse, and indeed, even within the context of their oral testimonies, they were commonly compelled to correct themselves for the sake of internal consistency. Nor are these alternative positions *per se* as clear-cut and dichotomous as they first appear. Those who insisted on a Romaic self-presentation were explicitly airing their grievances with the Greek state and its inhabitants, but the precise relationship between this Romaic self and a Hellenic identity remained somewhat ambiguous. Ilias explicated his Romaic identity by cryptically stating that he 'wanted to be a Hellene, but a proper Hellene', implying that the *Romiós* might, in fact, be considered the true Hellene. Vangelis, for his part, quite emphatically disconnected his community from the ancient Hellenes, but did not clearly pronounce on the identity of the contemporary Greeks of Greece, leaving open the possibility that they were to be considered as *Romioí* misidentifying themselves as Hellenes. Those who presented a Hellenic self, meanwhile, were concerned with demonstrating belonging in Greece and commonality with its inhabitants, but this did not necessarily prevent them from identifying differences between the Greeks of Greece and the Greeks of Turkey based on the latter's Byzantine heritage. Gerasimos generally played down cultural distinctions or social tensions between the two communities, but Thekla acknowledged them, characterising the *Polítes* as the 'remnants of Byzantium', though simultaneously stressing that these distinctions did not 'stop us from all being Hellenes'.

Indeed, for many of my informants, Hellenic sameness and Romaic distinctiveness were far from mutually exclusive, and to be a *Romiós* was to be Hellenic, but to be a distinctive kind of Hellene from the Greeks of Greece. Kyriakos was born in Istanbul in 1951, where he completed university before emigrating to Greece in 1975, partly as his partner had left to study in Athens, and partly as he struggled to find work as a Greek in the wake of the conflict on Cyprus in 1974. He had predominantly fond memories of growing up in Istanbul and positive relationships with his Turkish acquaintances, and also recalled that he was quickly integrated into Greek society after his arrival in 1975. He characterised both Istanbul and Greece as *patrídes*, and expressed an emotional attachment to both. When I asked him how he would describe himself, he responded: 'I would describe myself as an Orthodox Hellene of Our East [*i kath'imás anatolí*] [. . .] I mean, I'm not an *Elladítis* [. . .] I think of my identity as a *Romiós*. Not that I don't love Greece' (Kyriakos 03/02/2012). For Kyriakos, to be a *Romiós* was to be a Hellene of the *East* rather than a Hellene of *Greece*. Alexandros – born in Istanbul in 1962, and a resident of Turkey until his emigration to Greece in the mid-1970s – explained the usage of the self-descriptor '*Romiós*' in comparable terms:

> [When we were living in Turkey] we did not use the word Hellene, because Hellene was certainly a national entity and we did not want it. But we did use the word Hellenism, Greekness [*ellinikótita*]. 'The Hellene', meaning that you are a Hellenic citizen, is not something we said. We used the word '*Romiós*'. There was a distinction [. . .] We did not [use the term 'Hellene'] in a national sense, as in the state, but in a philosophical sense [. . .] It does not mean that you are Hellenic with the Greek flag, but that you are Hellenic because you respect the philosophy of Hellenism.
>
> (11/03/2014)

Stefanos, who was born in Istanbul in 1950 and came to Greece as a teenager in 1964, likewise drew a distinction between the Hellenes of Greece and those of Istanbul. Like Kyriakos, he placed emphasis upon the primarily harmonious relationships he enjoyed with other ethnic groups in Istanbul, as well as the positive reception his family received from the Greeks of Greece when they resettled in Greece, referring to Thessaloniki as his 'second *patrída*'. He defined himself as follows:

> Ethnicity: clearly Hellenic. For accuracy, we also have to separate the *Romiós*. The *Romiós* of Constantinople was a Hellene but he was something separate. He didn't think of his identity as Hellenic with the meaning of Greece. He thought of Greece as his *patrída*, if you like; yes, *patrída*. But the *Romiós* of Constantinople was something beyond Greece.
>
> (Stefanos 01/12/2011; see also Halstead 2014:273)

In a separate interview, Stefanos' younger sister, Tasoula, came to a similar conclusion. Tasoula was much less well reconciled to Turkey and Turks than her brother, although she too recalled having Turkish friends as a child, and whilst she felt that the Greeks of Greece had treated them well, she was angry with the Greek state for their failure to support the expatriate community in Greece (on which, see Chapter 4). I asked her how she would describe her ethnicity. After a long pause, she replied 'Hellene'. 'Not *Romiá*?' I countered. She responded: 'what does *Romiá* mean? Hellene, it means. Except it distinguishes that you are the community from Byzantium, from Constantinople. For that reason I am proud that I am a Constantinopolitan – because I am not a simple Hellene' (27/11/2011). Tasoula was proud to be a Constantinopolitan not because it distanced her from Hellenic identity, but because it marked out her distinctiveness as regards the Greeks of Greece: as a *Romiá*, she was a Hellene of Constantinople – of Byzantium – rather than just another Hellene of Greece.

Such distinctions are drawn not only to emphasise pride in a particular local heritage, but also as a counter to the narratives of ethnic and national *inauthenticity* aimed at the *Polítes* by segments of the Greek-born population. Spyros was born in Istanbul in 1930 and came to Greece in 1964. At the beginning of his narrative, detailing the difficulties that precipitated his emigration from Turkey, he used the words '*Romiós*' and 'Hellene' interchangeably to refer to his own community, and when asked to clarify explained that the two were one and the same. Later on in the interview, however, as he and Tasoula (no relation) began to work each other up when discussing the cultural differences between the *Polítes* and the Greeks of Greece – particularly in regard to etiquette, discipline, and piety – a clear terminological distinction emerged between the *Romioí* of Istanbul and the Hellenes of Greece. It was, nevertheless, emphasised by both informants that these Romaic distinctions made their community *more* rather than less Hellenic: the *Polítes*, it was alleged, showed greater respect for the Orthodox Christian religion, had a superior knowledge of the ancient Greek language, and positively influenced the culture of the Greeks of Greece after their arrival from Turkey. Spyros became particularly animated when describing what he perceived as the disinterested and disrespectful manner in which *Elladítes* behave in church (see Chapter 4), reflecting a broader feeling expressed by many *Polítes* that their community was more genuine in its religious belief than that of Greece. Narratives of this sort reverse accusations of ethnic and national illegitimacy aimed at the expatriates by some of the Greeks of Greece, by suggesting that the expatriates are not an alien body within the Greek nation but rather its more (or most) authentic members. As Spyros recalled, when *Elladítes* made fun of him by calling him a 'Turk', he would retort, 'I hope you are as Hellenic as I am! In terms of religion, in love for your *patrída*' (02/12/2011).

Assertions of Hellenic authenticity premised on Romaic particularity are common in expatriate testimony. Fotini, born in Istanbul in 1943, relocated to Greece in the 1970s with young Istanbul-born children. In her oral testimony, she recalled that her son was mocked as a 'seed of the Turks' by his classmates in Greece. Fotini went to her son's teacher to complain about this behaviour, protesting to her, 'look, we are more Hellenic than the Hellenes here!' (21/11/2011) Moments after she told this story, I asked Fotini how she would define herself. She replied:

> *Romiá.* [Pause] Not Hellenic, *Romiá.* There's a difference. What are the differences? Well, we had many [different] influences, because Constantinople is a cosmopolitan place. It wasn't a village, we didn't have animals. That's why we call it 'The City', with a big 'C'. It is the only city that is written with a capital 'C': Byzantium. And that's why we want to be Constantinopolitans.
> (Fotini 21/11/2011; see also Halstead 2014:275)[6]

At first glance, it may seem as though Fotini had contradicted herself: she initially claimed to be archetypically Hellenic, before moments later characterising herself as Romaic and *not* Hellenic. However, to borrow terms from Herzfeld, 'these usages are inconsistent only if one adheres to the absolutist logic of official ethnicity rather than to the entirely different theoretical underpinnings of ordinary talk' (1997:45). The ethnic shifter 'Hellenic/Hellenes' was deployed by Fotini both to refer specifically to the Greeks of Greece – from whom she wished to differentiate herself – and to a more transcendent Hellenic ethnicity – of which, due to her Romaic heritage, she was not only a part but a *distinctive* part.

These interviewees, when challenged to define their identities, were keen to separate themselves from a narrow association with the modern Greek state and its inhabitants, and to emphasise the specificity of their Byzantine or Constantinopolitan heritage, and accordingly adopted – to varying degrees – a Romaic persona. Yet this is a *particularisation* rather than a rejection of Hellenic identity: to be a *Romiós* or a *Romiá* was, for these informants, still to be ethnically Hellenic, but to be a different kind of Hellene from the Greeks of Greece. This difference was considered to be rooted, first, in the cosmopolitan and urban culture of Istanbul (see also Chapter 4 and Örs 2006), and, second, in an ethnic and religious authenticity deriving from the community's Byzantine history. In this way, the Greeks of Istanbul seek to affirm the authenticity of their Hellenic credentials and, consequently, their legitimacy as residents of Greece, by emphasising rather than downplaying the particularities of their own locality and its Romaic heritage. This Romaic legacy – sidelined in Greek nationalist historiography yet commanding considerable popular resonance amongst the modern Greek population (see above) – provides the *Polítes* with an identity that is quintessentially Hellenic yet distinct from Greece; Hellenic, but more than *simply* Hellenic (Halstead 2014:274).

Renée Hirschon has documented how the Orthodox Christian refugees who arrived in Greece after 1923 responded to xenophobia from the native Greek population by stressing their own cosmopolitan culture and origins: a 'knowledge of diversity' stemming from the refugees' experience of coexistence with Turks and other ethnicities in the Ottoman Empire, which provided them with a sense of identity that distinguished them from their native Greek detractors (2004:325–343; 2006:61–78). Örs has made similar observations about the expatriated *Polítes* in

Athens, suggesting that their knowledge of diversity from cosmopolitan Istanbul allows them to differentiate themselves from the Greeks of Greece (2006:87–89). Örs argued that the *Polítes* transcend the Greek–Turkish dichotomy, by rooting their sense of belonging not in Greek or Turkish ethnicity, but in a 'wider cultural sense of "belonging" [...] specifically centred on the urban cosmopolitan experience of being from Istanbul' (2006:81). This is an identity premised on claims to descent from Byzantium, a heritage taken to embody the civilised, urban, and cosmopolitan characteristics that make the community distinctive (Örs 2006:86–88). For Örs, the most noteworthy aspect of this cosmopolitan sense of belonging is that it can include Istanbul residents of all ethnicities/nationalities – including urbanite Muslim Turks – whilst excluding non-Istanbulite co-ethnics – i.e. *Elladítes* (2006:84–91). She argued that the *Polítes* occupy 'a conceptual space between and beyond categories', and exhibit a 'complex identity' that 'challenges nationalism' and 'shows the limits of established terminologies – including concepts such as diaspora, minority or homeland – which are formed within a nation-state-centred logic' (Örs 2006:90–92).

Örs was correct to identify that many *Polítes* see significant cultural differences between themselves and the Greeks of Greece, commonly expressed through the urban–rural and multicultural–monocultural dichotomies. As she observed, this cosmopolitan sense of belonging is often deployed to distinguish the *Polítes* from the Greeks of Greece, in certain contexts even excluding *Elladítes* at the expense of including non-Greek Istanbulites (see Chapter 4). She also accepted that many *Polítes* would be 'more than content' to be identified exclusively as Greeks and that few 'would accept that they are less than Greek' (Örs 2006:82, 85). Her emphasis, nevertheless, was on the 'non-negligible segment' of the community who exhibit 'a refusal to go along with confinement into one of two opposed camps, in other words, being either Greek or Turkish *only*' (Örs 2006:82). In this sense, her analysis was underwritten by a logic of transcendence: the adoption of either Greek or Turkish identity is taken to result in confinement and simplicity, and more nuanced understandings of self are only to be obtained by transcending these national categories. The possibility that there is considerable room for manoeuvre *within* national identity is therefore overlooked, resulting in a somewhat lopsided portrayal of the *Polítes*' understanding of self. For most of my interviewees, a cosmopolitan Romaic heritage, whilst distinguishing the *Polítes* from the Greeks of Greece in one sense, also made them *quintessentially* Hellenic: as the heirs to Byzantium, the *Polítes* could be both *included in*, yet *distinctive within*, the Greek *éthnos* or 'nation'.

Inclusive particularity (2): *Imvriótes* and Ancient Athens

> We too want to live as free people as Hellenes. And without having our Greekness [*ellinikótita*] doubted! We are more Hellenes than many Hellenes.
>
> (*Imvriakí Ichó* 1974)

Elder *Imvriótes*, such as reluctant Greek citizen Ilias (see above), as well as those who lived in Istanbul for substantial periods of time (see Loukas, below), sometimes joined the *Polítes* in categorising themselves as *Romioí* (Tsimouris 2008:300). Generally, however, my Imvrian interviewees preferred to describe themselves as Hellenes and/or simply *Imvriótes*. Tsimouris has suggested that a preference for Hellenic identity amongst younger *Imvriótes* may represent a 'strategic attempt' to assert their Greekness in the face of a sceptical native population (2008:300), reminiscent of the strategic change of name and colours by the refugee football team in Volos discussed at the beginning of the chapter. This may well be the case, although as I have argued above the use of the label *Romioí* by the *Polítes* might likewise be interpreted as an alternative strategy for demonstrating national authenticity. The comparative disinclination amongst my Imvrian interlocutors to refer to themselves as *Romioí* might also be accounted for by cultural and historical differences between them and the *Polítes*. Pavlos – who was born on Imbros in 1970, and moved to Istanbul in order to attend a minority school in 1975 – described something of a culture clash between the two communities. He recalled conflicts and fights at school between the children from Imbros and those from Istanbul, and as he grew up came to the conclusion that 'the *Polítes* thought of us as a lower class [. . .] In Constantinople the people were urban, they were a different class. They ate with a knife and fork, whilst we were villagers' (Pavlos 29/05/2013). In the mid-1960s, a young Fani similarly felt that the *Polítes* looked down on the children from Imbros and saw them as second-class, thinking of them 'in the same way that here [in Greece] they see the Vlachs' (i.e. as country bumpkins). 'We had that particular dialect that we spoke', she recalled, 'and the *Polítes* thought of themselves as cultured, regardless of the fact that they did not know how to speak Greek properly by comparison with us' (Fani 07/06/2013). As members of an agricultural island community, the *Imvriótes* may thus have comparatively little interest in claiming a cosmopolitan, urban identity rooted in the Byzantine legacy that might be associated with a Romaic self-presentation. At the same time, some may wish to differentiate themselves from the *Polítes* who *do* commonly characterise themselves as *Romioí*. From this point of view, Imvrian expressions of Hellenic rather than Romaic identity may have as much to do with differences between them and the *Polítes* as with attempts to demonstrate similarity with the Greeks of Greece.

Indeed, the commonplace use of the identity label 'Hellene' by the *Imvriótes* does not prevent them from drawing distinctions between themselves and the Hellenes who inhabit the Greek state. Loukas was born in Istanbul in 1967 to Imvrian parents who, as schoolteachers, had moved to the city after the prohibition on Greek language education on Imbros in 1964. He lived in Istanbul until his emigration to Greece in 1992, during which time he spent the summers on Imbros. He attempted to characterise his relationship to Greece as follows:

In Greece I am, okay – [hesitates] I am not an *Elladítis*. I am a Hellene. However, not an *Elladítis*. That is the only way I can describe it, with those words. Because to be an *Elladítis*, at least in the sense that I mean, means that you [. . .] are limited by experiences formed in a narrow country that is called, geographically, 'Greece'. I offer it as a contrast: if I must distinguish, if I have to say I am not something, I am not that, let's say. As a Hellene, I am not that.

(Loukas 03/07/2013)

Loukas' testimony uncouples the 'nation' from the 'state'. He saw himself as Hellenic, but was keen to underline that this sense of self was not narrowly defined by a relationship to the Greek state or its territorial boundaries; in fact, his Hellenic identity was defined as much in opposition to as through commensurability with the Greeks of Greece. In Loukas' case, this involved distinguishing the Greeks of Greece as '*Elladítes*', although as often as not my Imvrian informants differentiated themselves without making such terminological distinctions. Markos was born on Imbros in 1953, and initially emigrated to the USA with his family in 1967 before ultimately resettling in Greece as a grown man. Asked how he would describe himself, he responded, 'a Hellene of Imbros'. In this case, it is the *self* that is the Hellene. Explaining, however, why he felt that the *Imvriótes* required their own communal meeting place, he distinguished the Greeks of Greece as 'Hellenes':

One way for people who are migrants, who are from other *patrídes*, to find one another, was to build their own place to meet up. Because only here [in the Imvrian Association] can we talk amongst ourselves, about Imbros, let's say. If we go to another café, or restaurant, whatever, *there might be Hellenes*; and you cannot discuss things with them, because we do not have things in common. We want to have a place where we can talk and remember the past.

(Markos 04/05/2013; emphasis added)

In this context, the Hellenes become the other against which the *Imvriótes* are defined (see also Chapter 4), the two separated by a lack of common experience. Because the label 'Hellene' can mean different things in different performative contexts, Markos was able to differentiate himself from the Greeks of Greece without calling the 'Greekness' of either party into question. Coming from a different *patrída*, Markos' Hellenic self lacks *local* commonality with the Hellene of Greece, but both can, nevertheless, remain Hellenes on a *national* level. The variability of these identity labels typically went unacknowledged in my informants' testimonies, allowing them to indicate difference without explicitly flagging it up. Kostas, however, who was born on Imbros in 1963 and came to Greece in 1981, noticed that he had been using the word 'Hellene' both to refer to himself and to distinguish the residents of the Greek state, and remarked upon it as follows:

I don't know if you noticed, that there is a 'Hellene'. I am a Hellenic citizen, I feel Hellenic, but I do not think of myself as Hellenic with the same meaning as someone who was born in Kalamata [a large city in the Peloponnese] and lives in Athens thinks. To tell you something funny, when my mother hears on the television about some serious crime [that has taken place in Greece], she says, 'my my, what things are these Hellenes?'

(07/06/2013)

In Confino's terms, Hellenic identity for Kostas represents a 'common denominator of variousness' (1993:63): there are many different ways to be Hellenic, such that commonality on a national level can coexist with a significant degree of local particularity. In light of these comments, I asked Kostas precisely how he would describe his own identity. He pondered his relationship to both Hellenic and Turkish identity, before concluding that he felt more Hellenic because he was from Imbros:

> I would say that I was born on Imbros, I am a Hellene, I mean I feel ethnically Hellenic. No one has dared to ask me how I feel in relation to Turkey [. . .] I have asked to take my Turkish citizenship back [. . .] I willingly take Turkish citizenship, not only for some practical needs, but because I feel both Hellenic and Turkish [. . .] So I could belong to both countries and both sides. But, historically of course, I feel closer to the Hellenes, because I am an *Imvriótis*. Imbros was settled by Athenian colonists, okay.
>
> (Kostas 07/06/2013)

Kostas saw himself as ethnically Hellenic, but this identity became tangible and meaningful through the locality (Imbros) rather than through the nation-state (Greece). He did not feel Hellenic *despite* being from Imbros, but rather *because* he was from Imbros.

Indeed, as was the case with the *Polítes*, such local particularity is not only capable of existing alongside national commonality, but can itself *drive* narratives of national belonging. As Tsimouris has observed, the *Imvriótes* commonly deploy 'as compelling evidence of Greekness' the specificities of their island's demographics, history, and built environment: the preponderance of Greek-speaking Orthodox Christians prior to the 1960s, the sheer number of churches and chapels, and references to Imbros in Homer and other ancient texts (2008:185). The maintenance of these characteristics, despite the island's location within Turkish territory, is a source of particular pride for the community. As the newspaper *Imvriakí Ichó* put it in an appeal for support aimed at a domestic Greek audience:

> We were born Turkish citizens, but in the altar of our soul, we kept pure our Christianity and we preserved unaltered the Hellenic traditions. So as genuine Hellenes and Christians we ask the Hellenic press, the Hellenic Authorities to share our pain and to recognise our rights.
>
> (*Imvriakí Ichó* 1972)

In this way, the source of domestic Greek scepticism over the *Imvriótes*' Hellenic credentials – that they were born in Turkey rather than Greece – can be turned into an asset that asserts the depth and resilience of a Hellenic identity cultivated outside the embrace of the Greek state.

Nevertheless, appeals of this sort are not premised on a history of displacement from Greece, but on the notion that Imbros constitutes a centre of Hellenism in its own right. Just as the *Polítes* draw on the Byzantine legacy to emphasise their

Figure 6 The sign for the *Paipalóessa* café in the Imvrian Association, 2017.
Photograph by the author.

national and religious authenticity, so the *Imvriótes* mobilise histories of their island's distant past to bolster their claims to Hellenic identity. In Homer's Iliad, the island is referred to as 'rugged Imbros' (*Ímvros paipalóessa*), a characterisation that is often enthusiastically adopted by *Imvriótes*. A 1994 English-language article, for instance, began in the following terms: 'HOMER: "*Ímvros paipalóessa*. . .", "Iliad"[.] Greek, from the dawn of the History the Island of Imbros in the North Aegean Se[a] [. . .]' (*Ímvros* 1994b). The café of the Imvrian Association is itself named '*Paipalóessa*' (see Figure 6). Imvrian historical narratives typically place emphasis upon the island's subsequent colonisation by Athenians in c.480 BC, and stress that the history and culture of Imbros were thereafter closely intertwined with Athenian Hellenism despite repeated occupations by Spartans, Macedonians, Frankish crusaders, Ottomans, and others. Imvrian writer Giorgos Xeinos, for instance, in his history of Imbros and Tenedos, wrote of the former that 'all of the evidence points to the fact that from the moment that the island became an Athenian cleruchy, despite its hitherto unadulterated pre-Hellenic character, it was culturally transformed into a miniaturised Athenian state' (2011:28). In a 1977 article, the newspaper *Ímvros* voiced its objections to the Greek state's treatment of the expatriated *Imvriótes* as 'aliens' in similar terms: '[a]liens, those people who have the same roots in History (as is well known Imbros has been since antiquity a city of Ancient Greece with only small subjugations by the powers of the region) who have the same traditions, the same struggles, the same language, the same religion' (*Ímvros* 1977).

Writing in 1994, another author in *Ímvros* gave the following potted history of the island, again attempting to demonstrate the depth of its Hellenic identity, and its preservation from ancient to modern times, by highlighting references to Imbros by Homer, the intimacy of its relationship to both Classical Athens and the Byzantine Empire, and the resilience of its population in the face of foreign invaders:

Known as '*Imvrou ásty*' [i.e. 'the city of Imbros'] in Homeric times.[7] Opposite the Troad, where around its walls Achaeans and Trojans fought with spears for a decade, to give material to the timeless poet to write his immortal epic the *Iliad*, and why not, also his other epic the *Odyssey*. Its first settlers were Pelasgians. Cleruchs of Athens colonised it in the years in which the 'glorious city', was living the peak of its fame. Then, the Imvrian deme was organised according to the Athenian prototype, such that it was called 'Deme of Athens in Imbros'. Even the river-torrent of the island, the 'big river' as they call it today, was then called *Ilissós*[,] like one of the two rivers of the city [i.e. Athens] that Pallas [Athena] guarded. It encountered the Spartans, Philip [II of Macedon] and the Romans. It embraced Christianity. It was a region of the Byzantine Empire for centuries, not so far from the Queen of cities [i.e. Constantinople], like other parts of today's Greece. It knew the rule of the Franks and from 1460 the rule of the Turks. The expatriations and the persecutions did not stop. Imbros, however, retained its Greekness. And by 1893 it had 9357 Hellenes and only 99 – not even 100 – Turks!

(*Imvros* 1994a)

At a conference organised by the Imvrian Association in 1984, one of the speakers likewise deployed the ancient history of the island in an effort to establish the Hellenic credentials of the *Imvriótes*:

The Imvrian people, who happened to inhabit that tender and noteworthy geographic place [i.e. Imbros] for more than 3000 years, are purely Hellenic, descended from an ancient Hellenic race, derived from the crossing of the Hellenes with the pre-Hellenes [. . .] Its national history began in [. . .] 480 BC when it was occupied by the general Miltiadis I, he surrendered it to the Athenians, who settled it with Athenian cleruchs from Attica, and constituted it 'in the image and likeness of Athens' and thought of it as their adopted daughter.

(*Imvros* 1984a)

Similar origin stories were offered by some of my interviewees. Stamatios, who was born on Imbros in 1945 and relocated to Greece in 1963, offered a particularly in-depth narrative of the island's history. He began by answering his own rhetorical question:

What are the *Imvriótes*? Imbros, in the years of the Athenian democracy, and later in the Roman years, was a deme of Athens. The Athenians, realising that it was a very important location for their defence and for trade from the Black Sea, did that which the Turks have done today: they removed the inhabitants and settled new ones there [. . .] We *Imvriótes* are a mixture of pre-Hellenes and Athenians.

(Stamatios 30/05/2013)

Stamatios proceeded to argue that certain rituals and traditions derived directly from the Ancient Athenians, which had passed out of usage in Greece itself long ago, persisted on Imbros into the modern era:

> When I went to high school and started to study 'Introduction to Tragedy' and I read Homer, things seemed familiar to me [. . .] I said, 'this is all familiar, this is *our* way of life'. And what made a big impression on me was when I started to read Tragedy. Where does Tragedy come from? From the worship of Dionysus. We lived the Dionysian rites, exactly as they were described, until 1964! [. . .] The ban on public rituals issued by Justinian in 530 [AD] never reached Imbros [. . .] Another celebration which derives from antiquity [. . .] is the slaughter of the oxen [on 15 August, see Chapter 8], which is a memory of the hecatomb to Zeus and the gods in Athens [. . .] Even today, in our burial rites, we have traditions drawn from ancient religion and not Christian religion.
>
> (30/05/2013)

With these comments in mind, I asked Stamatios if he felt that he was moving to a 'second home' when he relocated to Athens in 1963, to which he replied in the negative, suggesting that no cultural or ceremonial legacy of the Ancient Athenians persisted in the modern Greek city. By claiming a ritual continuity with Ancient Greece allegedly lacking in modern Greece, Stamatios portrayed Imbros as a more authentically Hellenic space whose detachment from central authority had enabled ancient traditions to flourish. In this way, Imbros' geographic marginality is deployed to *reinforce* rather than undermine its inhabitants' national credentials: their position on the periphery places them on the margins of the Greek state but at the centre of the Greek national origin story.

Elif Babül has suggested that Imbros might be seen 'as an "exception" to the national order of things' within Republican Turkey (2004:3), insofar as the *Imvriótes*' sense of belonging on the island derives from 'pre-national forms of belonging through memory, spatiality and locality – in a word, nativity – rather than through citizenship' (2006a:50–51). In common with Örs, Babül discussed how her informants differentiated themselves from other Greek communities by 'claiming an identity based on a specific locality' and characterising themselves as 'Rums' (i.e. *Romioí*), which she interpreted as evidence of their sense of 'marginality' and 'in-betweenness' as regards nationalism and national categories (Babül 2006a:55–56; Babül 2006b:47). It is certainly true that the *Imvriótes*' claims to belonging on Imbros are not based on the possession of any particular citizenship. As Tsimouris has emphasised, however, the 'use of the term "*Romioí*" alternately with the term "Hellenes" amongst elder *Imvriótes* does not place the *Imvriótes* in an intermediate field between the Hellenes and the Turks, but rather *marks out their distinctiveness as Hellenes*' (2008:112). From this perspective, Imvrian attachment to the locality of Imbros, and their efforts to distinguish themselves from other Greeks, should not be interpreted as necessarily opposed or antithetical to ideas of national identity and national belonging. My Imvrian informants, in contrast to those from the Greek community of Istanbul, did not commonly present a Romaic persona or draw connections between their community and the legacy of Byzantium. Yet like the *Polítes*, these *Imvriótes* nevertheless emphasise their particularity as Hellenes vis-à-vis the Greeks of Greece by drawing on the specificities of their local heritage. Through narratives of ancient Athenian colonisation of the island and the preservation of its inhabitants' Hellenic traditions and Orthodox Christian religion under Turkish authority, the *Imvriótes* can portray themselves as legitimately Hellenic because of, rather than in spite of, their distinctive origins on an island outside the territory of the Greek state. In this way, they hope to demonstrate – to borrow terms from another speaker at the 1984 Imvrian Association conference – that 'the *Imvriótes* are not the poor relatives of the Hellenic people but the carriers and continuation of the genuine Aegean civilisation and its pure Hellenic Orthodox tradition' (*Imvros* 1984b).

Expatriate protoselves

I have sought to demonstrate that the choices expatriates make about whether to present themselves as Hellenes or *Romioí* are not simply random, and frequently serve to convey particular messages about themselves and their community. Unsurprisingly, however, it is also apparent that there are no static, clearly defined, or universally accepted parameters governing the meanings that might be associated with these identities. Building upon Ulric Neisser's concept of the 'remembered self',[8] the psychologist Craig Barclay argued that autobiographical remembering requires the continual construction of 'protoselves' that are developed through everyday social interactions and tested by the degree to which they are accepted by others (Barclay 1994:70). He wrote:

> [P]rotoselves are composed through a skilled process of improvisation such that what is created anew is referenced and firmly tied to the past [...] improvisations yield protoselves constrained by a life lived and a life being lived and by evolving social agreements regarding the range of culturally acceptable selves.
>
> (Barclay 1994:72)

This ongoing process of identity negotiation is clearly in evidence in expatriate autobiographical testimonies. Informants were constantly experimenting with different configurations of self (and other), improvising protoselves in their efforts to make sense of their own identity and to convey this sense of self to the interviewer. At the end of our interview, Andreas – born on *Chálki* in the Princes' Islands in 1943, and a resident of Greece since 1973 – played across the whole range of the Helleno–Romaic dichotomy in an attempt to arrive at a suitable self-description:

> Many of us Constantinopolitans, of course, feel that they are *Romioí*. They make a distinction, they take a stance, they say, 'I am a Constantinopolitan,

I am a *Romiós* from Constantinople, the others are *Elladítes*'. They make a distinction. But – I too want to be a *Romiós* of Constantinople. Not that it bothers me – I am Hellenic. Not *Ellaítis*. Constantinopolitan. *Romiós*. Hellenic Constantinopolitan. Hellenic Constantinopolitan doesn't bother me.
(11/02/2012)

Andreas' musings demonstrate that the performance of nationality is far removed from the superficial simplicity of national identity labels: his attempts to arrive at a suitable self-description are complicated by multiple and overlapping concerns with both distinctiveness and inclusiveness, resolved – in this case – with a protoself that combines a national identity (Hellenic) with a local one (Constantinopolitan).

The national self, nevertheless, is *far* from 'infinitely multifaceted' (Eriksen 2001:65). Daniel Albright has drawn a distinction between a 'conventional remembered self' and an 'unconventional remembered self': whilst 'the conventional vision of self offers me security; the unconventional one frightens me and frees me' (1994:39). Protoselves improvised along the lines of the Helleno–Romaic dichotomy could be conceived of as the expatriates' conventional remembered selves: whilst the hollowness and plasticity of these categories enables individuals to make identity meaningful on their own terms, their superficial stability imbues them with a comforting illusion of fixity and homogeneity that can be translated into a national commonality and solidarity. As I have discussed in more detail elsewhere – and as is in evidence in some of the testimonies considered above – sometimes expatriates have reason to escape temporarily this conventional self and access a more unconventional, Turkish self (Halstead 2014:280–283; see also Örs 2006:82).

Typically, this is done for humorous purposes, or to lampoon prejudices amongst the Greeks of Greece about the expatriate community (Halstead 2014:280–283). I witnessed such an event whilst having dinner at the house of *Polítes* Michalis and Alexandra. A Greek-born friend of mine, here called Achilleas, was also present. Michalis was listening to Turkish music, when a curious Achilleas asked him, 'what language is this? Turkish? Arabic?' 'What do you think?' Michalis responded, in a matter-of-fact tone, 'seeing as I am from Turkey'. At this point, Alexandra drifted into the conversation, and, grinning and pointing to Michalis, said to Achilleas, 'yes, he's a Turk him! He's a Turk!' Achilleas looked a little crestfallen. 'You're joking?' he implored. 'That's what [the Greeks of Greece] called us', Alexandra retorted. Achilleas turned to me and, in English, said, 'I feel uncomfortable now!' Alexandra here ascribed Turkish identity to her husband in order to critique sarcastically the manner in which the expatriates were treated by sections of the Greek-born population after their arrival in Greece. In cases like this, the expatriates are able to play upon the stigma that some of their detractors attached to their Turkish birthplace, accessing an unconventional self as Greece's ethnic other to tease or unsettle *Elladítes* (apparently with some success) (Halstead 2014:281). A few expatriates also claimed a Turkish aspect to their identity as part of their efforts to distinguish themselves from the Greeks of

Greece. Fotis, who was born in Istanbul in 1950 and came to Greece in 1976, felt that he could call himself both a Hellene and a Turk, and argued that unlike the Hellenes of Greece every *Romiós* has 'a percentage of Turk inside him'. This tied into the anti-nationalistic tenor of his narrative, in which he emphasised that he has no anti-Turkish sentiments, something he attributed to the fact that the *Polítes* 'didn't grow up at all like Hellenes, they grew up as *Romioí*' (Fotis 01/02/2012). In stating that he has no problem in calling himself a Turk, there is also a sense of defiance against those *Elladítes* who did just that; like Alexandra, Fotis calls their bluff (Halstead 2014:281).

These forays into unconventional selves, however, are generally cautious, partial, and temporary (Halstead 2014:283). Turkish protoselves run up against experiences of persecution in Turkey, as well as suspicions and prejudices both within and without the expatriate community, and informants generally stayed within the safer conceptual space of the conventional self, which still provided them with ample room for discursive manoeuvre. As Eriksen put it, identity cannot be created 'out of thin air', and its performative inflections must always be tested against the expectations of others and remain grounded in personal experience (Eriksen 2001:50, 61–66). The latter point can be illustrated by expanding upon the testimony of Loukas (see above), who was born in Istanbul to Imvrian parents. Asked how he would describe himself, Loukas indicated that he felt both Imvrian and Romaic:

> I am an *Imvriótis*, in terms of consciousness. That is to say, Imvrian *Romiós*. That is how I feel. There is also the Romaic child, because I grew up in Constantinople. I also feel like a child of Constantinople, understand? In spirit I am a child of Constantinople, but in body I am a child of Imbros.
> (03/07/2013)

He proceeded to characterise himself as Hellenic, but also to differentiate himself from the Greeks of Greece on the basis of their different life experiences. He concluded by ruminating on his relationship to Turkey:

> Beyond that, in relation to our discussion about the current [2013 Gezi Park] protests in Turkey, I feel very strongly about everything that is going on there. I mean, I feel like a part of that community, to the extent that they allowed me to, and to the extent that I am able to overcome those things through which we lived, in order to feel like a part of the contemporary community of Constantinople. And not of Turkey generally, specifically of Constantinople, because Constantinople has its own character which I think is much stronger than Turkey itself as a country.
> (Loukas 03/07/2013)

Loukas' testimony is an anatomy of expatriate taxonomies of belonging. He saw himself both as Imvrian (due to his parentage) and Romaic (due to his upbringing), which made him Hellenic but, nevertheless, distinct from the

Greeks of Greece. He also felt like a part of Istanbul's society, but emphasised that this sense of belonging was limited by his past experiences of discrimination in that city, and did not translate into a sense of belonging in Turkey generally. In this regard, his expressions of self were built upon, and made meaningful through, local experience: they could be stretched as far as this experience would allow, but no further.

Conclusions

In their discourses on self and belonging, my interviewees drew on two legacies that resonate strongly, if asymmetrically, in Greek nationalism: Romaic Byzantium and Ancient Hellenism. Within the expatriate community, there has often been debate over which of these two histories is most appropriate to the Greeks of Turkey, reflected in the preference shown by some informants for one self-categorisation over the other. Whilst those who felt alienated or even rejected in the Greek state often tended to emphasise their Romaic identity, others for whom Greece was a national refuge to which they escaped from Turkish persecution commonly gave salience to their Hellenic self. From this point of view, the Hellenic self represents sameness, and the Romaic self distinctiveness; one has a *patrída* in Greece, the other a *patrída* in Istanbul/Imbros; one self has been repatriated, whilst the other lives in exile. Delving beneath the surface of these terminological distinctions, however, reveals that individuals' notions of identity and belonging are not so easily pinned down. To be sure, many *Polítes* and *Imvriótes* are at pains to differentiate themselves from the Greeks of Greece, and commonly do so by placing emphasis on the particularities of their local heritages: respectively, the urban cosmopolitanism and Orthodox Christianity of Byzantine Constantinople, and the cultural legacy of Ancient Athenian colonisation of Imbros, portrayed as having survived in spite of repeated conquests and changes in political authority on the island. These efforts at distinction based on local particularity have led both communities to be interpreted through what we might call a 'cosmopolitan' approach to diaspora (Meinhof and Triandafyllidou 2006:200), which sees diasporic groups as 'caught up with and defined against [. . .] the norms of nation-states' (Clifford 1994:307), and views the former as characterised by a heterogeneity, hybridity, and in-betweenness absent in the latter.

Such perspectives are compelling insofar as they seek to move beyond the prejudices and exclusions associated with dichotomous and immutable understandings of group identity, but they are circumscribed by their assumption that attachment to the local is necessarily antithetical to attachment to the national, or, in other words, that 'a strong identification with locality [. . .] transgresses notions of ethnicity, religion and citizenship' (Örs 2006:86). I have sought to demonstrate that the expatriated Greeks of Turkey commonly draw on their identification with a particular local place of origin in order to authenticate their claims to national belonging, and, consequently, advocate for their presence in – and support from – the Greek state. This *inclusive particularity* is simultaneously an act of boundary-maintenance and one of boundary-erosion: it allows the expatriates to differentiate themselves from 'those Hellenes' of Greece whilst also establishing their distinctiveness *as* Hellenes (Tsimouris 2008:112). This is not to deny the friction that may be generated at the interface between local and national identities, but rather to suggest that there is often significant room for manoeuvre within the allegedly 'narrow confines of national categories' (Örs 2006:81). The Greeks of Turkey challenge their marginalisation in Greek national history, politics, and diplomacy by articulating their own narratives of national authenticity grounded in local particularity, drawing on history to bypass the modern Greek state and stake a more venerable claim to Hellenic identity.

Notes

1 Anna – born in Istanbul in 1923, and a resident of the city until emigration in 1937 – remembered her excitement when friends visiting from Greece brought two eggs with them: 'I still remember those eggs, because I ate eggs from *Greece*!' (28/11/2011).
2 Interestingly, as I have discussed elsewhere, rejecting Hellenic identity in this manner can even give expatriates a means to distance themselves from the stigma associated with Greece's current financial crisis (Halstead 2014:279).
3 This is a reference to five occasions on which Ilias has been a victim of mugging in Greece.
4 Vangelis' sense of disappointment with Greece was compounded when his Turkish citizenship came through, as he automatically received a Turkish pension, something he said he had thus far been unsuccessful in obtaining from the Greek state, despite being a Greek citizen (03/02/2012).
5 On the nomenclature of this community, see Chapter 7.
6 In the original Greek, Fotini said, 'That's why we call it *I Póli*, with a capital "P"' (21/11/2011).
7 This is a reference to a passage in book 14 of Homer's *Iliad* (Tzavaras 2005/2007).
8 The sense of self articulated when a past event is remembered in a specific present context (Neisser 1994:1–18).

References

(Items marked * are in the Greek language.)

Albright, D. (1994). Literary and psychological models of the self. In U. Neisser and R. Fivush (Eds.). *The remembering self: construction and accuracy in the self-narrative*. Cambridge; New York: Cambridge University Press, 19–40.
Anon. (2017). History. *Niki Volou F.C.* Available at: www.nikifc.gr/history [Accessed on 1 December 2017].*
Babül, E. (2004). Belonging to Imbros: citizenship and sovereignty in the Turkish Republic. Paper presented at the conference *Nationalism, Society and Culture in Post-Ottoman South East Europe*. 29–30 May 2004. St. Peter's College, Oxford. Available at: www.academia.edu/6707095/Belonging_to_Imbros_Citizenship_and_Sovereignty_in_the_Turkish_Republic [Accessed on 17 April 2016].
Babül, E. (2006a). Claiming a place through memories of belonging: politics of recognition on the island of Imbros. *New Perspectives on Turkey*, 34, 47–65.
Babül, E. (2006b). Home or away? On the connotations of homeland imaginaries in Imbros. *Thamyris/Intersecting: Place, Sex and Race*, 13(1), 43–53.

Barclay, C. (1994). Composing protoselves through improvisation. In U. Neisser and R. Fivush, (Eds.). *The remembering self: construction and accuracy in the self-narrative*. Cambridge; New York: Cambridge University Press, 55–77.
Brubaker, R. (2005). The 'diaspora' diaspora. *Ethnic and Racial Studies*, 28(1), 1–19.
Clifford, J. (1994). Diasporas. *Cultural Anthropology*, 9(3), 302–338.
Cohen, R. (1997). *Global diasporas: an introduction*. London: UCL Press.
Confino, A. (1993). The nation as a local metaphor: Heimat, national memory and the German Empire, 1871–1918. *History & Memory*, 5(1), 42–86.
Connor, W. (1986). The impact of homelands upon diasporas. In G. Sheffer (Ed.). *Modern diasporas in international politics*. New York: Croom Helm, 16–45.
Eriksen, T. H. (2001). Ethnic identity, national identity, and intergroup conflict: the significance of personal experiences. In R. D. Ashmore, L. J. Jussim, and D. Wilder (Eds.). *Social identity, intergroup conflict, and conflict reduction*. Oxford; New York: Oxford University Press, 42–68.
Fermor, P. L. (1983). *Roumeli: travels in Northern Greece*. London: Penguin Books.
Giossos, Y. (2008). Scoring for the homeland: the soccer team of the refugees of Volos. *Studies in Physical Culture and Tourism*, 15, 53–63.
Halstead, H. (2014). Heirs to Byzantium: identity and the Helleno–Romaic dichotomy amongst the Istanbul Greek migrant community in Greece. *Byzantine and Modern Greek Studies*, 38(2), 265–284.
Herzfeld, M. (1986). *Ours once more: folklore, ideology, and the making of modern Greece*. New York: Pella.
Herzfeld, M. (1997). *Cultural intimacy: social poetics in the nation-state*. New York: Routledge.
Heurtley, W. A., Crawley, C. W., Darby, H. C., and Woodhouse, C. M. (1965). *A short history of Greece from early times to 1964*. Cambridge: Cambridge University Press.
Hirschon, R. (2004). 'We got on well with the Turks': Christian–Muslim relations in late Ottoman times. In D. Shankland (Ed.). *Archaeology, anthropology, and heritage in the Balkans and Anatolia: the life and times of FW Hasluck, 1878–1920*. Istanbul: Isis Press, 325–343.
Hirschon, R. (2006). Knowledge of diversity: towards a more differentiated set of 'Greek' perceptions of 'Turks'. *South European Society and Politics*, 11(1), 61–78.
Holden, D. (1972). *Greece without columns: the making of the modern Greeks*. London: Faber and Faber.
Huyssen, A. (2006). Diaspora and nation: migration into other pasts. *Thamyris/Intersecting: Place, Sex and Race*, 13(1), 81–96.
Imvriakí Ichó. (1971). The 'Imvrian Echo', and its targets, October 1971.*
Imvriakí Ichó. (1972). The Imvriótes refugees: we ask for understanding and affection, October 1972.*
Imvriakí Ichó. (1974). How long will they go on ignoring us, January–February 1974.*
Imvros. (1977). Refugees and aliens, August–September 1977.*
Imvros. (1980). The *omogenéis Imvriótes*–Tenedians should not be thought of as aliens, December 1980.*
Imvros. (1984a). At the big meeting that happened in the hall of our Society: the first part of the speeches of our collaborators, May 1984.*
Imvros. (1984b). At the big meeting that happened in the hall of our Society: the second part of the speeches of our collaborators, June 1984.*
Imvros. (1994a). To the 'rugged' and 'sheer' . . . [Imbros] . . . a 'journey' that did not happen, May–June 1994.*

Ímvros. (1994b). Imbros, May–June 1994.
Just, R. (1989). Triumph of the ethnos. In E. Tonkin, M. McDonald, and M. Chapman (Eds). *History and ethnicity*. London; New York: Routledge, 71–88.
Karakasidou, A. (1997). *Fields of wheat, hills of blood: passages to nationhood in Greek Macedonia, 1870–1990*. Chicago, IL: University of Chicago Press.
Leontis, A. (1995). *Topographies of Hellenism: mapping the homeland*. Ithaca: Cornell University Press.
Mackridge, P. (2009). *Language and national identity in Greece, 1766–1976*. Oxford; New York: Oxford University Press.
Mackridge, P. (2012). The heritages of the modern Greeks. *British Academy Review*, (19), 33–41.
Meinhof, U. H. and Triandafyllidou, A. (2006). Beyond the diaspora: transnational practices as transcultural capital. In U. H. Meinhof and A. Triandafyllidou (Eds). *Transcultural Europe: cultural policy in a changing Europe*. Basingstoke: Palgrave Macmillan, 200–222.
Millas, H. (2008). History writing among the Greeks and Turks: imagining the self and the other. In S. Berger and C. Lorenz (Eds). *The contested nation: ethnicity, class, religion and gender in national histories*. Basingstoke; New York: Palgrave Macmillan. Available at: www.herkulmillas.com/en/hm-articles/76-on-historiography/439-history-writing-among-the-greeks-and-turks-imagining-the-self-and-the-other-.html [Accessed on 17 April 2016].
Neisser, U. (1994). Self-narratives: true and false. In U. Neisser and R. Fivush, (Eds.). *The remembering self: construction and accuracy in the self-narrative*. Cambridge; New York: Cambridge University Press, 1–18.
O Polítis. (1988). The '*Romioí*', April 1988.*
Örs, İ. R. (2006). Beyond the Greek and Turkish dichotomy: the *Rum Polites* of Istanbul and Athens. *South European Society and Politics*, 11(1), 79–94.
Özkirimli, U. and Sofos, S. A. (2008). *Tormented by history: nationalism in Greece and Turkey*. London: Hurst.
Peckham, R. S. (2001). *National histories, natural states: nationalism and the politics of place in Greece*. London; New York: I.B. Tauris.
Safran, W. (1991). Diasporas in modern societies: myths of homeland and return. *Diaspora: a Journal of Transnational Studies*, 1(1), 83–99.
Tsimouris, G. (2008). *Imvrioi*. Athens: Ellinikά Grάmmata.*
Tzanelli, R. (2006). 'Not my flag!' Citizenship and nationhood in the margins of Europe (Greece, October 2000/2003). *Ethnic and Racial Studies*, 29(1), 27–49.
Tzavaras, X. (2005/2007). Imbros amongst the ancient Hellenic writers. *Thrakikά*, 15(62), 10–38. Available at: www.imvrosisland.org/archives.php?subid=9 [Accessed on 6 May 2016].*
Xeinos, G. (2011). *Imbros and Tenedos: parallel histories*. Athens: Etaireía Melétis tis Kath' Imás Anatolís.*

4 Without barbarians

Turks and Elladítes

In the May–June 1994 issue of *Imvros*, Kyriakos Bakalis penned a reflective article on the relationship of the Imvrian community to both the Turks of Turkey and the Greeks of Greece (or *Elladítes*). Alluding to Constantine P. Cavafy's poem 'Waiting for the Barbarians', Bakalis wrote:

'AND NOW WHAT WILL WE BECOME WITHOUT BARBARIANS?'*
* C. Cavafy (1904)

Every people, every *éthnos*, every person in the final analysis faced and faces in each phase of its history or life some 'barbarians'. Someone who threatens their existence, their freedom, their autonomy.

We *Imvriótes* have had the misfortune to be faced with [. . .] two very clear and unscrupulous barbarians: on the one hand the Turk, who made a point of undoing us, and on the other the *Elladítis*, who not only took the decision to not take a stand against the work of the Turk, but even helped him! [. . .]

[W]e founded our [expatriate] associations [. . .] and we all gathered together, we talked, we amused ourselves and we remembered those past beautiful years on our island and in our village. And then we cursed and swore at the Turk (he who is uneducated and uncivilised) and the *Elladítis* (who is two times more uneducated and uncivilised) [. . .]

However, my dear *Imvriótis* – I regret that I will displease you – but things have changed somewhat [. . .] The barbarians have changed their attitude!

One of them, the Turk, allows us to go freely [. . .] to the island in the summers and to renovate our houses and our churches [. . .]

The other, the *Elladítis*, has awakened! Not a week goes by without Imbros being referred to either on TV, or on the radio, in magazines, in newspapers *et cetera* [. . .]

And now, however, what happens? What will we become without barbarians? 'Those people were a kind of solution'. What will we do without them? Who will we blame for that which happens from here on?

(*Imvros* 1994)

In Bakalis' eyes, recent Imvrian history had been determined by the actions (or inaction) of two others: the Turk and the *Elladítis*. Like the inhabitants of the unnamed city in Cavafy's poem, the *Imvriótes* might find in the presence of these 'barbarians' a solution of sorts: an explanation, in this case, for their current predicament, and justification for passivity and a sense of helplessness. Unlike Cavafy's protagonists, however, Bakalis saw in the unexpected disappearance of the 'barbarians' a major opportunity for the *Imvriótes*. No longer could they place blame for the situation on Imbros on Turkish aggression and Greek indifference, and they were now faced with the decision either to consign the island to history or to take action to reclaim it (on this dilemma, see Chapter 8).

The figures of the Turk and the *Elladítis*, however, provide the expatriated Greeks of Turkey with much more than just objects of blame for their community's plight. They also constitute points of reference through which, or in opposition to which, expatriates might process and articulate their experiences and cultivate a distinctive sense of self. In the previous chapter, we saw how expatriates commonly deploy their local particularities simultaneously to distinguish themselves from the Greeks of Greece and lay claim to Hellenic identity. In this chapter, I explore how representations of the Turkish other and the Hellenic other similarly allow many interviewees and expatriate writers to pursue both inclusiveness and distinctiveness as regards the Greek state and its inhabitants. Whilst stereotypes of Turkish barbarity, juxtaposed to Hellenic civilisation, serve to constitute the expatriates as national martyrs deserving of state support, alternative representations of Turks as honourable and industrious, set against allegations of unscrupulousness and indolence amongst the *Elladítes*, function as a critical mirror to spotlight shortcomings in Greek society. In both cases, narrators claim a *privileged knowledge* of the Turkish other acquired through lived experience, which they use both to sustain *and* challenge Greek nationalist stereotypes. I draw upon Brubaker *et al.*'s (2006) distinction between 'nominal' and 'experiential' ascriptions of ethnicity in order to consider how and why such stereotypes become expedient and meaningful in individuals' narratives.

Ethnicity as an 'interpretive prism'

Brubaker's criticism of 'groupism' has become a touchstone for studies of ethnicity and national identity, particularly amongst scholars interested in the salience of these concepts in everyday life (see Chapter 2). Brubaker insisted that the commonplace tendency – both popular and academic – to divide the world up into discrete ethnic groups was 'what we want to explain, not what we want to explain things *with*; it belongs to our empirical data, not to our analytical toolkit' (2004:9). For him, what we often refer to as groups – African Americans, Whites, Romanians, Hungarians – are, in fact, categories: 'not things *in* the world, but perspectives *on* the world' (Brubaker 2004:12, 17, 20, 24). Accordingly, he suggested an analytical shift from 'groups' – conceived of as concrete and bounded things-in-the-world – to 'groupness' – moments of cohesion and collective solidarity that *happen* in particular contexts without necessarily pointing to the existence of enduring and tangible *things* called groups (Brubaker 2004:7, 12). Based on ethnographic fieldwork in the Romanian city Cluj, Brubaker and colleagues thus conceived of ethnicity as 'an interpretive prism, a way of making sense of the social world' and 'a way of understanding and interpreting experience' (Brubaker *et al.* 2006:15, 358).

As Zsuzsa Csergo has observed (2008:395), Brubaker *et al.*'s attempts to explore ethnicity and nationalism without evoking the language of groups frequently ran into conceptual problems, due to the difficulty of categorising individuals for the sake of comprehensibility without referring to them as 'Hungarians' or 'Romanians' in a generalising manner. Brubaker *et al.* attempted to work around this issue by distinguishing between *nominal* claims to ethnic identity – i.e. the ethnic nationality an individual would consistently select if asked to choose – and *experiential* ethnicity – i.e. when ethnic nationality becomes experientially relevant and salient in a particular context (2006:209–210). They maintained that when they made reference to 'the Hungarians' or 'the Romanians' – as they often did – they were talking about individuals' nominal rather than experiential ethnicity (Brubaker *et al.* 2006:12). They found it understandably difficult, however, to follow this dictum consistently, sometimes writing as though individuals who nominally identify as Hungarian or Romanian might experience ethnicity in particular ways in given contexts, and thereby lapsing into treating Hungarians and Romanians, *pace* Brubaker, as 'things *in* the world' and not just 'perspectives *on* the world' (Brubaker 2004:17).

I do not intend to realise Brubaker's theoretically ambitious yet practically problematic call for scholars to abandon a 'groupist' language in their analyses. I do, however, concur with the argument that ethnicity is something one *does* rather than *possesses* (Brubaker *et al.* 2006:208). Ethnic and national identities are not simply straightforward labels for referring to specific, clearly demarcated groups of people, but are also devices for interpreting experiences, categorising situations and behaviours, and justifying contemporary stances and arguments about the past (Brubaker *et al.* 2006:15, 224–231). This is reflected in Sutton's study on Kalymnos (discussed above, see Chapter 2). Discussing Kalymnian views of outsiders, Sutton observed that perceptions of Americans, Europeans, and the residents of neighbouring islands were all deployed by Kalymnians in different ways 'as a foil for those parts of Kalymnian society people want to criticize' (1998:47). So whilst neighbouring islanders provided Kalymnians with 'an anatomy of how various foreign (European, Turkish, American) traits "look" when grafted onto a common Greek body', Europeans represented 'the "modernist" future' that Kalymnians saw with some ambivalence, and Americans stood in for the island's past, 'the good old days, when people were more straightforward' (Sutton 1998:47). Sutton found that he himself, despite being an American, was labelled 'European' by a neighbour based on the perception that he would require the facilities to wash every day. As he wrote, '[t]his example highlights how "European" is not used in any literal sense, since she well knew that I was from the United States; I was only "European" in my desire to bathe frequently' (Sutton 1998:37). To borrow Brubaker *et al.*'s terms, Sutton's neighbour was well aware that the American anthropologist would not identify himself as a European in a *nominal* sense, but nevertheless categorised him as European in an *experiential* sense due to his (presumed) attitude towards hygiene.

This indicates that whilst identity labels are evidently closely connected to stereotypes about others, they cannot always be interpreted narrowly as intending to indicate membership of a particular group, but may rather be an attempt to ascribe or explain a particular genre of behaviour. As several scholars have observed, it is not uncommon for a Greek to identify conceptually their own behaviour or that of another Greek as 'Turkish' (Brown and Theodossopoulos 2004:8; Delivoria 2009:111; Herzfeld 1997:30; Kirtsoglou and Sistani 2003:190, 203–206; Sutton 1998:38), without them necessarily meaning to claim or ascribe Turkish *ethnicity*. This is the metaphorical and analogical 'Turk *within*' who functions as a device to establish differentiations internally within Greek communities (Kirtsoglou and Sistani 2003:190) and can even act as a critique of the self (Brown and Theodossopoulos 2004:8). Indeed, it is common to hear people in Greece use the phrase 'I became a Turk' to mean 'I got mad'. During our interview, for example, Tasoula became agitated whilst describing the obstructive stance of the Greek government regarding work and residence permits for the expatriates. She then reprimanded herself for her anger by exclaiming, 'I am becoming a Turk!' Tasoula was not claiming to be ethnically Turkish, but rather drawing on Greek stereotypes of Turkish fanaticism (on which, see below) to characterise idiomatically her own emotional state. Cowan has made comparable observations about the use of ethnic symbols in the central Macedonian town of Sohos. She noted that whilst the Sohoians 'vehemently reject the insinuation that they are anything but Greek', in ritual and everyday life 'they frequently communicate through and place especial value upon linguistic, gestural and celebratory forms which [they] themselves identify as "not Greek"; that is, forms that incorporate Turkish or "Bulgarian" linguistic elements or are *conceptually identified* as Turkish or "Bulgarian"' (Cowan 1997:153). Cowan stressed the disjuncture between the inflections of these labels and the ethnic groups they supposedly evoked:

> Ironically, and importantly, what these purportedly 'ethnic symbols' seemed *not* to mark was 'ethnicity'! I encountered no evidence whatsoever that Sohoians wished to identify themselves as Macedonians (in a non-Greek sense) or Slavo–Macedonians or Bulgarians, nor any evidence that they considered their use of non-Greek forms as *constitutive*, or *evidence*, of one of these identities [. . .] Rather, they were viewed [. . .] as part of the normal fabric of everyday interaction, and as a code for Sohoians to articulate (largely to each other) complex identities, relationships and historical experiences.
>
> (1997:165)

As an intimate everyday 'code', ethnicity permits individuals to categorise and interpret the world around them, articulate their own sense of self and explain the behaviour of others, and make their experiences meaningful to themselves and intelligible to others. I develop these observations below by exploring the fluctuating and overlapping representations of Turks/Turkey and *Elladítes*/Greece in expatriate discourse.

Good Turk, bad Turks

It is a commonplace to observe that national identity requires an 'other' in contrast to which it is defined (Danforth 1995:20; Eriksen 1995:427; Hall 1996:3–4; Hirschon 2009:83; Mackridge and Yannakakis 1997:2; Millas 2004:144; Spyrou 2002:258–259; Triandafyllidou 1998:594, 598–599). In Anna Triandafyllidou's terms, nationalism is premised on the assumption that '[f]ellow nationals are not simply very close or close enough to one another, they are *closer* to one another than they are to outsiders' (1998:599). In modern Greece, the 'significant other' (Triandafyllidou 1998:600) has commonly been the Turks; as Spyros Spyrou put it, '*there are Greeks because there are Turks*' (2002:259). Negative stereotypes of this Turkish other have often been overwhelmingly prevalent in official, media, and popular representations (Kirtsoglou and Sistani 2003:194–195; Terzis 2004:174–175; Theodossopoulos 2004:29; Yerasimos 1988:40). Dimitris Theodossopoulos found that Greeks in the Peloponnesian town of Patras played 'Greeks versus Turks'[1] as children, with the weakest children taking on the role of the Turks, and when asked what the word 'Turk' had meant to them in childhood, most of his informants 'responded to this question with only one word: "fear"' (2004:31, 34). Nevertheless, an alternative narrative of harmonious coexistence between Greeks and Turks does exist, emerging particularly in 'private conservation or during nostalgic recollections' (Theodossopoulos 2006:16). Both Hirschon and Theodossopoulos have pointed to the lack of contemporary contact and shared experience between Greeks and Turks as central to the tenacity of mutually held negative stereotypes (Hirschon 2009:83; Theodossopoulos 2004:30). Indeed, narratives of harmonious Greek–Turkish coexistence were common amongst Greek refugees from the Ottoman Empire who had lived alongside Turkish people, in spite of their traumatic exodus from Turkey (Hirschon 2004; Hirschon 2006; Hirschon 2009:85–86), whilst Greeks who meet Turks abroad frequently express 'mutual amazement' at shared cultural traits (Hirschon 2009:91) and develop more favourable and differentiated perceptions of Turkish people (Bacas 2003; Kirtsoglou and Sistani 2003:202; Theodossopoulos 2004:38).

Unlike most residents of the Greek state, the expatriated Greeks of Turkey did have lived experience of the Turkish other. The degree of interaction that members of the Greek minority had with their Turkish fellow countrymen varied based on a number of factors (age, gender, occupation, area of residence, *et cetera*; see chapter 1). Men, for instance, generally had greater opportunities to interact with Turks than women, whilst those who lived in Istanbul had greater contact than those who lived (or remained) on Imbros. Interviewees sometimes portrayed majority–minority interaction in Turkey as limited and impersonal – particularly stressing that romantic entanglements with Turks were vociferously discouraged by parents – and remembered threats, insults, and physical clashes between the two communities. Several *Polítes*, for example, talked about being showered with abuse or bombarded by stones thrown by Turkish children *en route* to school. As Alexandra recalled:

> Every morning and every afternoon we lived with fear, because to get to school I had to pass through a Turkish neighbourhood, and the Turkish children – because we had to wear a uniform from school we stood out from them – they used to set up ambushes, and throw stones at us, shouting 'the infidels are passing'.
>
> (22/07/2011)

Accounts of intercommunal harmony were, however, also common in informants' narratives. Many – particularly, though not exclusively, residents of the Princes' Islands – were at pains to put across an impression of peaceable fraternity between the Armenian, Greek, Jewish, and Turkish communities, telling stories of interfaith mingling at important religious festivals, intercommunal support and protection during flashpoints such as the *Septemvrianá*, and close friendships that prevailed beyond the emigration of the Greeks. In the words of Andreas, a resident of *Chálki* until 1973, 'we played together, we grew up together with the Turks. We didn't have any problems, we were like brothers with the Turks' (11/02/2012). A number of interviewees recalled heart-wrenching farewells or emotional reunions with Turkish friends: Tasos, choking back tears of his own, told me that when his father left Turkey his Turkish fellow stallholders in the market in which he worked cried 'even though it was a competitor who was leaving' (13/03/2014); whilst Andreas recalled that when he was reacquainted with a childhood Turkish friend on a return visit to *Chálki* he embraced him so tight that a pencil he had in his shirt pocket bruised his chest (11/02/2012).

Some informants presented either overwhelmingly positive or unreservedly negative portrayals of Turks and Greek–Turkish intercommunal relationships, reflecting an internal debate within the expatriate community between those derogatorily labelled as 'Turk-lovers' for their supposedly idyllic impressions of Turks, and those lambasted as 'Hellenified' due to their allegedly 'uncritical' absorption of anti-Turkish vilification in the Greek state (Örs 2006:84). Commonly, however, positive representations of Turks coexisted with negative generalisations in expatriate testimony (Halstead 2014b). As the Istanbul-born sociologist Hercule Millas has argued in relation to his own father's discourse on Turks, it is too simplistic to dismiss such oscillation between positive and negative accounts as mindless contradiction (2006:47–48). Rather, for Millas, it reflects a tendency for narrators to 'compartmentaliz[e] their perceptions of the Turks in parallel, but not overlapping, domains of experience', such that stereotypes of the 'undifferentiated Turk as the ethnic Other' are kept separate from favourable impressions of 'actual, concrete people who happened to be the Others' (2006:48, 57). In an exploration of Greek Cypriot children's perceptions of Turks, Spyrou correspondingly observed that whilst the children often default to negative generalisations about the Turks such that '[t]here are no different kinds of Turks but "a Turk" who is homogenous, undifferentiated and captures the essential nature of all Turks', when asked to elaborate on these impressions most stress that 'there are both good and bad Turks', and often distinguish in this regard between Turkish Cypriots and mainland Turks (2002:260–261, 266). In Theodossopoulos' terms, this is a distinction between the particularised Turk – seen as human and similar to the self – and the generalised Turk – perceived as inhuman and hostile to the self (2006:9).

This tendency to differentiate between particular Turks and the generalised other was borne out in many of the oral testimonies I heard, including those of two of my younger, Greek-born Imvrian informants. Both recalled growing up with a somewhat negative impression of an abstract Turkish other. When, however, on later visits to Imbros with their parents, they encountered Turks as fellow human beings rather than as a 'faceless and nameless' mass, a 'particularization of the generalized Turk' took place (Theodossopoulos 2006:9–10). I asked Eva, who was born in Athens in 1991 to an Imvrian mother and a father from the Princes' Islands, if she remembered what impression she had of the Turks before she visited Imbros for the first time. She replied:

> I don't see the people themselves negatively, but generally when I say, 'that is a Turk' or 'Turkey', I might see it slightly negatively. But with an individual personally who is a Turk I do not think I have a problem.
>
> (Eva 13/08/2013)

Lia – also born in Athens in 1991 to an Imvrian mother – exhibited a comparable response. I asked her if she recalled what impression she had of the Turks whilst growing up, to which she replied:

> Err, yes [laughs]. Look, certainly it is not the same as 'he is a Frenchman, German'. I mean, I would say 'ah, *the Turk*'. I thought of him in a slightly derogatory manner [...] But I personally do not have a problem, because we are okay here, they have received us well, and because we are reconciled things are good.
>
> (Lia 13/08/2013)

In the narratives of both Lia and Eva, a distinction was drawn between actual people who happened to be – nominally – Turks, and 'the Turk', an abstract and somewhat ill-defined figure who represented fear and evoked wariness.

First-generation, Turkish-born interviewees often accounted for their mixed experiences of intercommunal relationships, and the discrepancies in their representations of Turks, by drawing similar distinctions between 'good' and 'bad' Turks. Some called attention to the attitudes of different groups within Turkish society, for instance contrasting educated or enlightened urban Turks with uneducated villagers or provincials; secularists and Kemalists with Islamists and fundamentalists; Westerners with Easterners or 'Anatolians'; or moderates/left-wingers with right-wing nationalists. Interestingly, however, others combined the figures of the 'good Turk' and the 'bad Turk' into the same individual, distinguishing between the positive behaviour typical of an individual *Turk* and the collective mob mentality of the same *Turks* together (Halstead 2014b:398–399). The following perspectives cannot be considered to be representative of the views of the expatriate community at large, but they do reflect a recurrent theme that I encountered in my research that can be productively analysed for insight into the nature of ethnic stereotypes.

Menelaos was born in Istanbul in 1946, and left for Greece in 1989 after his son finished primary school. When I asked him how he would characterise his relationships with his Turkish acquaintances, he responded:

> One person, one-on-one, is good. As a crowd, when the government stirs them up – [for instance,] a [Turkish] neighbour who knew that the *Septemvrianá* would happen, would not come to tell you, 'look, be careful, leave the house tonight, go elsewhere', nothing [like that].
>
> (Menelaos 06/02/2012)

Tryfon, who was born on Imbros in 1929 and emigrated to Greece after 1964 when the situation on Imbros began to deteriorate, put it rather more bluntly and crudely: 'one Turk is God, [but] if there are three, four together they provoke each other and become dogs' (21/05/2013). This alleged duality is commonly attributed either to the Islamic faith or to nationalist fanaticism. Lefteris, who was born in Istanbul in 1960 and left for Greece at the age of eight, maintained that the Turks' religion might cause them to go from friend to foe in an instant. As he put it, 'I think it is their religion that causes the problem. You might be a friend of theirs, a very close friend, but due to religion there might come a moment when they kill you, if you say something about their religion. They won't wait to ask you, they might just kill you. We are talking about the uneducated types now, of course, not about the educated people' (Lefteris 12/05/2013). Aris – born on Imbros in 1941, and a resident of Greece since 1969 – spoke favourably of the Turkish character, but likewise claimed that they were easily stirred up by their government:

> The Turks, the people, are good. Good? They are very patriotic. If the authorities say, 'you will not bother anybody', nobody will bother you. If they say, 'on your feet, kill them', they are on their feet. Such is their mentality. But if they are in the right frame of mind they are very good, honourable.
>
> (23/05/2013)

Alexandra, who lived in Istanbul from her birth in 1947 until her emigration to Greece in 1971, similarly juxtaposed the qualities of an individual Turk to the mob mentality of multiple Turks:

> The Turks are a people who are guided by their leaders. One-on-one, they are the best thing that God created. One-on-one. But more than two or three, they

start to think like a crowd, and if given some direction from the state, they cease to be friendly people, and whatever the country says, that's what they must do. There's no such thing as friend, or mother, or brother. They are a people guided by the leaders, the individual does not have his own free will. Those who think differently are very few. Those who think logically and are cultured people, are perhaps 1 million out of 90 million, and they are easily lost. That's difficult for someone to understand if they haven't lived there, and don't know their manner of thinking and behaviour.

(22/07/2011; see also Halstead 2014b:410)

This supposed propensity for extremes of behaviour is often used to account for both positive and negative experiences of living alongside the Turks. For example, in a written witness testimony to the *Septemvrianá*, Giorgos Gavriilidis wrote:

The Turk has a fanaticism within him, which he shows at bad and good moments. I remember, for example, female Turkish neighbours, helping my mother and embracing our family, our problems. I remember those same people showing the vandals the Greek houses, on that night [in 1955].

(Ekdóseis Tsoukátou 1999:169)

A stereotype of Turkish fanaticism was here used to account both for the lengths that the Turks will go to in order to lend assistance to their neighbours, and for their hostile behaviour at moments of intercommunal tension. It is, moreover, not uncommon for narrators to allege that the same Turkish individuals exhibited extremes of both honour and violence *on the same night* when the riots happened in 1955. Writing about her memories of the *Septemvrianá*, Maria Andreou Kanaki recalled that a group of rioters broke into her family home, forcing the majority of the family to escape into a neighbouring house, leaving behind her bedridden elderly mother. She described how '[t]he vandals got into the bedroom where we had placed my mother, and when they saw her in that state, they said to her: "you lie down there mother, do not worry" and they began to break and destroy [the property]' (Ekdóseis Tsoukátou 1999:66).

This story was also related to Turkish researchers by Veniamin Kanakis, the grandson of the bedridden woman, who remembered that many of the rioters were acquaintances of his father:

We heard a noise. Immediately a window was smashed [. . .] As soon as my father heard the noise he ran outside. Half of those gathered there were known to him [. . .] They said to my father, 'you leave, do not stay here, take your family and leave. Do not worry.' [. . .] The mob went into the house and devastated everything. They broke everything. Nothing remained standing [. . .] They did not touch my grandmother. 'Mama do not worry' they said to her.

(Turan *et al.* 2010:56–57)

96 *Local homelands and national belonging*

In this example, whilst as a crowd the Turks were portrayed as acting violently, obeying their instructions to destroy Greek property, as individuals they were seen to show respect for the sick elderly woman, ensuring that they did not harm her and even attempting to reassure her. In a testimony published by the Greek newspaper *Kathimeriní* in 2015, Michalis Vasileiadis similarly alleged that during the riots his Turkish doorman, having first protected Michalis' family – by standing outside the block of flats in which they lived waving a Turkish flag and telling the rioters that there were no Greeks living there – proceeded to join the rioters further down the road and participate in the looting of other Greek properties (Vasileiadis 2015:29–30). Michalis accounted for the doorman's behaviour in the following terms:

> Later I understood why he did it. It was the difference of identity: the unknown *Romiós* who he saw simply as a *Romiós* and I who was little Michalis, my mother Mrs. Katina who cooked and gave him food to eat, who sent him to shop [for her] and gave him a tip[,] and he felt an obligation towards us. The Turk as an individual is an exceptional person, and if you do him a kindness, he will not forget it for 40 years, as his proverb goes. His weakness is one: as a member of a crowd he is beastly.
>
> (Vasileiadis 2015:30)

Alexandra – who was a young girl at the time of the *Septemvrianá* and witnessed her mother being saved from sexual assault by the intervention of a Turkish friend of her father – made a comparable claim about the behaviour of her family's Turkish neighbours in 1955:

Alexandra: A Turk has a pride, a love that you won't find in a Hellene, or any other race. But once they become two, three, four, five, a crowd, they start to be dangerous.
Halstead: But some Hellenes were protected [during the *Septemvrianá*] by the Turks?
Alexandra: Our family was protected. '55 was organised from 1950. All the Turks promised to throw a stone at an infidel house. Our friend promised on the Qur'an to throw a stone. So, after protecting our family, he went to go and throw his rock [at another family].
(see also Halstead 2014b:398–399)

Through the good Turk/bad Turks dichotomy, these narrators find a rationalisation for their life experiences. Stereotypes of Turks as proud, honour-bound, and obedient to authority serve to explicate otherwise jarring memories: Turks as individuals – remembered from work, leisure, and the neighbourhood – are depicted as fanatically honourable; but the same people as a crowd – seen as implicated or complicit in attacks on the Greeks – are portrayed as liable to become fanatically violent if dishonoured. In this sense, being a 'good' or 'bad'

Turk is not an immutable quality inherent to particular individuals, but rather is dependent on the context in which they are remembered (Halstead 2014b:399).

Nominal and experiential Turks

I have elsewhere observed that in Greek Cypriot oral testimonies whether a Turkish character is classified as a 'Turk' – and therefore 'bad' and hostile to 'us' – or a 'Turkish Cypriot' – and therefore potentially 'good' and similar to 'us' – sometimes reflects not the actual birthplace of the subject but rather the context of their narration (Halstead 2014b:398). Turkish Cypriots remembered in benign or friendly settings – as fellow villagers or drinking partners – are generally called 'Turkish Cypriots', whilst other Turkish Cypriots remembered in antagonistic settings – such as in verbal confrontations on the dividing 'Green Line' – might be labelled as 'Turks' (Halstead 2014b:397–398). Spyrou has similarly noted that the Turkish Cypriot leader Rauf Denktash – who stands out in Greek Cypriot children's narratives as an archetypal 'bad Turk' – is generally seen by those children not as a Turkish Cypriot but as a Turk: '[f]or the children', he wrote, 'it makes much more sense to label Denktash as a Turk rather than a Turkish Cypriot because, unlike other Turkish Cypriots, he is seen as evil, similar in that sense to the Turkish occupiers' (2002:266). To adapt Brubaker's terms, individuals who would likely *nominally* be identified as Turkish Cypriots – that is, if the narrator is directly asked to identify their ethnicity – are classified as Turks in an *experiential* sense – that is, insofar as their reputed ethnicity becomes salient in categorising or explaining their behaviour.

I develop this view of ethnicity as an 'interpretive prism' (Brubaker *et al.* 2006:15) by exploring the ethnic identities imputed to others in narratives of intercommunal violence and protection during the *Septemvrianá*, drawing on the testimonial compilation *Septemvrianá 1955: the 'Kristallnacht' of the Hellenism of Constantinople*, published by Ekdóseis Tsoukátou (1999; see Chapter 1). Witness testimonies typically identify the perpetrators interchangeably as 'Turks', 'rioters', 'vandals', or 'barbarians', creating a casual equation between members of the mob and the Turkish population generally. One witness, for instance, described the riots as 'those events during which groups of *crowds Turks fanatics Muslims* destroyed whatever they came across that was Hellenic in Constantinople' (Ekdóseis Tsoukátou 1999:165, my emphasis), thereby equating Turkishness and the Islamic faith with fanaticism and a mob mentality. Rarely is there any serious attempt to discern the composition of the mob, apart from vague (and derogatory) references to 'Anatolians', and absent is the suggestion, sometimes found in expatriate discourse, that many of the rioters were Kurds (see Chapter 7). Every member of the mob was 'Turkish' and, indeed, in several of the testimonies the actions of the rioters are portrayed as *characteristically* 'Turkish'. One witness wrote that the Turks' 'wild instinct awoke, that afternoon of 6/9/1955', whilst another avowed that 'it is well-known that one can only expect such atrocities from the Turks' (Ekdóseis Tsoukátou 1999:117, 145). Two contributors quoted celebrated foreign writers in an effort to substantiate such claims:

[. . .] I remembered the philhellene V. Hugo, who wrote in one of his poems:
The Turks passed by here,
everything is in ruins,
plunged into mourning.
Yes, sirs, that is what happened on that ill-omened night.
(Ekdóseis Tsoukátou 1999:115)

[. . .] and then I took the big decision to leave, expatriated, and live elsewhere in another country, wherever in the world, leaving the holy earth where my forefathers lived and which was now trampled upon and contaminated by barbarians, 'the blight of Asia', as George Horton calls them [. . .].
(Ekdóseis Tsoukátou 1999:138)

Spyrou observed that for Greek Cypriot children the stereotypical 'bad Turk' is 'a minimised category which includes only those Turks they perceive as being "bad"', with the result that 'the national category itself (i.e. Turks) becomes a label for the negative [aspects] of the "other", not a label for the nation as a whole' (2002:269). In other words, whilst all Turks might be *nominally* Turkish in the eyes of the children in the sense that, if pressed, they would identify them as Turkish rather than Greek, it is only in the context of perceived negative behaviour that others become *experientially* Turkish; i.e. that their Turkishness comes to *matter*. Likewise, in the above examples, the ethnicity of the antagonists was significant for the narrators insofar as it explained their actions: the actual composition of the rioters and what their motivations might have been for engaging in acts of violence was disregarded in favour of the simpler answer that they did what they did because they were Turkish. What was significant, in a way, was less that the *people* were Turkish and more that the *behaviour* was 'Turkish'.

What, then, of nominal Turks who did *not* behave 'Turkishly'? As I mentioned in Chapter 1, oral accounts of the *Septemvrianá* frequently feature stories of Muslim neighbours, co-workers, and friends warning or protecting members of the Greek community. The testimonies in the Ekdóseis Tsoukátou compilation are no exception, and at least 19 of the 50 accounts contain some reference to intercommunal assistance.[2] In many of these accounts, the authors stressed that their saviours were Turks; in the words of one witness: 'the neighbours were Turks. We should not forget that the good people were good people and they have a conscience' (Ekdóseis Tsoukátou 1999:75). Some narrators, however, seemed to struggle to reconcile the violence of the mob with the assistance afforded by individual Muslims. Indeed, in 7 of the 19 intercommunal assistance stories, the protagonist is either explicitly presented as not ethnically Turkish or has their Turkish ethnicity 'qualified' in some way by the narrator. Of these, four stories feature Kurds. Petros Tsoukatos wrote that his apartment 'was saved, because our doorkeeper – a Kurd from Van [in eastern Turkey] – Memetis, as we called him, a very good young man of 25–30 years, protected the block of flats where our relatives were staying' (Ekdóseis Tsoukátou 1999:158). Another, anonymous witness was likewise keen to stress that their saviour was Kurdish:

At that moment, our doorkeeper Sadik came to ask us if we had a Turkish flag. However, as all of the tenants were Hellenes, we did not have a flag.

In the meantime, they [the rioters] had arrived and were breaking the outer door. Sadik, however, put his body in the way, holding with his two hands the frames of the door and shouting that everyone was away, that only his family was inside and that he would presently hang out a flag [. . .] And so we were saved.

Of course, our doorkeeper was a Kurd and the owner of our block of flats rewarded him the following day.

(Ekdóseis Tsoukátou 1999:107–108)

The house of Konstantinos Katsaros was similarly protected by the doorkeeper. In contrast to the two examples above, Konstantinos seemed unsure of the ethnicity of this doorkeeper, but nevertheless speculated that he might be of Kurdish extraction, writing '[w]hen we returned to Constantinople, our house [. . .] had been saved, because our doorkeeper Mr. Ömer, perhaps of Kurdish descent, prevented the barbarians from destroying it' (Ekdóseis Tsoukátou 1999:151). Simeon Vafeiadis, meanwhile, explained that his shop was saved by a man who was commonly thought to be a Kurd but was, in fact, descended from Armenians:

Our shop did not suffer great damage once again thanks to a Turkish neighbour, an accountant, who as soon as he heard about the events got in touch with a stevedore, Hasan, and told him to run immediately to save our shop. He along with another Kurd stood in front of the shop and did not allow the rioters to destroy it. Thus it was saved with only minor damages.

Everybody knew Hasan as a Kurd. In reality, however, he was of Armenian descent. In 1916, during the slaughters [i.e. the Armenian genocide], as a young child, he fetched up with a Turkish family.

(Ekdóseis Tsoukátou 1999:61)

Simeon also described how the neighbourhood in which he lived was saved from damage by a man named Ali Riza, twice stressing that he was a Turk from Crete (presumably a refugee from the 1923 exchange):

Our neighbourhood passed without damage, thanks to a neighbour and friend, Ali Riza [. . .] Ali Riza was a Turk from Crete and, as we learned later, he stood at the crossroads of our neighbourhood on the central road and did not allow the rioters to pass. Thus, thanks to that Turkish Cretan, the Hellenic houses of our neighbourhood were saved from the catastrophe.

(Ekdóseis Tsoukátou 1999:58)

Despoina Isaakidou similarly specified that the family living opposite her own that provided them with shelter in the middle of the riots was Turkish Cretan (Ekdóseis Tsoukátou 1999:147). Another anonymous witness, meanwhile, told the story of a neighbour who protected the women and children of the neighbourhood, and took care to point out that her mother was rumoured to be Greek: 'Mrs Chatzer, who had links with all of the Hellenic families there – they said that her mother was a Hellene – took almost all of the young mothers of the village with their children into her house and they stayed the night there' (Ekdóseis Tsoukátou 1999:90). Finally, in the testimony of Apostolis Nikolaidis – reconstructed by Leonidas Koumakis and excerpted from his book *The Miracle* (see Chapter 7, below) – it is emphasised that the wife of the Turkish Pontic neighbour who offered Apostolis' family shelter was a crypto-Christian, who clandestinely attended church every Sunday (Ekdóseis Tsoukátou 1999:188).

In each of these cases, the narrators placed special emphasis on the peculiar identity of their rescuers, seemingly so as to explain their 'motive' for intervening on behalf of the Greeks, or rather to offer an explanation as to why they did not behave 'Turkishly' like the 'Turkish' mob. It is, of course, quite possible that the protagonists of these stories genuinely were Kurdish (or Turkish Cretan or half Greek or crypto-Christian), even though it is clear in some of these cases that the narrators were drawing on speculation or hearsay rather than detailed personal knowledge of the individuals concerned (as in the case of Mr. Ömer who was 'possibly of Kurdish descent'). Each of these individuals may indeed have had special motivation to intervene on behalf of the Greeks – the half Greek and the crypto-Christian out of commonality, the Kurds and the crypto-Armenian out of solidarity, and the Turkish Cretans due to memories of living in Greece – although all could also have had good reason not to get involved. What is significant, however, is that these subtle discriminations of origin or family history appear only in the context of describing such acts of protection. These narrators felt it necessary to qualify the ethnicity of their saviours in this particular narrative context (even though some of these same individuals may well have been identified as Turks in other contexts). Their imputed ethnicity becomes experientially relevant insofar as it accounts for their exceptional behaviour: they were not complicit in the general violence of 'the Turks' because they were not 'really Turkish', or at least more than 'simply Turkish'. From this perspective, the ascription of a particular ethnic identity to others can be seen as a means to simplify and interpret experience, explaining behaviour both 'expected' and 'unexpected'.

Privileged knowledge (1): the 'bad Turks'

Alekos, who was born in Istanbul in 1971 but grew up in Athens, described to me how he had noticed that the Greeks of Istanbul habitually play devil's advocate in discussions relating to Turkey and the Turks. He observed that when *Polítes* talk amongst themselves they tend to reminisce nostalgically about the 'good old days' in Istanbul, whilst when they speak about the past with Greeks from Greece they emphasise the daily fear and persecution they experienced in Turkey. Yet if these conversations with other Greeks turn to Turkey or Greek–Turkish relationships more broadly, the expatriates will often take the Turkish side, prompting the Greeks of Greece to ask 'okay, if things were so good there and they treated you better there and the state was better there, why did you come over here?' In response, the expatriates frequently return to a narrative of strife, replying 'because they did not allow us to speak, we were afraid that our children might engage in mixed marriages and become Turkified, we did not know what would befall us the next day, *et cetera, et cetera*'. In Alekos' words, 'the repression that we had there as a minority and the repression that we feel here because everything is in a state of chaos become confused and agitate us' (28/05/2013).

As Alekos identified, fluctuations between positive and negative representations of the Turkish other in expatriate discourse reflect not only mixed and variable experiences of intercommunal relationships in Turkey, but also the ambivalent position of the expatriate community in regard to Greece, and their attempts to convey both sets of experiences in different social and narrative situations. In Spyrou's terms, stereotypes 'are not immutable attributions' but rather 'discursive strategies that take place within specific conversational contexts' (2002:267). For many expatriates, representations of the 'good Turk' serve to critique perceived defects in the character of the *Elladítes*, and thereby to express a sense of disillusionment with Greek society (see below). Stereotypes of the 'bad Turks', meanwhile, are, in particular, strategically expedient in the context of justifying the expatriates' presence in Greece and bolstering appeals for support from the Greek state.

In line with Alekos' observations, many interviewees substantiated their decision to emigrate by juxtaposing a sense of fear and repression in Turkey with one of freedom and security in Greece. Alexandra, for instance, characterised Turkey as 'a place where you feel enslaved, afraid to speak, to live as you want', and remarked that after 40 years of living in Greece – excluding 'a few unpleasant events' – 'for the most part I thank God that I am in Greece and that I am free. I'm not afraid to wear what I want, to wear my cross, to speak Greek' (22/07/2011). Expatriate writers often have recourse to similar dichotomies. In the newspaper *O Polítis*, stereotypes of Turkey as warmongering and untrustworthy – contrasted to the allegedly civilised and peaceable tendencies of Greece – frequently function as a discursive strategy for critiquing Turkish foreign policy (towards the Greeks of Turkey and towards Greece itself). In August 1976, for instance, the newspaper characterised Greece as a 'freedom-loving country *par excellence*' and admonished Turkey for conducting 'an undeclared war against Hellenism' in Istanbul, Imbros, Tenedos, and Cyprus, whilst in a March 1987 piece it asked whether it was possible for a peace-loving country like Greece to work cooperatively with a warmongering one like Turkey (*O Polítis* 1976b; *O Polítis* 1987).

At the same time, however, representations of Turkish aggression can also sustain a critique of Greek policy. In their early years of settlement in Greece, narratives of suffering in Turkey provided many of my interviewees with a means to respond to representatives of the Greek state who urged them to return to Turkey in the national interest. Tasoula, for example, who left Istanbul as a child with her family in 1964, recalled that her family's response to such suggestions was to invite the officials to try living in Turkey themselves. She told me:

We had to go every month to get residence permits. Imagine! And some of those people [the officials in the Aliens' Bureau] said to us, 'return home [to Turkey]'. And our response was, 'we've already eaten the cucumbers there. You, who is complaining to us, go there for a month and eat the Turkish cucumber yourself!

(Tasoula 27/11/2011)[3]

Similarly, *O Polítis* commonly prefaces complaints directed at the Greek state with accounts of the persecution the expatriates faced in Turkey. In a January 1979 article, the newspaper railed against Greek policy towards expatriates with Turkish citizenship by lamenting how those 'who were *de facto* forced, i.e. by every kind of unbearable Turkish pressure [. . .] to leave their homes' now 'in their own *patrída*, in Greece, suffer from myriad hardships' due to the state's reluctance to issue Greek citizenship (particularly when those expatriates 'who went to Canada, Sweden or other liberal countries, acquired the citizenship of the country they chose for their new *patrída*'). Forced to operate on their Turkish citizenship, the newspaper observed, these expatriates 'are driven like sheep to the slaughter to the Turkish Embassy to pay their poll tax [to the Turkish state],[4] so unnecessary because all of them are NOT going to return to the Turkish paradise' (*O Polítis* 1979).

In like manner, writers for *Ímvros* often contextualise their complaints towards the Greek state by first reminding their readers of the community's suffering at the hands of the national other, for example writing in 1977 that the *Imvriótes* were treated as aliens in Greece despite being 'victims of Turkish chauvinism', or in 1992 that Imbros was a casualty 'not only of Turkish beastliness, but also of non-existent Greek policies' (*Ímvros* 1977; *Ímvros* 1992). In the aftermath of Turkish military intervention on Cyprus in 1974, the newspaper likewise paralleled the experiences of the *Imvriótes* with those of the Cypriots (on such parallels, see Chapter 6) in order to provide context for a protest about Greece's reluctance to issue visas to the Greeks of Turkey. The author wrote:

When, thoroughly fed up and resentful from the barbarities of the Turk (that have now become famous in the Panhellenic world, due to Cyprus, although we tasted them long before), the *Imvriótes* asked for visas from the Embassy so as to come here [Greece], to save themselves from the endless torment and anguish, the officials turned them away in the worst way or teased them with the 'come tomorrow' and 'come the day after tomorrow', so that the people in the end would become weary and abandon their effort.

(*Imvriakí Ichó* 1974)

In 1993, *Ímvros* reprinted a letter from the Imvrian Association to the Undersecretary for Hellenism Abroad in the Greek government, objecting in similar terms to the charge applied by the Aliens' Bureau to those expatriates with Turkish citizenship for the renewal of their work and residence permits. The authors of this appeal asked the Undersecretary to put himself in their shoes:

Can you imagine, Mr. Undersecretary, the pain of our compatriots who suffered untold hardships at the hands of Turkish ferocity and vulgarity, who lived through the humiliations, the derisions, the degradations, the beatings, the rapes, the murders, the plunder of their houses, the confiscation of their properties, only because they were born Hellenes, because they wanted to call themselves Hellenes, to feel like Hellenes and act as Hellenes[?]

Those same people, Mr. Undersecretary, are called upon at the Aliens' Bureau to prove that they are Hellenes with the confirmation of the Hellenic Embassy in Constantinople! Those people who, if it were possible to examine them ethnically, would have written on their chromosomes only Greece and Hellenic.

(*Imvros* 1993)

In these examples, negative stereotypes of Turkish chauvinism were evoked in order to identify the expatriates as national martyrs deserving of support and compassion from the Greek authorities: because they suffered as Hellenes in Turkey, it was argued, they should be treated as Hellenes in Greece.

It is, furthermore, felt by some representatives of expatriate community organisations that this first-hand experience of the Turkish other places them in a unique position to advise the Greek government, and the wider Western world, on their diplomatic dealings with the Republic of Turkey. In a June 1976 article, for instance, *O Polítis* proclaimed that their own 'painful experience of Turkish tactics' gave them a duty to declare 'to all of the Christian world, the Islamic, everywhere, that the Turks live in their own world, with their political arsenal the lie, plunder, [and] treachery' (*O Polítis* 1976a). In particular, this is an argument often advanced by the Constantinopolitan Society, as part of their efforts to influence Greek and European policy towards Turkey. In 1998, for example, the Society prefaced an invitation to a Greek political party to attend a memorial ceremony to mark the anniversary of the Fall of Constantinople by declaring that the Society's committees

are sensitised to the issues related to Greek–Turkish relationships, [and] have a first-hand experience of the Turkish way of thinking and acting and therefore advance thoughts and perceptions to International Organisations [. . .] always in conjunction with the relevant political and diplomatic organs of the State.

(Constantinopolitan Society 1998)

Paris, a prominent member of the Constantinopolitan Society who was himself born in Greece in the early 1950s to a father from Istanbul, similarly argued that the *Polítes* were 'the only ones out of the Hellenes who live here [in Greece] who know in substance the character and behaviour of the Turks'. 'When you meet a Turk', Paris explained, 'be he a simple person or in some state capacity – diplomat, politician – you might think he is cosmopolitan, but in a given moment you understand that he has a guile that you cannot always immediately comprehend if you haven't lived through the behaviour of the Turks' (01/02/2012).

Nikolaos – born in Istanbul in 1939 and a resident of Greece since 1964 – likewise maintained that the Constantinopolitan Society was founded by 'people who had lived through both the *Septemvrianá* and the expulsions, and know the mentality of the Turk', something of which the Greek authorities were considered to be ignorant. Nikolaos elaborated as follows:

> As we were told by our parents, you cannot make a friend of the Turk, because they will catch you unawares. Turkish diplomacy sees many years ahead. Now it does not need to wage a war to defeat Greece, [it achieves it] with money and words [. . .] Here, the Hellenes, the Hellenic authorities, don't know that. That was the aim [of the Constantinopolitan Society], to be able to explain it to the Hellenic government so that they can understand.
>
> (30/01/2012)

Claiming a privileged knowledge of the Turkish other as first-hand witnesses, these narrators mobilised stereotypes of the 'bad Turks' to lend credence to their efforts to influence Greek foreign policy towards Turkey, and to present their community and its commemorative endeavours as an invaluable asset to the Greek state.

In the examples presented above, representations of the Turkish other as warmongering and treacherous were juxtaposed to stereotypes of the Greeks as peace-loving and honest. As Brown and Theodossopoulos have emphasised, however, '[s]tereotypes about ethnic neighbours can sustain a critique of the Self as much as the Other' (2004:8). Indeed, negative stereotypes of the Turks can sometimes be turned on the Greek state and its inhabitants. Testifying as a witness to the *Septemvrianá*, Iro Athinaiou made the following aside:

> I would like to insert a parenthesis here. The Turks regard the [Turkish] flag like a talisman, they worship it like a God. Not like us here, where we do not see it – unfortunately – not even at our biggest celebrations – 25.3 [Greek Independence Day], 28.10 [*Óhi* Day] – when the country should be submerged in the colour blue.
>
> (Ekdóseis Tsoukátou 1999:118)

In this case, a stereotype of the 'bad Turks' as fanatic nationalists was deployed to critique a perceived *lack* of patriotism in Greece. Michalis similarly utilised a stereotype of Turkish religious fanaticism in order to critique the discipline of the Greek Armed Forces:

> The Turkish soldier is illiterate. He does not have technical knowledge. If he is on his own, what can he do? But because of religion, he will do whatever

the officer tells him. Without offering any resistance, without having any opinion of his own. To compare with the Hellenic army, the Hellenic soldier, even if he is on his own, will manage, he will find solutions to problems [. . . but] there is not that obedience, because the soldier believes that he is equal with the officer, and that is not good in the military.

(29/01/2012)

The same stereotype of blind obedience to religious authority and lack of individual free will that was commonly used to account for the behaviour of the rioters during the *Septemvrianá* here served to raise questions of the normally cherished Greek values of defiance to authority and disregard for hierarchy. In this sense, attributes of the other that are typically presented as undesirable can nonetheless function as critical viewpoints on the idealised virtues of the self.

Privileged knowledge (2): the 'good Turk'

If members of the expatriated Greek community thus sometimes validate stereotypical Greek representations of the 'bad Turks' by citing lived experiences of persecution in Turkey, they also challenge them through their first-hand accounts of the 'good Turk' whose character is often portrayed as superior to that of the Greeks of Greece. As I have documented above (see Chapters 1 and 3), many expatriates were profoundly disappointed with the reception they received in Greece, and reported significant social and cultural differences between themselves and the Greeks of Greece. Interviewees sometimes distinguished in this regard between the Greek refugees from the Ottoman Empire/ their descendants and the 'native' Greeks, offering more favourable accounts of their interactions with the former, though as often as not they grouped all of the Greeks they encountered in Greece together as '*Elladítes*'. Those who had resided in Istanbul, in particular, perceived a contrast with the Greek cities of Athens and Thessaloniki in terms of modernity, urbanism, and cosmopolitanism, whilst informants from both Istanbul and Imbros commonly characterised the Greeks of Greece as impolite, lazy, and corrupt. Expatriate stereotypes of the 'good Turk' are frequently grafted onto these criticisms of the '*Elladítes*', functioning – to borrow terms from Sutton – as a foil for critiquing Greek society (1998:47).

In a 1978 article, *O Polítis* made the following implicit comparison between the *Polítes* and the *Elladítes*:

> [. . .] we remain aristocratic in our ways, which we also have an obligation to preserve in our new *patrída*. Blasphemy, the '*ré*' [a very informal form of address] and the use of the first person between those who are not closely acquainted are unknown to the Constantinopolitans.
>
> (*O Polítis* 1978)

This perception is reflected in the widespread complaint amongst my interviewees that the Greeks of Greece are rude, unchivalrous, and disrespectful in their day-to-day interactions, and comparisons were often made in this regard to the manners of the Turks. In a joint interview, Fotini and Rita – born in Istanbul in 1943 and 1948 respectively, and residents of Greece since the 1970s – were vocal on this point:

Fotini: One thing I didn't like when I came here [to Greece]: they spoke to me in the singular. I raised my children to speak to strangers in the plural. I go to a shop, and I address the young girl of 20 [the shop assistant] in the plural. And she turns to me and speaks to me in the singular, and it upsets me greatly. Here there was not the respect towards older people that there was in Constantinople. I mean, I get on the bus, if there was someone old on the bus, our mother would say to us, 'get up, get up'. Whereas here the mother sits down with the child, and the old lady is left standing.

Rita: I'm still in the habit of doing it, and one time I got up on the bus and I said [to an older woman], 'sit down, grandma'. And she said to me, 'who are you calling grandma?' There is no respect here.

Fotini: The Turks, even today, the young people will address the elder people in the plural [. . .] The Turks, when they see an older person, they go to kiss their hand. And we too, we kissed their hand.

(Fotini 21/11/2011; Rita 21/11/2011)

Dimitris, who was born on *Chálki* in 1956 and moved to Greece in 1975, was likewise disappointed by the behaviour of the *Elladítes*, remarking that 'the Hellenes were always very different compared to us'. He explained that he does not like to swear, whereas in Greece 'swearing is their bread-and-butter', and, like Fotini and Rita, he identified that in Greece

a young man on the bus would not get up for an old woman. Whilst in Turkey they still do that. If you go to someone's house, first you have to kiss their hand. Now maybe that is not a very good thing [i.e. maybe it is conservative/hierarchical], but it does show respect.

(Dimitris 30/11/2011)

Anastasia, who was born in Istanbul in 1939 and came to live in Greece in 1970, voiced similar complaints about the unchivalrous behaviour of her Greek-born concierge:

I knew Greece very well. However, I experienced difficulties in the beginning. Small things that were different. One thing, a small thing to which I had become accustomed from my doorman in Constantinople, was that he would help you with your shopping. When I came here, this is in 1970, I had a doorman in my block of flats, and I went shopping with my trolley, and [when I returned] there were stairs for me to get to the lift. And he was sitting there, watching me, he didn't even get up to help. That, for me, was something foreign. Come on now, he sees a woman struggling with her shopping, and he doesn't help?

(05/02/2012)

As I noted above, it is not uncommon for such positive accounts of the Turkish character to commingle with negative representations. Lefteris recounted a story in which he was looked after by two Turkish neighbours having badly injured his foot as a child in Istanbul. He concluded this anecdote as follows:

I want to tell you that as people they [the Turks] have a totally different character from the Hellenes. They are much better than us in terms of character. I mean, if you are in the streets and you go and ask somebody for directions, he will take you where you want to go, he will drop whatever he's doing and take you there, in order to look after you. Here in Greece, you won't find that. Or another thing. When you are on the bus. You get onto the bus, right, you are pregnant, you're very big, right? Here, the young people will run to take the seat before you can get there. In Turkey, the young person will get up so that you can sit. Here they will run to sit down before you. They have a very different mentality as compared to us. They will help you. But: Allah.[5] He might just kill you as well.

(Lefteris 12/05/2013)

Many expatriates were also exercised by a perceived lack of respect for the church and the Orthodox Christian faith in Greece. During our interview, Spyros – the octogenarian from Istanbul encountered alongside Tasoula in the previous chapter enumerating on the cultural differences between the expatriates and the Greeks of Greece – embarked upon a theatrical condemnation of piety in Greece by drawing comparisons with the way that Muslims in Turkey behaved in Christian places of worship (this despite having earlier characterised the Turks as fanatically Islamic). 'There [in Istanbul],' he began, 'we had respect for the church. Here I saw people going into the church with their hands in their pockets'. At this point, Spyros stood up, and offered an imitation of an *Elladítis* attending church, walking around with his hands in his pockets, shoulders hunched, looking bored and distracted. He continued: 'the Turks, when they go into the church, take off their hats. Kurds, who come in to see what the liturgy is like, he will take off his hat, sit down and watch' (Spyros 02/12/2011).

Another common grievance, particularly amongst male informants, was that the Greeks of Greece were lazy and dishonest in their work, looking for ways to shirk their responsibilities or to cut corners, and frequently depending upon clientelism (see Halstead 2014a:277–279). This, too, was a favourite topic for Spyros, who – betraying through his criticism of trade unionism a right-of-centre approach not uncommon amongst *Polítes* – contrasted the idleness of

108 *Local homelands and national belonging*

Greek workers to the thirst for knowledge demonstrated by the Turks who used to work in his shop in Istanbul:

> The Turks, and their children, will say to you, 'I don't know, I don't know, how do I do that?' Here in Greece, if you say, 'I'll tell you something', [the *Elladítis* says] 'I know, I know'. And the children. 'I know, I know'. That's how we withered away. 'I know, I know, I know' [. . .] The Turk will say, 'I don't know'. All of the Turks, who came from inner Anatolia to work in our shops, said, 'I don't know, how do I do that boss?' And they don't pay attention to what time they will knock off, like here [in Greece] with trade unionism and such.
>
> (02/12/2011)

Ilias – the elderly *Imvriótis* who defaced his Greek identity card (see Chapter 3) – railed against corruption in the workplace in Greece by similarly drawing a comparison with a Turkish sense of honour derived from their Islamic faith. He suggested:

> The Muslim is afraid of injustice, because of the *haram*[6] [. . .] In Turkey, if you were to give the doctor a little envelope [i.e. a bribe] as they do here, he would say no [. . .] If you treat the Turk to a coffee, he will remember it for 40 years. The Turk will not take money from you. Because he is afraid of the *haram*. Here? Don't ask. We have already said many things about how Greece has become spoilt.
>
> (Ilias 21/05/2013)

These criticisms of the work ethos of the *Elladítes* were sometimes used by informants specifically to explicate – and to distance themselves from – the ongoing Greek financial crisis (see examples in Halstead 2014a:277–279).

Several interviewees were also vexed by the political culture of Greece, which they felt tended unnecessarily towards partisanship, disunity, and anarchy. Istanbul-born *Imvriótis* Loukas, for example, spoke critically of political demonstrations in Greece, making contrasts with the (then ongoing) 2013 Gezi Park Protests in Istanbul:

> Whenever they have those protests here [in Greece], they break and loot everything. And they are not all agents of the deep state, as the left-wingers allege. It is the culture here, I would say. There is a culture of anarchy, a culture of destruction. A self-destructive mania. And they like to leave rubbish behind them and leave. With all of those things that have been happening in Constantinople in recent days, there has been a very strong community of demonstrators who remain there, after all of these days, to collect the rubbish, to clean up the place, they clean up the place before they leave. That shows a good manner of behaviour [. . .] And when you try and say that here in

Greece, they are bemused, they do not understand what you are saying. They think you are conservative, they will say that you are narrowminded.
(03/07/2013)

Just as stereotypes of the 'bad Turks' could be used to constitute the expatriate community as the latest martyrs to Greece's quintessential other, so representations of the 'good Turk' may function as a critical mirror directed at the inhabitants of the Greek state, permitting the expatriates to distinguish themselves from the '*Elladítes*' by drawing attention to virtues purportedly shared by the Turks and the Greeks of Turkey but lacking amongst the Greeks of Greece.

Conclusions

Ethnic stereotypes, as Brown and Theodossopoulos observed, have often been interpreted rather simplistically as 'products of a form of false consciousness', unselfconsciously reproduced by individuals who 'lack the critical capacity to see beyond rumour, hearsay, propaganda and pseudo-science' (2004:3). People, from this perspective, are passive sponges for a monolithic nationalist rhetoric that governs their interpretations and overrides their own experiences. The evidence presented in this chapter, however, would seem to support the notion that people 'continuously make choices on when and how to talk about "others"' (Brown and Theodossopoulos 2004:8); that, in other words, how and why the nominal ethnicity of others becomes experientially relevant varies in different discursive contexts. Ethnic stereotypes, like ethnic identities, rarely have fixed or unambiguous referents (Theodossopoulos 2003:178; Kirtsoglou and Sistani 2003:207–208), even though their continued usage doubtless contributes to the perpetuation of 'groupist' understandings of social organisation (Brubaker 2004:16). The narrators considered in this chapter often claimed a privileged knowledge of the Turkish other acquired through lived experience, which they mobilised sometimes to validate Greek nationalist stereotypes of the 'bad Turks' who are perpetually hostile towards the 'civilised Greeks', and sometimes to challenge these representations through their own stereotypes of the 'good Turk' whose sense of honour and duty stood in sharp contrast to the crudeness and idleness of the *Elladítes*. These stereotypes are not typically static or immutable categorisations of particular individuals, but rather function as malleable and contingent devices for explicating the behaviour of others, interpreting lived experiences, and plotting one's own place in the world. Stereotypes, as Spyrou put it, 'have depth, even if their depth is still to some extent stereotypical' (2002:269).

If ethnic stereotypes are durable and difficult for individuals to shed, it is, therefore, not simply because people are unwitting dupes of nationalist rhetoric. Rather, following Fox, people are 'thinking, sentient beings, capable of manipulating the nation in creative ways to suit their particular purposes', but also sometimes liable to operate 'on autopilot, with the nation supplying them with a pre-programmed cognitive map for negotiating a complex social world'

(2017:40). Theodossopoulos reported that his Greek informants from Patras were often keen to appraise critically their unfavourable portrayals of the Turkish other – typically blaming the education they received in school – but as they 'have no other patterns of historical causality to rely upon except those to which they have been exposed at school' their efforts 'rely heavily on the very sources they aspire to criticize', making it difficult for them 'to evade the conventional nationalism they would like to defy' (2004:30–31, 42). In Theodossopoulos' terms, stereotypes represent 'convenient guides to the behaviours expected from members of other ethnic groups', reflecting 'a strong desire to reach an explanation, an exegesis for events that involve other people' (2003:178–179). They provide, in other words, straightforward explanations for complex experiences (Spyrou 2002:267). The diverse range of behaviour exhibited by Muslim friends and neighbours during the *Septemvrianá*, for instance, could be accounted for through stereotypes of the Turks as fanatically proud and honour-bound. From this perspective, the violence of the mob, on the one hand, can be portrayed as a characteristically 'Turkish' response to a perceived threat to the Turkish nation: ethnicity provides an easy explanation as to why otherwise close acquaintances turned on the Greeks in 1955 and became complicit in mob violence. Those who went to sometimes dangerous lengths to protect the Greeks, on the other hand, might either be seen to be conforming to the stereotypical Turkish impulse to honour and respect those close to them, or be characterised as not (entirely) ethnically Turkish. In both cases, perceptions of others' ethnicity serve as an explanatory framework for experiences that are otherwise hard to process. It is crucial to note, however, that these easy answers 'also nourish our fears and prejudices, and divert our attention from evidence that might lead towards contradictory conclusions' (Theodossopoulos 2003:179). Explanations of intercommunal violence and solidarity based on ethnicity, for example, typically excused these particular narrators from seeking more complex interpretations of mob violence, and impeded them from developing more differentiated impressions of 'the Turks' generally.

Representations of the Turkish other, nonetheless, often have at least as much to do with negotiating the expatriates' place in the Greek state as with rationalising their experiences in Turkey. By presenting themselves as victims of Turkish chauvinism, juxtaposed to the civilised and democratic values of Greece, expatriate interviewees and writers can suture themselves into Greek national history, thereby challenging the apparent indifference of the Greek state towards the community and its problems in Greece. If it is thus correct to say that the national self is defined in relation to a significant other, it does not necessarily follow that the latter's defects serve solely to highlight the former's virtues. In the figure of the honourable and industrious 'good Turk', many interviewees find a potent and provocative discursive weapon with which to spotlight perceived deficiencies within Greek society, namely the alleged rudeness, discourteousness, and laziness of its members. Even stereotypical Turkish attributes otherwise presented as unfavourable could in certain contexts foster a reappraisal of idealised Greek values. The same sense of duty and deference to authority often used to account for a Turkish propensity towards mob violence, for instance, could also draw attention to a supposed lack of responsibility and respect in Greece deriving from the normally treasured Greek love of individual liberty and democratic equality. In this guise, the other becomes a critical mirror for the national self, opening up opportunities for contrast that not only define its unique attributes but also make conspicuous its flaws.

Notes

1 As well as 'Greeks versus Germans' (Theodossopoulos 2004:34), another 'significant other' at various points in Greek history.
2 My reading of these testimonies is that at least 19 – and as many as 23, depending on how you interpret some of the stories – contained references to protection and/or warnings provided by Muslims to members of the Greek minority (although these sometimes appeared alongside negative stereotypes of the Turks). Vryonis, analysing the same compilation, gave a slightly lower tally, writing that at least ten of the witnesses made reference to warnings or personal intervention by Muslims (2005:531). It is possible that Vryonis felt that some of these warnings were too cryptic to be counted.
3 In this context, the use of the word 'cucumbers' has phallic connotations.
4 I.e. the sum required for the renewal of their Turkish citizenship. The use of the term 'poll tax' or 'head tax' in this extract is probably intended to evoke the yearly tax or *jizya* levied on non-Muslims by the Ottoman Empire.
5 This is a pun in the original Greek: '*Allá* [but]: *Allách* [Allah].'
6 Sinful actions prohibited by Allah.

References

(Items marked * are in the Greek language.)

Bacas, J. L. (2003). Greek tourists in Turkey: an anthropological case study. *Journal of Mediterranean Studies*, 13(2), 239–258.
Brown, K. and Theodossopoulos, D. (2004). Others' others: talking about stereotypes and constructions of otherness in southeast Europe. *History and Anthropology*, 15(1), 1–22.
Brubaker, R. (2004). *Ethnicity without groups*. Cambridge: Harvard University Press.
Brubaker, R., Feischmidt, M., Fox, J., and Grancea, L. (2006). *Nationalist politics and everyday ethnicity in a Transylvanian town*. Princeton, NJ: Princeton University Press.
Constantinopolitan Society. (1998). Letter to *Synaspismós tis Aristerás kai tis Proódou* re. invitation to the event for the 545th anniversary of the Fall of Constantinople, 4 May 1998. Constantinopolitan Society Archive.*
Cowan, J. K. (1997). Idioms of belonging: polyglot articulations of local identity in a Greek Macedonian town. In P. A. Mackridge and E. Yannakakis (Eds). *Ourselves and others: the development of a Greek Macedonian cultural identity since 1912*. Oxford: Berg, 153–171.
Csergo, Z. (2008). Review essay: do we need a language shift in the study of nationalism and ethnicity? Reflections on Rogers Brubaker's critical scholarly agenda. *Nations and Nationalism*, 14(2), 393–398.
Danforth, L. M. (1995). *The Macedonian conflict: ethnic nationalism in a transnational world*. Princeton, NJ: Princeton University Press.
Delivoria, Y. (2009). The notion of nation: the emergence of a national ideal in the narratives of 'inside' and 'outside' Greeks in the nineteenth century. In R. Beaton and

D. Ricks (Eds). *The making of modern Greece: nationalism, Romanticism, and the uses of the past (1797–1896)*. Farnham: Ashgate, 109–121.
Ekdóseis Tsoukátou. (1999). Septemvrianá *1955: The* 'Kristallnacht' *of the Hellenism of Constantinople*. Athens: Ekdóseis Tsoukátou.*
Eriksen, T. H. (1995). We and us: two modes of group identification. *Journal of Peace Research*, 32(4), 427–436.
Fox, J. E. (2017). The edges of the nation: a research agenda for uncovering the taken-for-granted foundations of everyday nationhood. *Nations and Nationalism*, 23(1), 26–47.
Hall, S. (1996). Introduction: who needs identity? In S. Hall and P. Du Gay (Eds). *Questions of cultural identity*. London; Thousand Oaks: SAGE Publications, 1–17.
Halstead, H. (2014a). Heirs to Byzantium: identity and the Helleno–Romaic dichotomy amongst the Istanbul Greek migrant community in Greece. *Byzantine and Modern Greek Studies*, 38(2), 265–284.
Halstead, H. (2014b). Harmony and strife in memories of Greek–Turkish intercommunal relationships in Istanbul and Cyprus. *Journal of Modern Greek Studies*, 32(2), 393–415.
Herzfeld, M. (1997). *Cultural intimacy: social poetics in the nation-state*. New York: Routledge.
Hirschon, R. (2004). 'We got on well with the Turks': Christian–Muslim relations in late Ottoman times. In D. Shankland (Ed.). *Archaeology, anthropology, and heritage in the Balkans and Anatolia: the life and times of FW Hasluck, 1878–1920*. Istanbul: Isis Press, 325–343.
Hirschon, R. (2006). Knowledge of diversity: towards a more differentiated set of 'Greek' perceptions of 'Turks'. *South European Society and Politics*, 11(1), 61–78.
Hirschon, R. (2009). History's long shadow: the Lausanne Treaty and contemporary Greco–Turkish relations. In O. Anastasakis, K. Nicolaidis, and K. Öktem, (Eds.). *In the long shadow of Europe: Greeks and Turks in the era of postnationalism*. Leiden; Boston: Martinus Nijhoff, 73–94.
Imvriakí Ichó. (1974). Cyprus and Imbros, July–August 1974.*
Imvros. (1977). Refugees and aliens, August–September 1977.*
Imvros. (1992). Miscellany, November–December 1992.*
Imvros. (1993). Residence and work permits of the *Imvriótes*, March–April 1993.*
Imvros. (1994). And now what will we become without barbarians?, May–June 1994.*
Kirtsoglou, E. and Sistani, L. (2003). The other *then*, the other *now*, the other *within*: stereotypical images and narrative captions of the Turk in northern and central Greece. *Journal of Mediterranean Studies*, 13(2), 189–213.
Mackridge, P. A. and Yannakakis, E. (1997). Introduction. In P. Mackridge and E. Yannakakis (Eds). *Ourselves and others: the development of a Greek Macedonian cultural identity since 1912*. Oxford: Berg, 1–22.
Millas, H. (2004). The 'other' and nation-building: the testimony of Greek and Turkish novels. In N. K. Burçoğlu and S. G. Miller (Eds). *Representations of the 'other/s' in the Mediterranean world and their impact on the region*. Istanbul: Isis Press, 141–148.
Millas, H. (2006). *Tourkokratia*: history and the image of Turks in Greek literature. *South European Society and Politics*, 11(1), 47–60.
O Polítis. (1976a). Turkish deceit, June 1976.*
O Polítis. (1976b). As things are going . . ., August 1976.*
O Polítis. (1978). 6 September 1955, August 1978.*
O Polítis. (1979). The problems of the Constantinopolitans, January 1979.*
O Polítis. (1987). Greece remains a peace-loving country and a tough punisher when she is provoked, March 1987.*

Örs, İ. R. (2006). Beyond the Greek and Turkish dichotomy: the *Rum Polites* of Istanbul and Athens. *South European Society and Politics*, 11(1), 79–94.

Spyrou, S. (2002). Images of 'the other': 'the Turk' in Greek Cypriot children's imaginations. *Race Ethnicity and Education*, 5(3), 255–272.

Sutton, D. (1998). *Memories cast in stone: the relevance of the past in everyday life*. Oxford; New York: Berg.

Terzis, G. (2004). The 'other'/'Turk' in the Greek national media: the construction of 'oppositional metaphors'. In N. K. Burçoğlu and S. G. Miller (Eds). *Representations of the 'other/s' in the Mediterranean world and their impact on the region*. Istanbul: Isis Press, 169–186.

Theodossopoulos, D. (2003). Degrading others and honouring ourselves: ethnic stereotypes as categories and as explanations. *Journal of Mediterranean Studies*, 13(2), 177–188.

Theodossopoulos, D. (2004). The Turks and their nation in the worldview of Greeks in Patras. *History and Anthropology*, 15(1), 1–28.

Theodossopoulos, D. (2006). Introduction: the 'Turks' in the imagination of the 'Greeks'. *South European Society and Politics*, 11(1), 1–32.

Triandafyllidou, A. (1998). National identity and the 'other'. *Ethnic and Racial Studies*, 21(4), 593–612.

Turan, Ç., Pekin, M., and Güvenç, S. (2010). *Constantinople/Istanbul, my nostalgia: refugee narratives and the nostalgia of the* Romioí *of Constantinople/Istanbul*. Istanbul: Lozan Mübadilleri Vakfı. [In Greek and Turkish].

Vasileiadis, M. (2015). 'The deep state fooled the state itself'. In *The* Septemvrianá: *the persecution of the Hellenes of Constantinople*. Special issue of *Kathimeriní*, 10 September 2015, 29–31.*

Vryonis, S. (2005). *The mechanism of catastrophe: the Turkish pogrom of September 6–7, 1955, and the destruction of the Greek community of Istanbul*. New York: Greekworks.

Yerasimos, S. (1988). Les rapports gréco–turcs mythes et réalités. In S. Vaner (Ed.). *Le différend gréco–turc*. Paris: L'Harmattan, 35–40.

Part III
National and transnational histories

5 Everyday multidirectional memory

In a frequently cited passage from his posthumous volume *The Collective Memory*, the French sociologist Maurice Halbwachs – a pioneer of the notion that memory is socially determined – wrote that 'there is no universal memory. Every collective memory requires the support of a group delimited in space and time' (1980:84). For Halbwachs, the contours of an individual's memory are determined by that person's shifting relationships to different groups, such that even the 'most personal feelings and thoughts originate in definite social milieus and circumstances' (1980:33). Accordingly, the ease with which an individual can access a particular memory is dependent on their degree of contact with the relevant group, and, ultimately, a collective memory fades away when the group sustaining it ceases to be (Halbwachs 1980:30, 47, 78, 80). Halbwachs' notion that there is a direct correlation between the vitality of a given collective memory and the persistence of a particular, coherent group has underpinned much subsequent thought in the area of memory studies (Confino 1997:1392; Craps and Rothberg 2011:517); as Barbara Misztal stated in her 2003 survey of the field, Halbwachs' 'assertion that every group develops a memory of its own past that highlights its unique identity is still *the starting point for all research in the field*' (Misztal 2003:51, my emphasis).

In recent years, however, successive scholars have challenged the Halbwachian connection between particular groups and particular collective memories (Crownshaw 2011:1; Erll 2011a; Rothberg 2010:7; Silverman 2013:176), criticising Halbwachs for attaching a 'framedness' to memory connoting 'boundaries and a certain stability' (Erll 2011b:10; see also Rothberg and Yildiz 2011:43), and commenting on the unsuitability of his approach for a world marked by globalisation, mass media, and demographic mobility (Huyssen 2003:17; Huyssen 2011:615; Landsberg 2004:8). In particular, these interventions – which we might loosely group together as studies of 'transcultural memory' (Crownshaw 2011:2) – have attacked the supposition that there is a close link between a given collective memory and a national or ethnic group, a perspective that has typically been associated primarily with the French historian Pierre Nora.[1] Nora famously distinguished between *milieux de mémoire* ('environments of memory') and *lieux de mémoire* ('sites of memory'), arguing that the latter were consecrated by 'our hopelessly forgetful modern societies' to replace the natural and lived 'real environments of memory' that we had lost (1989:7–8). He edited an exhaustive series documenting sites of French national memory, which inspired a succession of subsequent scholars to seek out sites of memory in other national contexts (Erll 2010:310; Erll 2011c:25–26). Proponents of a transcultural approach to the study of memory have criticised this project for its 'nation-centredness' (Erll 2011c:26), taking Nora to task for entrenching an assumed connection between collective memory and the nation-state, ignoring the memories of minorities and migrants, and disregarding cultural exchange within Europe and with the French colonies (Craps and Rothberg 2011:517; Erll 2010:310; Erll 2011a; Erll 2011b:7; Erll 2011c:25; Graves and Rechniewski 2010:3; Huyssen 2003:97; Huyssen 2011:615; Rothberg 2010:7; Sundholm 2011:1). Under the influence of Nora and other late twentieth-century theorists, in the words of one critic, the analytical focus 'shifted from the dynamics of *memory in culture* to the specific *memories of* (allegedly stable and clearly demarcated) *cultures*', and as a result 'national memory studies' came to predominate the field (Erll 2011b:6).

Scholars working under the rubric of transcultural memory share a desire to break away from this 'methodological nationalism' (Erll 2011a; Levy and Sznaider 2006:103), and to explore the 'expanded field' (Huyssen 2003:97) in which memories cross or transcend national and cultural boundaries. Their studies have considered transcultural memory in a variety of different forms, including the 'migration' of concepts, terminology, or imagery from one context to another; the physical movement of 'memory-objects' across national borders (Bond and Rapson 2014:1–6); the construction of transnational memory networks and supranational political, cultural, economic, religious, or diasporic formations (Erll 2011b:8); the establishment of 'dialogic memory' between groups with histories of mutual violence, or mnemonic affinities in which one group takes up the memory and/or cause of another (Assmann 2014:553–554); and even the creation of universal, global, or shared memories (Alexander 2009; Assmann 2014:547–550; Levy and Sznaider 2006). These interventions have come from a variety of disciplines, but have been driven in particular by studies of Holocaust memory and mediated memory (Craps and Rothberg 2011:517; Erll 2011b:9).

Holocaust memory

Since the 1990s, there has been increasing interest in the transnational and transcultural proliferation of Holocaust memory. Besides survivors and their families, as Arlene Stein noted, 'other groups also tell Holocaust stories' (1998:519). Significant cultures of Holocaust commemoration have developed both in Germany, the country of many of the perpetrators, and in the United States, the country whose soldiers liberated many of the Nazi camps. As Hilene Flanzbaum observed, '[m]ost Americans seem so well acquainted with at least some version of the Holocaust that they freely invoke it in metaphor, and often with an inflammatory casualness' (1999a:96–97). Indeed, language and imagery derived from Holocaust memory have entered into diverse national, regional, and local vernaculars, leading one scholar to refer to the 'globalization of Holocaust discourse'

(Huyssen 2000:23). From this perspective, the Holocaust could be seen as a contemporary 'moral touchstone' (Kushner 2001; Levy and Sznaider 2002:93), a 'foundational past', in Confino's terms, 'that represents an age because it embodies a historical novum that serves as a moral and historical yardstick' (2012:5; see also Confino 2005:54).

Scholars have documented the use of Holocaust discourse in a vast range of geographical, situational, and discursive contexts. Analogies have repeatedly been drawn, for instance, between the Nazi Holocaust and European colonialism (Alexander 2009:52; Confino 2012:29; Hansen 1996:311; Rosenfeld 1999:46; Rothberg 2008:224–225; Rothberg 2009a). During and after the Algerian War of Independence, various groups drew parallels with the Holocaust and with the Nazi occupation of France, particularly in order to criticise the French colonial authorities (Cohen 2001:85–87; Confino 2012:29; House 2010:20–21, 26–27, 37; Prost 1999:171–172; Rothberg 2009a:196–266; Rothberg 2009b:130), but also to attack the Algerian National Liberation Front (Cohen 2001:85), and, on one occasion in 1987, to defend a Nazi facing trial by equating his crimes to those of the colonial French (Silverman 2013:18). The Holocaust was equally a common trope by which journalists, politicians, activists, and citizens alike framed conflict and genocide in Bosnia and Kosovo in the 1990s, and in Rwanda in 1994 (Alexander 2009:53; Assmann 2010:111; Flanzbaum 1999a:97; Huyssen 2003:13, 23, 73; Levy and Sznaider 2002:98–99; Stratton 2000:241). Whilst the Holocaust has frequently been deployed by Israeli politicians and journalists, for instance in the claims of right-wingers that Israel faces a 'second Holocaust' at the hands of its Arab neighbours (Moses 2011:96; Rothberg 2011:535), it has also been turned against the Israeli state, both by Palestinians and their supporters who compare the Palestinians to Jewish Holocaust victims and the Israeli authorities to Nazis (Alexander 2009:49; Levy and Sznaider 2006:24; Rothberg 2011:532), and by Jewish settlers in the Occupied Territories protesting against a lack of governmental support or efforts to dismantle illegal settlements (Katz and Katz 2009:164; Rothberg 2011:535). Holocaust memory has also been invoked in discussions about nuclear weapons (Alexander 2009:52–53; Minear 1995:354–357; Petrie 2000:52), political violence in South America (Feierstein 2014; Huyssen 2003:99; Jelin 2010:74; Molden 2010:80), murder and deportation of Republicans in Franco's Spain (Baer and Sznaider 2015:330–331, 338), abortion, women's rights, and gay rights (Assmann 2010:111; Rosenfeld 1995; Stein 1998:523–533), race relations in the United States (Flanzbaum 1999b:96–97), Japanese atrocity in China during the Second World War (Levy and Sznaider 2006:5), 9/11 and the War on Terror (Bond 2012:116–117, 121–122), post-war German expellees from Eastern Europe (Confino 2005:54–55), the Turkish minority in Germany (Huyssen 2011:622), the Great Famine in Ireland (Owen 2014:365–366), universal human rights (Alexander 2009:56; Levy and Sznaider 2004; Levy and Sznaider 2006:5), neoliberal capitalism (Saxton 2010:209), environmental disaster (Rosenfeld 1995), and many other contexts besides these.

The 'globalisation' and, more specifically, the 'Americanisation' of Holocaust discourse have had both their critics and their defenders. On the one hand, some scholars have deplored the metaphorical application of Holocaust memory to other contexts, variously arguing that it relativises the suffering of Holocaust victims (see examples in Petrie 2000:50; Rosenfeld 1999:34); that such appropriation is intrinsically uncritical, self-involved, and self-congratulatory (Rosenfeld 1995; Young 1999:73, 82); or that Holocaust memory might act as a screen memory obscuring other histories of violence and genocide (Craps and Rothberg 2011:518; Hansen 1996:311; Huyssen 2003:14, 16, 99). Yet scholars have also drawn attention to the ways in which Holocaust memory might contribute to the articulation of other, lesser-known atrocities, operating, in Huyssen's words, 'like a motor energizing the discourses of memory elsewhere' (2003:99; see also Craps and Rothberg 2011:518; House 2010:24, 31; Landsberg 2004:115; Levy and Sznaider 2002:98; Levy and Sznaider 2006:5; Rosenfeld 1999:44; Rothberg 2009a:6, 9, 196; Rothberg 2011:523–524). In an influential essay first published in 2002, sociologist Jeffrey Alexander argued that memory of the Holocaust had become 'free-floating rather than situated', creating a 'universalized symbol whose very existence has created historically unprecedented opportunities for ethnic, racial, and religious justice' (2009:3). He suggested that in the mid-1960s and 1970s – under the influence of widely circulated literary and media representations, the televised trial of Adolf Eichmann, and the consolidation of the label 'the Holocaust' – the Nazi genocide of the Jews came to be seen not simply as typifying Nazi atrocity, but rather as representing evil generally (Alexander 2009:28, 30–31, 38–43). As a result, what was 'once experienced as traumatic only by Jewish victims' came to be construed as a 'trauma for all humankind', and individuals and groups began to invoke the Holocaust in order to 'measure the evil of a non-Holocaust event' or to 'parse ongoing events as good and evil' (Alexander 2009:31, 36, 50, 59).

In their analysis of the trajectories of Holocaust remembrance in the United States, Israel, and Germany, fellow sociologists Daniel Levy and Natan Sznaider similarly argued that the Holocaust was on its way to becoming a 'cosmopolitan memory' (2006:4). They rejected the common assumption that 'memories, community, and geographical proximity belong together', and derided the suggestion that nations are the sole or principal repository of memory as a 'breathtakingly unhistorical assertion' (Levy and Sznaider 2002:89; Levy and Sznaider 2006:2). They claimed that in an increasingly globalised world the 'container of the nation-state' is 'slowly being cracked', and that accordingly the Holocaust 'has been dislocated from space and time, resulting in its inscription into other acts of injustice and other traumatic national memories across the globe' (Levy and Sznaider 2006:2, 5). Like Alexander, Levy and Sznaider placed emphasis upon the moral potential of this dislocated Holocaust memory, arguing that it 'harbours the possibility of transcending ethnic and national boundaries' and of becoming 'the cultural foundation for global human-rights politics' (Levy and Sznaider 2006:4). They boldly proclaimed, for example, that '[i]t does not take a huge leap to go from identifying with Schindler to taking the ensuing role of liberating Kosovo' (Levy and Sznaider 2006:141). They also made it clear, however, that they were not envisaging a universal memory that would hold the same meaning in every local context, and, to a greater extent than Alexander, stressed that global Holocaust memory must be 'reconciled with old national narratives' such that 'the result is always distinctive' (Levy and Sznaider 2006:3, 8).

Notions of the Holocaust's universality or cosmopolitan moral potential have been widely critiqued. Many commentators have questioned the predominantly optimistic accounts offered by Alexander and Levy/Sznaider by drawing attention to contrary examples in which the circulation of Holocaust memory promotes antagonism rather than solidarity, as in the case of the Israel–Palestine conflict where, according to A. Dirk Moses, it 'locks Palestinians and Israelis in a fatal embrace' (Moses 2011:103; see also Assmann 2010:107, 114; Erll 2011b:15; Jay 2009:108; Manne 2009:142; Rothberg 2009a:263–265). As Robert Manne put it, 'Israel is a society divided between a minority for whom the lesson of the Holocaust is the same as Alexander's – "It will never happen again" – and the majority for whom the lesson is, rather, "It will never happen to us again"' (Manne 2009:142).

Equally, several scholars have expressed wariness at the notion that Holocaust memory has become dislocated or free-floating, objecting, in Huyssen's terms, that 'discourses of lived memory will remain tied primarily to specific communities and territories' (2011:616; see also Assmann 2010:108; Assmann and Conrad 2010:8; Katz and Katz 2009:157; Manne 2009:144). Many critics have also pointed to the Eurocentric or Western-centric assumptions underpinning the notion that the Holocaust has become a global or universally intelligible symbol of atrocity (Assmann 2010:108; Assmann and Conrad 2010:8; Craps and Rothberg 2011:518).

Literary scholar Michael Rothberg made an influential contribution to these debates in his description of how Holocaust memory emerged in dialogue with discourses about decolonisation. Rothberg criticised what he saw as the dominant model for understanding the operation of memory in society, what he called 'competitive memory'. According to his analysis, it has long been taken for granted that in advancing one's own identity and memory, it is necessary to exclude others and suppress their memories (Rothberg 2009a:3–5). It is, therefore, typically assumed that particular memories attached to particular groups are locked in a 'zero-sum struggle', competing over 'scarce' mnemonic space in a contest with clear 'winners and losers' (Rothberg 2009a:3). Against this competitive model, Rothberg proposed a 'multidirectional' understanding of memory. He challenged 'the taken-for-granted link between collective memory and group identity' (Rothberg 2011:524), arguing that 'memories are not owned by groups – nor are groups "owned" by memories' (Rothberg 2009a:5). On the contrary, the borders of memory and identity are 'jagged', and different memories interact within a 'malleable discursive space' where they do not simply compete but are 'subject to ongoing negotiation, cross-referencing, and borrowing', which can take place even across antagonistic social boundaries (Rothberg 2009a:3, 5). From a multidirectional perspective, rather than competitively blocking one another from view, interacting memories of, for instance, the Holocaust, slavery, and decolonisation have contributed to each other's articulation (Rothberg 2009a:6).

In common with Alexander and Levy/Sznaider, Rothberg was at pains to emphasise the progressive moral potential of multidirectional memory. Whilst conceding that memory's multidirectionality might function 'in the interests of violence or exclusion' (Rothberg 2009a:12), he has repeatedly stressed that, 'solidarity [...] is a frequent – if not guaranteed – outcome of the remembrance of suffering' (Rothberg 2010:11), and that multidirectional memory's 'productive, intercultural dynamic' has the potential to create 'new forms of solidarity' (Rothberg 2009a:5). Rothberg distinguished his approach, however, by indicating that memory is not a 'one-way street', and that the Holocaust has not simply become a 'floating, universal signifier' (2009a:6, 244). He took Alexander and Levy/Sznaider to task for 'overlooking Holocaust memory's dialogic interactions' with other histories, and argued that the concept of the Holocaust's particularity and universality was in the first place produced by the ways in which it was evoked in emerging discourses surrounding slavery and decolonisation (Rothberg 2009a:118–119, 265).

Mediated memory

As Astrid Erll has remarked, 'research on mediated memory can boast a comparatively long record of thinking about how media disseminate versions of the past across time, space, and mnemonic communities' (2011b:9), even if here, too, the Holocaust has often been a central object of study. Since the early 1990s, Marianne Hirsch has been refining a theory of 'postmemory' as a means of describing, apropos the Holocaust, 'the relationship that the "generation after" bears to the personal, collective, and cultural trauma of those who came before – to experiences they "remember" only by means of the stories, images, and behaviors among which they grew up' (2012:5). Although these experiences are not, in a literal sense, personal memories for the 'generation after', they were nonetheless 'transmitted to them so deeply and affectively as to *seem* to constitute memories in their own right' (Hirsch 2012:5, 31). Hirsch distinguished two types of postmemory: the vertical 'familial' postmemory that is passed generationally from parent to child, and the horizontal 'affiliative' postmemory that is conveyed contemporaneously between unrelated members of the same generation (2012:36). In this sense, Hirsch challenged a central tenant of Halbwachs' theory, by suggesting that it was possible 'to *reactivate* and *re-embody* more distant political and cultural memorial structures', such that a postmemory might 'persist even after all participants and even their familial descendants are gone' (2012:33; cf. Kansteiner 2014:404).

The notion of an affiliative postmemory that might be taken up by individuals with little or no experiential or familial connection with an original event has been pursued by Alison Landsberg. Landsberg suggested that when people interact with 'an experiential site such as a movie theater or museum', they might develop 'prosthetic' memories, in the sense that they have not simply acquired new historical knowledge, but rather taken on a 'more personal, deeply felt memory of past events through which [they] did not live' (2004:2). Directly challenging the relevance of Halbwachs' model in a global world, Landsberg argued that prosthetic memories 'differ from earlier forms of memory' insofar as 'they do not emerge as the result of living and being raised in particular social frameworks' (2004:3, 19). Drawing on examples ranging from the American television series *Roots* to the film *Schindler's List* and the United States Holocaust Memorial Museum, she suggested that mass culture and mass media had enabled people to experience memories as genuine even if they 'are not naturally – ethnically, racially, or biologically – one's intended inheritance' (Landsberg 2004:11, 26). Though she conceded that this may 'not always produce utopian results', she nevertheless emphasised that because prosthetic memories 'feel real, they help condition how a person thinks about the world and might be instrumental in articulating an ethical relation to the other' (Landsberg 2004:21).

Andrew Hoskins has similarly argued that mass media have had a profound effect on the construction of memory, replacing 'old memory' with a 'new memory' that is increasingly 'manufactured, manipulated and above all, mediated' (2001:334). Hoskins has in his more recent work gone further than Landsberg, however, by turning to the significance of digital technology, theorising a 'connective turn' in the contemporary era (2009; 2011a; 2011b). He argued that the increasing 'abundance, pervasiveness and accessibility' of digital media and technology have given rise to a memory that is not simply 'a product of individual or collective remembrances', but is rather driven by the ways people connect with and through a shifting array of media, and, in doing so, encounter other times, places, and people (Hoskins 2011a:271–272, 278). Hoskins does not specifically associate his 'connective turn' with a 'transcultural turn', instead suggesting that the contemporary 'media-technological architecture of memory' indicates that memory is 'always already "transcultural"', insofar as it defies the 'biological, social and cultural divisions and distinctions of memory and memory studies' (2011b:21). Whether this applies only to the 'new mediatized age of memory' (Hoskins 2009:96), however, or is simply the most dramatic incarnation of an older phenomenon, is debated (Erll 2011c:132; Erll and Rigney 2009:7).

Erll, for instance, has argued that 'there is no such thing as a pure, pre-media memory' (2011c:132), and, with Ann Rigney, therefore writes that 'no historical document [. . .] and certainly no memorial monument [. . .] is thinkable without earlier acts of mediation' (Erll and Rigney 2009:4). According to Erll, this mediation happens in two principal ways: 'remediation', which is how particular events are 'represented again and again, over decades and centuries, in different media', and 'premediation', which is how 'existent media circulating in a given context provide schemata for future experience – its anticipation, representation and remembrance' (2009:111; 2011c:142). Significantly, these processes of mediation commonly take place 'across the boundaries of time, space, and culture', and did so even before the contemporary era of globalisation, mediatisation, and digitisation (Erll 2009:131). Erll examined, for instance, how Indian novels dealing with the 1857 Indian Rebellion extensively remediated contemporary British newspaper accounts filled with 'wild fantasies of rape and mutilation', accounts which were themselves premediated by the literary genre of Gothic horror and mediaeval/Renaissance imaginings of hell, i.e. by medial schemata with which the British journalists were familiar (2009:114, 121–124). More broadly, she has pointed out that even 'the very fundaments of what we assume to be Western cultural memory are the product of transcultural movements', from the 'Persian influence on the Old Testament' to the 'French origins of what the Grimm brothers popularized as "German" fairy tales' (Erll 2011b:11). Seen from this perspective, memory of a particular moment from the past 'usually refers not so much to what one might cautiously call the "original" or the "actual" events, but instead to a palimpsestic structure of existent media representations' (Erll 2011c:141). As a result, all *lieux de mémoire* are, ultimately, 'shared sites of memory' (Erll 2009:131).

The notion of memory as a palimpsest has more recently been taken up by Max Silverman, a scholar of Francophone film and literature. In common with Rothberg, Silverman was concerned with exploring the interconnectedness of supposedly distinct memories, focusing in particular on the mnemonic relationship between the Holocaust and colonialism. Silverman argued against an interpretation of memory as linear, proprietorial, and competitive, instead placing emphasis on 'interconnection, interaction, substitution and displacement' in the construction of memory (2013:28). Describing memory as 'palimpsestic', he called for a 'paradigm of hybrid and overlapping rather than separate pasts', which would not just identify the coexistence of, or comparison between, different histories, but would also recognise that 'the historical and physical base of cultural memory is a genuinely composite affair' (Silverman 2013:18, 179). Silverman shared Rothberg's conviction that uncovering the 'interconnecting traces of different voices, sites and times' might form the basis for 'new solidarities across the lines of race and nation', and, in contrast to Landsberg, emphasised that memory 'has always been deterritorialized in the sense of being a hybrid rather than pure category' (Silverman 2013:8). For Silverman, it is a fallacy to presume that 'memory loses its attachment to a particular identity [only] once it moves into the global sphere' (2011:627), an assumption that rests on the 'singularity, autonomy, specificity and authenticity of the memory in the first place' (2013:176).

An everyday history of multidirectional memory

To summarise the above, just as explorations of the transcultural circulation of Holocaust memory have helped to undermine the connection between collective memory and group identity – by demonstrating the mobility of a legacy previously assumed to 'belong' to a particular group and in a particular place – studies of mediated memory have destabilised the link between direct and indirect experience, and between originality and authenticity (Silverman 2013:176). These interventions open up important new vistas for memory studies. In what follows, I want to highlight several unresolved questions that will need to be addressed as these discussions develop, and to which I turn in the following chapters. In particular, I emphasise that the literature would benefit from incorporating greater awareness of the historical, local, and everyday aspects of transcultural memory.

Historians and anthropologists – who have been comparatively quiet (with some notable exceptions) in debates driven by outstanding contributions from the fields of sociology, literary studies, cultural studies, and media studies – may be particularly well-positioned to tackle these questions.

To begin with, there is debate as to whether the transcultural circulation of memories is a phenomenon peculiar to the modern, globalised, and mediatised world. Where some scholars see memory as loosed from its traditional moorings by the radical upheavals of globalisation, digitisation, and mass media, others challenge the idea that memory was ever firmly 'territorialised' to begin with. Erll has argued that 'transcultural remembering has a long genealogy', and that it is, in fact, 'since ancient times that contents, forms and technologies of memory have crossed the boundaries of time, space, and social groups, and been filled in different local contexts with new life and new meaning' (2011a). From this point of view, the transcultural approach to memory studies is not only suitable for 'our current globalizing age', but is rather 'a perspective on memory that can in principle be chosen with respect to all historical periods' (Erll 2011a). As Erll emphasised, a 'decidedly historical perspective on memory' would resolve this debate in short order (2011a). Some important work has already been done on the history of transcultural memory (though not always explicitly framed in these terms). For instance, in addition to Erll's observations on the Indian Rebellion (2009) and the transcultural origins of Western cultural memory (2011b:11), Geoff Cubitt has explored how nineteenth-century French polemicists detected 'contemporary French meanings in references to England's turbulent seventeenth-century history' (2007:74), whilst Confino has demonstrated that in the 1930s and 1940s opponents and proponents alike often measured the Nazi rise to power against the values of the French Revolution (2012:7).

For the purposes of the present study, however, what particularly interests me about Erll's intervention is the invitation to apply the concepts, critiques, and sensitivities of a transcultural approach to the study of national memory. If memory, to borrow terms from Rothberg, is 'structurally multidirectional' (Rothberg 2009a:35), then the commonplace distinction between a stable and homogenous national memory and a mobile and diverse transcultural memory becomes blurred, turning our attention to the 'great internal heterogeneity' and 'many fuzzy edges' of national memories (Erll 2010:311–312; Erll 2011b:8; Erll 2011c:65). We are led to the recognition that even sites of memory that appear quintessentially national are often in practice transnational and transcultural constructions (Sundholm 2011:2), both in that they rely on 'repurposing' older memory materials of diverse spatio-temporal origin (Erll and Rigney 2009:5), and insofar as they necessitate imaginative identification with people from the (distant) past who inhabited vastly different social and, sometimes, geographical worlds. I take these issues up in Chapter 6, exploring the palimpsestic layering of diverse 'memory traces' (Silverman 2013:28) that are inherent in the efforts of some expatriate activists to carve out a place within Greek national memory.

Moreover, precisely because every act of mnemonic 'de-territorialization' requires a subsequent process of 're-territorialization', as Levy and Sznaider themselves recognised (2006:8), it is always possible that the global circulation of memories will 'reinforce national memory communities that at first appearance they seem to supersede' (Assmann and Conrad 2010:9). As we have already seen, many scholars have (quite understandably) tried to identify and study the productive and ethical implications of memories crossing borders and boundaries. Others, however, have cautioned against an assumption that these 'travelling memories' (Erll 2011b) will necessarily replace exclusive national identities with cosmopolitan solidarities (Assmann 2014:546–548, 552; Erll 2011b:15; Huyssen 2011:621; Moses 2011). Lucy Bond, for instance, has demonstrated that analogies between 9/11 and the Holocaust are liable to generate 'insistent Americanism' rather than 'constructive cosmopolitanism', pointing, for instance, to inflammatory protestations by some American commentators that the proposed development of an Islamic cultural centre near Ground Zero would be tantamount to placing a swastika at the Holocaust Museum or a German cultural centre at Treblinka (2012:115–116). Similarly, Jacqueline Lo has expressed concern that contemporary Israeli commemoration of Aboriginal Australian William Cooper's 1938 Melbourne protest against *Kristallnacht* – on the surface, a quintessential example of a cosmopolitan, nation-transcending act of remembrance – has 'become part of the apparatus of the Israeli state', incorporating activities (such as tree planting) that in the Israeli context are laden with nationalist and statist associations (2013:349–350). As Rothberg has clarified in his more recent work, memory competition and power dynamics must be considered aspects of memory's multidirectionality (2011; 2014:655). If memory is indeed structurally multidirectional, then within this paradigm we must seek to explain not just instances in which the past is evoked to sustain transcultural solidarity and understanding, but also the construction and perpetuation of hostilities premised upon histories of national or ethnic conflict. Although I do not necessarily share Moses' assessment that the 'inescapable terror of history insists upon the constant instrumentalization of the Holocaust' and therefore invalidates a cosmopolitan take on transcultural memory (2011:104) – Moses' position could be said to represent a worst-case scenario where Levy and Sznaider's account constitutes a best-case scenario – I nevertheless address an imbalance in the literature by more systematically considering instances in which travelling memories serve to consolidate rather than dissolve antagonisms, and to sustain rather than challenge national myths and essentialist identities. This is a strand that I develop in Chapter 7.

Another area of ongoing debate concerns the specificity, or otherwise, of the Holocaust as a memory with transcultural reach. As Aleida Assmann has written, if the Holocaust has indeed become a global moral yardstick for measuring atrocity, the question remains as to 'whether this universal norm can only be accessed via the exemplary history of the Holocaust or whether other historic traumas can also serve to back these moral commitments and values' (2010:113). Levy and Sznaider might answer in the negative, and indeed they noted that the atomic bombing of Hiroshima by the United States has not become a 'medium for cosmopolitan remembrance' in the way that they felt the Holocaust had (2006:39). Alexander, meanwhile, pre-empting the criticism that his model might be seen as Western-centric, suggested that scholars might explore the extent to which non-Western communities have developed their own traumatic memories with the potential to underpin 'universalizing, supranational ethical imperatives' (2009:69). Rothberg's major contribution to the literature was to challenge such unidirectional perspectives, by suggesting that the apparently transcendent status of the Holocaust as a symbol of evil and suffering was in fact a symptom of the dialogic interactions between Holocaust memory and the memories of other atrocities. Rothberg focused on connections with decolonisation and slavery, though many years earlier Richard Minear had made a comparable claim that the term 'holocaust' came into use to refer to the Nazi genocide and the atomic bombings of Hiroshima and Nagasaki almost simultaneously, in part due to dialogic interactions between the two legacies (Minear 1995:354–357).

Nevertheless, it remains the case that Rothberg's arguments (and those of other scholars – such as Silverman – who have echoed his conclusions) were developed through reference to Holocaust memory as one of the principal nodes on the multidirectional memory network (and often, in Bond's terms, as 'the nexus to which all paths return' (2012:125)). There is, therefore, good reason for scholars to walk the 'crossroads of memory' (Bond 2012:125) a little more widely, and explore points of connection at which the Holocaust is not explicitly present. Some scholars have begun to do just that, considering other histories that may have taken on transnational resonance and become regional or global touchstones: the adoption of the Argentinian symbol of 'the disappeared' in discussions of Franco's victims in Spain (Assmann 2014:554–555; Mandolessi and Perez 2014); the use of the term 'ethnic cleansing' by Greek and Turkish Cypriots after the wars in Yugoslavia (Papadakis 2004:16); the evocation of the Vietnam War by socialist states and ordinary citizens in Eastern Europe in the 1960s and 1970s (Mark *et al.* 2015); or the development of the Larzac protest in southern France into 'an inspirational model to other communities facing the brutal power of the state' across France and as far afield as Japan, Latin America, and New Caledonia (Gildea and Tompkins 2015:600, 604). In Chapter 7, I seek to contribute to this broadening of the field. Although I do consider expatriate invocations of Holocaust memory, I also discuss the ways in which activists from the expatriated Greek community of Turkey articulate memories of suffering in dialogue with other traumatic legacies, most notably those of the Armenian genocide and the ongoing Kurdish-Turkish conflict.

As well as a tendency to focus, in one way or another, on Holocaust memory, pioneering studies of transcultural memory have commonly drawn their conclusions on the basis of formal and rehearsed representations of the past, often produced by elites, found in academic or intellectual texts, literature and film, political discourse, and museums. A shortcoming of a source base such as this for studying memory in society, as critics within the field had already noted in the late 1990s and early 2000s, is that we must either assume that 'facts of representation coincide with facts of reception' (Kansteiner 2002:195), or remain 'satisfied to recount how the past was publicly represented' at the expense of learning 'how collective memories were internalized by individuals' (Confino

2004:398, 409; see also Confino 1997:1392, 1395; Confino 2000:98; Confino and Fritzsche 2002:4; Erll 2011c:27; Erll and Rigney 2009:9; Novick 2007:28; Schudson 1997:3). Consequently, whilst we know a great deal, for instance, about the formal representation of the Holocaust by prominent politicians, filmmakers, and writers of academic and literary texts, we know comparatively little about the extent to which 'the Holocaust has really entered the life world of broader segments of the population and has repercussions in their "everyday local experiences"' (Assmann and Conrad 2010:8).

Equally, there has at times been an inclination to concentrate on the 'non-location' rather than the 'locatedness' of transcultural memories, and to fail to give sufficient attention to the variable, mutable, and unpredictable ways in which these memories are '*instantiated* locally' in different places and at different times (Radstone 2011:111, 117–118). The importance of studying this 'localizing aspect' of travelling memory (Erll 2011b:15; see also Assmann 2014:547; Crownshaw 2012:235–236; Kennedy and Radstone 2013:242; Rothberg 2014; Sierp and Wüstenberg 2015:323–324) is borne out in the findings of some more recent studies. Robert Gildea and Andrew Tompkins, for example, demonstrated that whilst the struggle of the Larzac sheep farmers (and their allies) to resist expropriation of their land by the French state became a transnational symbol of protest, the meaning of the Larzac struggle was interpreted differently in different local and national contexts, and, in the process, sometimes lost the non-violent aspect that had been so central to the original protests (2015:598, 604). Likewise, James Mark and colleagues showed that formal discourses of transnational solidarity with the Vietnamese articulated by state actors in Eastern European communist countries for their own political purposes were informally adopted and adapted by young people dissenting against officialdom (both those on the left who felt their governments' support for the Vietnamese communists was insufficient, and nationalists who saw parallels between US actions in Vietnam and Soviet hegemony in Eastern Europe) (Mark *et al.* 2015:458–459, 462–463). Such examples confirm, in Alejandro Baer and Natan Sznaider's words, that '[c]ommon narratives are not common in the sense that everybody would tell the same story' (2015:339).

Writing in 1997 to criticise the prevalence of what he saw as restrictively political understandings of memory's operation in society, Confino urged scholars to broaden 'the field from the political to the social and the experiential, to an everyday history of memory' (1997:1402). The everyday, in this sense, does not refer narrowly to the mundane activities and discourses of daily life, but more broadly to the 'anarchic quality' of remembrance that 'locates memory not only in monuments and museums but also in the ways people make it part of behaviour and of a mental world' (Confino 2004:412). In a similar vein, I suggest that we require an *everyday history of multidirectional memory*, which would explore 'what people actually "do"' (Confino and Fritzsche 2002:5) with the memories of other times, places, and people, and how these 'made a difference in people's lives' and were 'enacted on the local and private level' (Confino 1997:1394). I here prefer 'multidirectional' to 'transcultural' as it encompasses the travels and interactions of memory even where they do not explicitly cross national or cultural boundaries. This is a project for which anthropological, ethnographic, and oral history research may be particularly apposite. In Chapter 7, I embark upon this path, by considering, first, what representatives of a particular local community operating with particular agendas *actually do* with transcultural memories, and, secondly, the extent to which the transcultural dynamics of memory manifest themselves in people's personal narratives and understandings of the past. In doing so, I hope to shed light on the practical implications and local permutations of travelling memories.

Throughout Part III, I make reference to expatriate 'activists', by which I mean individuals from the expatriated communities of Istanbul and Imbros who are or have been actively involved in publicising the recent history of the Greeks of Turkey and in seeking recognition from Greek and international bodies. They might also be called 'memory activists' insofar as they seek to introduce and inscribe a certain set of memories in the public sphere, and indeed they often present themselves as preserving memories carrying important contemporary lessons that would otherwise be consigned to oblivion (see, especially, comments by representatives of the Constantinopolitan Society in Chapter 6). In particular, these are individuals working with expatriate community organisations and/or writing for expatriate newspapers. They would not necessarily self-define as activists, and their views should not be taken as representative of the range of positions taken up by members of the expatriate community at large (though, as we will see in Chapter 6, they equally do not all agree with one another as to the best way to represent their community's history). What I am primarily interested in is how, why, and when these individuals, in their efforts to represent and communicate their community's past, draw on memories of other times and places.

Note

1 It should be noted that Halbwachs himself was more interested in smaller-scale mnemonic communities, writing that 'the nation is too remote from the individual for him to consider the history of his country as anything else than a very large framework with which his own history makes contact at only a few points' (1980:77).

References

Alexander, J. C. (2009). The social construction of moral universals. In J. C. Alexander. *Remembering the Holocaust: a debate*. Oxford; New York: Oxford University Press, 3–102.

Assmann, A. (2010). The Holocaust – a global memory? Extensions and limits of a new memory community. In A. Assmann and S. Conrad (Eds). *Memory in a global age: discourses, practices and trajectories*. Houndmills, Basingstoke; New York: Palgrave Macmillan, 97–117.

Assmann, A. (2014). Transnational memories. *European Review*, 22(04), 546–556.

Assmann, A. and Conrad, S. (2010). Introduction. In A. Assmann and S. Conrad (Eds). *Memory in a global age: discourses, practices and trajectories*. Houndmills, Basingstoke; New York: Palgrave Macmillan, 1–16.

Baer, A. and Sznaider, N. (2015). Ghosts of the Holocaust in Franco's mass graves: cosmopolitan memories and the politics of 'never again'. *Memory Studies*, 8(3), 328–344.

Bond, L. (2012). Intersections or misdirections? Problematising crossroads of memory in the commemoration of 9/11. *Culture, Theory and Critique*, 53(2), 111–128.

Bond, L. and Rapson, J. (2014). Introduction. In L. Bond and J. Rapson (Eds). *The transcultural turn: interrogating memory between and beyond borders*. Berlin, Germany; Boston, MA: De Gruyter, 1–26.

Cohen, W. B. (2001). The sudden memory of torture: the Algerian War in French discourse, 2000–2001. *French Politics, Culture & Society*, 19(3), 82–94.

Confino, A. (1997). Collective memory and cultural history: problems of method. *The American Historical Review*, 102(5), 1386–1403.

Confino, A. (2000). Traveling as a culture of remembrance: traces of National Socialism in West Germany, 1945–1960. *History & Memory*, 12(2), 92–121.

Confino, A. (2004). Telling about Germany: narratives of memory and culture. *The Journal of Modern History*, 76(2), 389–416.

Confino, A. (2005). Remembering the Second World War, 1945–1965: narratives of victimhood and genocide. *Cultural Analysis*, 4, 46–75.

Confino, A. (2012). *Foundational pasts: the Holocaust as historical understanding*. Cambridge: Cambridge University Press.

Confino, A. and Fritzsche, P. (2002). Introduction: noises of the past. In A. Confino and P. Fritzsche (Eds). *The work of memory: new directions in the study of German society and culture*. Urbana, IL: University of Illinois Press, 1–24.

Craps, S. and Rothberg, M. (2011). Introduction: transcultural negotiations of Holocaust memory. *Criticism*, 53(4), 517–521.

Crownshaw, R. (2011). Introduction. *Parallax*, 17(4), 1–3.

Crownshaw, R. (2012). Response. In P. Vermeulen, S. Craps, R. Crownshaw, O. de Graef, A. Huyssen, V. Liska, and D. Miller (Eds) 'Dispersal and redemption: the future dynamics of memory studies – a roundtable'. *Memory Studies*, 5(2), 234–237.

Cubitt, G. (2007). The political uses of seventeenth-century English history in Bourbon Restoration France. *The Historical Journal*, 50(1), 73–95.

Erll, A. (2009). Remembering across time, space, and cultures: premediation, remediation and the 'Indian Mutiny'. In A. Erll and A. Rigney (Eds). *Mediation, remediation, and the dynamics of cultural memory*. Berlin; New York: Walter de Gruyter, 109–138.

Erll, A. (2010). Regional integration and (trans)cultural memory. *Asia Europe Journal*, 8(3), 305–315.

Erll, A. (2011a). Traumatic pasts, literary afterlives, and transcultural memory: new directions of literary and media memory studies. *Journal of Aesthetics & Culture*, 3.

Erll, A. (2011b). Travelling memory. *Parallax*, 17(4), 4–18.

Erll, A. (2011c). *Memory in culture*. Translated from the German by S. B. Young. Houndmills, Basingstoke; New York: Palgrave Macmillan.

Erll, A. and Rigney, A. (2009). Introduction: cultural memory and its dynamics. In A. Erll and A. Rigney (Eds.). *Mediation, remediation, and the dynamics of cultural memory*. Berlin; New York: Walter de Gruyter, 1–11.

Feierstein, L. R. (2014). 'A quilt of memory': the Shoah as a prism in the testimonies of survivors of the dictatorship in Argentina. *European Review*, 22(04), 585–593.

Flanzbaum, H. (1999a). The Americanization of the Holocaust. *Journal of Genocide Research*, 1(1), 91–104.

Flanzbaum, H. (1999b). Introduction: the Americanization of the Holocaust. In H. Flanzbaum (Ed.). *The Americanization of the Holocaust*. Baltimore, MD: Johns Hopkins University Press, 1–17.

Gildea, R. and Tompkins, A. (2015). The transnational in the local: the Larzac plateau as a site of transnational activism since 1970. *Journal of Contemporary History*, 50(3), 581–605.

Graves, M. and Rechniewski, E. (2010). From collective memory to transcultural remembrance. *PORTAL Journal of Multidisciplinary International Studies*, 7(1), 1–15.

Halbwachs, M. (1980). *The collective memory*. Translated from the French by F. J. Ditter and V. Y. Ditter. New York: Harper & Row.

Hansen, M. B. (1996). 'Schindler's List' is not 'Shoah': the second commandment, popular modernism, and public memory. *Critical Inquiry*, 22(2), 292–312.

Hirsch, M. (2012). *The Generation of postmemory: writing and visual culture after the Holocaust*. New York: Columbia University Press.

Hoskins, A. (2001). New memory: mediating history. *Historical Journal of Film, Radio and Television*, 21(4), 333–346.

Hoskins, A. (2009). Digital network memory. In A. Erll and A. Rigney (Eds). *Mediation, remediation, and the dynamics of cultural memory*. Berlin; New York: Walter de Gruyter, 91–106.

Hoskins, A. (2011a). 7/7 and connective memory: interactional trajectories of remembering in post-scarcity culture. *Memory Studies*, 4(3), 269–280.

Hoskins, A. (2011b). Media, memory, metaphor: remembering and the connective turn. *Parallax*, 17(4), 19–31.

House, J. (2010). Memory and the creation of solidarity during the decolonization of Algeria. *Yale French Studies*, (118/119), 15–38.

Huyssen, A. (2000). Present pasts: media, politics, amnesia. *Public Culture*, 12(1), 21–38.

Huyssen, A. (2003). *Present pasts: urban palimpsests and the politics of memory*. Stanford: Stanford University Press.

Huyssen, A. (2011). International human rights and the politics of memory: limits and challenges. *Criticism*, 53(4), 607–624.

Jay, M. (2009). Allegories of evil: a response to Jeffrey Alexander. In J. C. Alexander. *Remembering the Holocaust: a debate*. Oxford; New York: Oxford University Press, 105–113.

Jelin, E. (2010). The past in the present: memories of state violence in contemporary Latin America. In A. Assmann and S. Conrad, (Eds.). *Memory in a global age: discourses, practices and trajectories*. Houndmills, Basingstoke; New York: Palgrave Macmillan, 61–78.

Kansteiner, W. (2002). Finding meaning in memory: a methodological critique of collective memory studies. *History and Theory*, 41(2), 179–197.

Kansteiner, W. (2014). Genocide memory, digital cultures, and the aestheticization of violence. *Memory Studies*, 7(4), 403–408.

Katz, E. and Katz, R. (2009). Life and death among the binaries: notes on Jeffrey Alexander's constructionism. In J. C. Alexander. *Remembering the Holocaust: a debate*. Oxford; New York: Oxford University Press, 156–170.

Kennedy, R. and Radstone, S. (2013). Memory up close: memory studies in Australia. *Memory Studies*, 6(3), 237–244.

Kushner, T. (2001). Oral history at the extremes of human experience: Holocaust testimony in a museum setting. *Oral History*, 29(2), 83–94.

Landsberg, A. (2004). *Prosthetic memory: the transformation of American remembrance in the age of mass culture*. New York: Columbia University Press.

Levy, D. and Sznaider, N. (2002). Memory unbound: the Holocaust and the formation of cosmopolitan memory. *European Journal of Social Theory*, 5(1), 87–106.

Levy, D. and Sznaider, N. (2004). The institutionalization of cosmopolitan morality: the Holocaust and human rights. *Journal of Human Rights*, 3(2), 143–157.

Levy, D. and Sznaider, N. (2006). *The Holocaust and memory in the global age*. Translated from the German by A. Oksiloff. Philadelphia, PA: Temple University Press.

Lo, J. (2013). 'Why should we care?' Some thoughts on cosmopolitan hauntings. *Memory Studies*, 6(3), 345–358.

Mandolessi, S. and Perez, M. E. (2014). The disappeared as a transnational figure or how to deal with the vain yesterday. *European Review*, 22(04), 603–612.

Manne, R. (2009). On the political corruptions of a moral universal. In J. C. Alexander. *Remembering the Holocaust: a debate*. Oxford; New York: Oxford University Press, 135–145.

Mark, J., Apor, P., Vučetić, R., and Osęka, P. (2015). 'We are with you, Vietnam': transnational solidarities in socialist Hungary, Poland and Yugoslavia. *Journal of Contemporary History*, 50(3), 439–464.

Minear, R. H. (1995). Atomic holocaust, Nazi holocaust: some reflections. *Diplomatic History*, 19(2), 347–365.

Misztal, B. A. (2003). *Theories of social remembering*. Maidenhead, Berkshire; Philadelphia, PA: Open University Press.

Molden, B. (2010). Vietnam, the new left and the Holocaust: how the Cold War changed discourse on genocide. In A. Assmann and S. Conrad (Eds). *Memory in a global age: discourses, practices and trajectories*. Houndmills, Basingstoke; New York: Palgrave Macmillan, 79–96.

Moses, A. D. (2011). Genocide and the terror of history. *Parallax*, 17(4), 90–108.

Nora, P. (1989). Between memory and history: les lieux de mémoire. *Representations*, (26), 7–24.

Novick, P. (2007). Comments on Aleida Assmann's lecture. *GHI Bulletin*, (40), 27–31.

Owen, S. (2014). 'From one April to another': remembering and acknowledging the Holocaust in the poetry of Michael Longley. *Irish Studies Review*, 22(3), 358–373.

Papadakis, Y. (2004). Discourses of "the Balkans" in Cyprus: tactics, strategies and constructions of "Others". *History and Anthropology*, 15(1), 1–25.

Petrie, J. (2000). The secular word Holocaust: scholarly myths, history, and 20th century meanings. *Journal of Genocide Research*, 2(1), 31–63.

Prost, A. (1999). The Algerian War in French collective memory. In J. M. Winter and E. Sivan (Eds). *War and remembrance in the twentieth century*. Cambridge; New York: Cambridge University Press, 161–176.

Radstone, S. (2011). What place is this? Transcultural memory and the locations of memory studies. *Parallax*, 17(4), 109–123.

Rosenfeld, A. (1995). The Americanization of the Holocaust. *Commentary*, 99(6).

Rosenfeld, G. D. (1999). The politics of uniqueness: reflections on the recent polemical turn in Holocaust and genocide scholarship. *Holocaust and Genocide Studies*, 13(1), 28–61.

Rothberg, M. (2008). Decolonizing trauma studies: a response. *Studies in the Novel*, 40(1), 224–234.

Rothberg, M. (2009a). *Multidirectional memory: remembering the Holocaust in the age of decolonization*. Stanford, CA: Stanford University Press.

Rothberg, M. (2009b). Multidirectional memory and the universalization of the Holocaust. In J. C. Alexander. *Remembering the Holocaust: a debate*. Oxford; New York: Oxford University Press, 123–134.

Rothberg, M. (2010). Introduction: between memory and memory: from *lieux de mémoire* to *noeuds de mémoire*. *Yale French Studies*, (118/119), 3–12.

Rothberg, M. (2011). From Gaza to Warsaw: mapping multidirectional memory. *Criticism*, 53(4), 523–548.

Rothberg, M. (2014). Locating transnational memory. *European Review*, 22(4), 652–656.

Rothberg, M. and Yildiz, Y. (2011). Memory citizenship: migrant archives of Holocaust remembrance in contemporary Germany. *Parallax*, 17(4), 32–48.

Saxton, L. (2010). Horror by analogy: paradigmatic aesthetics in Nicolas Klotz and Elisabeth Perceval's *'La question humaine'*. *Yale French Studies*, (118/119), 209–224.

Schudson, M. (1997). Lives, laws, and language: commemorative versus non-commemorative forms of effective public memory. *The Communication Review*, 2(1), 3–17.

Sierp, A. and Wüstenberg, J. (2015). Linking the local and the transnational: rethinking memory politics in Europe. *Journal of Contemporary European Studies*, 23(3), 321–329.

Silverman, M. (2011). Between the local and the global. *Criticism*, 53(4), 625–628.

Silverman, M. (2013). *Palimpsestic memory: the Holocaust and colonialism in French and Francophone fiction and film*. New York: Berghahn Books.

Stein, A. (1998). Whose memories? Whose victimhood? Contests for the Holocaust frame in recent social movement discourse. *Sociological Perspectives*, 41(3), 519–540.

Stratton, J. (2000). Thinking through the Holocaust. A discussion inspired by Hilene Flanzbaum (ed.), The Americanization of the Holocaust. *Continuum*, 14(2), 231–245.

Sundholm, J. (2011). Visions of transnational memory. *Journal of Aesthetics & Culture*, 3(1), 7208.

Young, J. (1999). America's Holocaust: memory and the politics of identity. In H. Flanzbaum (Ed.). *The Americanization of the Holocaust*. Baltimore, MD: Johns Hopkins University Press, 68–82.

6 'The Third Fall'

Commemorations and national history

In his foreword to Dimitris Kaloumenos' *The Crucifixion of Christianity*, a photographic account of the 1955 Istanbul Riots, the Istanbul-born Greek sociologist Neoklis Sarris wrote:

> The real Fall of Constantinople, in the sense of the irreparable destruction of its culture and civilisation and its replacement with another city, inhospitable Istanbul [...] took place not on 29 May, 1453 but on the night of 6 September, 1955.
>
> (Sarris 2001:15–16)

In this chapter, I explore how expatriate activists create such linkages between temporally disparate moments from the past, relating their local experiences to pivotal events and archetypes from Greek national history. In particular, I focus on how and why organisations founded by expatriated Greeks from Istanbul commemorate two specific historical events: the 1955 Istanbul Riots or *Septemvriana* and the 1453 Fall of Constantinople. In discourse surrounding the 1955 anniversary, the two episodes often become palimpsestically linked (Silverman 2013), such that the events of 1955 come to be seen as a reliving or continuation of those of 1453. In commemorative narratives marking the anniversary of the Fall of Constantinople, meanwhile, the 1821 Greek Revolution is often superimposed over the last stand of the Byzantines against the Ottomans, so that contemporary Greek freedom is portrayed as dependent upon the sacrifices of the Greeks of Constantinople in 1453. By considering such 'knotted intersections' (Silverman 2013:8) in the efforts of some expatriate activists to write themselves into Greek national history, I aim to demonstrate memory's multidirectionality (Rothberg 2009) *within* as well as without national borders and ethnic boundaries.

'The 300 who stayed': thinking analogically

During his fieldwork on Kalymnos, Sutton noticed that it was commonplace for people to understand contemporary everyday experiences through 'analogic thinking', i.e. through both horizontal references to current political situations and vertical references 'appropriated from the length of Greek history' (1998:127).

For the islanders, Sutton wrote, 'no event stands on its own, but must always be understood in the wider context of similar events drawn from other times and other places' (1998:127). In their efforts to represent the persecution and displacement of the Greeks of Turkey, Greek-born and expatriate writers alike often share this impulse to explain contemporary experience through analogic reference to history. In the immediate aftermath of the *Septemvrianá*, for example, renowned Greek author and Asia Minor refugee Ilias Venezis, writing in the Greek periodical *Néa Estía*, characterised the riots by making comparisons to the flight of Greek refugees from Turkey following the Greek defeat in Asia Minor in 1922. He wrote:

> The unbelievable barbarities of the mob from the other side of the Aegean against Hellenism and Christendom awakens in everyone here in the *éthnos* a fearful memory. Greece remembers again the days of 1922 – the days of flames, and wild cries, and blood, and hunted flocks, uprooted people, women and children and the elderly [. . .]
> The days of September of 1955 take us back to the days of 1922.
> (Venezis 1955)

On its front page, the Greek newspaper *Emprós* similarly broke the news of the Istanbul Riots by juxtaposing an image of the hanging of Ecumenical Patriarch Gregory V in Istanbul in 1821 for his failure to quash the Greek Revolution with an artist's depiction of the arson of churches in Istanbul in 1955, under the headline 'History Repeats Itself' (*Emprós* 1955). The Thessaloniki-based newspaper *Makedonía*, meanwhile, compared the rioting to the Ottoman conquest of the city in 1453, writing:

> The clamouring of the frenzied crowd, the insults directed at the infidels, the threats of their slaughter, the sounds of shop windows being smashed and shutters being broken, the wailing of those that had been ruined, the futile cries for help of women and children gave the characterisation of a second 'Fall'.
> (*Makedonía* 14 September 1955; quoted in Kaloumenos 2001:230)

In 1993, Greek newspaper *Apogevmatiní* (not to be confused with the Greek-language newspaper of the same name printed in Istanbul) likewise marked the anniversary of the *Septemvrianá* with an article entitled 'Constantinople Has Fallen', likening 1955 to 1453, and writing that Hellenism had once again come 'face-to-face with the barbarians' (*Apogevmatiní* 1993). As for the Greeks of Imbros, nationalist rhetoric has often likened the few hundred islanders who remained on Imbros to the 300 Spartan warriors of Leonidas who made a last stand against the Persians at Thermopylae in 480 BC (Tsimouris 2001:8), reflecting a broader tendency in post-1821 Greek nationalism to associate the Persians and the Turks as the Asiatic others of Hellenism (Van Steen 2010:90; see also Chapter 7).

There is, as we have seen in earlier chapters, something of a disjuncture between this inclusive nationalist rhetoric that made the plight of the Greeks of Turkey a national concern, and the experiences of marginalisation recalled by many expatriates upon their arrival in Greece. As Babül observed, to take the example of the *Imvriótes*–Spartans analogy, whilst those Greeks who remained on Imbros might be characterised as the '300 Spartans' and as evidence of the Hellenic character of the island, members of the same community who sought refuge in Greece were commonly perceived as not being Hellenic enough (2006:55). Accordingly, the expatriate community sometimes eschews such rhetoric in their own discourse. In 1974, for example, the newspaper *Imvriakí Ichó* wrote disparagingly of rhetoric likening the elderly residents of Imbros to the Spartans at Thermopylae, condemning the recently departed Greek military junta who 'did not give us any importance, they sacrificed us saying: "stay in your land to guard Thermopylae. Stay as slaves, in the national interest"' (*Imvriakí Ichó* 1974a).

It is hardly surprising, however, that the expatriates often find such narrative frameworks to be compelling, 'link[ing] their own fate to that of the wider Greek nation' (Tsimouris 2001:8) in the hope of attaining support and empathy from the Greek state and populace, and to endow their struggles with broader meaning and intelligibility. In 1991, for instance, Imvrian Association president Christos Christoforidis, in a message published in *Ímvros* after the election of a new committee, extended his greetings to

> the Few, who in difficult times, the most difficult in our History [...] remained There. There, so that the church bell does not cease to chime in the village, so that the last candle does not go out [...] Those 300, like those then, 'obedient to their laws'[1] guarding Thermopylae.
>
> (*Ímvros* 1991a)

In this example, two histories separated by millennia are blended into a single moment, thereby transforming the elderly community of Imbros into heroic defenders of the nation. In the process, Imbros – geographically and politically marginal to the modern Greek state – is redeemed as the national first line of defence, the frontline in an ongoing struggle between 'Greeks' and 'Turks'. This is reflective of a wider trend in Imvrian discourse: as Christoforidis insisted in an interview with Greek television in 1991 on the occasion of the 28 October Greek national holiday, '[t]he borders of Hellenism are in Imbros, are in Fener [in Istanbul], are in Kyrenia [Northern Cyprus], are in Karpasia [Northern Cyprus]' (*Ímvros* 1991b). By thus expanding the borders of Hellenism from those of the contemporary Greek state to ones that encompass their own *patrída* (and those of other Greek-speaking communities), Imvrian activists call the bluff of Greek ideologues who evoked them by name from afar but failed to support and embrace them in practice, and in this way situate their own local history within the broader narrative of Greek national history.

However, whilst such palimpsestic images in one sense serve to incorporate the *Imvriótes* into the imagined national community, they can, nevertheless, simultaneously be used to critique the actions of the Greek state. In an editorial written in 1993 to coincide with the 70th anniversary of the signing of the Treaty of Lausanne, Christoforidis attacked 'Greek diplomatic timidity and inaction' on the issue of Imbros by once again comparing those remaining on the island to the 300 Spartans, but on this occasion he emphasised the solitary and unaided nature of the islanders' vigil. He wrote:

> For 70 years now the *Imvriótes*, left to our fate, fight an unequal struggle with a very powerful but also barbarous state.
>
> For 70 years we resist and we are not defeated.
>
> As then, so now, 300 remain to prevent the barbarous Asian from passing the 'opposing shore'.
>
> 300 remain to defend the holy and the sacred, our altars and our lands.
>
> 300 remain to defend the honour and the worth of the *Ethnos.*
> (*Imvros* 1993)

In this sense, the appeal of the national past as a discursive framework for orientating more contemporary experience lies not only in its inclusive and identity-affirming capacity, but also in its subversive or insubordinate potential (Herzfeld 1997:169). Reaching across time and space to cast themselves in the likeness of Leonidas' Spartans, the *Imvriótes* resist their marginalisation in Greek diplomacy by turning Greek national mythology on the Greek state, implying that the latter has fallen from a state of grace to which the former still aspires.

In common with Sutton's Kalymnians, the *Imvriótes* have recourse not only to archetypes from the distant past, but also to contemporary and unfolding political events. Greek media reports of atrocities committed against Greek–Cypriots by the advancing Turkish army in the summer of 1974, for instance, triggered a series of pessimistic comparisons between Imbros and Cyprus in the newspaper of the Imvrian Association. In the first issue published after the beginning of hostilities on Cyprus, the newspaper printed an article under the heading 'Cyprus and Imbros' extensively paralleling the experiences of the two communities (*Imvriakí Ichó* 1974a), and in a separate article in the same issue expressed a fear that similar violence was imminent on Imbros. 'We have ceased talking about schools, buildings and properties', the author wrote. 'We are gripped by the fear that maybe one evening they will slaughter everyone. Can anyone rule that out after what we have heard and seen committed on Cyprus?' (*Imvriakí Ichó* 1974b). Just as a legend of Spartan resistance to the Persians was remediated or 'repurposed' by Imvrian writers in their efforts to represent Imbros' dwindling Greek community, so the unfolding conflict on Cyprus operated as a premediator through which they anticipated the future fate of their own community (Erll 2011b:142; Erll and Rigney 2009:5). In the years following 1974, Imvrian writers continued to represent the expatriation of the *Imvriótes* in terms of the conflict on Cyprus. In 1977, *Imvros* marked the anniversary of the division of Cyprus by writing that '[w]e live and feel the drama of the Cypriots, because Attila[2] passed by our islands first', and a year later again drew comparisons not only between Turkish actions on the two islands, but also a perceived inaction on the part of the Greek state in both cases (*Ímvros* 1977; *Ímvros* 1978). My interviewees sometimes had recourse to similar analogies in their oral testimonies: Istanbul-born *Imvriótis* Loukas, for example, said of his childhood visits to Imbros in the 1970s that, 'we grew up going in the summers to an occupied Cyprus, in practice; because when you talk sometimes with Cypriots, those from the occupied part, you understand that it was the same thing, our experiences were the same' (03/07/13).

Similar palimpsestic discourses can be observed in the commemoration of the *Septemvrianá* and the Fall of Constantinople by organisations founded by the expatriated Greeks of Istanbul. I focus below on commemorative articles printed in the newspaper *O Polítis*, and, in particular, on the anniversary events orchestrated by the Constantinopolitan Society, both of which typically rely heavily on interpretations based on a perceived pattern governing Greek–Turkish relationships through the ages. The Constantinopolitan Society's events have sometimes been run in collaboration with the New Circle of Constantinopolitans and the Association of Hellenic Citizens Expelled from Turkey (on which, see Chapter 1), but most often have been organised independently (Isaakidis 2014; *O Polítis* 1998). As has already been noted, the Constantinopolitan Society represents a perspective on history and Greek–Turkish relationships that is far from universally accepted by the expatriate community at large, and that has sometimes resulted in disagreements with other expatriate organisations. Accordingly, at the end of the chapter, I consider the anniversary events that have been more recently organised by the Federation of Constantinopolitans, which tend to disassociate the community's experiences from the *longue durée* of Greek–Turkish bilateral relations, and instead to locate them within the context of Turkish domestic policy and international human rights legislation.

Commemorating the 1955 Istanbul Riots

The Constantinopolitan Society was founded in Athens in 1928 by Greek refugees displaced from Istanbul and its environs in the wake of the Greek–Turkish War (see Chapter 1). Since 1978, by which time post-1923 expatriates had risen to prominence within the organisation's administrative structure, the Society has organised an annual and public memorial day to mark the anniversary of the Istanbul Riots (Isaakidis 2014). The precise content varies year by year, but the central theme of bearing witness in order to preserve and disseminate memory of past persecution has been consistent, and the events form part of a broader effort to raise awareness of the experiences of the Greeks of Turkey both domestically and abroad (*O Polítis* 1998). The memorial day is generally centred around a photographic exhibition presenting images of the riots – seen by the organisers as essential in confirming the veracity of their claims – and a speech by an invited speaker relating to the *Septemvrianá* or to the history of the Greek community in Istanbul and Greek–Turkish relationships more broadly (Isaakidis 2014). Other features incorporated into the event over the years include a religious memorial for the victims of the rioting, roundtable discussions and panels of witness testimonies, readings from novels and academic studies dealing with the events, and audiovisual presentations and documentary film screenings. The Society makes a special effort to reach a wider audience amongst the Greek public, particularly on round-number anniversaries, which are commonly marked by a series of commemorative endeavours. On the 40th anniversary of the *Septemvrianá*, for instance, a full programme of activities was prepared in conjunction with the New Circle of Constantinopolitans and the Association of Hellenic Citizens Expelled from Turkey, including radio and television broadcasts and two photographic exhibitions hosted in the War Museum and the Cultural Centre of the City of Athens (Constantinopolitan Society *et al.* 1995a; Constantinopolitan Society *et al.* 1995c; Constantinopolitan Society *et al.* 1995d).

For the Constantinopolitan Society, these commemorative events serve two primary purposes. First and foremost, they are seen as a way to address the perceived ignorance amongst the population of the Greek state about the plight of the Greeks of Istanbul. As a former president of the Society, Giorgos Isaakidis, put it to me in an interview:

> The Hellenic state does not deal with its own history. The events [of September 1955] are part of the history of the Hellenes, and the people [in Greece] did not know about them. They did not even know if we in Constantinople were Christians, or if we were baptised, or why we spoke Greek. They knew nothing. So our intention, the basic purpose when we started in '78, was to inform people about those events and of the existence of a notable minority in Constantinople.
>
> (Isaakidis 2014)

Second, the Society is afraid that the grievances of the *Polítes* might be forgotten or disregarded as part of efforts to promote reconciliation with Turkey, what the president of the Society Antonis Lampidis derisively referred to in his introductory speech at the 2012 commemorative event as the 'genocide of memory' undertaken by certain 'well-known circles' within Greece (Lampidis 2012). The Society is concerned that this alleged historical amnesia might in turn breed a political complacency regarding the perceived threat to Greece posed by its Turkish neighbour, and/or be interpreted by the Turkish authorities as a sign of Greek weakness (Constantinopolitan Society 2012a). As the Society and its associates wrote on the 40th anniversary of the *Septemvrianá*:

> The forgetting of evil is a licence for its repetition and all those who lived through the atrocities of the Turks must remind [others] of them, in order to prevent similar situations in the future that can now be clearly discerned with 'the naked eye'[:] the aggression of Turkey in Cyprus, the Aegean and in Western Thrace.
>
> (Constantinopolitan Society *et al.* 1995a)

Accordingly, the Society has lobbied the Greek state to designate 6 September as an official national memorial day, which, they feel, would 'constitute the beginning of the awakening of Hellenism, in order that the expansive schemes of the Turkish chauvinists do not come to pass' (Constantinopolitan Society 1994b; Constantinopolitan Society *et al.* 1995b).

The newspaper *O Polítis*, particularly in its earlier years, has often pursued a similar line to that of the Constantinopolitan Society in the articles it prints to mark the anniversary of 1955. In September 1979, for instance, it wrote:

> The *Septemvrianá* is a fearsome moment in the life of *Romiosýni* [see glossary] that must not be forgotten, because it constitutes the continuation of the official Turkish policy of annihilation against Hellenism that has no end and that may be manifested elsewhere, if Hellenism does not stay alert and united. We see the truth of this today in Cyprus, in the Aegean.
>
> (*O Polítis* 1979)

On the 33rd anniversary of the Istanbul Riots, meanwhile, against the backdrop of Greek–Turkish bilateral talks taking place during the short-lived 'Davos process', *O Polítis* wondered 'whether the committees that are meeting in Ankara and Athens have remembered what happened in those days in Constantinople in 1955, in order to appreciate accordingly the weight of responsibility that they assume' (*O Polítis* 1988b). In common with the Constantinopolitan Society, writers for *O Polítis* have often portrayed themselves as responsible for preserving the memory of past persecution, and counteracting 'the apathy of all of the Hellenes, those in government and those not' towards the events of 1955 (*O Polítis* 1990). For both organisations, bearing annual witness to the Istanbul Riots, and calling on the Greek government to institute a national day of remembrance on 6 September, represents an attempt to inscribe the *Septemvrianá* formally onto the Greek memorial landscape. In this way, they hope to tackle a perceived popular ignorance about, and diplomatic indifference towards, the expatriate community, a situation that they see not only as the root cause of the *Polítes'* struggles in Greece, but also as a threat to Greece's future security.

Commemorating the 1453 Fall of Constantinople

There is no official national memorial day in Greece to mark the anniversary of the Fall of Constantinople, in the way that there is for the beginning of the 1821 revolution (25 March) or Greek resistance to Axis invasion and occupation during the Second World War (*Óhi* ('No') Day, 28 October). Writing in *O Polítis* in 1987, Kaloumenos (author of *The Crucifixion of Christianity*) lamented that the anniversary 'has been forgotten by the Hellenic state, the press, the church, and the people' (*O Polítis* 1987a). For some expatriates, this is symptomatic of a broader trend – deriving first from the desire to gain European support during the Greek Revolution, and secondly from the need for ideological re-centring after the Greek defeat in 1922 put an end to the 'Great Idea' of re-establishing the Byzantine Empire – to sideline the Eastern Romaic tradition in favour of the Western Hellenic legacy (see Chapter 3). Seen from this perspective, Greek disregard (on the formal level, at least) for the Byzantine past, and ambivalence towards, or lack of awareness of, the contemporary Greek community of Istanbul, are two components of a wider problem. This interpretation was put forward, for instance, by the president of the Federation of Constantinopolitans Nikos Ouzounoglou, who in an interview with me argued that when the Greek state was established in 1830 'one of its basic political doctrines was the disavowal of Byzantium'. As a result, after 1923 successive Greek leaders 'followed the doctrine that the issue of the minority in Constantinople should not upset Greek–Turkish relationships', and resisted only 'very tamely' the events of 1955 and the expulsion of Greek citizens in 1964. For Ouzounoglou, ignorance in Greece as regards the Fall of Constantinople and the *Septemvrianá* is accordingly closely connected to the 'disavowal of Byzantium' by the Greek state (Ouzounoglou 2014a). It is, to a significant extent, this perception that the *Polítes*' struggles are a by-product of a broader historical amnesia that led some expatriates to mark the anniversary of 1453, hoping in this way both to restore their community and Eastern Hellenism generally to the national historical narrative, and to disseminate knowledge about their more contemporary experiences of persecution.

As we saw in Chapter 3, many *Polítes* present themselves as the heirs to the Byzantine legacy. The Constantinopolitan Society is an institutional expression of this discourse, regarding itself as the 'successor to the Byzantine tradition' charged with preserving the memory of a period subordinated to the Classical Hellenic legacy in Greek historiography (Isaakidis 2014; Lampidis 2014; quote taken from Lampidis). Since 1931, the Society has correspondingly observed the anniversary of the Fall of Constantinople on 29 May 1453, when the city was taken by the Ottoman Sultan Mehmed the Conqueror, and the last Byzantine emperor Constantine XI Palaiologos was killed in battle (Constantinopolitan Society 2008:27). In the 1960s and 1970s, at a time when increasing numbers of *Polítes* were settling in the Greek capital, this anniversary memorial (sometimes co-organised with other expatriate organisations) consisted of the laying of a single wreath before a statuette of Palaiologos inside the old parliament building in central Athens, followed outside by a more extended wreath-laying ceremony in front of the statue of Greek revolutionary hero Theodoros Kolokotronis (Isaakidis 2014). In this guise, the commemoration produced an analogy between 1453 and 1821, assimilating the defenders of Constantinople to the liberators of the nation, but also in the process subordinating the former to the latter, thereby replicating the sidelining of Byzantium in the national narrative.

Several newer and younger members of the Constantinopolitan Society, including Isaakidis, accordingly sought to reconfigure the commemorative ceremony after their election to the executive committee in the late 1970s. They felt that commemorating 1453 in front of a monument to a hero from the Greek Revolution was not a fitting way for the *Polítes* to honour the memory of the Byzantine emperor and his compatriots. As Isaakidis put it, 'what do we Constantinopolitans, gathering together to commemorate the Fall, have to do with Kolokotronis?' (Isaakidis 2014). The format of the commemoration was therefore changed after 1978. In its new configuration, the event began with a liturgical memorial to the fallen emperor and his fellow fighters in the Metropolitan Cathedral of Athens, on the nearest Sunday to 29 May.

142 National and transnational histories

This was followed by a parade attended by members of the expatriate organisations, to which representatives of the Athenian municipalities, the Greek state and church, major political parties, and the Greek Armed Forces were invited. The parade culminated in the laying of wreaths at the Tomb of the Unknown Soldier outside the Hellenic Parliament in the central Syntagma Square, in honour of the nameless dead who fell in the defence of Constantinople, accompanied by a rendition of the Greek national anthem (see Figure 7). After the erection of a statue of Palaiologos in the square outside the Metropolitan Cathedral in 1990, the parade was extended to encompass a memorial service dedicated to the emperor, including speeches and an additional wreath-laying ceremony, again accompanied by the national anthem (see Figure 8). In its revamped format, the 1453 commemoration combined elements common to official Greek national holidays, such as the ceremony at the Tomb of the Unknown Soldier, the performance of the national anthem, and the attendance of important political and religious dignitaries, with features that emphasised the particularities of the *Polítes*, like the venerated hero Constantine Palaiologos and the flags carried by participants emblazoned with the double-headed eagle of Byzantium (see Figure 9). The central location in front of the bustling Syntagma Square, meanwhile, immediately made the event more conspicuous and striking, attracting the curiosity of both local Athenians and foreign tourists.

Figure 7 Leonidas Koumakis, author of *The Miracle* (see Chapter 7), lays a wreath at the Tomb of the Unknown Soldier on the anniversary of the Fall of Constantinople, 2004.

From the archive of the Constantinopolitan Society. Copyright Constantinopolitan Society. Reproduced with permission.

Figure 8 Speeches at the statue of Constantine Palaiologos in Metropolitan Square, 2013.
Photograph by the author.

Figure 9 Members of the Constantinopolitan associations, holding flags bearing the double-headed eagle of Byzantium, observe the wreath-laying ceremony at the Tomb of the Unknown Soldier, 2004.

From the archive of the Constantinopolitan Society. Copyright Constantinopolitan Society. Reproduced with permission.

By publicly observing an anniversary absent from the commemorative calendar of the Greek state, in a manner that both emphasised the expatriates' belonging to the Greek *éthnos* and the distinctiveness of their own origins, the Constantinopolitan Society and its associates aimed to fill a perceived void in Greek collective memory. This comes across in the invitations issued by the Constantinopolitan Society to dignitaries that they hoped would attend the event, which typically portrayed the memorial ceremony as a national duty undertaken by the organisation, and implicitly criticised the forgetfulness of the Greek state. Inviting the political party *Synaspismós tis Aristerás kai tis Proódou* (Coalition of the Left and Progress) to send a representative to the 1998 event, for instance, the Society wrote:

> [B]elieving that the past of our *Ethnos* must not be forgotten, every year we organise the memorial ceremony for the Fall of Constantinople, at which a commemorative prayer is performed for the last emperor of Byzantium and those who fell with him.
>
> (Constantinopolitan Society 1998)

In a 1999 invitation to the Archbishop of Athens, it was similarly declared that the Society, celebrating '71 years of presence in Greece and of contribution towards the *'Ethnos*', would be 'continuing the struggle for the preservation of the memory of the *'Ethnos*, this year, as every year, [by] put[ting] into practice the ceremony of remembrance for the FALL OF CONSTANTINOPLE honouring in that way the heroic sacrifice of the final emperor Constantine Palaiologos and his fellow heroic fallen' (Constantinopolitan Society 1999).

In this manner, the 1453 anniversary was reconfigured in the guise of an official national holiday that nevertheless highlighted the particularities of the Greek community from Istanbul. After 1978, the Fall of Constantinople commemoration was thereby subtly changed from one that silently subsumed the *Polítes* into an already established national memorial landscape, to one that visibly and publicly carved out a *distinctive* commemorative niche for the expatriates *within* this memorial landscape.

1453 and 1821

In the words of former Constantinopolitan Society president Isaakidis, the primary objective of these commemorative events is 'to show our presence': to raise their public profile in Greece, in other words, and thereby to tackle their marginalisation within Greek society and bolster their claims for support from the Greek authorities (Isaakidis 2014). They form part of a broader narrative of persecution commonly articulated in speeches and publicity materials relating to the anniversaries of 1453 and 1955, reflecting the Society's belief that the *Septemvrianá* was 'not an isolated accidental incident, but part of a series of measures of the Turkish government aimed at the annihilation and uprooting of the Hellenism of

Constantinople' (Constantinopolitan Society *et al.* 1995a). Archetypally, a poster distributed across Athens by the Constantinopolitan Society in 1979 under the heading 'The Annihilation of the Constantinopolitans' presented the expatriation of the *Polítes* as taking place over a period of some 500 years, beginning in 1453 with the Fall of Constantinople. Also included were the Greek defeat in Asia Minor and the subsequent refugee flight in 1922, the *Septemvrianá* in 1955 – referred to as the 'prologue to the complete extermination' – the expulsions in 1964 – dubbed the 'final extermination' – and finally the accusation that in 1979 the Ecumenical Patriarchate was under threat (Constantinopolitan Society 1979; see Figure 10).

As I suggested at the outset, expatriate activists often link such 'local' experiences to seminal moments from the national past, as in the 'brief historical detour' offered by *O Polítis* on the 33rd anniversary of the *Septemvrianá* under the title 'An eye on history that does not lie'. The author began by mentioning the Fall of Constantinople after which 'Hellenism struggled for more than four centuries to regain its freedom', before dealing in turn with the 'harsh and hostile' treatment of the Greeks of Constantinople, Imbros, and Tenedos; Turkish military action on 'martyred Cyprus' in 1974; the 'flourishing Hellenism' of the Pontus, Asia Minor, and Eastern Thrace that was 'lost thanks to the rapacious disposition of Turkey';

Figure 10 The Annihilation of the Constantinopolitans, 1979.

Poster produced by the Constantinopolitan Society. From the archive of the Constantinopolitan Society. Copyright Constantinopolitan Society. Reproduced with permission.

and Turkish attempts to control the Aegean, which 'has constituted, since the Homeric age, the soul of Greece' (*O Polítis* 1988a). Rather than suffering alone as a result of specific decisions taken by particular Turkish governments after 1923, the Greeks of Istanbul are through such 'strife narratives' (Halstead 2014) drawn into an historically and spatially deep national pantheon of Greek victims. From this point of view, marking the anniversaries of 1453 and 1955, and assimilating these events to a diachronic clash between Greek civilisation and Turkish barbarity, forms part of a general endeavour pursued by some expatriate activists to demonstrate that the *Polítes* were the victims of a systematic Turkish policy of de-Hellenisation in Istanbul.

Following Silverman, however, memory cannot be understood simply as a linear series of discrete events, but must rather be perceived as a 'composite structure' involving the 'superimposition and productive interaction' of diverse memory traces 'so that one layer of traces can be seen through, and is transformed by, another' (2013:3–4). Indeed, the significance that these expatriate activists draw from these historical events does not lie solely in their placement in a linear chronological narrative, but also in the ways in which they come to be palimpsestically linked, such that more recent memories are layered over, and reinterpreted through, moments from the distant past (and *vice versa*). To complement the 1453 commemorative parade, the Constantinopolitan Society organises speeches and produces publicity material expanding upon 'the significance of the Fall and the sacrifice of those who lost their lives' (Isaakidis 2014). Particular emphasis is placed on the last stand of Emperor Palaiologos and his soldiers on 29 May 1453, which was described as follows in a 2004 English-language flyer aimed at curious foreign tourists stumbling across the wreath-laying ceremony in Syntagma Square (and note the sense of immediacy and proximity conveyed by the use of the present tense):

> The Emperor Constantine Palaeologos fights his enemies bravely. There are only dead bodies of his soldiers around him. All the defenders are dead and the Emperor is completely by himself. He is badly wounded, full of blood, with torn clothes and he cries like Christ on the cross:
>
> 'Constantinople has fallen and I am still alive? Isn't there any Christian to take (cut) my head off?'
>
> Today, we Constantinopolitans, confer honour to Constantine Palaeologos and his soldiers.
>
> (Constantinopolitan Society 2004)

In such eulogies, it is frequently suggested that the defiant last stand of the emperor against the Ottoman Sultan in 1453 sowed the seeds for Greek revolution against the Ottoman Empire in 1821. Speaking at the commemorative ceremony in 2002, for example, the vice president of the Constantinopolitan Society Giorgos Gavriilidis addressed the following epitaph to the fallen emperor:

'The Third Fall' 147

Constantine Palaiologos we call you [the] Marbled [Emperor][3] but nevertheless immortal for ever, in mind, in soul, in our hopes and our dreams. Your heroic death gave courage, patience and fortitude under 400 years of slavery for the *éthnos*, so that the New Hellenic State would be reborn from its ashes.

(Gavriilidis 2002)

During the ceremony in front of the statue of Palaiologos outside the Metropolitan Cathedral in 2013, by which time the event was overseen by the Federation of Constantinopolitans (see below), a representative of a Laconian association in Athens[4] gave a similar speech in which he first equated Spartan resistance to the Persians in 480 BC with Byzantine resistance to the Ottomans in 1453, before linking both to contemporary Greek freedom. He characterised the Fall as 'the new Thermopylae where the enemy was allowed to pass only over the bodies of its defenders', and stressed:

If there had been no Leonidas or Palaiologos there would have been no 1821 and the freedom struggle that followed, there would have been no 'NO' [to the Italians] in 1940 and the resistance [to Axis] occupation, there would have been no free Greece.

(author's field notes 26/05/2013)

The expatriate newspapers have typically marked the anniversary in similar terms, tracing Greek insurrection against the Ottomans to the example set by Palaiologos on the walls of Constantinople in 1453. In 1973, for instance, *O Polítis* proclaimed:

The sacrifice of the Emperor was not in vain. The precious blood with which he watered that holy land sprouted the tree of freedom. Without the sacrifice there would have been no Resurrection [in 1821]. That sacrifice galvanised the souls of the Hellenes.

(*O Polítis* 1973)

In 1983, the newspaper comparably declared that the 'sacrifice of the Emperor was the seed for the resurrection of Hellenism' (*O Polítis* 1983), and again the following year wrote:

There in 1453, at the Gate of St. Romanus the Emperor Constantine, alongside other nameless heroes, with his heroic death, stood worthy for the *patrída*. He did not betray history and with his sacrifice cast the seed of the resurrection of Hellenism, which was reborn after 368 years with another sacrifice, this time in Fener, of the Patriarch Grigoris V.

(*O Polítis* 1984)

The newspaper *Palmós*, printed in Thessaloniki by the Union of Constantinopolitans of Northern Greece, wrote in similarly poetic terms in 1998:

Making a historical retrospection to the horrible day of 29 May we will see the shining example of sacrifice on the ramparts of the Queen of cities [i.e. Constantinople] by Constantine Palaiologos the last Hellenic emperor. His sacrifice became a legend and the legend brought about the rebirth of the *éthnos*. As a result today we live as free Hellenes.

(*Palmós* 1998)

Such discourses invert the analogy between 1453 and 1821 encapsulated in the older commemorative ceremony hosted in front of the statue of revolutionary fighter Kolokotronis, which subsumed the *Polítes* into an existing national narrative and silenced their local idiosyncrasy. Rather than basking in the reflected glory of the revolutionary heroes of 1821, these expatriate organisations put forward their own martyr–hero in the figure of the last Byzantine emperor, whose heroic sacrifice is presented as the spark that ignited the Greek Revolution. The putative ancestors of the *Polítes* are thus portrayed as the prototypical Greek freedom fighters, bestowing upon the expatriate community a privileged place within the national narrative. In this way, expatriate activists are able to out-manoeuvre their domestic detractors by staking a claim to Hellenic authenticity derived from the idiosyncrasies of their own local history (see also Chapter 3).

1453 and 1955

As we saw at the very beginning of the chapter, just as Byzantine resistance in 1453 comes to be seen as a rehearsal for Greek insurrection in 1821, so the Istanbul Riots are frequently portrayed as a reliving of the Fall of Constantinople. In a 1987 article, for example, *O Polítis* wrote:

The Hellenes of Constantinople, those uprooted from their homes during and after the wild persecutions of 6/7 September 1955 that they were subjected to by the Turks[,] will recall with pain the persecutions in the dark days that they lived in their historic birthplace, days that resemble the Fall, when the wild swarm of the Conqueror rushed into our Constantinople to loot.

(*O Polítis* 1987b)

More than simply implying, as in the above extract, a strong resemblance between these two events, such narratives commonly treat the *Septemvrianá* in 1955 as constituting the continuation or completion of the Fall of Constantinople that had begun in 1453. In 1978, *O Polítis* thus declared that '[o]n 29 May 1453 Constantinople was occupied politically. On 6 September it was occupied ethnically by the barbarian' (*O Polítis* 1978). In an interview with Greek newspaper *Ta Néa* in 1998, *Septemvrianá* victim Despoina Isaakidou similarly proclaimed that '[f]or me the Fall of Constantinople happened in '55. Because after those horrible events *Romiosýni* [i.e., in this case, the Greek population of Turkey] was roused, everyone left, [and] the uprooting happened' (*Ta Néa* 1998). Shifting the fall of the city from 1453 to 1955 in this manner not only restages the contemporary local experience of the Istanbul Riots in the guise of an infamous event from national history, but also carries an implied criticism of the Greek state. For if Constantinople fell not, as commonly supposed, in 1453 but in 1955, it follows that Greece gave the city up as lost prematurely when it might, even as late as 1955, have emulated the example of the Byzantines and resisted the Turkish 'occupation'.

By the logic of such equations, two events otherwise separated by 500 years and numerous differences in historical circumstance are reimagined as components of a single event. As Isaakidis of the Constantinopolitan Society put it, explaining the rationale behind publicity materials like the 1979 poster discussed above, 'we [always] write, "1453, 1922, 1941, 1942, 1955, 1964", and that is where the Fall finishes. It happened slowly' (Isaakidis 2014).[5] From this perspective, the Istanbul Riots came to be reframed in expatriate discourse as the 'Third Fall of Constantinople', the final act of a drama that was initiated in 1453 and for which the groundwork was prepared during the 'Second Fall' in 1923 when the city was passed from Allied control to that of the Republic of Turkey. On the 40th anniversary of September 1955, Archbishop Iakovos of America – who was born on Imbros in 1911 – accordingly penned an article about the *Septemvrianá* entitled 'The Third Fall' in Greek daily newspaper *Kathimeriní*. He wrote:

> Hundreds of shops were looted, whilst shopkeepers and employees were evicted and beaten and their merchandise burned to cinders. Churches and schools were looted and holy documents and books were given up to the flames and burned. So passed the third fall that was followed by the third refugee flight to Greece and the unjustifiable invasion of Cyprus and the occupation of two fifths of her land [. . .]
>
> The above lines are a sparing description of that abhorrent night of 1955, which in terms of persecution and plunder surpassed the night of St Bartholomew.
>
> (Archbishop Iakovos 1995)

Iakovos here conjured a memory of the *Septemvrianá* that is, to borrow terms from Silverman, 'contaminated by multiple elsewheres' (2013:5): the 1453 Fall of Constantinople, the 1922–1923 exodus of Greeks from Turkey, the 1974 conflict on Cyprus, and even the 1572 St Bartholomew's Day Massacre (on such transcultural cross-referencing, see Chapter 7).

James Young has observed that in Holocaust survivor Elie Wiesel's midrashic writings not only did religious texts provide him with a means to interpret his own contemporary trauma, but this trauma in turn led him to re-evaluate the ancient texts, such that 'his Holocaust experiences have had as great an effect on the ancient archetypes as the archetypes have had on his understanding of new experiences' (1990:106). In a comparable manner, the superimposition of 1453 and 1955 reconfigures the significance of *both* events. On the one hand, through its interpretation in terms of the Fall of Constantinople, the *Septemvrianá* ceases to be an isolated act of mob violence situated in the narrow context of policies undertaken by the then Turkish government or the burgeoning Greek–Turkish conflict over Cyprus, and instead becomes the 'Third Fall of Constantinople', the culmination of a sustained 'Turkish' assault on Greek Byzantine civilisation. In this sense, the Fall of Constantinople is not only remediated in these commemorative discourses, but also itself premediates memory of the Istanbul Riots, insofar as it acts as a paradigm 'to transform contingent events into meaningful images and narratives' (Erll 2009:114). This makes the comparatively less well-known events of 1955 recognisable and intelligible to a Greek domestic audience, casting the *Polítes* as victims of a barbaric Turkish other, and thereby furnishing expatriate organisations with a resonant language with which to narrate their displacement as a national martyrdom. If the archetype of 1453 thus makes the *Septemvrianá* more 'marketable' to an external audience, by the same token it renders it more 'thinkable' on an internal level, providing expatriate activists with a means to reconfigure raw personal experiences that defy simple exegesis into more readily graspable historical patterns that give that experience broader meaning and significance.

On the other hand, seen through the lens of 1955, the distant historical events of 1453 take on contemporary resonance and relevance, becoming, in Daniel Knight's terms, 'culturally proximate', insofar as they are evoked not simply as a dispassionate comparative framework, but because those concerned feel that they have in some sense relived the events of the past (2012:356). Personal memories of the Istanbul Riots are transposed onto, or superimposed over, the last stand of the city's defenders in 1453, such that individuals might come to speak or even feel as though they have a personal connection to events from the distant past. At the Constantinopolitan Society's 1981 memorial day, Greek journalist and invited speaker Giorgos Karagiorgas – who travelled to Istanbul in the immediate aftermath of the riots – closed his address by explicitly blurring 1453 and 1955, steeping his personal narrative in remediated language and imagery derived from archetypal representations of the Fall of Constantinople. He proclaimed:

> I have given to the photographs of Kaloumenos,[6] life as I tasted it in the streets of the city, in its alleys, when herds of breathless people ran hastily to avoid the slaughter, those hours of the second catastrophe of Hellenism after the Fall. And as then, the sun over Constantinople darkened, when the Queen of cities was delivered to the hands of the Turks, and I heard in those unspeakable hours a voice brought from THEN cry slowly and moan: 'sun shudder and earth groan, Constantinople has been overcome and the hour of our defence is over' . . .[7]
>
> The third night of the disaster fell. The dampness of the earth sent its heavy burnt scent across Constantinople. The fear of a repetition of the attack kept the Hellenes awake during the greater part of the night.
>
> (Karagiorgas 1981)

From this perspective, the commemoration of the Fall of Constantinople by expatriate organisations could be seen as a type of 'postmemorial work', in that it 'strives to *reactivate* and *re-embody* more distant political and cultural memorial structures by reinvesting them with resonant individual and familial forms' (Hirsch 2012:33). By identifying 1453 as their own, local historical heritage in this manner, these expatriate activists (and their Greek-born associates) simultaneously write themselves into a broader national history.

Yet the analogy between 1453 and 1955 is about more than simply establishing national inclusion. Although narratives of this kind are constructed in ostensibly normative forms, drawing heavily on recognisable nationalist rhetoric, they can nevertheless be deployed to express dissent from official readings of the past and to critique contemporary national diplomacy. In a document issued on the 39th anniversary of the Istanbul Riots, for instance, the Constantinopolitan Society made the following declaration:

> This year when we reach 39 years since the painful anniversary of the *Septemvriana* and 20 years since the invasion of Cyprus, Greece is obliged to not forget that there are still brothers of ours in their paternal lands who find themselves under the authority of Turkish politics and it [Greece] must follow a more dynamic politics.
>
> As the Constantinopolitan Society we once again this year address the Greek state and we exhort her to wake up and take responsibility for her obligations, because as a People we are strong and have both the power and the will to prevent the day from coming when we would shout alas! GREECE HAS FALLEN.
>
> (Constantinopolitan Society 1994a)

Mimicking the cry – 'Constantinople has fallen' – that purportedly rang out on 29 May 1453 when the walls of the city were breached (Runciman 1965:139), the Society suggested that if contemporary Greek diplomats did not follow the example set by Palaiologos and his fellow soldiers and take action on the perceived threat from Turkey, then ultimately Greece itself might fall to the Turks. In this sense, the Fall of Constantinople is transformed into a national morality tale, the defiant last stand of the Byzantines in 1453 serving as a critical mirror for a perceived *lack* of Greek diplomatic resistance in response to more recent crises such as that of 1955.

Transcending the national paradigm: the Federation of Constantinopolitans

In this chapter, I have focused primarily on commemorative events orchestrated by the Constantinopolitan Society. In the remainder of the chapter, I take a look at the more recent commemorative activities of the Federation of Constantinopolitans, which was established in 2006 with the aim of uniting all the expatriate associations in Greece and abroad, and providing a unified voice for the expatriate community (see Chapter 1). Although the Constantinopolitan Society is a founding member of the Federation, the two bodies put on separate events to mark the

152 *National and transnational histories*

anniversaries of 1453 and 1955, reflecting a divergent outlook on the future of the Greek community in Istanbul and Greek–Turkish relationships generally.

The Federation of Constantinopolitans has since 2010 pursued direct dialogue with the Turkish authorities, on matters such as the reissuing of Turkish citizenship to the expatriated Greeks and their descendants, the problems facing the Patriarchate and the Greek minority schools, and outstanding issues related to Greek property in Turkey (Ecumenical Federation of Constantinopolitans 2012:9; Ecumenical Federation of Constantinopolitans 2013b; Ecumenical Federation of Constantinopolitans 2015a:29–31; Ecumenical Federation of Constantinopolitans 2015b). Federation president Ouzounoglou explained the rationale of these negotiations to me as follows:

> We do not place our issues within national politics, because we do not believe in that road, but we take them [to the Turkish government] directly, because we are citizens of that country. Just because we are Hellenes does not mean that the Hellenic government has to express my opinions.
> (Ouzounoglou 2014a)

Ultimately, the Federation hopes that these talks will encourage Turkey to undertake 'a programme of repatriation, particularly for young people' in order to prevent the Greek community of Istanbul from disappearing entirely (Ouzounoglou 2014a).

The Constantinopolitan Society, by contrast, eschews direct communication with the Turkish authorities, maintaining that the plight of the Greek minority in Turkey is a component of Greek foreign policy and should therefore be discussed only through official diplomatic channels (Isaakidis 2014). In particular, the Society is concerned that Turkey might use such negotiations to turn the *Polítes* into a conduit for Turkish foreign policy, and thereby both damage the expatriates' reputation in Greece and weaken the diplomatic position of the Greek state (Constantinopolitan Society 2012b; Constantinopolitan Society 2013a; Constantinopolitan Society 2013c). They have protested, for instance, that the Federation's petition for Turkey to issue Turkish citizenship to the expatriates' descendants in Greece 'facilitates the plans of Turkish foreign policy to create a "Turkish colony" in Greece' (Constantinopolitan Society 2012b; Constantinopolitan Society 2013a). The Constantinopolitan Society is also comparatively sceptical about the feasibility of attaining lasting Greek–Turkish reconciliation, and of reinstating a sizeable Greek population in Istanbul, and considers an admission of responsibility on the part of the Turkish government to be a prerequisite for productive bilateral dialogue (Constantinopolitan Society and New Circle of Constantinopolitans 1997; Isaakidis 2014). As Isaakidis put it to me:

> A very simple thing that the Germans did, is that they asked for forgiveness from the Jews [. . .] For 30 years, we have been asking the Turks to ask for forgiveness, officially, for what they did. They do not even ask for

forgiveness from the Armenians. How can you become friends, when the other side does not take responsibility for the damage they have caused?
(Isaakidis 2014)

Accordingly, whilst the Society continues to organise its own memorial day for the *Septemvrianá*, the primary purpose of which is to keep the memory of 1955 in the forefront of Greek popular and diplomatic consciousness, the Federation has since 2008 marked the anniversary through an annual international conference that is more academic and scientific than commemorative (Ouzounoglou 2011). Rather than focusing on parallels with events from Greek national history such as 1453 or 1922, the Federation's conferences seek to identify commonalities between the Istanbul Riots and acts of anti-minority violence in other national contexts, in order to interrogate their common causes and consequences. The inaugural 2008 conference, for example, aimed 'to heighten international awareness of the mechanisms underlying acts of state-sponsored terrorism and ethnic cleansing as illustrated in the cases of *Septemvriana* (Istanbul, 6–7/9/1955), *Kristallnacht* (Crystal Night) (Germany, 8–9/11/1938) and other similar, but less well publicized, events' (Ecumenical Federation of Constantinopolitans 2008:104).

This reflects the Federation's belief that events like the Istanbul Riots 'had nothing to do with the Greek–Turkish bilateral relations but were related to the decline of the rule of law principles and democratic rights [in Turkey]' (Ecumenical Federation of Constantinopolitans 2013c). Between 2011 and 2014, the annual conferences similarly focused on how Turkey might provide remedy and reparation for the victims of the Istanbul Riots, in line with the United Nations' 2005 resolution (60/147) on the right for victims of human rights abuses to seek restitution within the framework of international law (Ecumenical Federation of Constantinopolitans 2013b; Ouzounoglou 2011; Ouzounoglou 2014b).

Although the Federation's anniversary conferences share with the Constantinopolitan Society's memorial days the stated aims of preserving the memory of the past and placing it within a wider historical framework, the reasons for doing so, and the salient framework to be used, are thus notably different. Whilst the Society believes that the experiences of the *Polítes* come firmly under the umbrella of a long-standing Greek–Turkish conflict, and therefore are best dealt with through a robust foreign policy, the Federation considers the issues facing the community as arising from a national homogenisation project connected with the decline of democracy and rule of law in post-1923 Turkey. Accordingly, in place of a language of national martyrdom, the Federation invokes a discourse of global human rights law.[8]

Since 2006, the Federation has also assumed responsibility for the ceremonial parade to commemorate the Fall of Constantinople. In principle, the format has remained largely unchanged, although the significance that the two organisations attach to the event differs somewhat. At the 2013 ceremony, for instance, speaking immediately before the Laconian representative who characterised the Fall as the 'new Thermopylae' (see above), Federation president Ouzounoglou placed

154   *National and transnational histories*

emphasis not on the connections between 1453 and Greek national freedom, but on the cultural contribution of Byzantium to contemporary civilisation. He told the gathering assembled at the statue of Constantine Palaiologos:

> The ultimate heroic resistance that was put up by the Hellenes of Constantinople, alongside their fellow fighters from the Christian West, has an exceptional significance for you to remember today, insofar as the defenders were fighting primarily not to protect the fortified Queen of cities, but for the values represented by its ancient tradition with its universal values. The defenders had a deep belief that they were the carriers of Christendom, of Orthodoxy, but also the synthesis of the Hellenic and Roman civilisation. That was the great historical achievement of the Eastern Roman Empire, that it created a synthetic universal civilisation [. . .] That is the primary reason why we are honouring Constantine Palaiologos and the fallen defenders after 560 years.
>
> (Ouzounoglou 2013)

The Constantinopolitan Society, meanwhile, has protested that under the auspices of the Federation the memorial ceremony no longer achieves the purpose that they had envisaged for it after 1978; that is, to stage a memorial day with the trappings of an official national holiday that would serve as a visible demonstration of the community's presence in Greece and emphasise their place within national history. In 2014, the Society accordingly wrote to the Federation expressing their disappointment with the level of attendance at the parade in recent years, maintaining that when they had organised the event they had always ensured a high turnout from members of the Society, 'exactly as happens at all national anniversaries' (Constantinopolitan Society 2014).

In line with these differing perspectives on the significance of the 1453 ceremonial parade, the Society and the Federation operate independent anniversary events, typically featuring talks by an invited speaker or speakers. These two events have much in common, but, as with the *Septemvrianá* commemorations, there are also perceptible differences to be discerned. On the 560th anniversary of the Fall of Constantinople in 2013, for instance, the Constantinopolitan Society hosted retired Greek general Frangoulis Frangos. His speech was preceded by greetings from the Society's president, who characterised the Fall as 'the most shocking event in the martyred journey of our race' (Lampidis 2013), and by the reading of a poem commemorating the heroic sacrifice of Palaiologos by *Prínkipos*-born poet Giorgos Aimilios Eden, accompanied by his daughter on the harp. In the first half of his talk, Frangos characterised Palaiologos as an exemplary Greek martyr whose sacrifice 'laid the foundations for the struggle in 1821' and 'inspires for all time the "NO" of Hellenism', before proceeding in the second half to advance the idea that a substantial population of crypto-Christians live in contemporary Turkey (Frangos 2013). His speech was later praised by the Society in the following terms: '[w]ith his directness of speech and the outspokenness that distinguishes him, he transported us to that ill-omened day, stressing that we must never forget all of the tragic events that followed up until today and sealed the fate of Hellenism, but also [that we must] demand our justice' (Constantinopolitan Society 2013b).

On the same day in 2013, the Federation – in conjunction with the municipality of *Palaió Fáliro*, a neighbourhood of Athens – hosted a talk by Greek professor of economics Michalis Psalidopoulos comparing the fall of various empires and nations from different eras. The event began with a memorial prayer to the fallen led by the bishop of *Palaió Fáliro-Néa Smýrni*, and an address by the mayor of *Palaió Fáliro*, who, according to a Greek journalist who was in attendance, emphasised that 'such historical moments must teach us about the mistakes that we made in the passing of the ages' so that they are not repeated in the future 'but, conversely, keep us united' (*Vima Online* 2013). After the main speaker, there was also a concert featuring the performance of dirges about the Fall of Constantinople (Ecumenical Federation of Constantinopolitans 2013a). This event seems to have been representative of the Federation's 1453 anniversaries more generally, in that whilst it incorporated aspects of a memorial day (such as the religious service) its scope extended beyond a narrow focus on Greek-Turkish relationships. If the Constantinopolitan Society is concerned principally with making the Fall 'culturally proximate' as a national trauma and cautionary tale for the future, in an effort to ensure that the *Polítes* are not sidelined in Greek history or diplomacy, the Federation of Constantinopolitans shows a greater interest in historicising the Fall, by viewing it within a broader historical context rather than primarily through the cipher of Greek national history.

Conclusions

In this chapter, we have seen that it is common for expatriate (and Greek-born) commentators to interpret the contemporary experiences of the Greeks of Turkey by analogic reference to archetypes from Greek national history. For expatriate activists, adopting such rhetoric provides a means to counteract their sense of marginalisation in Greek society and abandonment by Greek diplomacy. Drawing upon the coincidental numerical equivalence of Leonidas' Spartan warriors in 480 BC and Imbros' extant elderly Greek population after the 1970s, as well as perceived similarities between Turkish militarisation and resettlement policies on Imbros and Turkish military action in Cyprus in 1974, Imvrian activists can rewrite their own local suffering as a national drama. In like manner, by identifying themselves with the defenders of Byzantium in 1453, linking this defiant last stand to Greek Revolution in 1821, and delaying the ultimate Fall of Constantinople until their own experiences in 1955, the Constantinopolitan Society and other like-minded activists can portray the *Polítes* as both the prototypical Greek freedom fighters against, and archetypal national martyrs to, Turkish aggression and expansionism. By constructing linkages between their own experiences and seminal moments from Greek national history, these expatriate activists thus draw on the local particularities of their own communities to establish their belonging as part of the Greek *éthnos*.

If the examples presented here are thus ostensibly normative, replicating Greek nationalist rhetoric for inclusive purposes, they also, following Herzfeld, demonstrate that 'people know how to adopt the rhetoric of normativity in order to achieve non-normative ends' (1997:44). By casting themselves in the likeness of iconic and recognisable heroes and martyrs from the recent and distant national past, expatriate activists implicitly and sometimes explicitly cast aspersions on Greece's contemporary diplomatic record towards the Greeks of Turkey, indicating, for instance, that if the Greek state had resisted in 1955 as the Byzantines did in 1453 then the city might never have definitively 'fallen'. In any case, it is noteworthy that although 'the Turks' are superficially the chief antagonists in many of the narratives discussed above, efforts to mark the anniversaries of events like 1453 and 1955 have at least as much to do with expatriate complaints towards the Greek state, and a lack of awareness on the part of the Greek public, as with their grievances with Turkey. The fact that normative representations can sustain insubordinate discourses helps account for the resilience of national(ist) readings of the past, as even when expressing dissent from national policy or history local actors often rely upon a national interpretive framework. In this sense, expatriate activists might 'participate through their very discontent' (Herzfeld 1997:2) in the consolidation and perpetuation of the national frame of reference, reflecting Sutton's observation that 'even those [. . .] who implicitly or explicitly challenge the content of national history, do not [necessarily] challenge its form' (1998:128).

Though expatriate activists' uses of history in this chapter might often seem measured and deliberate – archetypes from the past conjured up in very particular contexts to serve quite clear discursive purposes – it may not necessarily follow that the past is being evoked cynically and dispassionately simply as expedient packaging for personal experience (Knight 2012:356; Schudson 1997:5, 15). In some of these cases, it may be that the individuals concerned not only saw *convenient comparisons* between different historical moments, but also felt that they were *reliving* – or were *fated* to relive – the events of the past (Knight 2012:356). From this perspective, widely available historical schemata might *implicitly* govern the reception and representation of new experiences in ways in which individuals are only partially in control (Erll 2011b:174; Schudson 1997:13). So, for instance, whilst comparisons between Imbros and Cyprus might in one sense be viewed as cynical attempts to harvest the widespread indignation in Greece about Turkish actions in order to generate sympathy for the struggles of the *Imvriótes*, it is also quite possible that omnipresent Greek media representations of unfolding events on Cyprus seemed so frighteningly plausible to Imvrian writers as a model for future experience on Imbros that they *presented themselves* as a 'common sense' frame of reference.

To borrow terms from Kostis Kornetis, however, in many of the instances discussed in this chapter the relationship to the past was marked less by 'proximity or affinity', as in Knight's case, and more by 'temporal and semantic distance' (2010:190–191). Indeed, it was in some ways the distance of 1453, and hence its hollowness and malleability, that made it a compelling interpretive framework for the contemporary experiences of 1955. In this case, the past, to paraphrase

Kornetis, was made present not in the form of detailed historical knowledge, but in terms of a more abstract repertoire of resonant symbols (2010:190). These symbols can then be applied to contemporary events in order to give broader meaning, significance, and intelligibility to personal experience, and are subsequently (and consequently) backfilled with personal resonance such that the events of the past *appear* temporally and semantically proximate. In this way, the palimpsestic relationship between 1453 and 1955 mutates the memory of both events: the Istanbul Riots become the Third Fall of Constantinople, directing their interpretation in terms of a diachronic and interminable Greek–Turkish conflict, whilst the Fall of Constantinople is reactivated but also absorbed by the more recent occurrences of 1955, obscuring much of what Erll 'might cautiously call the "original" or the "actual" events' from view (2011b:140–141). If the past thus indeed 'seeps into the cracks of the present' (Sutton 1998:210), equally the present seeps into the cracks of the past, as individuals attempt to make sense of their experiences, and make them intelligible to others, by thinking analogically.

As this chapter has sought to demonstrate, memory is from this perspective 'multidirectional' (Rothberg 2009) regardless of whether or not it happens to cross artificial ethnic or national borders. If, as Erll argued, 'all cultural memory must "travel" [. . .] in order to stay alive' – must, in other words, be repurposed or reused to transcend the original context of its articulation – it invariably follows that these travels consist 'only partly in movement across and beyond territorial and social boundaries' (2011a:12). Moreover, once we peer beneath its linear, unidirectional surface, we can perceive that national history is itself a palimpsest, drawing together, in the case presented here, such disparate times and places as fifth century BC Thermopylae, fifteenth-century Byzantium, mid-twentieth-century Istanbul, and late-twentieth-century Cyprus. It is through such multidirectional memory work that a group of expatriate activists excavates a commemorative niche within Greek memorial culture, reconfiguring the already well-trodden journeys across space and time carved out by national history. The national, then, is also fundamentally transcultural: in Jie-Hyun Lim's terms, '[t]he most frequent misunderstanding of nationalism is that nationalism is national' (2010:138).

The national palimpsest, nevertheless, is not the only mnemonic framework to which expatriate activists have recourse when narrating their experiences of persecution. We have already seen how the Federation of Constantinopolitans – less concerned with integrating the expatriates within Greek national history, and more interested in facilitating restitution, reparation, and repatriation within the framework of international law – typically structures its commemorative activities not so much through analogic reference to the national past, but by drawing connections across national boundaries in order to place the Greeks of Turkey within the context of global human rights discourse. In the next chapter, I turn my attention to such transcultural cross-referencing, demonstrating that memory is indeed a frequent flyer. I also observe, however, that the articulation of local experience within a transcultural frame of reference is far from incompatible with the maintenance of a national outlook or reading of the past, and may strengthen rather than undermine the assumptions of national(ist) historical narratives.

Notes

1 This is a fragment from the Epitaph of Simonides honouring the sacrifice of the 300 Spartans at Thermopylae.
2 Turkish military action on Cyprus in 1974 was codenamed 'Operation Attila'.
3 The emperor's body could not be found after the battle, giving rise to the legend that he was turned to marble by God and secreted near the Golden Gate, to one day arise and take back the city (Herrin 2008:319; Nicol 2002:101–102).
4 Who was in attendance, presumably, because Constantine had been the Despot of Morea at Mystra in Laconia before ascending to the throne in Constantinople.
5 These dates, in order, refer to the Fall of Constantinople, the exodus of Greek refugees from Turkey, the conscription of non-Muslims into forced labour battalions, the wealth tax, the *Septemvrianá*, and the expulsion of Greek citizens from Turkey.
6 Kaloumenos' photographs, which were taken in the aftermath of the *Septemvrianá* and documented the damage to Greek property and churches, constitute a significant part of the corpus of material used by the Constantinopolitan Society for the photographic exhibitions that are a central feature of their commemorative events (the photographs can be found in Kaloumenos 2001).
7 I cannot be sure of the precise provenance of the words quoted by Karagiorgas in this extract, but it seems probable that he intended to evoke similar words purportedly spoken by one Italian soldier to his brother on the walls of Constantinople on 29 May 1453 upon seeing that the Ottoman forces had breached the city's defences, as reported in the *Chronicon Maius*, an account of the Fall of Constantinople traditionally attributed to the Byzantine writer Georgios Sphrantzes but now thought to have been authored by Makarios Melissenos in the sixteenth century.
8 This is not to say that the Constantinopolitan Society necessarily eschews a more transnational frame of reference: see Isaakidis' comparisons with the Holocaust and the Armenian genocide, and Chapter 7.

References

(Items marked * are in the Greek language.)

Apogevmatiní. (1993). 'Constantinople has fallen', 6 September 1993.*
Archbishop Iakovos. (1995). September 1955: the third fall. *Eptá Iméres, Kathimeriní*, 10 September 1995. Reprinted in *O Polítis*, September 1997.*
Babül, E. (2006). Claiming a place through memories of belonging: politics of recognition on the island of Imbros. *New Perspectives on Turkey*, 34, 47–65.
Constantinopolitan Society. (1979). *The annihilation of the Constantinopolitans*. Poster. Constantinopolitan Society Archive.*
Constantinopolitan Society. (1994a). *Chronicle of the events of 6–7 September 1955*. Publicity pamphlet. Constantinopolitan Society Archive.*
Constantinopolitan Society. (1994b). Letter to Christos Naskas re. responses to questions, 2 September 1994. Constantinopolitan Society Archive.*
Constantinopolitan Society. (1998). Letter to *Synaspismós tis Aristerás kai tis Proódou* re. invitation to the event for the 545th anniversary of the Fall of Constantinople, 4 May 1998. Constantinopolitan Society Archive.*
Constantinopolitan Society. (1999). Letter to Archbishop Christodoulos re. invitation to the event for the 546th anniversary of the Fall of Constantinople, 19 April 1999. Constantinopolitan Society Archive.*
Constantinopolitan Society. (2004). *The conquer [sic] of Constantinople*. Publicity flyer, 6 June 2004. Constantinopolitan Society Archive.

Constantinopolitan Society. (2008). *Constantinopolitan Society: 1928–2008 80 years of contribution*. Athens: Constantinopolitan Society.*

Constantinopolitan Society. (2012a). *Constantinopolitan Society event for the Septemvrianá*. Press release, 11 September 2012. Available at: www.cpolitan.gr/news/εκδηλωση-συλλογου-σεπτεμβριανα [Accessed on 12 May 2014].*

Constantinopolitan Society. (2012b). *Response of the Constantinopolitan Society to the announcement of the executive committee of the Ecumenical Federation of Constantinopolitans and to the joint announcement of the Constantinopolitan Associations*, 5 November 2012. Available at: www.cpolitan.gr/wp-content/uploads/2012/11/apantisi-syllogou-pros-oiomko.pdf [Accessed on 12 May 2014].*

Constantinopolitan Society. (2013a). *Declaration and proposals of the Constantinopolitan Society to the general assembly of the Ecumenical Federation of Constantinopolitans on 19/01/2013*, 22 March 2013. Available at: www.cpolitan.gr/news/δηλωση-συλλογου-κωνσταντινουπολιτω [Accessed on 12 May 2014].*

Constantinopolitan Society. (2013b). *Event of the Constantinopolitan Society for the anniversary of 560 years since the Fall of Constantinople and the completion of 85 years since its foundation*. Press release, 30 May 2013. Available at: www.cpolitan.gr/news/εκδήλωση-επετείος-560-χρόνων-άλωση-πόλης [Accessed on 12 May 2014].*

Constantinopolitan Society. (2013c). *Declaration of the Constantinopolitan Society to the extraordinary general assembly of the Ecumenical Federation of Constantinopolitans on 12 October 2013*, 9 October 2013. www.cpolitan.gr/wp-content/uploads/2013/10/Cpolitan-12-10-2013.pdf [Accessed on 12 May 2014].*

Constantinopolitan Society. (2014). Letter to the Ecumenical Federation of Constantinopolitans re. the commemorative event for the Fall of Constantinople, 16 May 2014. Constantinopolitan Society Archive.*

Constantinopolitan Society and New Circle of Constantinopolitans. (1997). Letter to Dr. Gürbüz Çapan (Mayor of Esenyurt) re. declining invitation to Greek–Turkish reconciliation event in Istanbul, 2 September 1997. Constantinopolitan Society Archive.

Constantinopolitan Society, New Circle of Constantinopolitans, Association of Hellenic Citizens Expelled from Turkey, Union of Constantinopolitans of Northern Greece, Thracian Association of Imbros, Constantinople, Tenedos, and Eastern Thrace, and Society for the Advancement of National Heritage. (1995a). *40 years: 6–7 September 1955 Constantinople*. Publicity material and resolution issued by the organising committee. Constantinopolitan Society Archive.*

Constantinopolitan Society, New Circle of Constantinopolitans, Association of Hellenic Citizens Expelled from Turkey, Union of Constantinopolitans of Northern Greece, Thracian Association of Imbros, Constantinople, Tenedos, and Eastern Thrace, and Society for the Advancement of National Heritage. (1995b). *To protest the ethnic cleansing perpetrated by Turkey against the Greeks of Istanbul in 1955*. Resolution. Constantinopolitan Society Archive.

Constantinopolitan Society, New Circle of Constantinopolitans, Association of Hellenic Citizens Expelled from Turkey, Union of Constantinopolitans of Northern Greece, Thracian Association of Imbros, Constantinople, Tenedos, and Eastern Thrace, and Society for the Advancement of National Heritage. (1995c). *Constantinople memorial day 6–7 September 1955*. Invitation to the photographic exhibition at the War Museum. Constantinopolitan Society Archive.*

Constantinopolitan Society, New Circle of Constantinopolitans, Association of Hellenic Citizens Expelled from Turkey, Union of Constantinopolitans of Northern Greece,

160 National and transnational histories

Thracian Association of Imbros, Constantinople, Tenedos, and Eastern Thrace, and Society for the Advancement of National Heritage. (1995d). *Constantinople memorial day 6–7 September 1955*. Invitation to the photographic exhibition at the Cultural Centre of the City of Athens. Constantinopolitan Society Archive.*

Ecumenical Federation of Constantinopolitans. (2008). *Proceedings of international conference: Septemvriana 6-7/9/1955 an act of annihilation of the Greek community of Istanbul*. 13 September 2008. Athens. Available at: www.conpolis.eu/Septemvriana/2008/Πρακτικά%20Συνεδρίου%20Σεπτεμβριανών%20ΟΙ.ΟΜ.ΚΩ%202008.pdf [Accessed on 15 May 2014].

Ecumenical Federation of Constantinopolitans. (2012). *The Greek Orthodox minority of Turkey: history of human rights violations and the need of remedy and reparations*. PowerPoint presentation, May 2012. Available at: www.conpolis.eu/uploadedNews/Human%20rights%20of%20the%20Greek%20Orthodox%20minority%20of%20Turkey-May%202012b.pdf [Accessed on 15 May 2014].

Ecumenical Federation of Constantinopolitans. (2013a). *560th anniversary of the Fall of Constantinople*. Programme for the anniversary event. Available at: www.conpolis.eu/uploadedNews/Oi.Om.Kw%20Ekdiloseis%202013%20Alwsi.pdf [Accessed on 15 May 2014].*

Ecumenical Federation of Constantinopolitans. (2013b). *The petitions that have been submitted to the Turkish Government for restitution and remedy of the mass scale violations of human rights against the Greek-Orthodox community of Constantinople*. PowerPoint presentation at the Ecumenical Federation of Constantinopolitans event for the 58th anniversary of the *Septemvrianá*, 7 September 2013. Available at: www.conpolis.eu/uploadedNews/Presentation%20%207.9.2013.pdf [Accessed on 15 May 2014].*

Ecumenical Federation of Constantinopolitans. (2013c). *Statement of the administrative board of the Ec.Fe.Con done by its president Prof. Nikolas Uzunoglu towards the Minister of Foreign Affairs of Republic of Turkey Prof. Ahmet Davutoglu*, 13 December 2013. Available at: www.conpolis.eu/uploadedNews/Statement%20Meeting%20of%20Ec.Fe.Con%20with%20MFA%20of%20Turkey%20in%203%20languages.pdf [Accessed on 15 May 2014].

Ecumenical Federation of Constantinopolitans. (2015a). *60 years on from the 6–7 September 1955: the organised attack by the Turkish state with the aim of the annihilation of the Hellenism of Constantinople*. PowerPoint presentation at the Ecumenical Federation of Constantinopolitans event for the 60th anniversary of the *Septemvrianá*, September 2015. Available at: www.conpolis.eu/uploadedNews/H%20Tragiki%20Epeteios.3.pdf [Accessed on 15 May 2014].*

Ecumenical Federation of Constantinopolitans. (2015b). *60 years on from the pogrom of 6–7 September 1955 against the Greek-Orthodox community of Istanbul: time for remedy and reparation for the survival of the community*. PowerPoint presentation to the European Parliament, 12 October 2015. Available at: www.conpolis.eu/uploadedNews/European%20Parliament%20-%20Monday%2012%20October%202015.pdf [Accessed on 15 May 2014].

Emprós. (1955). History repeats itself, 10 September 1955.*

Erll, A. (2009). Remembering across time, space, and cultures: premediation, remediation and the 'Indian Mutiny'. In A. Erll and A. Rigney, (Eds.). *Mediation, remediation, and the dynamics of cultural memory*. Berlin; New York: Walter de Gruyter, 109–138.

Erll, A. (2011a). Travelling memory. *Parallax*, 17(4), 4–18.

Erll, A. (2011b). *Memory in culture*. Translated from the German by S. B. Young. Houndmills, Basingstoke; New York: Palgrave Macmillan.

Erll, A. and Rigney, A. (2009). Introduction: cultural memory and its dynamics. In A. Erll and A. Rigney, (Eds.). *Mediation, remediation, and the dynamics of cultural memory.* Berlin; New York: Walter de Gruyter, 1–11.

Frangos, F. (2013). *The fall of the Queen of cities and the crypto-Christians.* Speech at the Constantinopolitan Society event for the 560th anniversary of the Fall of Constantinople, 30 May 2013. Available at: www.youtube.com/watch?v=Wsp_H4IV-R8 [Accessed on 22 November 2015].*

Gavriilidis, G. (2002). *The siege and the fall . . . Constantine Palaiologos.* Speech at the Constantinopolitan Society event for the 549th anniversary of the Fall of Constantinople. Constantinopolitan Society Archive.*

Halstead, H. (2014). Harmony and strife in memories of Greek-Turkish intercommunal relationships in Istanbul and Cyprus. *Journal of Modern Greek Studies*, 32(2), 393–415.

Herrin, J. (2008). *Byzantium: the surprising life of a medieval empire.* London: Penguin.

Herzfeld, M. (1997). *Cultural intimacy: social poetics in the nation-state.* New York: Routledge.

Hirsch, M. (2012). *The Generation of postmemory: writing and visual culture after the Holocaust.* New York: Columbia University Press.

Imvriakí Ichó. (1974a). Cyprus and Imbros, July–August 1974.*

Imvriakí Ichó. (1974b). Our island is fading away forever, July–August 1974.*

Imvros. (1977). Events of July, June–July 1977.*

Imvros. (1978). The black anniversary of the Cyprus issue, June–July 1978.*

Imvros. (1991a). Greetings-message from the president of the executive committee, January–April 1991.*

Imvros. (1991b). Activities of the pan-Imvrian committee during the month of October, October 1991.*

Imvros. (1993). 70 years on from the Treaty of Lausanne, July–August 1993.*

Isaakidis, G. (2014). Interview with author. Athens, 22 March 2014.*

Kaloumenos, D. (2001). *The crucifixion of Christianity: the historic truth concerning the events in Constantinople of 6–7 September, 1955.* Athens.

Karagiorgas, G. (1981). Untitled. Speech at the Constantinopolitan Society event for the 26th anniversary of the *Septemvrianá*. Constantinopolitan Society Archive.*

Knight, D. M. (2012). Cultural proximity: crisis, time and social memory in central Greece. *History and Anthropology*, 23(3), 349–374.

Kornetis, K. (2010). No more heroes? Rejection and reverberation of the past in the 2008 events in Greece. *Journal of Modern Greek Studies*, 28(2), 173–197.

Lampidis, A. (2012). Greetings. Speech at the Constantinopolitan Society event for the 57th anniversary of the *Septemvrianá*, 10 September 2012. Available at: www.cpolitan.gr/events/ομιλία-λαμπίδη-σεπτεμβριανά-2012 [Accessed on 22 November 2015]*

Lampidis, A. (2013). Greetings. Speech at the Constantinopolitan Society event for the 560th anniversary of the Fall of Constantinople, 30 May 2013. Available at: www.youtube.com/watch?v=Wsp_H4IV-R8 [Accessed on 22 November 2015].*

Lampidis, A. (2014). Greetings. Speech at the Constantinopolitan Society event for the 561st anniversary of the Fall of Constantinople, 28 May 2014. Available at: www.cpolitan.gr/news/εκδηλωση-μνημησ-τησ-αλωσεωσ-τησ-πολησ [Accessed on 22 November 2015]*

Lim, J.-H. (2010). Victimhood nationalism in contested memories: national mourning and global accountability. In A. Assmann and S. Conrad (Eds.). *Memory in a global age: discourses, practices and trajectories.* Houndmills, Basingstoke; New York: Palgrave Macmillan, 138–162.

162 National and transnational histories

Nicol, D. M. (2002). *The immortal emperor: the life and legend of Constantine Palaiologos, last emperor of the Romans*. Cambridge; New York: Cambridge University Press.

O Polítis. (1973). 29 May . . ., June 1973.*

O Polítis. (1978). 6 September 1955, August 1978.*

O Polítis. (1979). A date of horror: the 6–7 September, September 1979.*

O Polítis. (1983). 29 May: the anniversary of the great sacrifice, May 1983.*

O Polítis. (1984). 29 May 1453, May 1984.*

O Polítis. (1987a). 29 May 1453 and Mystras, June 1987.*

O Polítis. (1987b). Opinions and thoughts, September 1987.*

O Polítis. (1988a). An eye on history that does not lie, September 1988.*

O Polítis. (1988b). An unforgettable night of terror, October 1988.*

O Polítis. (1990). The black anniversary of the *Septemvrianá*: the uprooting of Hellenism, October 1990.*

O Polítis. (1998). There are no Constantinopolitans who would not want to publicise the events. Interview with Mr. Giorgos Isaakidis, President of the Constantinopolitan Society, March 1998.*

Ouzounoglou, N. (2011). Greetings. Speech at the Ecumenical Federation of Constantinopolitans event for the 56th anniversary of the *Septemvrianá*, 10 September 2011. Available at: www.conpolis.eu/uploadedNews/Πρακτικά%20Ημερίδας%20Σεπτεμ%202011.pdf [Accessed on 2 December 2015].*

Ouzounoglou, N. (2013). Address at the statue of Constantine Palaiologos. Ecumenical Federation of Constantinopolitans ceremonial parade for the 560th anniversary of the Fall of Constantinople, 26 May 2013. Personal observation.*

Ouzounoglou, N. (2014a). Skype interview with author. Athens/York, 16 May 2014.*

Ouzounoglou, N. (2014b). Greetings. Speech at the Ecumenical Federation of Constantinopolitans event for the 59th anniversary of the *Septemvrianá*, 6 September 2014. Available at: www.conpolis.eu/uploadedNews/Praktika%20Hmeridas%20Septembriana%202014.pdf [Accessed on 2 December 2015].*

Palmós. (1998). 29 May 1453–29 May 1998, May–June 1998.*

Rothberg, M. (2009). *Multidirectional memory: remembering the Holocaust in the age of decolonization*. Stanford: Stanford University Press.

Runciman, S. (1965). *The Fall of Constantinople 1453*. Cambridge: Cambridge University Press.

Sarris, N. (2001). Foreword. In D. Kaloumenos. *The Crucifixion of Christianity: the historic truth concerning the events in Constantinople of 6–7 September, 1955*. Athens, 15–16.

Schudson, M. (1997). Lives, laws, and language: commemorative versus non-commemorative forms of effective public memory. *The Communication Review*, 2(1), 3–17.

Silverman, M. (2013). *Palimpsestic memory: the Holocaust and colonialism in French and Francophone fiction and film*. New York: Berghahn Books.

Sutton, D. (1998). *Memories cast in stone: the relevance of the past in everyday life*. Oxford; New York: Berg.

Ta Néa. (1998). The black September of '55, 12 January 1998.*

Tsimouris, G. (2001). Reconstructing 'home' among the 'enemy': the Greeks of Gökseada (Imvros) after Lausanne. *Balkanologie*, 5 (1–2).

Van Steen, G. (2010). *Liberating Hellenism from the Ottoman Empire: Comte de Marcellus and the last of the classics*. New York: Palgrave Macmillan.

Venezis, I. (1955). Tuesday, 6 September 1955. *Néa Estía*, 7 September 1955.*
Vima Online. (2013). They honoured the anniversary of the Fall of Constantinople, 3 June 2013. Available at: www.vimaonline.gr/20/article/11112/timhsan-thn-epeteio-ths-aloshs-ths-konstantinoypolhs [Accessed on 25 October 2015].*
Young, J. E. (1990). *Writing and rewriting the Holocaust: narrative and the consequences of interpretation*. Bloomington; Indianapolis: Indiana University Press.

7 *Kristallnacht* in Constantinople'
Parallel and analogous histories

In this chapter, I focus on how expatriate activists and writers, in their efforts to articulate and communicate their own narratives of persecution, frequently draw parallels and analogies between the experiences of the Greeks of Turkey and those of other communities, most notably Turkey's Armenian and Kurdish communities, and Europe's Jews. Such mnemonic cross-fertilisation supports the notion that representations of the past are commonly articulated within a transcultural field of reference, and that different histories of suffering need not necessarily be locked in a competition for primacy (Rothberg 2009:3–6). Indeed, my analysis lends credence to the suggestion that analogic thinking on a transcultural level might lead to the elaboration of solidarities between different victim communities, or even lay the groundwork for reconciliation between historical antagonists. At the same time, however, I demonstrate that memory's extraterritorial journeys do not necessarily have 'cosmopolitan' (Levy and Sznaider 2006) or even 'post-national' implications, and may frequently serve to consolidate rather than undermine national identities and intercommunal antagonisms. I suggest, moreover, that scholarship on transcultural memory would benefit from more explicitly recognising the variable strength and depth of the 'knotting' (Rothberg 2010:7; Silverman 2013:8) that connects different histories. This, in turn, may have implications for our understanding of how transcultural memory is experienced by individuals on local levels, and how it finds meaningful expression in their narratives and understandings of the past.

Parallel histories: Armenians and Kurds

As we have already seen, the newspapers *O Polítis* and *Ímvros* have since their foundation been engaged in a struggle to counteract the marginalisation of the Greeks of Turkey in Greek society, history, and diplomacy, and to preserve and publicise their memories of persecution in Greek, European, and international forums. These efforts often involve the adoption and adaptation of archetypes from Greek national history (see Chapter 6) and/or stereotypes of Turkish aggression or fanaticism (see Chapter 4), which can serve to give expatriate local histories national meaning and intelligibility by assimilating them to a broader, diachronic conflict between Greeks and Turks. For many expatriate activists, nevertheless, it also makes sense to interpret and present the persecution of the Greeks of Turkey within a broader frame of reference that includes the experiences of other minority communities in Turkey and the Ottoman Empire. In the mid-to-late 1970s, against the backdrop of the rise of the Kurdistan Workers' Party (PKK) and the Armenian Secret Army for the Liberation of Armenia (ASALA) as well as increasing activism by Armenian and Kurdish diaspora communities, expatriate newspapers began to carry sympathetic articles discussing the 1915 Armenian genocide, Armenian efforts to obtain international recognition for its occurrence, and the armed conflict between Turkey and the PKK. In 1975, for instance, *O Politis* responded to reports in the Turkish press that Armenian, Greek, and Kurdish diaspora groups were working cooperatively in opposition to Turkey, by declaring on its front page that Greeks should support the efforts of these other communities. This appeal for solidarity is couched in terms of commonality, the author paralleling the experiences of the Armenians and Kurds with those of the Greeks, and placing all three histories within the shared context of a long-standing Turkish strategy to remove non-Turkish peoples from its lands:

> It is about time for these two ancient peoples [the Armenians and the Kurds] to be vindicated. The Turkish chauvinists for centuries now since their arrival in Asia Minor, have thought of nothing but how to exterminate the ethnic groups that they found on the land that they conquered by fire and sword. The genocide of the Armenians 60 years ago is famous throughout the world just like the persecutions of the Hellenes and the Kurds whom for centuries the Turks have treated with so much moral and humane disregard, starting with that barbarous *devşirme* that formed the Janissaries, after the Fall of Constantinople and the dissolution of the Hellenic Byzantine Empire, the stronghold of this civilization.
>
> (*O Politis* 1975)

This article appeared in the specific context of discussion about intercommunal cooperation, but before long both the Armenians and the Kurds were making regular appearances in expatriate newspapers, even when the piece in question had no direct relevance to either community. In 1977, for example, *O Politis* printed an article entitled 'History Repeats Itself', which begins by enumerating ancient Greek victories against the Persians – the Battle of Marathon, the Battle of Salamis, and the campaigns of Alexander the Great and Eastern Roman Emperor Heraclius – before equating these confrontations with a contemporary conflict between Greeks and Turks. Within this protracted narrative of Greek–Turkish antagonism, the Armenians and Kurds feature as fellow victims of Turkish aggression:

> The place of the Great King [Persian Xerxes I] has been taken by the Turkish invader. For 500 years he has pillaged Hellenic Asia Minor and the Aegean. Various circumstances prevented Hellenism from giving the appropriate lesson to that conqueror. By contrast [due to] their conflicting interests various

[presumably Western] countries did not only support [the Turk] but also covered up the genocides he committed against the Hellenes, the Armenians, and the Kurds, genocides that still cast their shame on our world today. And we arrive at the drama of Cyprus and the disregard by the Turkish invaders of all of the votes and decisions of the United Nations [. . .] Kurds, Armenians and Hellenes ask for justice, awaiting the liberation of their lands on which they have inalienable rights.

(*O Polítis* 1977b)

Cutting across huge swathes of history, the author of this article drew equivalences between the Persian Wars, the 1919–1922 Greek–Turkish War, the Armenian genocide, the Kurdish–Turkish struggle, and Turkish military action on Cyprus in 1974, thereby crafting a simplified historical narrative that condenses centuries or even millennia into a straightforward clash between Greeks, Armenians, and Kurds (any historic enmities conveniently passed over) and oriental Turkish/Persian invaders. A comparable (if less chronologically ambitious) narrative was articulated in a 1983 *Imvros* article entitled 'From Lausanne to Cyprus', in which the author wrote of Turkish actions on Imbros:

Same formula, same execution. Lausanne [i.e. the Greek–Turkish population exchange] and afterwards our uprooting. Zürich [i.e. the agreements that established an independent Cyprus guaranteed by the UK, Greece, and Turkey] and then 40% of Cyprus under occupation. Similar of course applies both for the Armenians previously and the Kurds more recently [. . .] Turkey found in the following decade the opportunity to achieve the final blow on Imbros (the events of 1964, the expropriations, the closure of the schools, terrorism, and much more).

(*Imvros* 1983)

In this extract, the experiences of the Greek refugees from the Ottoman Empire in 1922–1923, the Greek Cypriots in 1974, the Armenians in 1915, and the Kurds in more recent decades are equated with those of the Greeks on Imbros after 1964, in an effort to demonstrate that the *Imvriótes* were simply one in a series of victims of a familiar Turkish tactic.

Comparisons with Armenian and Kurdish experience offer expatriate activists something that recourse to Greek national history alone could not: a means to make their own persecution more broadly recognisable and intelligible to non-Greek audiences. Correspondingly, the articulation of these parallel histories is particularly common in expatriate efforts to raise awareness internationally. In 1995, the Constantinopolitan Society – in conjunction with the New Circle of Constantinopolitans, the Association of Hellenic Citizens Expelled from Turkey, the Union of Constantinopolitans of Northern Greece, and two other organisations – marked the 40th anniversary of the *Septemvrianá* by issuing a resolution in English with the aim of exposing Turkey 'in the eyes of global opinion' (Constantinopolitan Society *et al.* 1995b). They wrote:

WE PROTEST Turkish expansionist policies, militarist practices and flagrant violations of international treaties regarding the basic human rights of minority populations as well as the ethnic cleansing this country is presently undertaking against minority populations such as the Kurds, the Armenians and the (remnants of) Greeks and a number of religious denominations which are denied the free assertion of their identity.

(Constantinopolitan Society *et al.* 1995b)

The cooperating Constantinopolitan organisations released a similar declaration in Greek, appealing 'once again to Greek and international Public Opinion, Governments, and Parliaments of all civilised countries' to recognise that 'even if Turkey tries to put on a European Mask, it continues to be indifferent and to unreservedly trample on human rights'. They condemned 'the ethnic cleansing programme of the Turkish government' that began with the Young Turk Revolution in 1908 and unfolded in several phases: 'the genocide of millions of Armenians, Hellenes and other people in Asia Minor'; Turkey's 'expansive politics, invading Iraq, as Cyprus in 1974 and Syria in 1938, with the intention on that occasion of exterminating the Kurds'; and '[t]he final phase [. . .] the annihilation of the Hellenism of Constantinople' (Constantinopolitan Society *et al.* 1995a).

In a 1994 English-language article, *Imvros* likewise published an appeal to international audiences that incorporated both the Armenians and the Kurds alongside the Greeks and Greek Cypriots as victims of Turkish actions:

[T]o the civilized World: the Treaty of Lausanne must be respected by Tur[key], RESPONSIBLE FOR TWO EXTERMINATIO[N]S in our century: of the Armenians in 1915, and of Greeks of Pontus in 1922. Although only 551 years dates the presence of the Turks in the land, that was glorified for 1000 years by the Byzantine Empire, and for another 1000 years before the [B]yzantines by the Ancient Greeks – now it is time for the Tur[key] to be initiated to the Civilization, guarantor of the human rights. IMBROS and TENEDOS, CYPRUS, the KURDS – a TOUCHSTONE fo[r] the Civilized World to taste his civilization.

(*Imvros* 1994c)

In a 1995 article discussing Turkey's relationship with the EU under the headline 'Let's Not Allow the European to Forget the Atrocities of the Turk', *O Polítis* similarly wrote, '[o]ur neighbours [i.e. the Turks] do not change tactic. Only the people and the victims change: Armenians, Greeks, Kurds' (*O Polítis* 1995). In 1997, meanwhile, it printed a gruesome cartoon in which a caricatured Turk, complete with fez and a blooded scimitar, stands at the gates of Europe proclaiming to be European, whilst behind him lie four severed heads labelled, respectively, as the Cypriots, the Kurds, the Armenians, and the Greeks (*O Polítis* 1997; see Figure 11). There is, in this illustration, no effort to prioritise the suffering of the Greeks – who, lying in the background, are in fact the least visible of the victims – because the implication that the 'true nature' of the Turks is hidden behind a

168 National and transnational histories

European façade is made more arresting by broadening the field of victims, and subsuming Greek victimhood within historical atrocities more recognisable to European ears.

By the 1990s, transcultural cross-referencing of this sort had become commonplace in formal expatriate discourse, persistently cropping up in discussions that largely remained focused on Greek suffering, often accompanied by little (if any) explanatory context. Expatriate writers were evidently confident that their readers would immediately appreciate the relevance of bringing up these two communities, so much so that they were often content simply to mention them in passing by name, as in a 1990 *Polítis* article that referred to the 'characteristic acquaintance of the Turkish race with genocide (*Hellenes, Armenians, Kurds*)', or a 1996 editorial from *Imvros* that characterised the uprooting of the *Imvriótes* as one of the '"works of love" of the Turks whose sensitivities have been registered in history towards the minorities of the twentieth century (*Armenians, Pontics, Hellenes, Kurds et cetera*)' (*Imvros* 1996; *O Polítis* 1990; my emphasis). Repeatedly name-dropped as fellow sufferers of Turkish atrocity, the Armenians and Kurds became part of a regular cast of persecuted minorities totemically cited by expatriate writers whenever they had cause to articulate their own grievances with Turkey. The Armenian genocide and the Kurdish–Turkish conflict fill in the empty background space surrounding seminal moments in Greek national history, thereby providing expatriate narratives of persecution with greater spatial breadth and temporal depth. The memories of others serve as tropes through which expatriate writers seek to validate, explicate, and communicate their own experiences and ideological stances, both to themselves and to unfamiliar third-parties, and to reassure themselves that they have not suffered alone, but are rather victims of a diachronic Turkish policy of national homogenisation.

Figure 11 'Open the gate. I'm a European!' Cartoon by Zavikos from *O Polítis* November 1997.

Copyright Ekdóseis Tsoukátou. Reproduced with permission.

Analogous histories: Jews and Nazis

The parallels that expatriate writers draw between their own persecution in the 1950s, 1960s, and 1970s and that of the Armenians earlier and the Kurds (primarily) later suggest that memory of the Holocaust may not be unique in offering persecuted communities a point of reference through which to understand and represent their experiences. Nevertheless, in this case at least, we are dealing with regional rather than global touchstones, and with the Armenian genocide and the Kurdish–Turkish conflict as metonyms for *Turkish* atrocity rather than atrocity *per se*. In this sense, the examples presented above are somewhat different from Alexander and Levy/Sznaider's description of the Holocaust as a global 'cosmopolitan' memory (2006), and even from the characterisation by Silvana Mandolessi and Mariana Eva Perez of 'the disappeared' (see Chapter 5) as a diffuse figure in both Latin America and Spain (2014:610), in that the symbols derived from Armenian and Kurdish experience still remain interconnected and rooted in a particular geographic context. I treat these examples as transcultural articulations of memory, in that they involve reaching across significant (and, in some cases, antagonistic) cultural and national boundaries, but, to varying degrees, they are also *entangled* histories, particularly in the case of the Armenians and the Ottoman Greeks, insofar as they unfolded largely within the common context of the dissolution of the Ottoman Empire and Turkish nation-building.

A perception of the Holocaust as 'a standard of evaluation for judging the evility of other threatening acts' (Alexander 2009:58), however, does sometimes incline expatriate activists to draw analogies between Turkish actions and the Nazi genocide. In a 1979 article entitled 'the Holocaust', for example, *O Politis* paralleled the experiences of the Greeks and the Jews as victims of persecution, and likened the Turks to the Germans as perpetrators of genocide (*O Politis* 1979). Under the heading 'And Yet . . . The Nazi-esque Crimes Continue', a 1985 *Politis* article similarly 'established polluting analogies with Nazism' (Alexander 2009:45) by rhetorically asking its readers:

> What differences are there between the Nazi crimes and those that have been committed and continue to be committed, for twenty years now, against the Cypriots by the Turks? Perhaps Turkey is excused, as the first teacher of genocide, with the extermination of the Armenians, whose blood still asks for justice, and we must leave her free to commit crimes against humanity?
> (*O Politis* 1985)

In June 1988 the newspaper likewise stated that Turkish military action on Cyprus in 1974 'resembles Nazi methods, such as when Hitler attacked Czechoslovakia to liberate, allegedly, the Sudeten Germans', and in April 1994 commented that the recent arrest of seven Kurdish deputies by Turkey 'takes us back to the era of Hitlerism' (*O Politis* 1988a; *O Politis* 1994).

As well as such general comparisons between Turks and Nazis (and occasionally between Greeks and Jews), expatriate activists also sometimes make more explicit analogies between Nazi violence and the persecution of the Greeks of Istanbul/Imbros. A 1992 English-language article in *Imvros* aimed at second-generation *Imvriótes* living outside Greece thus dubbed Turkish actions on Imbros the '"final solution"' for the island, whilst in a 1993 speech reprinted in *Imvros* one prominent member of the Imvrian Association declared that Turkish policy towards the Greeks of Imbros was so crafty that 'even Hitler's Nazi regime against the Jews would envy it' (*Imvros* 1992b; *Imvros* 1993). In a 2015 press release coinciding with the 60th anniversary of the Istanbul Riots, the Constantinopolitan Society likewise wrote that the *Septemvrianá* 'can be compared only to the atrocities of the Nazis of Germany' (Constantinopolitan Society 2015). Levy and Sznaider suggested that because 'Jewish victims can come to represent victimhood in general' it becomes possible for 'diverse oppressed groups to recognize themselves in the role of the Jewish victims' (2006:43, 46). Equally significant, however, is that diverse oppressed groups can also recognise their antagonists in the role of the Nazis, and thereby establish the culpability and villainy of their oppressors within a widely-intelligible narrative framework. Indeed, expatriate activists generally seem more concerned with establishing the comparability of Nazi and Turkish villainy than of Greek and Jewish victimhood, and for the most part these discourses do not lead to the sort of explicit solidarities seen in relation to the Armenians and the Kurds, nor to any consideration of the specific fate of the Greek Jews during the Second World War (something about which there has been considerable public silence in Greece (Droumpouki 2016)). In this context, it is curious to note that the Jews as a minority community *within Turkey* are not very commonly mentioned by expatriate activists, in spite of a history of anti-Semitic persecution in Republican Turkey (though there are some exceptions, for instance a 1991 *Polítis* article that made reference to the persecution of the Jews in Eastern Thrace in the late 1930s, and noted that the 1942–1944 discriminatory wealth tax was directed 'against the Hellenes, Jews and Armenians' (*O Polítis* 1991b)).

The Federation of Constantinopolitans persistently deploys one particular analogy with Nazi violence: the comparison between the Istanbul Riots and *Kristallnacht*. The Federation likened these two events in their inaugural annual conference to mark the anniversary of the *Septemvrianá* (see Chapter 6), observing in the conference proceedings that the Istanbul Riots have been 'described by some as the "*kristallnacht of Romiosyni*"' (Ecumenical Federation of Constantinopolitans 2008:104). In 2013 and 2014, the Federation pursued this comparison further by advertising the annual conference as the 'anniversary of the *Kristallnacht* 6–7/9/1955 for the Hellenism of Constantinople' (Ecumenical Federation of Constantinopolitans 2013; Ecumenical Federation of Constantinopolitans 2014b), and in public presentations consistently draws attention to similarities between the two events. A 2007 English-language PowerPoint presentation available on the organisation's website, for instance, contained a slide that made the following observations:

THE SIMILARITY OF THE 'SEPTEMBRIANA' WITH THE KRISTAL NIGHT OF NAZI GERMANY

- There is a very high degree of similarity between the Kristal Night Riots [that] occurred against the Jewish Minority in Nazi Germany in 8–9/11/1938 and the Events of 6–7/9/1955 in Constantinople.
- The similarities are:
  - The involvement of Provocation
  - Action of Para-state mechanisms and use of storming troops
  - Attack to pre-marked shops and houses
  - The attack to sacred Places and Cemeteries
  - The orders of not massacres [i.e. instructions to rioters not to kill anyone]

(Ecumenical Federation of Constantinopolitans 2007)

The next slide of the presentation staged a photographic dialogue between *Kristallnacht* and the *Septemvrianá*, juxtaposing an image of the broken shop window of a Jewish business in Berlin in 1938 with one depicting rioters throwing merchandise from a shop into the streets of Istanbul in 1955, and a photograph of the ruined Fasanenstrasse Synagogue in Berlin with one of Patriarch Athenagoras I standing in the looted Church of Saints Constantine and Helen in Istanbul. In another PowerPoint authored in 2012, the Federation similarly wrote that the 'size of the pogrom is comparable to the Crystal Night in Nazi Germany against the Jewish community 9–10 November 1938', whilst in a 2014 presentation marking the 50th anniversary of the 1964 expulsions the Istanbul Riots were described as 'very much resembling the 1938 Crystal Night in Nazi Germany' (Ecumenical Federation of Constantinopolitans 2012:2; Ecumenical Federation of Constantinopolitans 2014a).

The Federation maintains that identifying commonalities between events like 1938 and 1955 might contribute to academic understanding of how state-sponsored acts of mob violence are organised and put into practice, in order that similar incidents might be averted in the future (Ecumenical Federation of Constantinopolitans 2008:104). Perhaps equally significantly, however, analogies between 1938 and 1955 can be seen as part of the Federation's efforts to separate the Istanbul Riots from narrow association with Greek–Turkish bilateral relationships, and instead to place the events within a broader framework of ethnic cleansing and human rights discourses, hoping in this way to secure greater international recognition and bolster claims for restitution (see also Chapter 6). From this perspective, presenting the Istanbul Riots as 'Kristallnacht in Constantinople' could be described as a process of 'remediation' by which an older mnemonic form is 'repurposed' in order to 'to make sense of "new" and different experience' and to 'make the past intelligible' (Erll 2011a:14; Erll 2011b:143; Erll and Rigney 2009:5), both for those who were there (insofar as it provides an established language and imagery through which to interpret and represent their experiences) and for unfamiliar external audiences (who, in the West at least, are more likely to

172 *National and transnational histories*

be familiar with *Kristallnacht*, and for whom the comparison will likely direct an interpretation of the *Septemvrianá*). This explanation was put forward by former president of the Constantinopolitan Society Isaakidis in his interview with me, discussing the challenges faced by expatriate activists seeking to raise European and international awareness about the Istanbul Riots:

> The whole world knows about the Jews. There is not a corner of the world that does not know that the Jews were burned by the Germans. About the rest? About the Roma, the homosexuals, about Greece that they burned, about Yugoslavia that they destroyed, about Russia where they killed 3 million. Next to the Jewish Holocaust, that – nobody knows [. . .] Somebody from China, for instance, will not know about the slaughter of the Armenians or the Christians of Anatolia, but he knows that the Jews were burned in Germany [. . .] For someone who is foreign, a third party, one must make a comparison.
> (Isaakidis 2014)

I indicated earlier that the drawing of parallels between Armenians, Greeks, and Kurds is somewhat different from analogies with the Holocaust, insofar as the former are also to a significant degree entangled histories. Interestingly, however, it is apparent that many expatriate activists do not see Turkish violence and Nazi violence as altogether disconnected. Federation president Ouzounoglou, in particular, has sought to emphasise that the 'amazing similarity' in terms of techniques and execution between the events of 1955 in Istanbul and those of 1938 in Germany might reflect a direct knowledge exchange between the SS organisers of *Kristallnacht* and the architects of the Istanbul Riots (Ouzounoglou 2013; Ouzounoglou 2014). Likewise, it is sometimes suggested by expatriate activists that the Nazis took inspiration from the Turkish genocide of the Armenians in their own efforts to destroy Europe's Jews. Isaakidis, for instance, seeking in his interview with me to convey the importance of preserving the memory of past persecution, paraphrased the infamous quotation from Hitler's 1939 Obersalzberg Speech in which the Nazi leader supposedly suggested that the world had already forgotten the slaughter of the Armenians (and, by implication, would thus also forget the Nazis' planned destruction of the Poles) (Isaakidis 2014). In a 1977 article, *O Polítis* similarly associated Nazi actions with the example set by the Turks in 1915, writing:

> The Armenian genocide found its imitator in the face of Hitler who followed the Turkish example with the genocide of the Jews during the Second World War. Another genocide was committed by the Turks against the Cypriot people, and by the very same [Turks] human rights have been flagrantly violated in Cyprus, Constantinople, Imbros, [and] in Anatolia against the Kurds.
> (*O Polítis* 1977a)

In this sense, expatriate activists may not simply be seeing a passing resemblance between these two histories, but rather envisaging them as interconnected through

'Kristallnacht *in Constantinople*' 173

a multidirectional network of genocidal violence (and possibly genocidal prototypes) that transcends national and territorial boundaries.

Asymmetric histories: the Western Thracian minority

There is one other community that makes regular appearances in formal expatriate discourse: the Turks/Muslims of Western Thrace, exempted from the 1923 Greek–Turkish population exchange as a counterweight to the Orthodox Christians of Istanbul, Imbros, and Tenedos. Officially characterised as Muslims by the Treaty of Lausanne, the composition and nomenclature of this community is highly contested: Greece typically resists the appellation 'Turkish minority', preferring to classify the entire community as the 'Muslim minority' and/or to emphasise its multi-ethnic character (Turks, Slavic-speaking Pomaks, Roma), whilst Turkey refers to the whole community as the 'Turkish minority', considering sub-groups such as the Pomaks to be Turks (Akgönül 1999:16; Demetriou 2006:298; Dragonas 2012:140). Perhaps unsurprisingly, many expatriate activists follow the Greek convention, referring to the minority as the Muslims of Western Thrace. Members of the Western Thracian minority have their own grievances with their treatment by the Greek state, particularly as regards denial of ethnic identity, restrictions on freedom of movement, deprivation of citizenship, interference in religious institutions, and difficulties associated with education, driving licences, buying land/property, and rebuilding/repairing mosques and minority schools (see, for instance, Akgönül 1999; Alexandris 2004; Helsinki Watch 1990; Oran 2004).

In contrast to the discourses of solidarity and commonality aimed at the Armenians and Kurds, expatriate activists' comparisons between their own experiences and those of the minority in Western Thrace most often fall under the rubric of what Rothberg calls 'competitive memory' (2009:3). In the expatriate newspapers, such comparisons commonly emerge in response to claims about the persecution of the Western Thracian minority made elsewhere (for instance, in the Turkish press, by Turkish politicians, or occasionally in international forums: in 1991, *Ímvros* reprinted a letter signed by the Pan-Imvrian Committee[1] to *The Guardian* responding to comments made in that newspaper by Dr Ahmet Sadık, a Greek MP and prominent member of the Western Thracian minority (*Ímvros* 1991)). Typically, these articles involve some combination of the following: 1) a statistical demographic comparison (i.e. that since the Treaty of Lausanne the number of Orthodox Christians in Turkey has declined from over 100,000 to only a few thousand, whereas the Muslim population of Western Thrace has remained more or less stable at 110,000, which, in the words of one writer in *O Polítis*, 'prove[s] that the human rights of the Muslim minority have never been deprived' (*O Polítis* 1991b));[2] 2) the accompanying suggestion that the present-day populations should be equalised ('[e]ither all of the Muslims of W. Thrace will leave or the Hellenes of Constantinople will remain and even increase in number', as one writer for *O Polítis* put it (*O Polítis* 1982); 3) a blanket statement asserting, along the lines of the following example, that members of the minority in Western Thrace 'have all of the freedoms and rights of all other Greek citizens';

4) an enumeration of the injustices experienced by the Greeks of Turkey, often juxtaposed to the freedoms allegedly enjoyed by the minority in Western Thrace; and/or 5) a denunciation of Turkish hypocrisy in protesting about Greek actions in Western Thrace whilst remaining silent on the treatment of non-Muslim minorities in Turkey. Rarely is there any concerted effort to engage with the specific complaints of the Western Thracian minority, which are dismissed as trivial as compared to those of the Greek minority in Turkey.

To give an illustrative example, in March 1992 *Imvros* printed a satirical list of "'rightful'" (in scare quotes) demands for the minority in Western Thrace, seeking to highlight what the author saw as the asymmetrical experiences of the two minority communities exempted from the 1923 population exchange. The list contains nine types of discrimination experienced by the Greeks of Turkey that the author, directly addressing the minority in Western Thrace, inverts as supposed justification for that community's grievances with the Greek state. These include:

> [. . .] 2. You are right to protest, because:
>
> The Greek State never IMPOSED ON YOU A SPECIAL WEALTH TAX – CALCULATED ARBITRARILY IN SUCH A WAY AS TO GUARANTEE YOUR ECONOMIC ANNIHILATION, SELECTIVELY, BECAUSE YOU ARE MUSLIMS.
>
> Turkish example: 'VARLIK VERGISI' [i.e. the wealth tax], 1942 [. . .]
>
> 3. You are right to protest, because:
>
> Hordes of indignant Greek citizens, directed by state agencies, never DESTROYED IN ONE NIGHT ALL OF YOUR LIVELIHOOD – YOUR HOMES, SHOPS, FACTORIES, MOSQUES, SCHOOLS, GRAVEYARDS, NOR RAPED YOUR DAUGHTERS AND WIVES, NOR BURNT ALIVE ANY OF YOUR MUEZZINS.
>
> Turkish example: SEPTEMVRIANA 1955 [. . .]
>
> 5. You are right to protest, because:
>
> The Greek State never EXPROPRIATED WHOLE VILLAGES OF YOURS IN ORDER TO CONVERT THEM INTO OPEN PRISONS.
>
> Turkish example: Imbros, 1970s [. . .]
>
> 6. You are right to protest, because:
>
> The Greek State never GUIDED SO-CALLED PATRIOTS WITH RABID HATRED AND PASSION TO STOP YOU IN THE ROAD AND TO FORBID YOU FROM SPEAKING TURKISH AMONGST YOURSELVES.
>
> TURKISH EXAMPLE: 'VATANDAS TÜ[R]KÇE KONUŞ!' [i.e. the 'Citizen, speak Turkish!' campaign] [. . .]
>
> (*Imvros* 1992a)

On rarer occasions, some expatriate activists are prepared to depart from such discourses of incomparability, and to explicitly recognise the potential for expressing common cause with the minority in Western Thrace (at least rhetorically). In 1994, the Pan-Imvrian Committee wrote an open letter to Deniz Baykal, then leader of the Republican People's Party in Turkey, after hearing that he would be visiting the minority in Western Thrace. The Committee expressed their desire to meet with Baykal and representatives of the Western Thracian minority, in order to 'assure you that *together* we will demand the full application of the principles and terms of the Treaty [of Lausanne] on the part of the Hellenic government' (my emphasis). By the same token, the Committee also called on Baykal and the Western Thracian representatives to accompany them on a visit to Imbros and Tenedos, and reciprocally to assist the Committee in appealing their case to the Turkish government. The letter concluded by drawing a parallel between the two minorities: '[j]ust like the Muslims of Thrace so we, the *Imvriótes* and *Tenédioi* [i.e. the Greeks of Tenedos], are determined to claim our rights, exactly as derived from the Treaty of Lausanne' (*Imvros* 1994a). In this particular case, the Pan-Imvrian Committee was able to move away from a competitive narrative of asymmetry for the sake of issuing a compelling and deft appeal for action on anti-minority persecution. Such an approach, nevertheless, does appear to be something of an exception rather than the norm in formal expatriate discourse, and most often comparisons between the two Lausanne minorities lead not to mutual recognition of injustice within a shared context of Greek/Turkish nationalism and nation-building, but rather to the competitive weighing up of experiences of persecution.

From 'pogrom' to 'genocide': classifying the persecution of the Greeks of Turkey

As well as making these explicit comparisons between their own experiences and those of other communities, expatriate activists also sometimes implicitly place their narratives within a transnational frame by borrowing terminology developed in other contexts to classify or categorise Turkey's actions against its Greek minority. In formal writing, as well as in many oral testimonies, it is common for *Polítes* to refer to the *Septemvrianá* as a 'pogrom', adopting terminology originally associated with anti-Jewish violence in the Russian Empire but used in this case (as in contemporary general usage more widely) as a descriptor for a planned attack on an ethnic/religious group. More rarely, some *Polítes* refer to the Istanbul Riots as 'a night of St Bartholomew', using the 1572 St Bartholomew's Day Massacre of Huguenots as shorthand for a targeted and religiously motivated assault. In the October 1988 edition of *O Polítis*, for example, a regular contributor and witness to the *Septemvrianá* wrote, 'I remembered, today 6 September 1988, the night of horror of 6–7.9.1955, which I lived and suffered, as all of [my] fellow citizens, in Constantinople, that night of St Bartholomew' (*O Polítis* 1988b). In the testimonial compilation *Septemvrianá 1955*, one anonymous witness similarly commented, '[f]rom the *Septemvrianá* of 1955 I have a lot to write.

176 *National and transnational histories*

It was a night of St Bartholomew', whilst another declared, '43 years have passed since then, but those who experienced the night of St Bartholomew first-hand hold onto the memory' (Ekdóseis Tsoukátou 1999:97, 181). This particular analogy may well originate in an article written by Andreas Lampikis on 10 September 1955 in the Istanbul-based Greek-language newspaper *Eléftheri Phoní*, in which he characterised the riots as the 'night of St Bartholomew of *Romiosýni* [see glossary]' (Alexandris 1992:261; Sarioglou 2015:86).

Yiannis Papadakis has drawn attention to the tendency, in the aftermath of the wars in Yugoslavia in the 1990s, for Greek and Turkish Cypriots on both official and popular levels to adopt the term 'ethnic cleansing' to describe events on Cyprus, particularly when attempting to appeal to 'outside powers' or to 'official, or other, ears' (2004:16). In the mid-1990s, some activist *Polítes* and *Imvriótes* followed suit, making use of rhetoric that, in Papadakis' terms, 'has the advantages of being established, well known and difficult to refute or disavow, since it is itself used by those towards whom it is addressed' (2004:16). In 1994, for instance, the president and the general secretary of the Imvrian Association published an appeal to the Greek government in the pages of *Imvros*, in which, amongst other things, they called on Greece to denounce on an international level the ethnic cleansing undertaken by Turkey on Imbros and Tenedos (*Imvros* 1994b). As we saw earlier in this chapter, the Constantinopolitan Society and its associates likewise adopted the language of ethnic cleansing in both Greek and English-language declarations issued on the 40th anniversary of the *Septemvrianá* with the aim of influencing domestic and international public opinion (Constantinopolitan Society *et al.* 1995a; Constantinopolitan Society *et al.* 1995b).

Expatriate activists also occasionally (and typically somewhat cautiously) use the term 'genocide' to refer to their own persecution. For example, in a 1973 article responding to Turkish complaints about the treatment of the minority in Western Thrace, *O Polítis* accused Turkey of committing 'the genocide of Imbros'; in 1984 it characterised the 1941–1942 conscription of non-Muslims into forced labour battalions as an attempt to conduct 'a "mini genocide" of the *Romioí* in the depths of Anatolia', foiled only by 'the victory of the Allies against [the Turks'] "soulmate" the Nazis'; and in 1991, in an article accusing Turkey of agitating the minority in Western Thrace, the newspaper referred to the Turks as 'those responsible for genocides from Erzurum [i.e. the Hamidian Massacres of Armenians] to Imbros and from *Sampsoúnta* [Samsun, i.e. massacres of Pontic Greeks] to Constantinople' (*O Polítis* 1973; *O Polítis* 1984; *O Polítis* 1991a). Towards the end of the article 'From Lausanne to Cyprus' (mentioned above), *Imvros* likewise labelled the persecution of the *Imvriótes* 'our genocide' (*Imvros* 1983).

Generally, however, expatriate activists shy away from explicitly labelling the persecution of the Greeks of Istanbul and Imbros as 'genocide', much to the irritation of Vasilis Kyratzopoulos, an outspoken expatriate from Istanbul and writer for the nationalist website *Antívaro*. In his 2006 book *Unregistered Genocide: Constantinople September 1955*, Kyratzopoulos wrote disapprovingly of the tendency for Greek and foreign writers to use the terms 'pogrom' or '*Kristallnacht*' to characterise the *Septemvrianá*, which, he felt, generated a distorted impression of the Istanbul Riots, and risked obfuscating the particularity of the experiences of the Greeks of Turkey as compared to those of the Jews in Russia and Germany (2006:22, 77–79). Amongst other reasons, and with an often startling and provocative disregard for historical accuracy, he objected to the label 'pogrom' on the basis that the Jews in Russia had immigrated from abroad whilst the Greeks in Istanbul were indigenous, and to the moniker '*Kristallnacht*' because the perpetrators in Germany were primarily members of the Nazi party whereas those in Istanbul came from various strata of Turkish society and had different ideological dispositions (2006:77–78). He suggested that the *Polítes* are wrong to assume that 'because I am alive, there was no genocide', and argued that the *Septemvriuná* should instead be classified as a genocide in terms of international law (Kyratzopoulos 2006:20, 23). He accordingly embarked upon an extensive effort to demonstrate how the Istanbul Riots, along with other measures targeting the Greeks of Turkey, satisfied the definitions of genocide as laid out by the International Criminal Court and by Genocide Watch (Kyratzopoulos 2006:100–103, 115–131; see also de Zayas 2007), which finished with a controversial (to say the least) statistical comparison with the Holocaust and the Rwandan genocide:

> [L]et's compare in numbers the Genocide of the *Septemvriuná* with its counterparts of the Holocaust (1933–1945) and Rwanda (1959–1963, 1993–1994).
>
> During the Holocaust the Jewish population was to be found in the lands of 33 modern-day European countries. The number of their victims ranges from 3,800,000 to 6,500,000. Taking into account both of these figures, and the number of Jews who live today in the same areas (1,375,000), we see that around 3% of the population is Jewish. So, by 2005 the Jewish population had been replenished by between 21% and 36% respectively.
>
> At the beginning of the 1990s the population of Rwanda amounted to around 7,000,000 of which around 1,800,000 were Tutsi. Today, the number of Tutsi amounts to 1,250,000 around 15% of the total population. The population has been replenished by 66%. At the beginning of 1950 the number of Hellenes in Turkey amounted to around 145,000 and constituted around 6.9% of the total population of Turkey. Today the Hellenes comprise 0.025% of the total population of Turkey.
>
> (Kyratzopoulos 2006:129)

Kyratzopoulos proceeded to make further comparisons based on the contemporary economic situation of these three groups, before concluding that 'in the second half of the twentieth century the genocide of the Constantinopolitan Ethnic Group is, from a sociological perspective and in terms of International Jurisprudence and in substance, a reality' (2006:130–131). Whilst some other expatriates seem to envisage (often tentative) comparisons with the Nazi Holocaust and other atrocities as a vehicle for interpreting and articulating their own experiences of suffering, Kyratzopoulos was not prepared to assimilate the *Septemvriuná* to other more infamous acts of violence for the sake of demonstrating commensurability. In his effort to ensure that memories of the

178 *National and transnational histories*

Septemvrianá were 'written into global history as befits them', he accordingly placed the expatriation of the Greeks of Turkey into explicit competition with the genocide of the Jews and the Tutsi, hoping in this way to demonstrate its reality as an act of genocide in the face of alleged indifference from the European community (Kyratzopoulos 2006:18). Kyratzopoulos' argument is a strong reminder that competition is always a possible outcome of the multidirectional trajectories of memory (Rothberg 2011; see below).

Transcultural memory in personal testimony

Explicit transcultural thinking is also sometimes in evidence in personal testimony. Expressions of commonality and/or solidarity with the Armenians and Kurds were offered by a few of my interviewees. For instance, when I asked Istanbul-born *Imvriótis* Loukas if he had had any Kurdish acquaintances whilst living in Turkey he replied, 'I have never met anyone in my life speaking Kurdish. They were afraid, of course. As I was afraid to speak Greek in the street, so they too were afraid to speak Kurdish' (03/07/2013). Reminiscing about the Kurds who used to work in his shop in Istanbul, Spyros similarly exclaimed, 'the Kurds are another race, they are not Turks. Now they are trying to make them into Turks [. . .] we also had two Armenians [in the shop], and great damage befell them also, the Armenians: 1.5 million'. In his life history narrative – structured around moments of persecution – Spyros broadened the field of victims to include Armenians and Jews, taking care to mention that these communities were also targeted during the forced conscription into labour battalions in 1941–1942, the 1942–1944 wealth tax, and the Istanbul Riots in 1955 (02/12/2011). Fotis, born in Istanbul in 1950, likewise proclaimed that the Kurds 'are a different people, they should have their own country' (01/02/2012), whilst Michalis explicitly grouped together the Armenian genocide, the Greek–Turkish population exchange, the Kurdish–Turkish conflict, and the persecution of the Greeks of Istanbul as part of a systematic Turkish policy to rid itself of its minorities (29/01/2012).

Analogies between Turkey and Nazi Germany also cropped up in a few of my interviewees' testimonies. Markos, for instance, discussing Turkish actions during the 1922 war with Greece, remarked, 'you win a war, but you do not kill everyone, we are not Hitler, only Hitler killed people. But the Turks did that: they slaughtered, they killed, they burned' (04/05/2012). Gerasimos similarly accused the Turks of implementing 'Hitler-esque methods' in their dealings with the Kurds, stated that when he lived in Turkey 'it was like a fascist regime, like living in Germany under the Nazis and being a communist', and likened Mustafa Kemal to Adolf Hitler ('I don't call him "Atatürk", because Atatürk means "father of the Turks". Hitler, I don't call him the "Führer", I call him "Adolf Hitler", so why would I call Mustafa Kemal "Atatürk"?') (06/02/2012). Gerasimos was also one of a handful of interviewees to make comparisons between their own experiences and those of the minority in Western Thrace. Whilst he saw certain commonalities – remarking that 'many times I have been able to speak to such people, and I understand them' – his narrative nonetheless took on a competitive dimension when he argued that the Western Thracian minority enjoys 'ten times greater freedom than we did' and dismissed their complaints as 'stupidities' (06/02/2012). *Imvriótis* Kostas likewise felt that the minority in Western Thrace had not suffered as much as his own community, but nevertheless criticised some of his compatriots for suggesting that Greece should have taken punitive measures in Western Thrace in response to Turkish actions on Imbros ('because after all they are ordinary people [. . .] how is the ordinary Mehmet in Komotini to blame?') (07/06/2013; see also Evangelos' comments in Chapter 3).

Nevertheless, in the case of my interviewees, at least, transcultural comparisons and analogies – and terms such as 'genocide' or 'ethnic cleansing' – were not commonplace features of personal testimony in the way that they often are in the formal written discourse of expatriate memory activists. Where such references did occur, they were often made by interviewees closely involved in expatriate memory activism, and/or were made by individuals who felt that they needed to justify a perspective that was being called into question. For instance, when I queried Menelaos' suggestion that Turks are easily incited by their government (see Chapter 4) by asking whether he felt this was something unique to Turkey, he responded by discussing Turkish persecution of the Armenians. Similarly, on one occasion I witnessed a conversation between one of my interviewees and another expatriate, in which the former was attempting to convince the latter that there was no viable future for a Greek minority in Istanbul because of Turkey's history of persecuting minorities in its territory. Having failed to talk the other man around to his point of view by enumerating Turkish actions against Greek communities, my interviewee proceeded to introduce the additional examples of the Armenian genocide and the Kurdish–Turkish conflict, hoping that by doing so his argument would carry more weight and win through. From this perspective, it is not that transcultural cross-referencing is in some sense unique to formal written discourse – indeed, I have elsewhere explored similar narratives in the more informal (and frequently acrimonious) setting of peer-to-peer debates between Greeks and Turks on the Internet (Halstead 2018) – but rather that such cross-referencing may be most expedient, and therefore most common, in rather particular discursive contexts.

To further this point, I will examine an autobiographical testimony by an expatriate from Istanbul that does engage in a particularly systematic effort to parallel the experiences of the Armenians, the Greeks, and the Kurds: Leonidas Koumakis' semi-autobiographical novel *The Miracle* (first published in Greek in 1993). Koumakis was born in Istanbul in around 1950, where he lived until his father was expelled from Turkey as a Greek citizen in 1964. *The Miracle* incorporates both the personal experiences of the author and his father, and extended historical narratives, the latter typically delivered by characters within the story. In one passage, for instance, the author reconstructs his father's inner monologue as he sits waiting to learn of his fate at a Turkish police station on one Tuesday in

1964, a day that 'my father had always considered to be an unlucky day because 29 May, 1453, when Constantinople fell to the Turks, was a Tuesday' (Koumakis 1996:19). In the book, Koumakis senior ruminates at length on the plight of the Greeks of Turkey whilst he waits, ultimately arriving at the conclusion that the Armenian genocide and the persecution of the Greeks of Istanbul were components of a broader Turkish policy:

> Any decisive blows meted out by Turkey during the course of the twentieth century have been inflicted by taking advantage of a 'suitable opportunity'. The Armenian genocide that took place during the First World War, the Capital Tax known as *Varlık Vergisi* that was imposed mainly on Turkey's Greek population in the Second World War, the pogrom of 1955 and the expulsions in 1964 – all these occurred at times when circumstances were 'suitable'.
>
> 'Are you Gerasimos Koumakis?' a stern voice asked in Turkish, bringing my father back from his thoughts with a bump. It was the afternoon of 9th July, 1964.
>
> (Koumakis 1996:24)

Historical interludes of this sort recur throughout *The Miracle*. The longest occurs towards the end of the story, as the Koumakis family are preparing to leave Istanbul for good. A young Leonidas Koumakis is unexpectedly summoned to the apartment of an elderly Greek neighbour, Mr Kleopas, who proceeds to deliver an extended lecture on Turkish history from which the author quotes verbatim for 18 pages. Mr Kleopas begins by declaring that '[t]he Turks [. . .] are a barbaric people', who for 600 years have 'practised the only skill nature has endowed them with: destruction and pillage' (Koumakis 1996:75, 77). Amongst other things, his narrative then touches in detail upon the Armenian genocide,

> '[. . .] the greatest cold-blooded genocide in the history of mankind. Within the space of just a few months [in 1915], one and a half million Armenians were mercilessly wiped out at the hands of the Turks [. . .]
>
> Here Mr Kleopas paused again, quite clearly overcome, drank a few more sips of water and then went on [. . .].
>
> (Koumakis 1996:82)

massacres of Greeks during the First World War and the Greek-Turkish War,

> '[o]n 9th September, 1922 the Turks invaded Smyrna and spent the next five days in a frenzy of destruction, conflagration and slaughter. Over 150,000 Greeks were massacred by the Young Turks when Kemal entered Smyrna. Between 1914 and 1922 they killed 323,000 Greeks in the Pontus region and more than 400,000 living on the Asia Minor coast [. . .].
>
> (Koumakis 1996:90)

and the Kurdish-Turkish conflict,

> '[n]ext it was the turn of the Kurds, but they proved to be considerably tougher. After holding out for 79 days, the Kurdish revolution ended in a bloodbath in July, 1924. The Kurds are an ancient and historic people who are mentioned by Xenophon [...] The Kurdish uprisings began long before the Greek Revolution of 1821 [...] they paid with their blood for their longing for freedom [...].
>
> (Koumakis 1996:90–91)

Mr Kleopas' account concludes by alluding to more contemporary events and by making pessimistic predictions about the future:

> '[...T]he age–old Turkish philosophy that applies at any time and in any place occupied by the Turks: "The Turks are the only masters in this country. Anyone who is not a genuine Turk has only one right in this country: the right to be a servant, the right to be a slave."
>
> 'And the Kurds who are still living in Turkey today, my boy, have this right only. The Greeks who stayed on in Turkey were all wiped out after the events of 1955. The final act of this terrible Greek tragedy is now being played out [...]
>
> '[...] Sooner or later, having resolved the Kurdish problem by massacring innocent civilians, they will turn their attention to Cyprus, Western Thrace, and to the Greek islands in the Aegean. The next generation of Greeks will have to do better than the previous one [...]
>
> Slowly, I stood up. My head was spinning with all that I had just heard.
>
> 'Thank you for telling me all this, Mr Kleopas,' I mumbled. 'I promise I'll never forget it.'
>
> (Koumakis 1996:91–92)

In common with the style of the book generally, this section weaves together two different narrative modes: the first a personal story of how the author left Turkey and bid farewell to his neighbour, and the second an historical narrative that uses this farewell as a means to place Koumakis' personal and familial memory within a broader history. The latter narrative systematically assimilates personal experiences of the Istanbul Riots in 1955 and the expulsion of Greek citizens in 1964 to a chronic history of repression, injustice, and bloodshed in Turkish lands.

According to the blurb on the inside cover of the 1996 English-language reprint, Koumakis wrote *The Miracle* in order 'to communicate, through both historical evidence and my personal experience, the Turkish policy against Hellenism and beyond'. It is, perhaps, this stated purpose – i.e. the explicit desire to make the author's charges against Turkey intelligible and compelling to an external, public audience – that in particular accounts for the explicitly transcultural frame of reference adopted by Koumakis. Whether in formal and public expressions of grievance, institutional awareness-raising materials, vitriolic online debates

(Halstead 2018), or (more rarely) in personal testimony, narrators seem to reach for transcultural analogies to other violent histories most readily when attempting to validate their narratives and/or to communicate them concisely and clearly to a broad public audience.

Transnational nationalism?

As Rothberg observed, it has often been assumed that the memories of different victim communities must interact competitively in a battle over the scarce resource of public recognition; that '[a]s I struggle to achieve recognition of *my* memories and *my* identity, I necessarily exclude the memories and identities of others' (2009:5). If this assumption was accurate, we might expect the juxtaposition of different memories of atrocity in the examples presented above to generate a competitive hierarchy of suffering, what the author Daniel Mendelsohn has aptly termed the 'my-genocide-was-worse-than-your-genocide thing' (Hartman *et al.* 2011:119). Competitive victimhood is certainly an aspect of memory's multidirectionality, as Rothberg himself made clear in a later piece of work (2011), and as expatriate references to the Western Thracian minority and, in particular, Kyratzopoulos' arguments above vividly demonstrate. Generally, however, cross-referencing with Armenian, Jewish, and Kurdish experience actually follows an *anti*-hierarchical logic: expatriate activists seem more concerned with constructing rhetorical solidarities premised on the equality and interchangeability of victimhood than with establishing competitive victim stratification, and, accordingly, routinely compromise the specificity of their own experience by asserting its commensurability with that of other oppressed groups. This provides them with a means to legitimate their narratives of persecution by asserting that other communities had similar experiences at the hands of the same perpetrators, and/or represent comparatively obscure events such as the *Septemvrianá* through more well-known and concrete analogies familiar to European and international audiences. In this sense, *including* the memories of others in their narratives serves to bolster rather than undermine their efforts to achieve recognition of their own memories.

The question remains, however, as to whether such transnational cross-referencing simply functions to structure and buttress narratives about the self, or whether it also has a transformative effect on perceptions of others. To be sure, invocations of the Armenian genocide and the Kurdish–Turkish struggle are not restricted to totemic name-dropping within narratives of Greek suffering, and sometimes find expression in impassioned proclamations of empathy, angry denunciations of Turkish actions (and international indifference) towards these communities, or appeals for readers and the Greek public to support their campaigns for recognition or liberation. In 1999, for instance, PKK leader Abdullah Öcalan was captured by Turkish intelligence services in Kenya *en route* from the Greek embassy in Nairobi to the airport. There was a strong outpouring of support for the Kurdish leader in *O Polítis*, and in the March edition one writer responded to the arrest – and to rumours of Greek complicity – by reflecting on her own prejudices towards Kurdish and other political refugees who had taken shelter in Greece. She recalled how, as a young girl, she felt that the Kurds should 'stay in their own country to fight for their rights', and complained that 'they are dirty, they smell [. . .] they will give us lice', for which she was reprimanded by her mother – an expatriated Greek from Istanbul – who reminded her that '[w]e were the same when we first came as little children to the homeland [that is, Greece]'. On the day of Öcalan's arrest, the author found her mother 'shedding tears whilst watching the news':

> – We ended up handing him over, [my mother said], we forced him to leave the embassy, everything has been revealed. Poor Öcalan, the Turks are torturing him now.
>
> I, however, did not believe it and I sat down [. . .] and watched the news, for many hours [. . .] searching to find an explanation, which would justify our actions. And then I saw ARO [nickname for Öcalan] the powerful leader of 30 million repressed people, fatigued, distressed and with the look of a small child who had become lost and was afraid. And I too began to cry. And I know that shortly, when the noise has died down [. . .] I too will have forgotten that look [. . .]
>
> There is, however, that burning that remains in the stomach and the guilt that weighs heavily on me. And I know that every time my gaze meets that Kurd, that Iranian, that Albanian and whichever repressed person on this planet, I will be the first one to bow her head in shame. And that hurts. Good morning Kurdistan, good morning ARO. One thousand times sorry.
>
> (*O Polítis* 1999)

Landsberg suggested that when we hear the testimony of another we 'construct a memory triggered by the testimony that also is closely connected to our own archive of experience' (Landsberg 2004:137). Indeed, in this extract, it was precisely by equating the past experiences of her parents as Greeks in Turkey with the contemporary plight of the Kurds that the author of the article came to re-evaluate her prejudice towards political refugees in Greece: a postmemory (Hirsch 2012) of her parents' suffering acted as a cipher for engaging with the otherwise intangible suffering of others.

Significantly, the rhetorical solidarities extended to the Armenians and Kurds by expatriate activists were frequently reciprocated by Armenian and Kurdish diaspora organisations in Greece. On the 78th anniversary of the Armenian genocide, for instance, the Armenian National Committee of Greece wrote the following in their newsletter:

> The chain of the Turkish expansionist policy begins in **1915** with the extermination of 1.5 million Armenians. **1916–1923** is the turn of 700,000 Hellenes of the Pontus. **1922** the catastrophe of Smyrna and the civilisation of the Hellenes of Asia Minor. **1955** catastrophe in Constantinople and the extermination of 250,000 Hellenes. **1974** invasion of Cyprus and the occupation

of 40% of its land. **1980–1990** a decade of persecution and extermination of the Kurdish people. **1993** threats against Armenia and Nagorno-Karabakh.

(*Armeniká Chroniká* 1993)

In January 1997, the Balkan branch of the National Liberation Front of Kurdistan (ERNK) sent words of support to the Constantinopolitan Society that similarly paralleled the experiences of the *Polítes* and the Kurds:

> The peoples who were victims of Turkish Kemalist racism do not differ from one another. We are the children of the same land of Asia Minor, whatever religion and whatever language we might have. Victims of the same barbarity, we strongly believe that every Kurd is today also a Constantinopolitan of 1941–44, of 1955, of 1964 [...] The Kurdish rebel of the National Liberation Front of Kurdistan carries in his heart the pain and the hope of the Constantinopolitan.
>
> (*Phoní tou Kourdistán* 1997)

In this extract, contemporary Kurdish guerrilla fighters were portrayed as embodying the persecuted *Polítes* of the past, or as present-day auxiliaries for past Greek victims, carrying into their fight with Turkey not just their own pain but also an affiliative postmemory (Hirsch 2012:36) of Greek suffering in mid-twentieth-century Istanbul. As such examples demonstrate, by the 1990s writers representing all three communities had become fluent in each other's languages of victimhood, trading iconic dates such as 1915 and 1955 from each other's mnemonic repertoires and displaying them as badges of solidarity and tropes to demonstrate the universality of minority experience in Turkey. Such rhetorical solidarities could also be translated into real-world actions: in 1988, for instance, Greek expatriate organisations worked collaboratively with Armenian and Kurdish diaspora groups in Athens to organise a protest to coincide with the diplomatic visit of Turkish Prime Minister Turgut Özal during the Davos process (*Ímvros* 1988a; *Ímvros* 1988b; Isaakidis 2014). The discursive practice of paralleling Greek and Armenian experience with that of the Kurds, furthermore, lends some credence to Landsberg's suggestion that the transcultural circulation of memories 'might serve as the grounds for unexpected alliances across chasms of difference' (2004:3). Both Armenian and Greek writers and activists have in the past held the Kurds accountable for participating in both Ottoman-era and later Turkish anti-minority persecution, in particular the Armenian genocide, atrocities during the Greek–Turkish War, and – to a lesser degree – the *Septemvriná* (although cf. the discussion in Chapter 4). From this perspective, incorporating the experiences of all three communities into a narrative of shared victimhood might help to promote intercommunal reconciliation, by foregrounding their commonality as victims over their differences as antagonists.

There are, nevertheless, reasons to be cautious about the emphasis in recent scholarship on the tendency for the remembrance of suffering along transcultural lines to challenge essentialist national identities and replace these with nation-transcending solidarities. To begin with, the chasm of difference between the Armenians and the Greeks, on the one hand, and the Kurds, on the other, is not always so easily overcome, and historical enmities may continue to simmer beneath the surface in spite of rhetorical and public expressions of solidarity and communality. Former president of the Constantinopolitan Society Isaakidis, for instance, had the following recollections of planning meetings between the three communities for the 1988 protest:

> What is the funny thing, however? The Armenians were slaughtered by the Kurds! So when we had the first meetings, the representatives of the Armenians were sitting next to me, and the Kurds were sitting opposite [. . .] I said to the Armenian woman, 'now we are all sitting down together and we are speaking in a friendly manner, but don't forget that those Kurds opposite us slaughtered you, and others during the *Septemvrianá*'.
>
> (Isaakidis 2014)

Narratives that cut across boundaries and call received historical knowledge into question may encounter severe resistance, and it cannot necessarily be assumed that the historical analogies individuals draw in particular discursive contexts will carry over into other social situations and have a lasting effect on individual subjectivity. As Jim House has observed, whilst 'for some people, there are connections between historical events that appear "self-evident"', for others these links 'are either refused (due to "competing memories") or genuinely not understood as being connected' (2010:37). Indeed, the transcultural comparisons that are fairly common in the formal writing of expatriate activists seeking to publicly advance and justify their representations of the past are comparatively uncommon in oral testimonies offered to me by expatriate interviewees, raising a question mark over the extent to which these connections have been internalised by individuals and become part of their mental apparatus for understanding their lives.

If the practice of transcultural cross-referencing is thus to a significant extent the domain of memory activists seeking to achieve recognition of their own memories, we must confront the possibility that such comparisons might sometimes be as much (if not more) about the *subject* making the connections as the *objects* of those connections. Although in some contexts expatriate activists draw on perceived parallels with the experiences of others to call for mutual intercommunal support, or even to re-evaluate their own preconceptions about these communities, in other cases the Armenians, Jews, and Kurds appear in these activists' narratives not so much as distinctive communities with distinctive identities and histories, but rather as truncated contextual depth for a protracted narrative of Greek suffering. In such cases, *pace* Landsberg, expatriate activists do not 'suture [themselves] into a larger history' (2004:2) so much as suture compelling motifs onto their *own* history.

This highlights certain limitations to the productive moral potential of multi-directional mnemonic engagements. First, as Silverman cautioned, there is an inherent risk of 'clothing ourselves in others' victimhood, which we have neither experienced nor properly understood, for the purpose of identity and, consequently, participating in a banal culture of empathy which is often more self- than other-oriented' (2013:174). Second, the effort to find counterparts to Greek suffering often leads narrators to disregard the historical particularities of different past occurrences. In an effort to account for 'some of the more difficult and even troubling cases of multidirectionality', Rothberg proposed that connections between different histories might be plotted along both an 'axis of comparison' – with equation at one extreme and differentiation at the other – and an 'axis of political affect' – ranging from solidarity to competition (2011:524–525). He emphasised that discourses located in the differentiation-solidarity quadrant, 'in which transcultural comparison does not simply produce commensurability out of difference', held the greatest potential for recognising and redressing injustices (2011:538). Most of the examples in this chapter could be placed in the solidarity-equation quadrant, as, in the process of articulating solidarities between the Armenians, Greeks, and Kurds, and drawing parallels between Nazi persecution of the Jews and Turkish treatment of other ethnic groups, they tend to a greater or lesser degree to elide these different histories. As Rothberg identified, although such discourses might be preferable to those governed by a logic of competitive victimhood, they nevertheless carry certain dangers, not only of distortion and misrepresentation, but also, more seriously, the imposition of reified moral absolutes of good versus evil on complex contemporary problems, and the importation of 'a dangerous model of victimization' from one context to another (2011:534). For instance, there is a risk that equating frozen or ongoing conflicts, like the division of Cyprus or the Kurdish–Turkish struggle, with historical atrocities like the Armenian genocide or the Holocaust might make the former seem intractable and bound for a catastrophic conclusion.

A competitive logic is also discernible in some of the above examples, in those discourses that disrupt the solidarity between Armenians, Greeks, and Kurds by equating contemporary Kurdish suffering with that allegedly inflicted *by* the Kurds on the Armenians and Greeks (competition-equation); in Kyratzopoulos' controversial efforts to demonstrate the severity of Greek suffering through competitive contrast with other historical atrocities (competition-differentiation); and in the way in which some expatriates seek to establish the specificity of their own experiences through contrast with those of the Western Thracian minority (competition-differentiation). The 1999 *Politis* article '*Dozmpas* Kurdistan, Sorry Aro' that proclaimed solidarity with Öcalan and the Kurds, meanwhile, might tentatively be plotted in the solidarity-differentiation quadrant. Although at first glance it may seem that this text is in the business of equation, the author likening her parents' experiences to those of Kurdish political refugees, there is also a sense in which the author did not simply compare Greek and Kurdish histories in order to reaffirm a preconceived perception of the Turkish other, but rather drew on the experiences of her parents as *Polítes* to reappraise her perspective on Kurdish suffering and that of other persecuted communities. As such, the text seems to harbour greater potential for developing a more differentiated awareness of victimhood generally (Rothberg 2011:526). At any rate, however, it is notable (amongst my material at least) that discourses that could be placed in Rothberg's coveted solidarity-differentiation quadrant are few as compared to those that tend towards competition and, particularly, equation. This suggests that although (rhetorical) solidarities may indeed be a 'frequent – if not guaranteed – outcome of the remembrance of suffering' (Rothberg 2010:11), the 'harnessing of the[se] legacies of violence in the interests of a more egalitarian future' (Rothberg 2009:21) may be comparatively uncommon as compared to the harnessing of these solidarities in a manner that distorts or blurs different histories and/or risks perpetuating historical enmities in relation to a common antagonist. Put differently, it may be much easier to develop solidarities based on a pre-existing and mutual antagonism with a third party (Armenians/Greeks/Kurds versus Turks, for example) than it is to articulate solidarities that require received knowledge and stereotypes about others to be rewritten and challenged (as would be the case, for instance, for a transcultural solidarity between the Greeks of Istanbul/Imbros and the Turks/Muslims of Western Thrace).

Indeed, there is ample evidence in this chapter to suggest that transcultural connections between different violent histories might be as likely to strengthen as to abrogate existing national identities and frameworks of remembrance. Staging Greek suffering as part of an unchanging pattern of Turkish behaviour stretching from the Armenian genocide to the contemporary conflict with the Kurds may only serve to fortify hostility towards the Turks, and to consolidate the rhythms of Greek national history. Discussing Turkey's relationship with the EU, *O Polítis* symptomatically declared that the Turks 'do not change tactic. Only the people and the victims change: Armenians, Greeks, Kurds' (*O Polítis* 1995). Sharing memories of suffering may thus also involve sharing abstract enmities. Similar risks apply to the drawing of parallels between Turkey and Nazi Germany. Though analogies between *Kristallnacht* and the Istanbul Riots represent for the Federation of Constantinopolitans an attempt to move *away* from a narrow national perspective, discourses that liken Turkish actions to those of Nazi Germany are always potentially liable to reinforce negative nationalist perceptions of the Turkish other as a homogenous community of perpetrators. Although (rhetorical) solidarities may be a common product of multidirectional thinking, these may often go hand-in-hand with the perpetuation of historical enmities in relation to a common antagonist, demonstrating that transcultural 'entanglements' (Conrad 2003:86–87) between different memories might 'reinforce national memory communities that at first appearance they seem to supersede' (Assmann and Conrad 2010:9).

Conclusions

The connections (and sometimes divergences) between the persecution of the Greeks of Turkey and the histories of other communities envisaged by expatriate writers and activists in their efforts to rationalise and represent their own experiences confirm the implausibility of 'maintain[ing] a wall, or *cordon sanitaire*, between different histories' (Rothberg 2009:313). Whilst broadening the field of victims to include the Armenians and the Kurds helps to visualise and substantiate expatriate activists' narratives of victimisation, analogies with Nazism function to assert the indisputability and severity of Greek suffering and Turkish guilt. Such transcultural cross-referencing might draw certain national groups closer together – perhaps even promoting reconciliation between historical antagonists such as the Armenians and the Kurds – as well as helping to bring comparatively marginalised or poorly recognised histories to light. Yet there is also a danger that such transcultural comparison will 'simply block insight into specific local histories' (Huyssen 2003:14) – eliding sometimes quite different historical circumstances for the sake of demonstrating commonality – or, worse, contribute to a radicalisation of discourse that might entrench a generalised hostility towards the Turks, and thereby hamper any prospects of productive intercommunal dialogue. The evidence presented in this chapter, moreover, would tend to suggest that transcultural connections may be stronger and smoother when they validate rather than challenge existing histories and identities. Insofar as these transcultural flows of memory have been internalised by individuals, it is more as a language for talking about (their own) suffering than as 'privately felt public memories' (Landsberg 2004:19) that might drastically restructure their perceptions of history, others, or their own identity.

In a discussion of First World War poetry, Geoff Dyer argued that the image of war as horrific had become so clichéd that it had lost its power to express that horror: '[w]ar may be horrible', he wrote, 'but that should not distract us from acknowledging what a horrible cliché this has become' (1995:27). Dyer termed these instinctive clichés '[o]ff-the-peg formulae [that] free you from thinking for yourself about what is being said', and warned that '[w]henever words are bandied about automatically and easily, their meaning is in the process of leaking away or evaporating' (1995:29). In a similar vein, we might describe many of the transcultural references considered in this chapter as 'off-the-peg memories': abstracted and simplified formulae, often accompanied by little historical baggage, that are temporarily adopted by expatriate activists, without necessarily triggering, or indicating, any particularly in-depth engagement with the experiences of the others concerned. These off-the-peg memories typically come across as knee-jerk reactions to particular discursive situations, and often stand in for substantive independent thinking about Greek–Turkish relationships and histories of violence more generally. At the same time, however, such off-the-peg memories free expatriate activists from thinking about history *on their own*. On the one hand, the construction of parallel histories with Armenians and Kurds serves to endorse and rationalise Greek victimhood, by suggesting that other communities had similar experiences at the hands of the same perpetrators, and thereby multiplying the witnesses able to 'testify' to the accused's record of atrocity. Meanwhile, analogising with other, more well-known historical atrocities such as Nazi genocide makes these claims evocative and intelligible for unfamiliar audiences.

My intention here is not to create a false dichotomy between 'off-the-peg' and 'bespoke' or 'tailor-made' memories; to reinforce, in other words, Landsberg's problematic distinction between 'natural' and 'prosthetic' memories (see also Silverman 2013:176). It is not the transcultural nature of these references that leads me to characterise them as off-the-peg memories, but rather their *simplicity* and *homogeneity*, and their *transience* and *disposability*. *Simple* and *homogenous* because they appear as ready-made, decontextualised, and often functionally interchangeable motifs, picked up from the public mnemonic domain largely divorced from their historical context. *Transient* and *disposable* because they are 'bought in' primarily in the context of memory activism, and may be 'returned' in other contexts when they are no longer needed. This is not to suggest, however, that the use of these transcultural parallels and analogies is necessarily frivolous or irrelevant. Indeed, I have highlighted examples of reciprocal solidarities between Armenians, Greeks, and Kurds, as well as transcultural discourses that come closer to realising Rothberg's favoured coupling of solidarity and differentiation. Even when this cross-referencing is not explicitly accompanied by detailed contextual understanding of the complexities of others' histories, it does not necessarily follow that its usage is dispassionate, disingenuous, or cynical. Comparatively hollow off-the-peg memories, stripped of their historical specificity, may still be filled with new and personal meaning by individuals who see their own experiences paralleled in those of other victimised communities.

What I do want to draw attention to is the fact that not every act of cross-referencing is necessarily evidence of lasting and pervasive 'knotting' between different histories that might radically challenge existing national(ist) understandings of the past, and that the discursive connections drawn by narrators in certain contexts will not necessarily carry over into other settings and reconfigure their perceptions of past, self, and other. Indeed, it is notable that transcultural cross-referencing often serves to reaffirm what narrators thought they already knew about the Turks, and to make the articulation of more differentiated representations of the Turkish other less likely. These 'off-the-peg memories' provide frameworks through which expatriate experiences can be represented or communicated in particular contexts, but could likely be abandoned if necessary – placed 'back on the peg' – without major surgery to self-understanding or received historical knowledge. This is not to preclude the possibility that such cross-referencing may sometimes have a discernible impact on expatriate activists' narratives: the comparisons, for instance, they envisaged with the histories of the Armenians, Kurds, and Jews may well have played a significant role in developing the tendency to present Greek experiences in Istanbul and Imbros in terms of human rights discourse. What it does suggest, however, is that multidirectional thinking may often produce transnational translations of national(ist) narratives, or even contribute to their consolidation and ongoing explanatory appeal, rather than producing more reflective and inclusive understandings of the past.

Notes

1 A Pan-Imvrian Committee was first established after the 1973 Pan-Imvrian Conference, and the idea was revived in 1991. On both occasions, the intention was to provide a

common voice for all of the Imvrian organisations in Greece and abroad (Chortaras 1993:229–230; Xeinos 1990:28).

2 Some observers provide a contrary interpretation of these data, pointing to a high birth rate amongst the minority population in Western Thrace, and accordingly arguing that the lack of population increase must indicate that hundreds of thousands have emigrated (primarily to Turkey) since 1923 (Helsinki Watch 1990:2; Oran 1988:145–146; Oran 2004:101).

References

(Items marked * are in the Greek language.)

Akgönül, S. (1999). *Une communauté, deux états: la minorité turco-musulmane de Thrace occidentale*. Istanbul: Éditions Isis.

Alexander, J. C. (2009). The social construction of moral universals. In J. C. Alexander. *Remembering the Holocaust: a debate*. Oxford; New York: Oxford University Press, 3–102.

Alexandris, A. (1992). *The Greek minority of Istanbul and Greek–Turkish relations, 1918–1974*. Athens: Centre for Asia Minor Studies.

Alexandris, A. (2004). Religion or ethnicity: the identity issue of the minorities in Greece and Turkey. In R. Hirschon (Ed.). *Crossing the Aegean: an appraisal of the 1923 compulsory population exchange between Greece and Turkey*. New York: Berghahn Books, 117–132.

Armeniká Chroniká. (1993). Our opinion, April 1993.*

Assmann, A. and Conrad, S. (2010). Introduction. In A. Assmann and S. Conrad (Eds.). *Memory in a global age: discourses, practices and trajectories*. Houndmills, Basingstoke; New York: Palgrave Macmillan, 1–16.

Chortaras, P. (1993). Pan-Imvrian Committee. Achievements, prospects. In *Imvrian two-day conference: Imbros today. Problems, prospects*. Athens: Imvrian Association, 229–234.*

Conrad, S. (2003). Entangled memories: versions of the past in Germany and Japan, 1945–2001. *Journal of Contemporary History*, 38(1), 85–99.

Constantinopolitan Society. (2015). *60 years, 6–7 September 1955, memorial day of the Hellenism of Constantinople*. Press release, 4 September 2015. Available at: www.cpolitan.gr/news/δελτιο-τυπου-60-χρονια-6-7-σεπτεμβριου-1955-η [Accessed on 12 May 2014].*

Constantinopolitan Society, New Circle of Constantinopolitans, Association of Hellenic Citizens Expelled from Turkey, Union of Constantinopolitans of Northern Greece, Thracian Association of Imbros, Constantinople, Tenedos, and Eastern Thrace, and Society for the Advancement of National Heritage. (1995a). *40 years: 6–7 September 1955 Constantinople*. Publicity material and resolution issued by the organising committee. Constantinopolitan Society Archive.*

Constantinopolitan Society, New Circle of Constantinopolitans, Association of Hellenic Citizens Expelled from Turkey, Union of Constantinopolitans of Northern Greece, Thracian Association of Imbros, Constantinople, Tenedos, and Eastern Thrace, and Society for the Advancement of National Heritage. (1995b). *To protest the ethnic cleansing perpetrated by Turkey against the Greeks of Istanbul in 1955*. Resolution. Constantinopolitan Society Archive.

Demetriou, O. (2006). Streets not named: discursive dead ends and the politics of orientation in intercommunal spatial relations in northern Greece. *Cultural Anthropology*, 21(2), 295–321.

Dragonas, T. (2012). The vicissitudes of identity in a divided society: the case of the Muslim minority in Western Thrace. In K. Featherstone (Ed.), *Europe in modern Greek history*. New York: Columbia University Press.

Droumpouki, A. M. (2016). Shaping Holocaust memory in Greece: memorials and their public history. *National Identities*, 18(2), 199–216.

Dyer, G. (1995). *The missing of the Somme*. London: Penguin.

Ecumenical Federation of Constantinopolitans. (2007). *The tragic anniversary of the 6–7 September 1955 Turkish State organised ethnic cleansing night of the Greek community of Istanbul*. PowerPoint presentation, 2007. Available at: www.conpolis.eu/Septemvriana/Septemvriana.aspx [Accessed on 15 May 2014].

Ecumenical Federation of Constantinopolitans. (2008). *Proceedings of international conference: Septemvriana 6–7/9/1955 an act of annihilation of the Greek community of Istanbul*. 13 September 2008. Athens. Available at: www.conpolis.eu/Septemvriana/2008/Πρακτικά%20Συνεδρίου%20Σεπτεμβριανών%20ΟΙ.ΟΜ.ΚΩ%20 2008.pdf [Accessed on 15 May 2014].

Ecumenical Federation of Constantinopolitans. (2012). *The Greek Orthodox minority of Turkey: history of human rights violations and the need of remedy and reparations*. PowerPoint presentation, May 2012. Available at: www.conpolis.eu/uploadedNews/Human%20rights%20of%20the%20Greek%20Orthodox%20minority%20of%20Turkey-May%202012b.pdf [Accessed on 15 May 2014].

Ecumenical Federation of Constantinopolitans. (2013). *Invitation to the day-conference on the 58th anniversary of the* Kristallnacht *6–7/9/1955 for the Hellenism of Constantinople*. Invitation to the conference. Available at: www.conpolis.eu/uploadedNews/Σεπτεμβριανά%20Εκδήλωση%202013.pdf [Accessed on 15 May 2014].*

Ecumenical Federation of Constantinopolitans. (2014a). *16 March 1964: the banishment of the Greek community of Istanbul through deportations and expatriation*. PowerPoint presentation, February 2014. Available at: www.conpolis.eu/uploadedNews/16%20Mart%201964-Eng.pdf [Accessed on 15 May 2014].

Ecumenical Federation of Constantinopolitans. (2014b). *Invitation to the day-conference on the 59th anniversary of the* Kristallnacht *6–7/9/1955 for the Hellenism of Constantinople*. Invitation to the conference. Available at: www.conpolis.eu/uploadedNews/Septembriana%202014.pdf [Accessed on 15 May 2014].*

Ekdóseis Tsoukátou. (1999). *Septemvrianá 1955: The 'Kristallnacht' of the Hellenism of Constantinople*. Athens: Ekdóseis Tsoukátou.*

Erll, A. (2011a). Travelling memory. *Parallax*, 17(4), 4–18.

Erll, A. (2011b). *Memory in culture*. Translated from the German by S. B. Young. Houndmills, Basingstoke; New York: Palgrave Macmillan.

Erll, A. and Rigney, A. (2009). Introduction: cultural memory and its dynamics. In A. Erll and A. Rigney (Eds). *Mediation, remediation, and the dynamics of cultural memory*. Berlin; New York: Walter de Gruyter, 1–11.

Halstead, H. (2018). 'Ask the Assyrians, Armenians, Kurds': transcultural memory and nationalism in Greek historical narratives about Greek–Turkish relationships'. *History & Memory* 30(2), 3–39.

Hartman, S., Hoffman, E., Mendelsohn, D., and Miller, N. K. (2011). Memoirs of return. In M. Hirsch and N. K. Miller (Eds). *Rites of return: diaspora poetics and the politics of memory*. New York: Columbia University Press, 107–123.

Helsinki Watch. (1990). *Destroying ethnic identity: the Turks of Greece*. New York: Human Rights Watch.

Hirsch, M. (2012). *The Generation of postmemory: writing and visual culture after the Holocaust*. New York: Columbia University Press.

House, J. (2010). Memory and the creation of solidarity during the decolonization of Algeria. *Yale French Studies*, (118/119), 15–38.
Huyssen, A. (2003). *Present pasts: urban palimpsests and the politics of memory*. Stanford, CA: Stanford University Press.
Imvros. (1983). From Lausanne to Cyprus, September 1983.*
Imvros. (1988a). Extraordinary Panhellenic Imvrian conference, June–July 1988.*
Imvros. (1988b). Big march during the visit of Özal, June–July 1988.*
Imvros. (1991). Letter of the Pan-Imvrian Committee to the editor of the newspaper *The Guardian*, July–August 1991.*
Imvros. (1992a). List of 'rightful' demands for the Western Thracian Muslims, March 1992.*
Imvros. (1992b). Violations of treaties and accords, June 1992.
Imvros. (1993). Violations of human rights and the Treaty of Lausanne on the islands of Imbros and Tenedos, November–December 1993.*
Imvros. (1994a). Pan-Imvrian Committee letter to Deniz Baykal, January–February 1994.*
Imvros. (1994b). Declaration, May–June 1994.*
Imvros. (1994c). Imbros, May–June 1994.
Imvros. (1996). *Responsibilities*, October–November–December 1996.*
Isaakidis, G. (2014). Interview with author. Athens, 22 March 2014.*
Koumakis, L. (1996). *The miracle: a true story*. Translated from the Greek by P. Tsekouras. Athens.
Kyratzopoulos, V. (2006). *Unregistered genocide: Constantinople September 1955*. Athens: Ekdóseis Tsoukátou.*
Landsberg, A. (2004). *Prosthetic memory: the transformation of American remembrance in the age of mass culture*. New York: Columbia University Press.
Levy, D. and Sznaider, N. (2006). *The Holocaust and memory in the global age*. Translated from the German by A. Oksiloff. Philadelphia: Temple University Press.
Mandolessi, S. and Perez, M. E. (2014). The disappeared as a transnational figure or how to deal with the vain yesterday. *European Review*, 22(04), 603–612.
O Politis. (1973). The uproar in Turkey about repression of the Muslims in W. Thrace, May 1973.*
O Politis. (1975). They must be vindicated, September 1975.*
O Politis. (1977a). Two magic words, June 1977.*
O Politis. (1977b). History repeats itself, September 1977.*
O Politis. (1979). The Holocaust, May 1979.*
O Politis. (1982). Death rattle, September 1982.*
O Politis. (1984). A stop, June 1984.*
O Politis. (1985). And yet . . . the Nazi-esque crimes continue, June 1985.*
O Politis. (1988a). The non-existent Turkish rights on Cyprus, June 1988.*
O Politis. (1988b). It is paramount that Greek–Turkish collaboration acquires firm foundations, October 1988.*
O Politis. (1990). The new Omer [i.e. Homer] and the Omerika [i.e. Homeric] epics, March 1990.*
O Politis. (1991a). Ankara arouses the minority, March 1991.*
O Politis. (1991b). Answer to the falsehoods: systematic persecution of Turkey's minorities, September 1991.*
O Politis. (1994). Opinions and thoughts, April 1994.*
O Politis. (1995). Let's not allow the European to forget the atrocities of the Turk, April 1995.*

O Polítis. (1997). Open the gate. I'm a European! [cartoon], November 1997.*

O Polítis. (1999). *Dozmpas* Kurdistan, sorry Aro, March 1999.*

Oran, B. (1988). La minorité turco-musulmane de la Thrace occidentale (Grèce). In S. Vaner (Ed.). *Le différend gréco-turc*. Paris: L'Harmattan, 145–161.

Oran, B. (2004). The story of those who stayed: lessons from articles 1 and 2 of the 1923 convention. In R. Hirschon (Ed.). *Crossing the Aegean: an appraisal of the 1923 compulsory population exchange between Greece and Turkey*. New York: Berghahn Books, 97–115.

Ouzounoglou, N. (2013). Address at the statue of Constantine Palaiologos. Ecumenical Federation of Constantinopolitans ceremonial parade for the 560th anniversary of the Fall of Constantinople, 26 May 2013. Personal observation.*

Ouzounoglou, N. (2014). Skype interview with author. Athens/York, 16 May 2014.*

Papadakis, Y. (2004). Discourses of "the Balkans" in Cyprus: tactics, strategies and constructions of "Others". *History and Anthropology*, 15(1), 1–25.

Phoní tou Kourdistán. (1997). Message for the event of the Constantinopolitan Society, January–February 1997.*

Rothberg, M. (2009). *Multidirectional memory: remembering the Holocaust in the age of decolonization*. Stanford, CA: Stanford University Press.

Rothberg, M. (2010). Introduction: between memory and memory: from *lieux de mémoire* to *noeuds de mémoire*. *Yale French Studies*, (118/119), 3–12.

Rothberg, M. (2011). From Gaza to Warsaw: mapping multidirectional memory. *Criticism*, 53(4), 523–548.

Sarioglou, E. (2015). The '*Eléftheri Phoní*' of the *Septemvrianá*. In *The* Septemvrianá: *the persecution of the Hellenes of Constantinople*. Special issue of *Kathimeriní*, 10 September 2015, 85–86.*

Silverman, M. (2013). *Palimpsestic memory: the Holocaust and colonialism in French and Francophone fiction and film*. New York: Berghahn Books.

Xeinos, G. (1990). Investigating the historical course of the emigration of the *Imvriótes* in the 20th century and mapping their settlements. In *Symposium proceedings: the emigration of the Imvriótes in the 20th century and mapping their settlements*. Thessaloniki: Etairía Melétis 'Imvrou kai Tenédou, 11–29.*

de Zayas, A. (2007). The Istanbul pogrom of 6–7 September 1955 in the light of international law. *Genocide Studies and Prevention*, 2(2), 137–154.

Part IV
Homelands new and old

8 Welcome to Gökçeada
The Greek return to Imbros

When a visitor arrives on the island that the Greeks call Imbros, they are likely to be greeted with the Turkish words: *Gökçeada'ya hoşgeldiniz*, 'welcome to Gökçeada'. In the casual summer tourist, this gesture is unlikely to provoke any negative reaction. For many *Imvriótes*, however, returning to their place of birth after years or even decades of exile, to be welcomed to Gökçeada by residents who mostly arrived on the island after 1964 represents an affront to their sense of belonging on the island as natives. Two elderly returnees described this sentiment to me as follows:

> I will not allow anybody to say to me 'welcome'. Where are you welcoming me? You are welcoming me to my own house? [. . .] Who are you welcoming? I who have been here for 3000 years?
>
> (Antonis 10/08/2013)

> [When I come to the island] I feel both like a native and like a foreigner. When I come and they welcome me to the place, it offends me. Because he who is welcoming me really is a foreigner. And I say to him, 'welcome to you too! I was born here, I have been here for 4000 years. How long have you been here? 30 [years]?' [. . .] Who are you welcoming?
>
> (Themis 11/08/2013)

These proclamations of ancestral belonging phrased in the first person singular give a sense of the perturbations and tribulations experienced by those *Imvriótes* who, after a period of exile sometimes lasting decades, return to the island of their birth. This return movement, primarily seasonal but also semi-permanent and even permanent, has been gathering momentum since the early 1990s, after restrictions on travel to Imbros were eased. It somewhat distinguishes the Greeks of Imbros from the Greeks of Istanbul, for whom there has been no comparable large-scale seasonal or permanent return (though many former residents of the Princes' Islands do return to spend their summer vacations in their former places of residence). In part, this is because the *Polítes*, unlike many *Imvriótes*, have not typically kept possession of their properties in Turkey, and many of the former Greek neighbourhoods of Istanbul have changed beyond recognition, such that there are no places in Istanbul comparable to the Greek villages on Imbros in which to stage an *en masse* communal return.

In this chapter, I explore narratives of belonging and legitimacy in the Greek return to Imbros, based on oral and written expatriate testimonies as well as my own visit to the island in the company of the Imvrian Association in August 2013. The possibility of return has had a significant influence on the Imvrian expatriate community, reconfiguring their relationship with Greece and Greek national history, facilitating the transmission of an Imvrian identity to the second generation, and permitting a reconnection not just with lost places but between long-estranged people. Yet the return has also been laden with anxiety and ambivalence, as the community faces everyday challenges to their sense of belonging on Imbros, villages reinvigorated by people but still littered with ruins, and a resurgent but uncertain future on the island.

In recent years, there has been a revival of academic interest in return migration, with a particular focus on the 'return' of the second or subsequent generation(s) to the birthplaces of their parents, which has been dubbed 'roots migration' (Wessendorf 2007) or 'counter-diasporic migration' (King and Christou 2008; King and Christou 2010). Notable studies have concentrated on counter-diasporic migration to the Caribbean (Potter 2005; Potter, Conway, and Phillips 2005), Greece (Christou 2006; Chryssanthopoulou 2015; Christou and King 2010; Hess 2008; King and Christou 2010), Italy (Baldassar 2001; Wessendorf 2007; Wessendorf 2010), Japan (Tsuda 2003), and Pakistan/Kashmir (Cressey 2006). This literature has considered permanent return migration but also shorter return visits lasting days (e.g. for weddings and funerals) or weeks/months (e.g. for summer holidays) (Chryssanthopoulou 2015:80; King and Christou 2011:452, 458). Many of the findings indicate, amongst other things, that a disjuncture between nostalgic (post)memories of the homeland and the reality of return may lead to disillusionment and a 'reverse nostalgia' (Wessendorf 2010:376) triggering a reevaluation of the pre-return place of residence (Christou 2006:139; Christou and King 2010:643; Hess 2008:289, 307; King and Christou 2010:111–112; King and Christou 2011:454; King, Christou, and Ahrens 2011:488, 491, 498; Wessendorf 2007:1097–1098).

There has also been a small amount of specific interest in the Greek return to Imbros. This scholarship has focused in particular detail on the festival for the Assumption of the Virgin Mary celebrated in the village of *Agrídia* on 15 August. At this festival, oxen – donated or paid for by members of the community – are sacrificed as offerings to the Virgin Mary, and their meat, cooked overnight, is freely distributed in the yard of the village church after the morning liturgy on 15 August (Asanakis 2017:29–30).[1] Turkish anthropologist Babül and Greek anthropologist Tsimouris have explored how the festival, since the beginnings of the Greek return, has emerged as a site of contestation for competing claims over history and belonging. On the one hand, the 15 August celebration constitutes a symbolic demonstration of Imvrian belonging on the island, a ritual 're-membering' of place in Tsimouris' words

(Babül 2004:11; Babül 2006a:58–59; Babül 2006b:48–49; Tsimouris 2001:6; Tsimouris 2008:194; Tsimouris 2014:41–43, 48–50). The attendance of Turkish officials at the festival as guests of the Greek hosts provides an opportunity for the *Imvriótes* to establish belonging on the island as natives, and to forge cordial relationships with the local authorities so as to facilitate the continuing return movement (Babül 2004:11; Babül 2006a:59; Babül 2006b:49; Tsimouris 2008:237–239). The Turkish authorities, on the other hand, promote the festival as a demonstration of the island's cultural diversity, and – in light of the permits they issue for the event each year – as evidence for their tolerance of minority communities (Babül 2004:11; Babül 2006a:58–59; Babül 2006b:48–49; Tsimouris 2008:240; Tsimouris 2014:42). Babül has also explored Greek returnees' claims to belonging in relation to official Turkish discourse, arguing that whilst the Turkish state's claims to ownership over the island are premised on sovereignty and law, Imvrian counter-claims draw on memory and narratives of nativity (Babül 2004:2–3, 10–14, 15–19; Babül 2006a:50–51, 57–64; Babül 2006b:45–46, 48–51).

My focus, however, is not on the 'self-conscious memory site[]' (Schudson 1997:3) of the annual festival in *Agrídia* as a ritual of belonging, nor on official or legal channels of belonging, but rather on the negotiation and contestation of belonging in the everyday experience of the return. This is in part because the size and permanence of the return movement, and by extension the range of settings and situations in which belonging is asserted or called into question, has grown far beyond the centrepiece on 15 August. More broadly, it reflects my interest in how belonging is experienced and made meaningful in the mundane settings of daily life, rather than more specifically how it is represented in (or around) public ceremony and official discourse. Though Tsimouris has focused on narratives surrounding the 15 August celebration as a reflection of contests over belonging on the island, he has also touched upon the ways in which 'the past is painfully actualized' on a daily basis for the returning *Imvriótes* as they walk familiar routes, meet familiar faces, and repair their damaged properties (2014:54–55). It is this aspect of the Greek return to Imbros with which I am primarily concerned in this chapter. I explore how the *Imvriótes* themselves talk about the return and the ruins they see around them, the internal debates and schisms that emerge in the course of everyday life, and feelings of belonging and alienation expressed in banal rather than exceptional commemorative settings. In particular, I consider the quotidian challenges to returnee belonging that emerge from the demographic and topographic changes that have taken place on the island, the returnees' relationships both with the extant local *Imvriótes* and the island's Muslim settlers, and – especially for the summer vacationers – the manner of their return as visitors rather than permanent residents. I also contribute to the burgeoning literature on second-generation 'return' by focusing more specifically than in previous studies on the second-generation descendants of the expatriated *Imvriótes*, their experiences of visiting Imbros, and how their presence is received by older generations.

Between 'New Imbros' and 'Old Imbros'

When the Greeks of Imbros left the island in droves during the 1960s and 1970s, many feared that they would never be able to return. In 1973, the newspaper of the Imvrian Association wrote that those remaining on the island in anticipation of a reversal of fortunes were living with a 'futile hope' (*Imvriakí Ichó* 1973). The 1970s and 1980s were for the *Imvriótes* the decades of exile, during which time it was difficult to make even brief return visits. Aside from financial and psychological barriers, return journeys were complicated because Turkey had designated the island a restricted military zone. In order to set foot on Imbros, any returning *Imvriótes* were obliged to obtain a special permit from Çanakkale before boarding a boat for the island, and to surrender their passports for the duration of their stay (Xeinos 2011:76).[2] According to informants who did make the trip, those who were successful in obtaining visas for Imbros were commonly permitted only short stays on the island, whilst others were turned away altogether. Those who did make it to Imbros often recalled a sense of indignation at having to obtain permits to visit the place of their birth. As Vasillis – born on Imbros in 1938 – put it, remembering his visits to the island from Germany in the 1970s:

> I came here and I had to go to Çanakkale to take a *visa*, to come to my *home*. Those were difficult times [. . .] You come to your house and they keep your

Figure 12 Cartoon by Nikos Koilos from *Ímvros* May 1985.

A family of Imvriótes is depicted standing in the Aegean Sea contemplating two signposts, one labelled 'New Imbros' the other 'Imbros'. Copyright Imvrian Association. Reproduced with permission.

passport. Because I had come to my house. *My* house! [. . .] That bothered us a *great* deal

(12/08/2013)

Moreover, male expatriates who had left Turkey before undergoing their military service and had not yet acquired Greek citizenship were fearful of returning to Turkey lest they be detained by the authorities and compelled to fulfil their obligations as Turkish citizens (Christoforidis 1993:165). During this period, the Greek villages on Imbros suffered from decline and neglect: few of the departing *Imvriótes* sold their (remaining) properties, and with no one to look after the empty residences many buildings fell into disrepair (through a combination of natural causes and looting/vandalism).

Faced with the prospect of permanent estrangement from their place of origin, the *Imvriótes* set about reconstructing their community in their new places of settlement. They founded a cultural association (the Imvrian Association), congregated in coffee shops owned by compatriots, wrote and read nostalgic pieces about Imbros in their community newspaper, sought to continue traditions such as the 15 August festival (most notably on the island Salamis),[3] and discussed the establishment of a 'New Imbros' in Greece where they could settle *en masse* and return to a rural style of life (Xeinos 1990:20). In doing so, they were adhering to the well-established Greek ideology of 'lost homelands' (*chaménes patrídes*), which emerged from a nostalgic longing for place expressed in the memories, writings, and toponyms of Greek refugees displaced by the Greek–Turkish population exchange, and had by the 1960s become a central feature of Greek nationalist discourse (Liakos 1998; Liakos 2007:214–215). In February 1965, in light of the deteriorating situation on Imbros, the Imvrian Association took the decision that the construction of a New Imbros was the only way to ensure the community's survival (*Imvros* 1995b), and began to appeal to the Greek government to grant them agricultural land in Western Thrace where the *Imvriótes* could 'revive our lost *patrída* from its ashes, offering to Mother Greece a New Imbros' (*Imvros* 1977). This ambition was premised on the notion that 'Old Imbros' was a lost cause, as was made plain in the October 1972 edition of *Imvriakí Ichó*:

> [U]nited and tightly bounded, with one belief and one conviction, one hope and one dream: to acquire a second *patrída*, a 'NEW IMBROS'. Let us not wilfully blind ourselves with false hopes and comforts to the sick. The game is lost. Imbros has escaped our hands [. . .] A 'NEW IMBROS' must howsoever be established.
>
> (*Imvriakí Ichó* 1972)

Creating a New Imbros, the Imvrian Association emphasised, was about recreating an Imvrian locality:

Without a New Imbros, it is not possible to preserve the name of the old one, let's not delude ourselves, if we do not have our own church and our own school, our own organised community, where the idea of Imbros will be continually cultivated, even our own earth, to bury our dead.

(*Imvros* 1982a)

By 1980, a rural area near Komotini in Western Thrace had been earmarked as the future location for New Imbros, which was first visited by the Imvrian Union of Macedonia–Thrace in May 1980, and afterwards by the Imvrian-born Archbishop Iakovos of America alongside the societies of Athens and Thessaloniki in August 1981 (*Imvros* 1980a; *Imvros* 1980b; *Imvros* 1981a). The land, it was hoped, would be granted to the *Imvriótes* by the Greek state, and in November 1981 *Imvros* printed the prototype plans for the first and second phases of the settlement, intended to cover over 400,000 m² (*Imvros* 1977; *Imvros* 1981b; Pavlos, pers. comm., 4 November 2015). The Imvrian community associations had even begun to solicit applications from expatriated *Imvriótes* who were interested in being allocated plots of land in New Imbros (Asanakis 2016b; *Imvros* 1980c).

The large-scale resettlement of the *Imvriótes* in Thrace, however, never came to fruition, and ultimately the idea of New Imbros disappeared from the agenda altogether (*Imvros* 1994). Financial and practical difficulties were in the main decisive,[4] but the demise of the New Imbros movement also coincided with the re-emergence of 'Old Imbros' (Stelios 27/05/2013). After 1988, many of the impediments that had prevented the *Imvriótes* from visiting their island began to dissipate. Since the early 1980s, the Greek government had begun to grant citizenship to the Greeks of Turkey (see Chapter 1), permitting those who had lost their Turkish citizenship, and/or left without completing their military service, to cross the border into Turkey without fear of arrest. In around 1993, the Turkish authorities lifted the restricted access to the island, marking the transition of Gökçeada in the eyes of the Turkish government from a military zone to a touristic area (Babül 2004:7; Babül 2006a:56; Babül 2006b:48).[5] By this point, the open prisons near *Schoinoúdi* (see Chapter 1) had also been closed down, and the prisoners relocated off the island (*Imvros* 1992a). A brief period of Greek–Turkish reconciliation after the 1988 Davos process also helped to give expatriates the courage to return to Turkey. In line with these developments, the *Imvriótes* began to make tentative return visits, first in the late 1980s (Tsimouris 2001:5), then with increasing frequency throughout the 1990s.

These early returnees were mostly those born in the late 1950s or 1960s, who had migrated either to Istanbul or abroad at a relatively young age (Tsimouris 2001:6). Many had not seen each other since childhood, and they congregated on the island during the month of August. Such inaugural visits were marked by caution and nervousness. For many, the first return provoked a reliving of the trauma of their original departure, as described by Kostas, who returned in 1989 having left Imbros as a teenager in 1981:

[When I left for Greece] there was a climate of fear. [On the bus] I was waiting to pass the border to be free [. . .] The return had similar characteristics. When I return, my eyes are trying to be very keen. I am afraid once again, about what I will encounter, how they will treat me [...] For the first ten years, every time that we crossed the bridge on the way back to Greece from Turkey, we said 'oof! We have been saved again!'

(07/06/2013)

Unsure of how long the favourable climate would last, the young returnees were initially relishing the moment rather than making long-term plans, but when these fleeting pilgrimages became a regular summer tradition the returnees started to look to the future. In the words of Giorgos, a contemporary of Kostas, who first returned in 1991:

> We had the impression that we probably wouldn't come again. And so we got on very well in those years, because in essence we were just relaxing [...] We had parties, every day. But when Greek–Turkish relations improved and we realised that we will continue to come to Imbros, all that was shelved. We became serious.
>
> (14/08/2013)

In August 1992, a group of 104 young returnees drafted and signed an open letter appealing for others to join them in following summers (Christoforidis 1993:167–169), couched in terms of a return to roots and a simpler way of life:

> Friends, we are a group of young people whose only common characteristic is our Imvrian identity. This identity did not mean much for most of us and this appeal letter might never have been written. This year, however, we experienced something extraordinary: we came to Imbros [...] As young people we all face every day the problems placed upon us by stress, pollution, commercialism and even human relationships. We believe that this place, with its unique genuineness, its pure soul, and its – as yet – unpolluted nature, provides a unique opportunity for us to escape and simultaneously re-evaluate the impersonal society of our age. Come to our *patrída* so that we can get to know one another, so that we can discover human warmth again and feel the ancient soul of Imbros [...] Let us meet in the land of our fathers. Come to Imbros.
>
> (*Imvros* 1992c)

As the return movement became larger and more sustained, many *Imvriótes* set about rebuilding and refurbishing their family houses that had fallen into disrepair, in order to make them habitable for seasonal or even permanent residence. The mountainous *Agrídia* and its neighbour *Ágios Theódoros* – birthplace of Ecumenical Patriarch Bartholomew I – have probably seen the most dramatic revival, and although there are still ruined houses many have been restored: the Imvrian Association calculated that by 2007 in *Agrídia* alone around 180 houses had been rebuilt at a cost of over €4 million (Imvrian Association 2007). A greater proportion of the properties lie in ruin in the sprawling *Schoinoúdi* (over 80% according to Tsimouris 2014:47), although here too many returnees have taken pains to rebuild damaged family homes. In these three villages, a summer visitor is thus confronted by an incongruous blend of functioning, inhabited houses and ruined, half-collapsed buildings (see Figure 13, and below).

The number of summer returnees increased throughout the 1990s, and by the turn of the century between 2000 and 3000 *Imvriótes* could be found on the island in mid-August, travelling not just from Greece but also from Australia, Germany, North America, and elsewhere, and usually staying for between one and four weeks (Tsimouris 2001:5). A growing number of these are drawn from the foreign-born generation, who visit the island with their families during the summer vacation, and are henceforth referred to as the second generation. Some might be characterised as 'trailing travellers' (King and Christou 2011:459) too young to make choices about whether or not to take part, but many others actively and enthusiastically elect to make the annual journey. Many developed an emotional relationship to Imbros (and to one another) before their first physical encounter with the island through their attendance at Imvrian cultural associations (Xeinou 1993:190), although for others it was the visits themselves that sparked a particular interest in their origins and a stronger sense of commonality with their Imvrian compatriots (see below). Since the 1990s, an increasing number of *Imvriótes* – particularly retirees – have made a semi-permanent return, coming to the island at Easter and staying until October, then wintering in Greece or elsewhere; these returnees are known locally as 'six-monthers'. Others – again predominantly retirees – have returned to live permanently on the island; I call these individuals 'permanent returnees', distinguished from 'local *Imvriótes*', which is the term commonly used by expatriates to refer to those who never left. A significant number of expatriates, nevertheless, have never returned to the island, or did so only to sell/claim whatever remaining property they possessed or to collect sick and elderly relatives (Tsimouris 2008:212). Many of these non-returnees are those who left as adults, who prefer to preserve their memories of the island as it was before they left (*Imvros* 1990; Tsimouris 2001:6). According to estimates by the president of the Imvrian Association, after the opening of the minority schools in *Ágios Theódoros* in 2013 and in *Agrídia* in 2015 (on which, see below), the number of permanent Greek residents on the island reached 350 (of which around 50 are 'locals' who never left). Those Greeks who are resident on the island for six months or more of the year now number over 100, and in August there are typically between 2000 and 3000 Greeks on the island. In 2016, Greek residents were in a majority in the villages *Agrídia, Ágios Theódoros, Glyký*, and *Schoinoúdi* (significantly fewer Greeks remained in, or returned to, the capital *Panagía* and the villages *Kástro* and *Evlámpio*, the latter of which has been absorbed by the capital) (Asanakis 2016a).

If at the beginning of the 1980s Imbros seemed lost to its expatriate population, by the year 2000 seasonal and even permanent return had thus become a real possibility: as Imvrian Association president Christoforidis put it in a speech in 1997, for the young returnees 'Imbros is not a nostalgic past that we are attempting to revive', but 'a reality, a substantial portion of our life' (*Imvros* 1997). This, in turn, led to a re-evaluation of the discourse of 'lost homelands' and of the community's relationship to the Greek state. On 8 March 1988, the president of the

Figure 13 Panoramic view of *Schoinoúdi* (Imbros), 2013.
Note the juxtaposition between renovated and whitewashed houses and those lying in disrepair and ruin. Photograph by the author.

Imvrian Association met with Greek Deputy Foreign Minister Yiannis Kapsis to express his frustration that Imbros had not been raised by the Greek side during recent bilateral meetings between the Greek and Turkish prime ministers Andreas Papandreou and Ozal (the aforementioned Davos process). Kapsis responded to this criticism by assuring the Imvrian Association that the plight of the *Imvriótes* had not been forgotten, and would be brought to the attention of the Turkish authorities in future meetings (although he also declared that the expropriations of land and property on Imbros were a matter of Turkish domestic policy in which Greece could not intervene, much to the dismay of the Association) (*Imvros* 1988b). *Imvros* cautiously welcomed Kapsis' pledge, but also expressed concern as to whether or not the Greek authorities considered the situation on Imbros to be an 'open question' and one that might yet be reversible, and accordingly appealed to the Greek government to recognise that 'Imbros and Tenedos do not constitute "lost *patrídes*"' (*Imvros* 1988a). In a 1991 article calling on the *Imvriótes* to pull together to 'rebuild our *patrída*' rather than selling their remaining property on the island, and appealing for support from the Greek state and tolerance from the Turkish state, the Imvrian Association likewise declared that 'THE *IMVRIÓTES* do not accept "lost *patrídes*"' (*Imvros* 1991). In 1994, *Imvros* similarly complained that Greece 'prematurely and without a fight, included Imbros and Tenedos in the lost *patrídes*' (*Imvros* 1994). As the return movement became a reality, representatives of the Imvrian Association became increasingly dissatisfied with the assimilation of the *Imvriótes* and their recent history into a nationalist discourse of 'lost homelands', which they identified as both a symptom and possible cause of Greek government indifference towards the community. Many came to feel that their only true *patrída* was to be found on Imbros, not in a 'New Imbros' within the Greek *patrída* (see Figure 14): as the Association declared in a new regular

Figure 14 The caption reads: 'The tragic fate of the majority of the Imvriótes who live today in some big city: The houses do not differ greatly from jails, whilst those that they were compelled to leave by force, have already converted to 'beautiful ruin'. Left: an elderly Imvriótissa in her 'home', in Athens. (Photograph G. Xeinos). Right: That was once her real HOME. (Photograph Vaso Xeinou).' Copyright Imvrian Association. Reproduced with permission.

Photographs by Giorgos Xeinos and Vaso Xeinou from Imvros October–November 1987.

banner that appeared in the newspaper in 1993, 'the *Imvriótes* have a *patrída*. They have an identity and a 3000 year history' (*Imvros* 1993).

Confronting 'the real Imbros': challenges and prospects

It is the great hope of the Imvrian Association and many of the expatriated *Imvriótes* that the summer pilgrimages to Imbros by its former inhabitants might be metamorphosed into a larger, more permanent and sustained presence for the community on the island. Realising this ambition requires the expatriates to confront what Pavlos – born in *Ágios Theódoros* on Imbros in 1970, and a regular seasonal returnee since the late 1980s – called 'the real Imbros'. I asked Pavlos whether he had considered making a permanent return to the island, to which he responded:

> I have thought about it, and not just now that I have a family, but always [. . .] On the other hand, things are not simple [. . .] All of us have the image of the holiday: in August you go, there are people in the villages, all of the doors are open, you go to the sea, *et cetera*. Yes. But if I return, it means that I will be there for at least eleven months, and for one month I will go on vacation elsewhere. There is the reality. The real Imbros starts there.
>
> (29/05/2013)

Once the month of August is over, the population in the Greek villages dwindles, dropping off dramatically during the winter months. According to residents of *Agrídia* interviewed in 2013, for instance, whilst there might be as many as 500 people in the village in the summer, in winter there are just 25 (Miltos 06/08/2013; Orestis 06/08/2013; Stamatios 07/08/2013). As permanent returnee Antonis put it, in the winter in *Schoinoúdi* 'it is the wind that keeps you company' (10/08/2013).

There are several practical obstacles standing in the way of the re-establishment of a sizeable year-round Greek population on the island. First and foremost, there is the struggle to retain whatever property titles remained in the hands of the *Imvriótes* after the expropriations of the 1960s. In 1994, Turkey embarked upon a cadastral survey on the island, requiring property owners to present themselves and prove that they had been the legal owners for at least 20 years and were continuing to make active use of the property (Babül 2004:11–12; Council of Europe Resolution 1625 (2008); Imvrian Association no date; *Imvros* 1995a; Tsimouris 2008:126). The *Imvriótes*' long-term exile, coupled with the loss of Turkish citizenship by many, greatly complicated this endeavour (Babül 2004:12; Babül 2006a:57; Babül 2006b:48; Tsimouris 2008:126–127). Properties that were not successfully claimed in this manner passed into the ownership of the state, and challenging such decisions through the courts was an expensive process with no guarantee of success (Babül 2004:12; Babül 2006a:58; Council of Europe Resolution 1625 (2008)). The Imvrian Association has accordingly urged each individual to take personal responsibility for their own estates and to ensure that their properties do not pass into the hands of any non-Imvrian, maintaining that '[n]obody has the right to be indifferent' about property ownership on the island

(*Imvros* 1995a; see also Tsimouris 2008:126, 211–212). It was in order to ensure that they had the right to claim or inherit property that many expatriates retained, or took pains to reacquire, their Turkish citizenship, and the Imvrian Association has called on all those who can reacquire Turkish citizenship 'without great sacrifices' to do so (*Imvros* 1992b).

Preserving property titles in the Greek villages greatly facilitates the return of retirees and vacationers in the summer months, but a more sustainable Greek community would also have to encourage working-age people and their children to (re)establish themselves on Imbros. Language, citizenship, and socio-cultural differences between urban centres such as Athens and Thessaloniki and rural Imbros are all pertinent issues in this regard, but the two obstacles most consistently identified by potential Imvrian returnees concern work and education. Although a handful of returnees are able to work in agriculture – Christos, for instance, has assisted with his father's animal husbandry since his permanent return in 2011 (08/08/2013) – the majority of the cultivable fields and olive groves owned by the *Imvriótes* were confiscated by the state during the 1960s and 1970s, making the re-establishment of a large-scale agricultural economy amongst the returning Greeks difficult. The recent touristic awakening of the island might provide alternative employment opportunities, and indeed some returnees have established small businesses on the island: Savvas, for instance, has opened a cafe in one of the Greek villages (14/08/2013). In a paper delivered at an Imvrian Association conference on the future of Imbros in 1993, Yiannis Politis strongly advocated for the *Imvriótes* to take advantage of the tourism industry, urging his compatriots to return to the island not only as 'guests-tourists' but also as 'entrepreneurs' (1993:155). There is, however, some concern amongst the community that large-scale Greek involvement in business might create tensions with the resident Turkish population. As café owner Savvas put it:

> Many people want us to form large businesses here [. . .] [But] if three or four of our people open businesses and become competitors [with the Turkish residents], I think there will be a problem. They will look at us a bit like, 'ah, we did this and this to get you to leave, and now you return and raise your head again.' For that reason I would prefer people like me to set up small shops, so as not to bother other people so much.
>
> (14/08/2013)

As I indicated in Chapter 1, the abolition of Greek-language education on Imbros was one of (if not the most) significant trigger for the exodus of its Greek-speaking population, and for most young Greek families who might resettle on the island it is a precondition that their children would be able to receive an education taking place half in Greek in accordance with the Lausanne provisions. In September 2013, after almost 50 years without any Greek-language education on the island, the Turkish authorities granted a permit for the opening of a new minority primary school in *Agios Theódoros*. This development was the result of many years of negotiations involving both Greek and Turkish officials, the expatriate societies, the European Union, and the Ecumenical Patriarchate in Istanbul. It was followed by the opening of a secondary school and a high school in September 2015, and for the academic year 2015–2016 there are at least 14 students attending the minority schools on the island. The opening of the schools was a hugely significant moment for the community both symbolically and practically, a 'dream of half a century [that has] become a reality', in the words of the Imvrian Association, which provides 'hope for a new beginning on the troubled land of Imbros' (Imvrian Association 2013b). The reopening of the minority schools has been a cause for great optimism for many, but has also provoked anxieties about the community's long-term prospects on the island. Some returnees expressed to me their fears that they would not be able to attract sufficient numbers of students to make the schools viable, and that in turn the schools would serve as a visible demonstration of the community's uncertain future. Speaking in 2013 before the opening of the primary school in *Agios Theódoros*, permanent *Schoinoúdi* resident Antonis even speculated that the granting of the permit might be a ploy of the Turkish authorities:

> I am afraid. Maybe I am wrong, but I'm afraid it will remain an anecdote [. . .] The Turks behaved cleverly here. 'They [the *Imvriótes*] want the school, we [the Turkish authorities] will issue a permit to open their own school'. Now they will say, 'come on, you were shouting for so many years about how you don't have a school. I have opened one for you. What is going on? Where are the children?'.
>
> (10/08/2013)

It is hard to overstate, however, the enthusiasm with which the new schools have been received by many *Imvriótes*, for whom the presence of children on Imbros is a necessary and exciting first step towards creating a future for the Greek community on the island. As six-monther and *Agrídia* resident Kleopas argued:

> It is a chain, one thing will bring another. When you start something, you have to build upon it slowly, you cannot do everything in one go [. . .] If those children spend their childhood years on the island, they will always come, even 50 years later.
>
> (09/08/2013)

In sum, the post-1988 Greek return to Imbros has been a time of great optimism for the expatriated Imvrian community, tempered, however, by a sense of anxiety regarding its sustainability. As I prepared to take my leave from the Imvrian Association in Athens after a research expedition in June 2013, news filtered through from the island of the murder of a Greek woman by a Turkish woman in *Schoinoúdi*. The attack was a 'crime of passion' unrelated to broader Greek–Turkish relations or the problems of the past (Imvrian Association 2013a), but nevertheless triggered an immediate concern amongst Association members that the tragic incident might damage intercommunal relationships and jeopardise the position of the Greek community on the island. The Imvrian Association moved quickly to issue a press release the following day, stressing that 'this isolated incident should not affect the efforts for reestablishing the links of the Imvrian Community with its native island and the return of as many Imvriotes to the island as possible' (Imvrian Association 2013a). To the best of my knowledge, no major destabilising repercussions emerged from the murder, but the incident testifies to an unshakeable fear amongst the *Imvriótes* that at any moment something might occur to destabilise the precarious momentum of the return movement.

'Native tourists': belonging in the Imvrian return

Since 1988, the returning *Imvriótes* have been engaged in a struggle not only to address the practical difficulties associated with seasonal and permanent return, but also to re-establish their own sense of belonging on an island greatly transformed during their period of exile. The renovation of family homes (see above) is an important component of this effort. Indeed, many returnees recalled great distress when they were unable to stay in their own homes on their first return to the island. Panagiota – born in 1927 and a migrant to Greece in 1980 – made a return journey to the island in 1989, but was compelled to stay in a hotel as her own house in *Panagía* was leased to a Turkish resident. She described the experience as follows:

> One year, we came with my son, and we stayed in a hotel. And when I went out walking and saw our [family] home up there, whilst I was staying in the hotel, I went crazy. I said, 'my son, I am leaving, I cannot stay here. Either find me a house to stay in until the rental term is up, or I am leaving'.
>
> (Panagiota 07/08/2013)

It was to avoid this feeling of alienation that Vasillis – returning to visit the island in 1993 after a 15-year absence – chose to sleep amongst the ruins of his family home in *Agrídia* rather than seek out rented accommodation. As he explained it to me, 'I could not pick up my suitcase and go to another house; I wanted to sleep here' (Vasillis 12/08/2013).

Even once individual family homes are renovated, however, returnees still face daily reminders of the island's traumatic recent history through their encounters with ruined houses whose owners never returned, and expropriated lands that used to belong to the community. When I asked Dimitra – who was born in 1939 and is now a six-monther on the island – how the ruins in *Agrídia* made her feel, she responded with a rich description of life in the village in the 1950s and 1960s, before making the following contrast with the contemporary situation:

> I remember all of that, you understand? Good things, lovely things. And yesterday, when I passed by the house of my cousin, I lent on the fence of the

yard with both of my hands, and I thought, 'what is man, and what becomes of him?' The buildings, and the houses, everybody leaves, the people die, and the houses have become ruins. What can you say? I remembered the olden days, at that moment.

(09/08/2013)

Antigoni – born in *Schoinoúdi* in 1975, a resident of Greece since 1983, and today a seasonal returnee to Imbros – similarly described how the ruins and expropriated areas provoked in her a feeling of disinheritance, saying to me:

> My feelings are mixed [. . .] You feel that the house in which you live is yours: that is mine and nobody can touch it. You see, however, the ruins, the bits that they have taken, and I don't know if they can ever become ours once again [. . .] I mean, it is theirs. As much as we might want to believe otherwise, it used to be Hellenic but they have conquered it.
>
> (13/08/2013)

Panagiota likewise recalled with anger and dismay one particular summer when she spotted one of her father's former fields out of a bus window, which had been expropriated by the state and given to Turkish settlers to cultivate. She told the story as follows:

> I mentioned that it was our field, and somebody on the bus said to me, 'get down there and harvest it, if it belongs to you'. I said, 'I should go down there and steal from my own field?' I was struck by tears. There was a pear tree in that field, which my father had planted. Below the field they [the new owners] had a grocery, and I asked those Turkish ladies, 'that tree, did it bear fruit this year?' 'It was full,' they replied. And I said, 'did you not leave one pear for me to eat, it was my father that planted that tree. It is our field'. And they said to me, 'it was yours; now it is ours'.
>
> (Panagiota 07/08/2013)

On one afternoon during my own stay on Imbros, I went out walking with summer returnee Kostas in *Agrídia*, who beckoned me to follow him along a shortcut. After we had struggled up a narrow, ascending gap between two ruined houses littered with roof tiles and fallen masonry, Kostas turned to me and said, 'sorry I brought you this way. I always remember it from when I was a child, as a path lined with people drinking coffees' (author's field notes 08/08/2013; see Figure 15). Operating in the 2010s on memories from the 1950s, 1960s, and 1970s, the returning *Imvriótes* experience an uncanny encounter with a place in which familiarity and strangeness collide awkwardly (Tsimouris 2008:212). For the returnees, the ruins literally and figuratively disrupt the flow of everyday life in the villages, conjuring up unbidden memories of the past and those who peopled it, and threatening to derail their renewed sense of belonging on the island.

Figure 15 Looking back along the path in *Agrídia* (Imbros) walked by Kostas and the author in August 2013.

Photograph by the author.

Surveying the juxtaposition between the lively streets bustling with tourists and the ruined houses of *Ágios Theódoros* in mid-August, Pavlos remarked to me that 'sometimes you have the unpleasant feeling of being a tourist' (author's field notes 08/08/2013). Indeed, for seasonal returnees such as Pavlos, the brevity of the summer sojourns, and the fact that they coincide with the peak of the tourism season on the island, often heighten the disorientating notion that they have become, in the words of one writer in *Ímvros*, a 'foreigner in the land where you were born [. . .] in your own *patrída*!' (*Ímvros* 1992b). Panagiota coined the term 'native tourists' to describe these concurrent and paradoxical sentiments of belonging and alienation:

Panagiota: Now people come, as you know, from all the corners of the earth. Native tourists [chuckles].
Halstead: Native tourists?
Panagiota: I call them native tourists, because they left for faraway places, yet most come in the summer. Some have houses, some ruined, some do not [. . .]
Halstead: Do you feel like that, like a tourist?

Panagiota: Yes, yes. I mean, I feel like a foreigner. When we meet [Turkish people] on the boat, and they ask, 'where are you from? Are you natives or not?' I say 'I was born here, where are *you* from?' [...] This is our *patrída*, home.

(07/08/2013)

It is not uncommon for the local *Imvriótes* who never left the island to characterise the summer returnees in comparable terms (Tsimouris 2008:217). These few hundred, primarily elderly islanders are proud at having remained on the island, and have often for years resisted their relatives' attempts to transport them to Greece (or elsewhere) (Tsimouris 2001:9). When I asked Patroklos, a nonagenarian and local resident of *Agios Theódoros*, whether he had ever considered leaving, he replied in no uncertain terms, thumping the table for emphasis: 'I leave? I never once thought that I could leave from here. I did not think once about leaving from here. And nor did I leave. I did not go anywhere' (08/08/2013). Katerina, a local resident of *Agrídia*, similarly exclaimed to me in jest: 'I say, "until the last, I will hold aloft the flag, I will not abandon the Hellenic flag!"' (06/08/2013) These local *Imvriótes* experience a somewhat ambivalent relationship to the summer returnees. Though they are undoubtedly happy to see old familiar faces, particularly returning relatives and children who have resettled abroad, it was often suggested to me by both returnees and elderly locals that the summer sojourners spoil the serenity for those that remained: as Katerina put it, when I asked if she was pleased that the *Imvriótes* had started to return, 'I will tell you: I am not so much because, you know, when you have become accustomed to your peace and quiet [laughs]' (06/08/2013).

For many of these local *Imvriótes*, yearly witnesses to the disjuncture between the carnivalesque month of August and the hardships of winter, the summer returnees are simply 'tourists'. Fokas, who left for Greece in 1975 but now once again lives permanently on the island, recalled that in the 1990s 'the older people saw us as strangers, even our own people. "The tourists have come," they would say. Old people. Our people. Of course, they had lived many years here alone, and they saw us as tourists' (13/08/2013). Babis – who emigrated to Australia in 1970 and now returns on-and-off in half-year stints – reported a similar indifference amongst the local population towards the returnees, suggesting that the former felt the latter had acquired pretensions in their host countries:

Now the old people say, 'ah, they [the returnees] will all leave. They are tourists'. [But] they don't think of me as a tourist, they see me as a local. Why do they see me as a local? Because I don't return as though I went to Australia and now I'm 'Somebody'. I return and I become exactly the same as them.

(12/08/2013)

The perception that the presence of the seasonal returnees is purely recreational and makes little contribution to the long-term prospects of the community was even shared by permanent returnee Miltos, who had left the island for Greece in 1969 in his twenties but now resides on Imbros permanently. He had the following to say:

> Now people come to the village, but they come as tourists. And tourism is not what we want, for me to come to my *patrída* as a tourist. I have to come to do something, to sow something, to take advantage of whatever has remained. Not the 10 days, 'tra la la, bla la la', we come, we sing and dance, and we leave again, and we throw our money about. If I was coming for tourism, I would go to some other island [. . .] Six-monthers are tourists [too]. If they want a touristic programme, they should go elsewhere. They do not help at all.
>
> (Miltos 06/08/2013)

Not surprisingly, many returnees vociferously reject their appellation as 'tourists'. In the words of permanent *Schoinoúdi* returnee Mimis: 'I never felt like a tourist, because a man does not feel like a tourist at home. He must not feel so. Regardless of the fact that some of our people called us tourists [. . .] The older people called us tourists, for them, of course, we are tourists, but I do not accept being a tourist in my house' (13/08/2013). Permanent *Schoinoúdi* resident Antonis similarly remarked that 'I never felt like a tourist, I didn't allow myself to feel like a tourist' (10/08/2013), whilst seasonal returnee Babis, asked if he had ever felt like a tourist, responded, 'no, I feel like a real *Imvriótis*, because I am *real*' (12/08/2013). Running through statements of this sort is not only a strong sentiment of belonging to Imbros, but also a defiant insistence in not allowing that sense of belonging to be called into question.

The returnees' daily interactions with the island's Muslim settlers, as well as the former's perception of how the latter see the returning Greeks, present further occasions for the assertion and contestation of belonging. Since 1960, the island has been extensively settled by Anatolian Turks and Kurds, who took up residence in the capital, five new settlements, and some of the Greek villages (particularly *Kástro*, but also in smaller numbers in villages with extant Greek populations such as *Ágios Theódoros* and *Schoinoúdi*) (Babül 2004:14–16). My interviewees almost unanimously agreed that the island's Muslim residents were friendly and welcoming towards the returning *Imvriótes*, and several observed that the opportunity for the returnees to interact with Turks on a daily basis had helped to replace a negative image of the generalised Turk as a hostile other with a more positive impression of particularised Turks as human beings (Theodossopoulos 2006:9; see also Chapter 4). In Istanbul-born *Imvriótis* Loukas' terms:

> We gather together there [on Imbros] in the summer, and we recycle not just the bad things and the hatred and such, but also new experiences and needs. And we have our houses, and you must get a builder, a Turk, [you must] speak to the taxi driver, as a friend, afterwards at your wedding his wife brings you a present, she knits a jacket for your child, and after that they become people.
>
> (03/07/2013)

For their part, the island's Turkish authorities have formally welcomed the return of the Greeks, portraying their presence as a demonstration of Gökçeada's multiculturalism (in a manner that nevertheless typically sidelines Imvrian experiences of persecution and expatriation in favour of a narrative of equality and tolerance) (Babül 2006a:60, 63; Babül 2006b:50; Tsimouris 2014:40–41, 47–48). In a 2013 interview with the newspaper *Çanakkale Olay*, for instance, Gökçeada's Turkish mayor Yücel Atalay encouraged the *Imvriótes* to return and take their place in the local economy:

> That is our biggest dream. With luck they will come. It is our great expectation. At the moment, we are able to accommodate around 500 families [. . .] We must make them entrepreneurs [. . .] With them Imbros will move forward [. . .] We have always treated everyone equally, we have not separated anyone. We behaved the same towards everyone. We gave everyone the opportunity to work. Until now no incident has occurred. Imbros can become a very beautiful model, a model applicable across the whole country.
>
> (*Gökçeada Gazetesi* 2013)

The returnees' reactions to such expressions of welcome are somewhat ambivalent. On the one hand, cordial intercommunal relationships have greatly facilitated the return movement, and invitations for the Greeks to participate in the touristic development of the island present a possible means by which the seasonal return might be made more permanent and sustainable (echoing Politis' arguments at the 1993 Imvrian Association conference; see above). As was noted at the beginning of the chapter, however, accepting this invitation also means tacitly acknowledging that it is the Turkish authorities who have the right to welcome or 'accommodate' the *Imvriótes* rather than *vice versa*, an implicit challenge to the returnees' sense of historical belonging and nativity on the island. As permanent *Schoinoúdi* resident Mimis put it when I asked about his relationships with the village's Muslim inhabitants: 'they have welcomed us. Now, you will say to me, "*they* have welcomed *you* in your *patrída*?" Unfortunately, that is the way it is' (13/08/2013).

The returning Greeks also provide a significant seasonal injection into the local economy (Babül 2004:10; Babül 2006a:57; Babül 2006b:48), buying produce from shopkeepers and stallholders in the capital, hiring local labour to renovate their houses, travelling around the island in taxis driven by Turks, and when necessary renting hotel rooms operated by settlers. This fact is not lost on the returnees, many of whom feel that the island's Muslim population sees them as visiting tourists rather than returning natives. In the words of six-monther Vasilis:

> Now they want us. Especially those that have businesses and shops. They wait for us, saying, 'when will August arrive when all of those Hellenes will come?' [. . .] Many say, 'if you Hellenes don't come, the following year we will leave' [. . .] Especially us six-monthers, every Sunday we go to the market.
>
> (12/08/2013)

Cafe owner Savvas concurred, attributing the settlers' positive reception of the *Imvriótes* to the latter's economic contribution: 'the Turks have accepted our return', he declared, 'because they think of us as tourists. They say, "great, come here, leave your money". That was the idea of the authorities. We come for three or four weeks, spend plenty of money, and we leave' (14/08/2013).

If the returnees are thus afraid that they are nothing more than touristic consumers in the eyes of the island's authorities and settler populace, they simultaneously have to confront the possibility that they themselves have become *objects* of touristic curiosity. As Politis remarked in his 1993 speech (see above), '[a]s strange as it may seem to you, the only touristic interest which Imbros has to offer, are the half-ruined houses and the handful of Christian traditions of the few inhabitants of the island' (1993:151). Gökçeada's mayor estimated that, in the year 2012, 320,000 Turkish tourists visited the island (*Gökçeada Gazetesi* 2013). Though it would be inaccurate to suggest that these huge numbers were drawn solely by the island's Greek history (most come for the beaches and the windsurfing), it is nonetheless part of the appeal for many Turkish tourists (Babül 2004:7), who not only attend ceremonial events like that on the 15 August in *Agrídia*, but also make daily visits to the Greek villages throughout the month of August, soaking up the atmosphere and taking photographs of the Greek houses (reflecting something of a broader multicultural nostalgia amongst some sections of contemporary Turkish society (Babül 2004:8)). Characteristically, a Turkish journalist who visited the island in 2012 affectionately wrote about the 'picturesque' backstreets of *Agrídia* and the cheerful Greek-speaking old ladies (*Today's Zaman* 2012). As Babül has discussed, a number of Istanbul Turks have even bought houses in some of the Greek villages, and see themselves as part of the effort to preserve the Greek cultural heritage of the island (2004:9).

Permanent returnee Christos spoke favourably to me about the 'cultivated' and 'educated' Turks who had recently acquired former Greek houses in *Ágios Theódoros*, observing:

> They attempt to preserve the physiognomy of the village in the old-style, for it to be recognisable as a Hellenic village. They too do not want it to change from that perspective: I can tell you that they work harder to preserve it than our people!
>
> (08/08/2013)

Several of my interviewees also saw the influx of Turkish tourists as an opportunity to inform ordinary Turks about the plight of the island's Greek community that is conspicuously absent from official pronouncements and tourist brochures: Antonis, Fokas, and Savvas each had stories of eliciting sympathetic and even tearful responses from visiting Turks who had sought an explanation for the ruined and abandoned Greek villages (Antonis 10/08/2013; Fokas 13/08/2013; Savvas 14/08/2013). Nevertheless, these visitations are sometimes a cause of discomfort for the returnees. Yiannis, a member of the young second generation summering in *Agrídia*, offered me the following impressions about the presence of Turkish tourists in the village:

> First of all I think it is good because the island becomes more well known, tourism will increase [. . .] On the other hand, I can say that I don't like it so much, sometimes when I see them taking photographs, because I feel that they are doing it because we are something totally different from them, something so strange, with the negative meaning of strange.
>
> (15/08/2013)

Pavlos similarly lamented that when he sees Turkish tourists circulating with cameras in *Ágios Theódoros* he sometimes feels 'like the Native Americans on their reservations' (author's field notes 08/08/2013). As we walked together through the village on an August afternoon, we passed a delicatessen blaring out Greek music. When I remarked that it was interesting that the *Imvriótes* had started to open businesses like these, Pavlos corrected me: 'that is a Turkish shop. It is run by Turks. They probably play the Hellenic music to appeal to the Turkish tourists' (author's field notes 08/08/2013). Six-monther Themis, meanwhile, explaining his reservations about the 15 August celebration in *Agrídia*, told me that he had the uncomfortable feeling that it had become a staged performance:

> We come here, for parties and dances, I see it and I am saddened even more. I don't know how other people see it. They go and they force themselves to dance. Where did they find that good humour? Inside their souls are crying. It is like they put us on a stage, the Turks put us on a stage to watch us, and when the performance finishes they leave.
>
> (11/08/2013)

The Greek returnees to Imbros experience an island transformed not only by the decay of its Greek villages, but also by its touristic awakening. Whilst the possibility of participating in this tourism industry might provide the *Imvriótes* with employment opportunities and therefore make permanent return more feasible, it also generates anxieties amongst those uncomfortable with the notion that their return to the place of their birth is simply feeding the local Turkish economy. Equally, though they may feel affronted by the suggestion that it is they who must be welcomed by the settlers rather than the other way around, in turn the flow of Turkish tourists into the Greek villages provides the *Imvriótes* with the opportunity themselves to play the role of hosts to Turkish outsiders. In this sense, the returnees' everyday interactions with the growing tourism industry simultaneously undermine and strengthen their sense of belonging on the island: treated as tourists in the capital, they are themselves visited as natives in their villages.

'When you return to your *patrída*': the second generation

In Athens, many second-generation *Imvriótes* develop a strong emotional attachment to the island of their parents' birth from afar under the auspices of the Imvrian Association, dubbed a 'little Imbros' by one second-generation interviewee

(Natasha 07/06/2013). In the words of Paschalis, who was born in Athens in 1976 to Imvrian parents and had not yet (at the time of our interview) visited Imbros, 'hearing constantly about Imbros, seeing photographs of the island, we feel like we are on the island when we come here [to the Assocation]'. Having grown up around the Association and other Imvrian families, Paschalis emphasised that 'I think of [Imbros] as my *patrída*, even if I was not born there and have not been' (07/06/2013). Maximos – who was born in Athens in 1999, and had family from both Imbros and Tenedos, but had by 2013 only managed to visit the latter – exhibited a similar emotional bond to Imbros. When I sat down to talk with Maximos, who was sporting a necklace in the shape of Imbros, he quickly began to offer a wistful and involved description of the island that would not have seemed altogether incongruous coming out of the mouth of a much older, first-generation *Imvriótis*:

> Imbros has seven villages, each of which is very beautiful. Whatever season you visit Imbros, it is beautiful; each season has its own beauty. August, of course, is the nicest, because you can go and swim and other things: it's the season of the youth.
>
> (06/06/2013)

I then asked him where he would say he was from, to which he responded:

Maximos: From Imbros, I think of myself as being from Imbros, it is more in my heart than Tenedos. If somebody asks me, the first word I will say is 'Imbros'.
Halstead: And Athens, when would you say that?
Maximos: Athens? Towards the end.

(06/06/2013)

He reinforced this sense of belonging later in our interview when, replying to a question about the image of the island that he has in his head, he stated 'I personally am from *Ágios Theódoros*', a village in which he has never actually set foot (Maximos 06/06/2013). For Paschalis and Maximos, the prospect of being able to visit the island in the near future was eagerly anticipated, a sentiment that was only enhanced by the fact that many of their friends have already made the trip. In Peggy Levitt and Nina Glick Schiller's terms (2004:1010–1011), these second-generation *Imvriótes* demonstrate not only 'transnational ways of being' (that is, having connections with another place of origin) but also 'transnational ways of belonging', insofar as they explicitly foreground these connections and consciously identify with Imbros as a homeland.

It is clear, nevertheless, that visiting Imbros, and in the process meeting other compatriots, has often significantly strengthened second-generation *Imvriótes*' transnational ways of belonging. In a 2012 speech given in Istanbul to mark the publication by a Turkish university of a monograph about the *Imvriótes*, Imvrian Association president Christoforidis described what he called a 'modern Imvrian identity' that had been inculcated amongst foreign-born and foreign-raised *Imvriótes* through the 'to-and-fro between foreign countries and the village on the island' (Christoforidis 2013). For Christoforidis, it was hugely significant that this second-generation Imvrian identity had been developed through physical encounters with the island rather than purely in cultural associations abroad, permitting the second generation to develop their own relationship to Imbros as a contemporary place (Christoforidis 2013). Indeed, interviewees from the second generation who were regular visitors to the island unanimously concurred that they had developed a strong sense of belonging on Imbros derived from their experiences. Many of them travel to the island habitually for the summer holiday, most often with parents or other relatives, but also in some instances independently of their families. Eva, for instance, first visited the island with her mother in 2011, but has since continued to make the annual excursion in the company of a friend's family. Asked to describe her feelings when she visits the island, she explained:

> When I come to Imbros I feel very at ease [. . .] It may not be my home here, but I feel like I am at home on the island. And there may be Turks here, and I may not know the language or be able to talk, but I feel very nice, I do not feel like I am in a foreign place.
> (Eva 13/08/2013)

Yiannis – born in Thessaloniki in 1996, and a regular visitor with his family since 2000 – exhibited similar sentiments. When I asked him where he was from, he hesitated briefly before answering in a manner that foregrounded his parental origins rather than his own place of birth, belying the 'dual allegiance' (King and Christou 2010:110) characteristic of second-generation counter-diasporic travellers: 'my mother is from Imbros, and my father is from a village in Langadas near Thessaloniki'. It was only when I sought clarification that he specified his own birthplace as Thessaloniki, and he nevertheless sought to emphasise that 'I've been to Imbros plenty of times'. Asked about his experiences of visiting Imbros, he described how he developed a feeling of homeliness in *Agrídia* as the summer population of returnees grew larger, interestingly characterising his first excursion as a 'return':

Halstead: How would you describe your first trip to Imbros?
Yiannis: I think it was amongst my favourite visits [. . .] When you return to your *patrída*, both the trip and the memories that it brings are lovely.
Halstead: And have you ever felt at all like a tourist when you come here?
Yiannis: Look, in the beginning, I felt like a guest, because most of the houses were in ruins, and the Turkish population was dominant [. . .] Now, in the last few years, because most of the houses are inhabited again, and with the six-monthers the Greek population has become more prevalent, especially in our village, I feel like I belong to this community.
(15/08/2013)

Later on in the same interview, Yiannis explained that he had decided to apply for Turkish citizenship in order to be able to inherit his family home in the future (something that many of his peers were also considering). I asked him whether he had any fears that his friends in Greece would react badly to this decision, to which he responded:

> If we had had this conversation two years ago, I would have been very certain that I did not want to take Turkish citizenship, because I believed that I would 'become a Turk'. But afterwards I sat down and thought about it, and, slowly slowly, I came to feel more Imvrian than Hellenic. So I thought that whatever they may say in Greece, it doesn't bother me [. . .] Because as I told you the Hellenes behaved towards the *Imvriótes* as though they were Turks, and the *Imvriótes* isolated themselves somewhat, they became like a different family, embedded, of course, within the Hellenic community, but somehow different. And now that we come to the island, and I start to learn the history and meet other young people, I feel Imvrian [. . .] So I feel Hellenic, of course, but increasingly I feel Imvrian.
> (Yiannis 15/08/2013)

Through the experiences and friendships he has gained on the island, Yiannis has developed a local Imvrian 'inflection' (Cowan and Brown 2000:20; see Chapter 2) to his Hellenic ethnic identity, which has not led him drastically to re-evaluate his relationship to the country of his birth, but rather allowed him to feel distinctive within it; Hellenic, that is to say, but different from other Hellenes (see Chapter 3). In his own words:

> [My grandfather told me] that the Hellenes [of Greece] were very ambivalent, and treated the *Imvriótes* not as Hellenes but as Turks [. . .] Us, as *Imvriótes*, we belong: we are Hellenes, we simply didn't have the fortune to join the Hellenic state [. . .] We are in some way, not different exactly, simply as *Imvriótes* we are otherwise united [i.e. they have a distinctive kind of solidarity]. When you see an *Imvriótis* you think of him as your fellow countryman more than you would a Hellene [. . .] So certainly I feel that Imbros is my *patrída*, and Thessaloniki too, simply Imbros is something separate.
> (Yiannis 15/08/2013)

In his aforementioned 2012 speech in Istanbul, Imvrian Association president Christoforidis expressed a hope that this second-generation Imvrian identity, 'precisely because it continues to be developed *also* in Turkey', might enable the *Imvriótes* to 'continue in some way to remain a part of modern Turkish society and attempt to establish a dialogue with Turkish society' (Christoforidis 2013). For him, the permanent resettlement of second-generation *Imvriótes* on the island 'constitutes perhaps the last opportunity for the rebirth of a culture that belongs to Turkey that it might continue to offer something to Turkey' (Christoforidis 2013). Regardless of whether or not this represents a plausible scenario for the future, however, it was clear that for my second-generation interviewees the prospect of acquiring a wider sense of belonging in contemporary Turkish society was some way off. In common with their parents and grandparents, they tended mentally to separate Imbros from the rest of Turkey, or even, more specifically, to separate the Greek villages on the island from the rest of Gökçeada. In summer visitor Lia's words, 'as familiar as we feel in the village, where we feel like natives, when we are at the border we feel foreign, I personally feel like a foreigner' (in interview with Eva 13/08/2013). Eleni likewise observed that 'I do not feel like a tourist here [in my village], but if I go across to Çanakkale I am a tourist' (15/08/2013), whilst her friend Takis, during the same conversation, explained that 'when I am in my village [...] and I feel that I am with Hellenes, and people that I know, I do not feel like a tourist [...] I feel like I am in my place, but when I am with the Turks, I feel like I am in another country' (15/08/2013). This somewhat spatially constricted sense of belonging made it harder for the second-generation *Imvriótes* to envisage their permanent resettlement on the island, and although all expressed a desire to continue their seasonal visits, most were hesitant about the prospect of living on Imbros permanently (at least during their working lives). Some of the obstacles they cited are common to Greeks all over Greece whose parents or grandparents migrated from rural to urban settings (such as the lack of employment opportunities, or the cultural differences between cities and villages), but others are particular to the case of Imbros (the language barrier, for instance, and the scarcity of Greek residents on the island). In Eva's terms, 'it is not the same thing to live alone with the Hellenes, and to live with the Turks that you do not know well' (13/08/2013). In this sense, we might say that the youth of Imbros is torn between a desire to belong on Imbros and the difficulties of belonging on Gökçeada.

The participation of the second generation in the Greek return to Imbros was a source of great enthusiasm for many of my older interviewees. Retired six-monther Stamatios, for instance, approvingly pointed out to me that on one day in August 2013 he had been able to count 45 children in the central square of *Agrídia*, more than the total number of permanent residents of all ages in the winter months (07/08/2013). Permanent *Schoinoúdi* returnee Mimis likewise praised the efforts of the second generation, even if their exuberance might spoil the peace and quiet of the older returnees:

> I have spent many Augusts here – celebrations, parties for the youth, all of that – I guess you could say that I'm tired of it [...] It is lovely because it enlivens the island [...] It is lovely regardless of the fact that I have grown tired of it. But it must happen. It is our culture and tradition, and our *patrída* is brought to life by its traditions.
>
> (13/08/2013)

There was, nevertheless, for some of my first-generation interviewees a nagging concern that the second generation's presence on the island is impermanent, and that their youthful parties will not outlast the passing of their parents and grandparents. Antonis, for example, felt it most unlikely that many of the summer visitors would become permanent residents, remarking:

> The young people come here. On 13 August [at a party for the youth in *Schoinoúdi*] you will find a *dámpa doúmpa* [i.e. deafening club music]. Nothing more [. . .] It would be a great surprise if two or three of those – it won't be more than two or three who will take root here. It is not possible [. . .] Eh, as long as it lasts.
>
> (10/08/2013)

Permanent returnee Miltos concurred, suggesting that the second generation would cease to visit Imbros once their parental safety net disappears:

> They like to come here for the freedom of the 'la la la, bla bla bla'. Within a month, they want to leave, they become bored [. . .] If I leave, I who does the cooking, looks after the house, *et cetera et cetera*, and they cannot come and find everything ready, they will not come again.
>
> (06/08/2013)

For their part, the second-generation *Imvriótes* readily acknowledge that the character of their visits differs somewhat from that of their parents and grandparents, but also emphasise that their desire to prolong their relationship with the island is genuine. As Lia put it:

Lia: For us young people it is a bit different, because the truth is we come for holidays. But we get on very well because kids from all over the world come. We might not socialise during the year but we gather every summer here, and we make very close friends [. . .] and a summer does not pass that we do not think of going to Imbros.
Halstead: So for you it is tourism?
Lia: Yes, truth be told it is more touristic in my mind than [for] my mother who comes here for work, to do things with the house and such, whilst we come for holidays, because we go swimming, we see our friends: it is different, certainly. But there are other parameters, because this house will pass to us when we grow up, we want to continue to come, even if our parents cannot.

(13/08/2013)

Indeed, to dismiss the second generation's attachment to Imbros as purely recreational would be to do them a disservice. Many are intending to acquire Turkish citizenship so as to be able to inherit parental properties (well aware that this might be frowned upon or misunderstood by some in Greece), are making efforts to learn Turkish (sometimes through classes given at the Imvrian Association), and – notwithstanding their scepticism about its practicality – have often given serious thought to the possibility of more permanent settlement (some, for instance, talked about retiring to the island). Their own accounts of the role that they play in the summer return are marked by a clear self-awareness as regards both the ways in which their activities might be perceived by older *Imvriótes* and the inevitability that they must connect with the island on their own terms. In Yiannis' words:

> The older people, who were born here, who lived the traditions traditionally, for them it was a reality. Now we who come here, we want to live them as they lived them, but simply things have changed [...] We never lived the times that they lived, and nor was there video for us to be able to see how they lived, how they celebrated, we simply know the tradition. And so we, as young people, celebrate in our own manner, as *Imvriótes* who are coming back to their *patrída*.
>
> (15/08/2013)

Indeed, whilst the passage of time, the changes it has brought, and the second generation's own rather different upbringing away from the island may prevent them from practising 'the traditions traditionally', ultimately if their presence on Imbros is to be lasting they will have to (re)create traditions contemporaneously on their own terms, fusing values and ways of life developed in 'host' countries with their understanding of the Imvrian 'homeland'. As Christoforidis argued in Istanbul in 2012, in order for the Imvrian community 'to envision a new future on the island' it is essential that the second generation be able 'to create a new narrative of their own upon the contemporary soil of their *patrída*' (Christoforidis 2013).

Conclusions

The Greek return to Imbros is one that is still developing and mutating, as the number of seasonal visitors grows and the prospect of more extensive and sustained return migration begins to materialise. The narratives of those *Imvriótes* who have participated in this movement confirm that return does not simply put an end to displacement or unmake diaspora (Hess 2008:289; King and Christou 2008:20, 22). Even for those who have relocated (semi-)permanently to the island, but perhaps particularly for the summer visitors, return is an ongoing process of 'homing' (Christou and King 2010:640), triggering great joy and gratification but also anxieties and tensions not altogether dissimilar to those experienced during the original displacement from Imbros. For those who left Imbros at a young age or were born abroad, travel to Imbros certainly seems to have reaffirmed and strengthened a sense of belonging on Imbros and to the Imvrian community, yet at the same time is accompanied by an awareness that permanent return may be something of a 'chimera' (King and Christou 2011:454), as the 'real Imbros' may be radically different from that remembered, imagined, or experienced during the buoyant summer sojourns (see also King and Christou 2010:111; King, Christou, and Ahrens 2011: 488, 491). Return, from this point of view, might be better conceptualised as part of the pathology of displacement rather than its antithesis or its panacea.

Discussing international policy on refugee repatriation, Elazar Barkan lamented that the *right to return* for refugees enshrined in the Universal Declaration of

Human Rights had become a *rite of return*, a rhetorical stance rather than a practical response to expatriation: '[t]he right of return', he wrote, 'becomes more of a rite than a right when politicians support the demand rhetorically and use it as an easy escape from finding an actual solution to real crisis' (2011:236). Such *rites of return* have certainly been practised by Turkish politicians as regards Turkey's expatriated Greek minority: Turkish Prime Minister Recep Tayyip Erdoğan has on several occasions invited the Greeks to return to Turkey (Ecumenical Federation of Constantinopolitans 2012:8), and as we saw above Gökçeada's Turkish mayor has specifically called on the *Imvriótes* to come back to the island. Over the last quarter of a century, the expatriated Greeks of Imbros have been engaged in a struggle to turn these *rites of return* into a concrete and sustainable *right to return*. This has involved addressing not only practical difficulties relating to property rights, citizenship, language, education, and employment, but also the question of how to reconcile a sense of belonging to Imbros with the contemporary reality of Gökçeada: the ruins, the tourists, the expropriated lands and those who now live and work there, the perception of the returnees in the eyes of the local *Imvriótes* and Turks alike, and the ways in which the second generation's Imbros might differ from that of their parents and grandparents. Recalling his first return to Imbros in 1996 after a 20-year absence, six-monther Themis spoke of the difficulty he had retracing once familiar paths:

> I went to our buildings, our outhouses, I went to our fields: unrecognisable. Because I knew the area very well – I even used to know which trees were where – I used to be able to walk the path at night without lights. But now I go there in the day and I cannot walk it, because everything has fallen into ruin.
> (11/08/2013)

Since 1988, the expatriated *Imvriótes* have walked once again on the island of their birth. Yet for now at least, they must do so along paths littered with ruins, both literal and psychological.

Notes

1 Traditionally the sacrifices were performed by the villagers themselves in the village, although in recent years the animals have been killed in a slaughterhouse in the capital at the insistence of the authorities. The animals were usually donated by those seeking help from the Virgin Mary, for instance in the case of illness of the donor or a family member, or in the hopes of securing a good marriage for the donor's children (Asanakis 2017:29). Since the early 1990s, the composition of the festival's attendees has transformed dramatically, as increasing numbers of 'outsiders' – Greek and Turkish tourists, Turkish residents of the island, foreign researchers – began to attend, such that by 2000 the *Imvriótes* were somewhat 'lost in the crowd of tourists' (Tsimouris 2008:228).
2 There is no direct transport link between Greece and Imbros, and returnees travelling from Greece come through Turkey (usually by road through Thrace or sometimes by plane to Istanbul) and then take a boat from Çanakkale to the island.
3 A number of *Imvriótes* had bought summer houses on Salamis, and, beginning in 1980, they decided to revive the annual 15 August celebration (Asanakis 2017:34–35).

4 The Imvrian Association laid the blame firmly with the Greek authorities for prematurely withdrawing their support for the establishment of a New Imbros near Komotini (*Imvros* 1982b; see also Xeinos 1990:37). The movement finally foundered in the early 1990s, when migrants of Greek descent from post-Soviet states settled in the area that had been earmarked for New Imbros (Asanakis 2016b).
5 Babül dated the lifting of the restricted zone to 1993, although a March 1992 *Imvros* article included the end of the restricted zone in a list of promising developments that had already occurred (*Imvros* 1992a).

References

(Items marked * are in the Greek language.)

Asanakis, A. (2017). Panagía Imvriótissa *of Salamis: its history*. Athens.

Asanakis, P. (2016a). Email to H. Halstead re. Greek population of Imbros, 12 May 2016.*

Asanakis, P. (2016b). Email to H. Halstead re. New Imbros, 12 May 2016.*

Babül, E. (2004). Belonging to Imbros: citizenship and sovereignty in the Turkish Republic. Paper presented at the conference *Nationalism, Society and Culture in Post-Ottoman South East Europe*. 29–30 May 2004. St. Peter's College, Oxford. Available at: www.academia.edu/6707095/Belonging_to_Imbros_Citizenship_and_Sovereignty_in_the_Turkish_Republic [Accessed on 17 April 2016].

Babül, E. (2006a). Claiming a place through memories of belonging: politics of recognition on the island of Imbros. *New Perspectives on Turkey*, 34, 47–65.

Babül, E. (2006b). Home or away? On the connotations of homeland imaginaries in Imbros. *Thamyris/Intersecting: Place, Sex and Race*, 13(1), 43–53.

Baldassar, L. (2001). *Visits home: migration experiences between Italy and Australia*. Melbourne: Melbourne University Press.

Barkan, E. (2011). The politics of return: when rights become rites. In M. Hirsch and N. K. Miller, (Eds.). *Rites of return: diaspora poetics and the politics of memory*. New York: Columbia University Press, 227–238.

Christoforidis, K. (1993). The Imvrian youth in relation to the *patrída* today, tomorrow. In *Imvrian two-day conference: Imbros today. Problems, prospects*. Athens: Imvrian Association, 165–170.*

Christoforidis, K. (2013). *Speech of the President of the Imvrian Association Kostas Christoforidis at the presentation of the book 'the Romioí of Imbros' (Bahçeşehir University)*, 12 November 2012. Available at: www.imvrosisland.org/news_det.php?id=847 [Accessed on 20 October 2013].*

Christou, A. (2006). American dreams and European nightmares: experiences and polemics of second-generation Greek-American returning migrants. *Journal of Ethnic and Migration Studies*, 32(5), 831–845.

Christou, A. and King, R. (2010). Imagining 'home': diasporic landscapes of the Greek-German second generation. *Geoforum*, 41(4), 638–646.

Chryssanthopoulou, V. (2015). Reclaiming the homeland: belonging among diaspora generations of Greek Australians from Castellorizo. *Diaspora: A Journal of Transnational Studies*, 18(1–2), 67–88.

Council of Europe. Parliamentary Assembly (2008). *Gökçeada (Imbros) and Bozcaada (Tenedos): preserving the bicultural character of the two Turkish islands as a model for co-operation between Turkey and Greece in the interest of the people concerned*. Resolution 1625 (2008). Available at: assembly.coe.int/nw/xml/XRef/Xref-XML2HTML-en.asp?fileid=17668&lang=en [Accessed on 10 April 2016].

Cowan, J. K. and Brown, K. S. (2000). Introduction: Macedonian inflections. In J. K. Cowan, (Ed.). *Macedonia: the politics of identity and difference*. London: Pluto Press, 1–27.
Cressey, G. (2006). *Diaspora youth and ancestral homeland: British Pakistani/Kashmiri youth visiting kin in Pakistan and Kashmir*. Leiden: Brill.
Ecumenical Federation of Constantinopolitans. (2012). *The Greek Orthodox minority of Turkey: history of human rights violations and the need of remedy and reparations*. PowerPoint presentation, May 2012. Available at: www.conpolis.eu/uploadedNews/Human%20rights%20of%20the%20Greek%20Orthodox%20minority%20of%20Turkey-May%202012b.pdf [Accessed on 15 May 2014].
Gökçeada Gazetesi. (2013). A wide-ranging interview with the mayor, 10 June 2013. Translated by Valeria Antonopoulou, 26 July 2013. Interview originally conducted by *Çanakkale Olay*. Available at: www.imvrosisland.org/news_det.php?id=926 [Accessed on 7 January 2016].*
Hess, C. (2008). What are 'reverse diasporas' and how are we to understand them? *Diaspora: A Journal of Transnational Studies*, 17(3), 288–315.
Imvriakí Ichó. (1972). New Imbros, October 1972.*
Imvriakí Ichó. (1973). On the threshold of a new history, March 1973.*
Imvrian Association. (2007). *Concerns for the future*, 12 May 2007. Available at: www.imvrosisland.org/news_det.php?id=187 [Accessed on 20 January 2016].*
Imvrian Association. (2013a). *Murderous assault at Schinoudi (Dereköy), Imvros (Gökçeada): appeal to respect the family of the victims and support the return of the Imvrian Community to its native island*. Press release, 8 June 2013. Available at: www.imvrosisland.org/UserFiles/File/Deltyp/Press_Release_Imbros_080613_Eng.pdf [Accessed on 10 September 2013].
Imvrian Association. (2013b). *Commencement of lessons at Greek school on Imbros*. Press release, 17 September 2013. Available at: www.imvrosisland.org/news_det.php?id=952 [Accessed on 5 January 2016].*
Imvrian Association. (no date). *Calendar of important events*. Available at: www.imvrosisland.org/imvros.php?subid=15&catid=1 [Accessed on 12 December 2015].*
Imvros. (1977). From our point of view: let there be a solution, April 1977.*
Imvros. (1980a). Bound to the land of Greece, March 1980.*
Imvros. (1980b). Exploratory excursion to 'New Imbros' in *Pagoúria* near Komotini, July–August 1980.*
Imvros. (1980c). The *Imvriótes* of Melbourne for the resettlement in *Pagoúri*[a] near Komotini, July–August 1980.*
Imvros. (1981a). Archbishop Iakovos at the settlement 'New Imbros', September 1981.*
Imvros. (1981b). The street plan of the model settlement 'New Imbros', November 1981.*
Imvros. (1982a). Trumpet call, November 1982.*
Imvros. (1982b). Questions that remain unanswered, December 1982.*
Imvros. (1985). Untitled cartoon, May 1985.*
Imvros. (1987). Untitled image and caption, October-November 1987.*
Imvros. (1988a). The [Imvrian] Association promotes the demands of the *Imvriótes* and Tenédioi: the Imbros question on the stage, March 1988.*
Imvros. (1988b). Meeting of the President [of the Imvrian Association] with Yiannis Kapsis, March 1988.*
Imvros. (1990). Untitled image and caption, January–February 1990.*
Imvros. (1991). Into the print of the nails . . ., July–August 1991.*
Imvros. (1992a). Changes that give rise to hope, March 1992.*
Imvros. (1992b). Imbros in development, July–August 1992.*

Imvros. (1992c). Letter-appeal of the young *Imvriótes* compiled in August 1992, September–October 1992.*
Imvros. (1993). The *Imvriótes* have a patrída. They have an identity and a three-thousand year history, March–April 1993.*
Imvros. (1994). Declaration, May-June 1994.*
Imvros. (1995a). Protect your properties! March–April–May 1995.*
Imvros. (1995b). 'Imvrian Association' 1945–1995: '50 years of contribution and activity', September–October–November 1995.*
Imvros. (1997). The four-day conference of May, April–May–June 1997.*
King, R. and Christou, A. (2008). Cultural geographies of counter-diasporic migration: the second generation returns 'home'. *University of Sussex, Brighton, Sussex Migration Working Paper, 45*.
King, R. and Christou, A. (2010). Cultural geographies of counter-diasporic migration: perspectives from the study of second-generation 'returnees' to Greece. *Population, Space and Place*, 16(2), 103–119.
King, R. and Christou, A. (2011). Of counter-diaspora and reverse transnationalism: return mobilities to and from the ancestral homeland. *Mobilities*, 6(4), 451–466.
King, R., Christou, A., and Ahrens, J. (2011). 'Diverse mobilities': second-generation Greek-Germans engage with the homeland as children and as adults. *Mobilities*, 6(4), 483–501.
Levitt, P. and Schiller, N. G. (2004). Conceptualizing simultaneity: a transnational social field perspective on society. *International Migration Review*, 38(3), 1002–1039.
Liakos, A. (1998). The ideology of the 'lost *patrídes*'. *To Vima*, 13 September 1998.*
Liakos, A. (2007). Historical time and national space in modern Greece. In T. Hayashi and F. Hiroshi, (Eds.). *Regions in Central and Eastern Europe: past and present*. Sapporo: Slavic Research Centre, Hokkaido University, 205–227.
Politis, Y. (1993). Possibilities for the émigré *Imvriótes* in the touristic and economic development of Imbros. In *Imvrian two-day conference: Imbros today. Problems, prospects*. Athens: Imvrian Association, 145–157.*
Potter, R. B. (2005). 'Young, gifted and back': second-generation transnational return migrants to the Caribbean. *Progress in Development Studies*, 5(3), 213–236.
Potter, R. B., Conway, D., and Phillips, J. (2005). *The experience of return migration: Caribbean perspectives*. Aldershot, Ashgate Publishing.
Schudson, M. (1997). Lives, laws, and language: commemorative versus non-commemorative forms of effective public memory. *The Communication Review*, 2(1), 3–17.
Theodossopoulos, D. (2006). Introduction: the 'Turks' in the imagination of the 'Greeks'. *South European Society and Politics*, 11(1), 1–32.
Today's Zaman. (2012). *Return to Imbros: a new look at Gökçeada*, 3 June 2012. Available at: www.todayszaman.com/news-282293-return-to-imbros-a-new-look-at-gokceada.html [Accessed on 13 September 2013].
Tsimouris, G. (2001). Reconstructing 'home' among the 'enemy': the Greeks of Gökseada (Imvros) after Lausanne. *Balkanologie*, 5 (1–2).
Tsimouris, G. (2008). *Imvrioi*. Athens: Ellinikà Grámmata.*
Tsimouris, G. (2014). Pilgrimages to Gökçeada (Imvros), a Greco-Turkish contested place: religious tourism or a way to reclaim the homeland? In J. Eade and M. Katić, (Eds.). *Pilgrimage, politics and place-making in Eastern Europe: crossing the borders*. Farnham: Ashgate Publishing, 37–56.
Tsuda, T. (2003). *Strangers in the ethnic homeland: Japanese Brazilian return migration in transnational perspective*. New York, NY: Columbia University Press.

Wessendorf, S. (2007). 'Roots migrants': transnationalism and 'return' among second-generation Italians in Switzerland. *Journal of Ethnic and Migration Studies*, 33(7), 1083–1102.

Wessendorf, S. (2010). Local attachments and transnational everyday lives: second-generation Italians in Switzerland. *Global Networks*, 10(3), 365–382.

Xeinos, G. (1990). Investigating the historical course of the emigration of the *Imvriótes* in the 20th century and mapping their settlements. In *Symposium proceedings: the emigration of the Imvriótes in the 20th century and mapping their settlements*. Thessaloniki: Etairía Melétis Ímvrou kai Tenédou, 11–29.*

Xeinos, G. (2011). *Imbros and Tenedos: parallel histories*. Athens: Etaireía Melétis tis Kath' Imás Anatolís.*

Xeinou, V. (1993). The *Imvriótes* in Greece and the diaspora. In *Imvrian two-day conference: Imbros today. Problems, prospects*. Athens: Imvrian Association, 179–192.*

Conclusions

> Coming here [to Greece], the first thing you feel is the freedom that you are in your place: a Hellene in Greece. Because that is how we felt over there: Hellenes without Greece. When we came here, suddenly we were Hellenes in Greece, wherever you went it was Hellenic, in the churches, in the schools, in the hospitals, wherever. You constantly hear and speak Greek, you are not afraid.
>
> (Markos 04/05/2013)

> The mentality of the Hellene was totally different from the *Romiós* [. . .] They called us 'seeds of the Turks'. We left there as infidels, and we came here as seeds of the Turks [. . .] We are a group of people who essentially have two *patrídes* and none.
>
> (Maria 09/05/2013)

These two quotations capture something of the range of ways in which the expatriated Greeks of Turkey interpret and represent their disorientating and often fragmentary experiences of belonging and alienation in two nation-states: Turkey, the country of their birth, where they were periodically persecuted on the basis of their ethnic and religious identity; and Greece, their purported national *patrída*, in which they encountered both reassuring similarities and striking differences between themselves and the Greeks of Greece, who were sometimes ill-acquainted with their plight or viewed them with suspicion due to their Turkish birthplace. In this book, I have sought to demonstrate how the Greeks of Turkey respond to these ambivalent experiences by emphasising the specificities of their own recent and more distant local historical heritages.

Inclusive particularity

In some cases, members of the expatriated communities of Istanbul and Imbros counteract this sense of alienation by either emphasising sameness to establish inclusion within Greece, or stressing difference to demonstrate distinction from the Greeks of Greece. This is often reflected in the choice and use of particular identity labels. For some expatriates, especially those with particular grievances towards the Greek state, a Romaic identity separates the expatriates from the

Hellenic residents of Greece, a discursive position that sometimes finds concrete expression through a preference for using, retaining, or regaining Turkish citizenship rather than relying on Greek identity papers. This stance prompts others within the community, fearful of opening up a chasm between the Greeks of Turkey and the Greeks of Greece, to eschew the label *Romioí* and emphasise their Hellenic selves. Actively seeking to lose Turkish citizenship and to acquire/possess only Greek citizenship, ordering coffee rather than tea when in the company of *Elladítes*, or marking the anniversary of 1453 in front of a statue of a hero of the 1821 Greek Revolution, all represent further means by which expatriates might seek inclusion through sameness.

I have argued in this book, however, that national belonging can also be sought through strategies of *inclusive particularity* that approach inclusion in the imagined national community from the standpoint of local distinctiveness. Expatriate interviewees frequently expressed belonging both to Greece as a national homeland and to Istanbul or Imbros as local homelands, and whilst these two identifications sometimes existed in tension with one another, as often as not they were mutually reinforcing, such that informants felt that they belonged in Greece precisely because of their Constantinopolitan or Imvrian identity. For many *Polítes*, a Romaic self-identification rooted in the Byzantine legacy – officially sidelined yet popularly resonant within Greece, and according to Greek national history the period when pagan Hellenism merged with Orthodox Christianity, a cornerstone of modern Greek identity – serves as a means to *simultaneously* differentiate themselves from the inhabitants of Greece *and* affirm that they themselves are particularly Hellenic. My informants from the agriculturalist Imvrian community were generally less inclined to characterise themselves as cosmopolitan *Romioí*, but nonetheless drew on the particularities of their own locality in an effort to demonstrate the authenticity, specificity, and venerability of their Hellenic credentials through tales of their island's colonisation by Ancient Athenians, and the preservation of its Hellenic traditions in spite of repeated occupations and the absence of protection from the Greek state. Furthermore, even for those born *inside* Greece, national identity and statehood are not inextricably bound together, and the relationship between the locality and the nation is not invariably a zero-sum conflict between competing and incompatible claims on individual belonging and selfhood. For my interviewees from the younger, second generation of *Imvriótes*, experiences of visiting Imbros alongside their parents and grandparents certainly have fostered a greater emotional identification with the locality of the island as a contemporary physical place as opposed to a bygone cultural or historical inheritance. But this does not seem to prompt them to supplant a national Hellenic sense of self with a local Imvrian one, so much as to incline them to reimagine their Hellenic identity in terms of a different locality (i.e. Imbros rather than Athens or Thessaloniki).

The strategy of inclusive particularity is further in evidence in the efforts of some expatriate activists to counteract their marginalisation within Greek society by presenting themselves as exemplary national heroes and national martyrs. As we have seen, expatriate interviewees and writers often claim a 'privileged knowledge' of the Turkish other acquired through their personal experiences of living in Turkey, and deploy ethnic stereotypes supposedly derived from this intimate knowledge to both explicate historical occurrences and substantiate contemporary claims about self and other. In some contexts, some members of the expatriate community endorse Greek nationalist stereotypes through representations of the 'bad Turks' who are violent, impulsive, and readily roused by nationalist ideologues. This serves not only to explain their experiences of persecution in Turkey by individuals that sometimes included those they had thought of as friends, but also to counteract a perceived indifference on the part of the Greek state and populace by depicting the expatriates as martyrs to Greece's quintessential other. Representatives of expatriate community organisations sometimes go further, suggesting not only that their experiences of persecution in Turkey constitute them as particularly legitimate residents of Greece, but also that their particular expertise in diagnosing the behaviour of the Turkish other makes them a particular asset to the Greek state in its diplomatic dealings with Turkey.

Similar concerns underpin the commemorative activities orchestrated by some of the prominent expatriate organisations. In the late 1970s, the Constantinopolitan Society and its associates began to publicly mark the anniversaries of the Istanbul Riots and the Fall of Constantinople, hoping in this manner to raise awareness amongst the Greek public of the expatriates' experiences of discrimination in Turkey. In these commemorative ceremonies, as well as in associated publicity materials and articles printed in community newspapers, expatriate activists often compare their own experiences during the riots in 1955 to the last stand of the Byzantines against the Ottoman Empire in 1453, and present the latter as a necessary precursor to the Greek Revolution in 1821. Through this palimpsestic layering of the Fall of Constantinople and the *Septemvrianá*, the nationally resonant history of 1453 also becomes a local history for the *Polítes*, whilst in turn the local history of 1955 takes on national significance as a restaging of the historic Fall. At the same time, the nexus between 1453 as a local history and the 1821 Greek Revolution writes the *Polítes* and their community into Greek national history, not as subordinates to the heroes of 1821 but as their inspirational historical archetypes. Comparable analogies are drawn by some *Imvriótes* between the political and demographic changes instituted by Turkey on Imbros during the 1960s and the aftermath of Turkish military action on Cyprus in 1974, and between the few hundred remaining elderly residents of their island and the 300 Spartan warriors of Leonidas who stayed to defend Thermopylae from the Persians. In this manner, Imvrian activists join their counterparts from Istanbul in casting themselves in the likeness of exemplary heroes and martyrs from Greek national history. Such discourses reframe local experience as a national cause, and in doing so construct the Greeks of Turkey not just as legitimately Greek but as archetypally Greek. They again demonstrate that it is distinctiveness as much as sameness that expatriate activists evoke to establish inclusion and tackle their marginalisation in Greece. This inclusive particularity indicates that ordinary people's sense of national belonging may be constructed through attachment to the local rather than simply in opposition to it, and through the accentuation of local heterogeneity as well as the assertion of national commonality.

The past as a critical mirror

The potential of these acts of past presencing, however, lies not simply in their ability to produce national inclusion, but also in their capacity to simultaneously sustain a critique of the national self. My interviewees drew on their 'privileged knowledge' of the Turkish other not only to construct narratives of the 'bad Turks', but also to place emphasis upon the virtues of the 'good Turk' who is honourable, respectful, and industrious, a representation that commonly functions as a means to critically appraise the alleged untrustworthiness, crudeness, and idleness of the inhabitants of Greece. These contrasting stereotypes of the Turkish other are not necessarily targeted at separate and clearly demarcated groups within Turkish society, but are rather used to explain the contingent behaviour of others in particular situations, such that an individual who was said to exhibit the tendencies of the 'good Turk' in one context might be depicted as complicit in the violence of the 'bad Turks' in another. By the internal logic of such stereotypes, it is the same fanatical sense of honour amongst the Turks that accounts for both extremes of violence and extremes of courtesy, in much the same way as the Greeks' archetypal love of individual liberty and democratic equality clarifies their irreverent and anarchic tendencies. From this point of view, as well as constituting a point of reference in opposition to which one might establish positive aspects of the self, the national other is also an equally compelling tool for collective self-criticism and for spotlighting perceived defects amongst one's co-nationals.

In like manner, national history and nationalist rhetoric can be used by local communities to express dissent as well as assent in regard to official policy and interpretations of the past. The palimpsest of 1453 and 1955, and the rendering of the last *Imvriótes* on Imbros as the 300 Spartans, both serve in one sense to place local experience within a national context, but also carry an implicit criticism of contemporary Greek diplomacy for its failure to live up to the archetypes of the past. Further evidence for the malleable and subversive potential of nationalist rhetoric can be found in changing Imvrian attitudes towards the ideology of the 'lost homelands'. During the 1970s and 1980s, when even short-term return to Imbros seemed implausible, the expatriated *Imvriótes*, in common with other Greek communities with origins outside the territory of the contemporary Greek state, focused on commemorating their locality as part of the national pantheon of lost *patrídes*, and attempting to establish a 'New Imbros' on Greek soil. After 1988, however, the growing possibility of return, and the realisation that Imbros might not be 'lost' to its former Greek inhabitants, provoked in Imvrian activists an increased sense of dissatisfaction with the diplomacy of the Greek state. This led not so much to the *abandonment* of the rhetoric of 'lost *patrídes*', but rather its *redeployment* as a discursive device for criticising a perceived inactivity or fatalism on the part of Greek politicians and diplomats. As the Imvrian Association declared in its newspaper in 1982, in a strongly worded article complaining that the Greek state had failed in its duty to the *Imvriótes* by withdrawing its support for the New Imbros settlement: '[w]e wish firstly to remind everyone that Imbros is the latest in a series of 'lost *patrídes*' [...] and afterwards to express our bitterness about the disregard for [our] sacrifice on the altar of the national interest in difficult hours' (*Imvros* 1982).

This book has demonstrated that ethnicity, national identity, and national history are domains of active and varied use, negotiation, and contestation in the oral and written narratives of expatriated Greeks from Turkey. By asserting the particularity of their own local relationship to both the national past and the national other, many expatriates seek to establish their authenticity as residents of Greece and members of the Greek nation whilst simultaneously maintaining a sense of their distinctiveness vis-à-vis other Greeks. These individuals are not narrowly confined or stifled by national categories, which offer them significant leeway to express heterogeneity, differentiation, and dissent, even if they are sometimes somewhat reliant upon them as explanatory frameworks for their life experiences. Nation-states strive for homogeneity, which frequently leads to the exclusion and persecution of people perceived to be incompatible with this national sameness, as the Greeks of Turkey found out to their great cost. It is, nevertheless, important to recognise that this homogeneity is itself constructed and illusory, and in practice the success of nationalism is premised on the incorporation as well as the rejection of local particularity, and on the culturally intimate space (Herzfeld 1997) where dissent can occur *through*, rather than in opposition to, national categories and symbols. This is crucial for our understanding of the resilience and continuing salience of nationhood, and how it becomes meaningful in people's lives: what would otherwise be abstract national concepts are invested with local and personal meanings, to the extent that local agents can see themselves as more authentically national than the representatives of national authority. The Greeks of Turkey demonstrate that there are multiple – though not infinite – local pathways to national belonging.

Excavating and backfilling the past

Greeks without Greece has exemplified Macdonald's characterisation of past presencing (2013) as a two-way process that, to adopt an archaeological metaphor used in Chapter 6, involves first the *excavation* of the past and then its *backfilling* with the present. In this way, although the past is once again brought into view, it is not transported into the present unchanged, but, to borrow terms from Cubitt, is rather 'annexe[d . . .] to a present social conception' (2007:17). Whilst memories certainly travel – and often do so across as well as within national and cultural boundaries – it is often the form more than the content that moves, which may result in *off-the-peg memories* that have more to do with the self in the present than others in the past, and may be limited in their capacity to transform or revise ideas and identities. Those expatriate activists who have recourse to abstracted motifs borrowed from the histories of other communities typically do so precisely when they feel the need to articulate more forcefully and recognisably their own grievances towards Turkey, and then in fairly invariant and interchangeable forms. Although this confirms that memories – often thought of as being aligned with particular groups of people or rooted in certain temporal or spatial contexts – frequently migrate and interact with one another, we should be cautious about interpreting such references to other times, places, and people as necessarily reflecting complex and deep-rooted mnemonic entanglements that might significantly impact upon people's understandings of self, others, and history in local and everyday contexts. Likewise, through its commemoration by expatriate organisations and its placing alongside the *Septemvrianá*, the Fall of Constantinople is granted renewed visibility and significance in the present, and at his statue in Metropolitan Square the last Byzantine emperor receives eulogies over 500 years after his death. In the process, however, the events of 1453 may be subsumed within those of 1955, losing their historical complexity and becoming part of a diachronic conflict between Greeks and Turks, national entities that did not even exist in their present form when the walls of Constantinople were breached and Palaiologos fell.

We might refer to this as a kind of *façadisme*, a term I adapt from David Jordan's discussion of attempts to modernise Parisian architecture whilst preserving the aesthetic quality of the Haussmann era. *Façadisme* refers to the gutting and renovation of a building from the inside, in theory without tampering with its outside appearance. Jordan is sceptical about these efforts, writing that the buildings are in essence destroyed rather than protected, losing their overall 'architectural integrity' whilst at the same time

> important features on the outside are destroyed: old windows are replaced, a garage door is added where originally there were shops, the passage from street to courtyard is sealed. The skeleton, with some of the bones missing, is all that remains to testify to the past.
>
> (2004:112)

By the same token, pasts brought into the present undergo a process of historical *façadisme*: their skeleton may remain recognisable, and thereby convey a certain gravitas through the authority of venerability, but their historical content has been gutted and their *façade* altered in the service of present needs and functions.

Yet if the past is thus excavated and hollowed out in the process of being brought into new, contemporary contexts, it does not follow that the past becomes meaningless or vacuous. Instead, put to new usage in the present, events from the past can come to be backfilled with new meaning and, potentially, new personal resonance. In this way, people may come to identify themselves with others from the recent or distant past, potentially leading to transcultural and/or trans-historical solidarities that may in certain contexts even have real-world implications, irrespective of how dependent the solidarities are on historical truncation and elision. The paralleling, for instance, of Greek experience with that of the Armenians and Kurds can generate reciprocal solidarities or even promote reconciliation between erstwhile antagonists, rather than leading inevitably to competitive and acrimonious clashes over the singularity or specificity of victimhood. Likewise, the anniversary of 1453 is marked by the Constantinopolitan

Society not simply as a dispassionate strategy to influence Greek governmental and popular opinion, but with a degree of reverence that reflects the way in which participants might see their own experiences mirrored in the events of the past. The Federation of Constantinopolitans, meanwhile, seeks to imbue the hollowness of 1453 with its own, alternative meaning, presenting Palaiologos and his soldiers as defenders of a broader Christian and Helleno-Roman civilisation in order to disassociate the Fall – and, by extension, the contemporary *Polítes* – from the *longue durée* of Greek–Turkish relationships. Past presencing, from this point of view, is often a question of personalising the past, which involves not only making the past intelligible and expedient in the present, but also investing something of ourselves in the past; and, in the process, perhaps repairing the fracture between *façade* and content.

Everyday multidirectionality

Greeks without Greece has sought to demonstrate not only the shortcomings of a methodological nationalism that reflexively places the nation at the centre of scholarly analyses of identity and memory, but also the potential pitfalls of approaches that, in a laudable effort to evade this national(ist) analytical lens, run the risk of exclusively locating heterogeneity and complexity *between* and *beyond* rather than *within* established categories. My findings do not necessarily call into question the salience of ethnicity and nationhood as prominent paradigms through which the Greeks of Turkey orientate their identities and memories. For many of those with whom I spoke and whose writings I read, these categories form something of a conceptual and explanatory horizon within which their life experiences are habitually plotted and made meaningful; and whilst I did encounter individuals who felt that their experiences and origins in some way place them betwixt Greek and Turkish identities, most of my interviewees articulated a sense of self that does not explicitly transgress the Helleno-Romaic dichotomy. What my discussion does suggest, however, is that there is greater room for manoeuvre *within* these horizons than is sometimes supposed, and that ethnicity and nationhood can be reworked and re-tasked by 'ordinary people' in order to express a fairly diverse range of discursive positions, some of which may be partially or wholly at odds with the identities or histories formally proliferated by the organs of the state. Nationhood, like memory, is multidirectional, and our analyses should pay attention to the different and mutable ways in which it becomes significant (or otherwise) in diverse local contexts.

This is not to undermine, however, the critical contribution of studies that explicitly hone in on actions, discourses, or people that transgress or muddy the interface between familiar categories and groups. On the contrary, I suggest that we adopt the conceptual arsenal offered by these studies to interrogate the dynamics of memory and identity 'within' *as well as* 'between and beyond' (with the ultimate aim, perhaps, of dissolving these very distinctions). In this book, we have seen that the idealised 'either/or' of nationalist rhetoric frequently translates in practice into a more variegated 'both/and' (though certainly not '/and everything'). Studying the expatriated Greeks of Turkey from this standpoint means avoiding the assumption that they must either see themselves as unambiguously and simplistically Greek or transcend ethnic and national identifications through stronger attachment to a particular locality. Rather, in cases like this an increasing sensitivity to multiplicity, experimentation, and 'as-well-as' thinking (Beck 2008:31) can lead us to a fuller understanding of the complexity of nationalism itself. In turn, we can offer not only a more realistic appraisal of nationalism's strengths, but also, by belying claims to fixity and homogeneity, its limitations and contradictions.

Likewise, memory studies and related fields have been driven in important new directions in recent years by scholars who have posited more dynamic, interconnected, and transcultural understandings of social memory and its relationship to group identity, and have even suggested that these perspectives might herald novel, post-national, and/or more morally productive ways for people to understand the past (and the present). This book has suggested that ethnographic and historical research can make an important contribution to this analytical paradigm shift, by proffering an *everyday history of multidirectional memory* that more systematically considers how these theoretical models – developed in large part through reference to macro-level socio-historical processes, and literary or mass-mediated representations of the past – might apply to the study of particular local communities in particular historical contexts. In *Greeks without Greece*, this approach has led to the recognition that the mobility of memory and the dynamic interplay between spatially and temporally distant moments highlighted in recent scholarship applies equally to the construction and reconfiguration of the past *within* nation-states, and not just to memories that conspicuously traverse artificial national, cultural, or social boundaries (themselves often erected through the multidirectional memory work of nation-builders who equated contemporary communities with those of the distant past). Furthermore, it has shown that transcultural cross-referencing may frequently reinforce existing national(ist) understandings of the past rather than encouraging new and more ethical or cosmopolitan histories, and perpetuate negative representations of a shared antagonistic other in spite of (or, in this case, perhaps because of) its capacity to simultaneously facilitate intercommunal solidarities between different groups of victims. The everyday history of multidirectional memory should thus not focus solely on memories that happen to cross artificial social or cultural borders, but rather begin by recognising that the multidirectional dynamics of memory might be as complicit in the maintenance of national boundaries as they are necessary for their tearing down.

References

(Items marked * are in the Greek language.)

Beck, U. (2008). Mobility and the cosmopolitan perspective. In W. Canzler, V. Kaufmann, and S. Kesselring (Eds). *Tracing mobilities: towards a cosmopolitan perspective*. Aldershot: Ashgate Publishing, 25–35.

Cubitt, G. (2007). *History and memory*. Manchester: Manchester University Press.
Herzfeld, M. (1997). Cultural intimacy: social poetics in the nation-state. New York: Routledge.
Imvros. (1982). Questions that remain unanswered, December 1982.*
Jordan, D. P. (2004). Haussmann and Haussmannisation: the legacy for Paris. *French Historical Studies*, 27(1), 87–113.
Macdonald, S. (2013). *Memorylands: heritage and identity in Europe today*. London; New York: Routledge.

Appendix
Tables

Table 1 List of interviewees: Polites*

Pseudonym	D.O.B.	Place of birth	Gender	Date of migration	Reason for leaving	Citizenship (in Turkey/present)	Date of Interview
Adamantios	1978	Istanbul (Agios Stéphanos/Yeşilköy)	M	1996	Family reasons	Turkish/Turkish	10/05/13
Alekos	1971	Istanbul (Péra/Beyoğlu)	M	1971	Parents' decision	Turkish/Greek (*1981*)	28/05/13
Alexandra	1947	Istanbul	F	1971	Discrimination/fear	Turkish/Greek	22/07/11
Alexandros	1962	Istanbul (Agios Stéphanos/Yeşilköy)	M	*1978*	Discrimination/economic situation after 1974 Cyprus conflict	Turkish/Greek	11/03/14
Anastasia	1939	Istanbul	F	*1970*	Deteriorating situation after 1964	Turkish/Turkish	05/02/12
Andreas[a]	1943	Chálki/Heybeliada (Princes' Islands)	M	1973	Deteriorating situation (associated with tensions on Cyprus)	Turkish/Greek and Turkish	11/02/12
Anna	1923	Istanbul	F	1937	Education/family left	Greek/Greek	28/11/11
Apostolis	1955	Istanbul (Péra/Beyoğlu)	M	1975	Discrimination (associated with nationalism)	Turkish/Greek (*1986*)	03/02/12
Artemis	1987	Istanbul	F	2005	Studies in Greece	Turkish/Turkish	15/05/13
Dimitris	1956	Chálki/Heybeliada (Princes' Islands)	M	1975	Seeking new experiences	Turkish/Greek (Turkish pending)	30/11/11
Evangelos	1945	Prínkipos/Büyükada (Princes' Islands)	M	*1963*	Expulsions (indirectly)	Turkish/Greek (*1973*)	08/05/13
Fotini[b]	1943	Istanbul	F	*1973*	Deteriorating situation	Not specified	21/11/11
Fotis	1950	Istanbul (Péra/Beyoğlu)	M	1976	Deteriorating situation/partner left	Turkish/Greek (*1980*)	01/02/12
Gerasimos	*1949*	Istanbul	M	1964	Father expelled as Greek citizen	Turkish/Greek (*1964*)	06/02/12
Ioanna	1944	Istanbul	F	1964	Parents' decision	Turkish/Greek (*1982*)	21/11/11; 23/11/11
Iraklis	1947	Istanbul	M	1964	Father expelled as Greek citizen	Greek/Greek	11/02/12
Konstantinos	1944	Istanbul	M	1959	Father expelled as Greek citizen	Greek and Turkish/Greek	05/02/12

(*continued*)

Table 1 (continued)

Pseudonym	D.O.B.	Place of birth	Gender	Date of migration	Reason for leaving	Citizenship (in Turkey/present)	Date of Interview
Kyriakos	1951	Istanbul	M	1975	Discrimination in employment/partner left	Turkish/Greek (1982)	03/02/12
Lazaros	1948	Prinkipos/Büyükada (Princes' Islands)	M	1964	Father expelled as Greek citizen	Greek and Turkish/Greek	10/05/13
Lefteris	1960	Istanbul (Yedikule)	M	1968	Discrimination/fear	Turkish/Greek	12/05/13
Manos	1941	Istanbul (Şişli)	M	1972	Deteriorating situation/friends left	Turkish/Turkish	05/02/12
Maria	1959	Prinkipos/Büyükada (Princes' Islands)	F	1971[c]	Fear	Turkish/Greek and Turkish	09/05/13
Marios	1941	Istanbul	M	1966	Fear/friends left	Turkish/Greek (1980)	29/01/12
Menelaos	1946	Istanbul (Skoutári/Üsküdar)	M	1989	Deteriorating situation	Turkish/Turkish	06/02/12
Michalis	1940	Istanbul (Péra/Beyoğlu)	M	1971	Deteriorating situation	Turkish/Greek	29/01/12
Milena	1950	Istanbul (Şişli)	F	1964	Deteriorating situation	Turkish/Greek (1972)	30/11/11
Mitsos	1976	Istanbul	M	1982	Parents' decision	Turkish/Greek	06/06/13
Nikolaos	1939	Istanbul	M	1964	Relatives left	Turkish/Greek (1982)	30/01/12
Panagiotis	1946	Istanbul (Péra/Beyoğlu)	M	1963	Deteriorating situation	Turkish/Greek and Turkish (2011)	24/11/11
Petros	1946	Istanbul (Péra/Beyoğlu)	M	1964	Deteriorating situation/reached age for military service	Turkish/Greek (1985)	26/11/11
Rita[b]	1948	Istanbul (Péra/Beyoğlu)	F	1976	Deteriorating situation	Turkish and Greek/not specified	21/11/11
Sofia[a]	1955	Istanbul (Péra/Beyoğlu)	F	1975	Not specified	Turkish/Turkish	11/02/12

Sotiris	1946	Istanbul	M	1970	Love (*érotas*)	Turkish	08/02/12
Spyros	1930	Istanbul (Chalkidóna/ Kadıköy)	M	1964	Fear/partner left	Turkish/Greek (*1971*)	02/12/11
Stavros	1947	Istanbul (Yedikule)	M	1963	Discrimination	Turkish/Greek (*1974*)	29/11/11
Stefanos	1950	Istanbul (Péra/Beyoğlu)	M	1964	Parents' decision	Turkish/Greek (1982)	01/12/11
Tasos	1949	Istanbul	M	1964	Father expelled as Greek citizen	Greek and Turkish/ Greek	13/03/14
Tasoula	*1953*	Istanbul (Péra/Beyoğlu)	F	1964	Parents' decision	Turkish/Greek (*1980*)	27/11/11
Thanasis	1953	Istanbul	M	1971	Discrimination	Turkish/Greek (1981)	06/02/12
Theodora	1967	Istanbul (Péra/Beyoğlu)	F	1971	Parents' decision	Turkish/Greek	19/04/12
Theodoros	1951	Istanbul	M	1973[d]	Studies abroad/threat to family home	Turkish/Greek	07/02/12
Tomas	1928	Istanbul (Yedikule)	M	1964	Deteriorating situation	Turkish/not specified	21/11/11
Vangelis	1934	Istanbul	M	1980	Declining minority population/ partner wanted to leave	Turkish/Greek (1981) and Turkish	03/02/12
Thekla	1950	Istanbul (Yedikule)	F	1977	Not specified	Turkish/Greek (1992)	21/08/12

* Dates in *italics* are approximate. [a] Interviewed together. [b] Interviewed together. [c] 1971 (school in Greece); 1975 (as a family). [d] 1973 (studies in England); 1976 (to Greece).

Table 2 List of interviewees: *Imvriótes**

Pseudonym	D.O.B.	Place of birth	Gender	Date of migration	Reason for leaving	Citizenship (in Turkey/present)	Date of Interview
Amarillis[b]	1934	Imbros (Schoinoúdi)	M	1963	Declining minority population	Turkish/Greek	21/05/13
Antigoni	1975	Imbros (Schoinoúdi)	F	1983	Discrimination	Not specified	13/08/13
Antonis	1941	Istanbul	M	1964 – 1974 (Australia)	Deteriorating situation	Not specified	10/08/13
Argyris[a]	1927	Imbros (Agios Theódoros)	M	1984	Son taken ill in Greece	Turkish/not specified	08/08/13
Aris	1941	Imbros	M	1969	Declining minority population/discrimination	Turkish/Greek and not specified	23/05/13
Babis	1951	Imbros (Agrídia)	M	1970 (Australia)	Not specified	Not specified	12/08/13
Christos	1958	Imbros (Agios Theódoros)	M	1977	Deteriorating situation/lack of Greek language education	Turkish/Greek (1988) and Turkish (2012)	08/08/13
Damon	1936	Imbros (Agrídia)	M	1975	Deteriorating situation	Not specified	08/08/13
Despoina[c]	1926	Imbros (Agios Theódoros)	F	1966 (Istanbul); 1970 (Greece)	Lack of Greek language education	Turkish/not specified	12/08/13
Dimitra	1939	Imbros (Agrídia)	F	1974 (Istanbul); 1982 (Greece)	Lack of Greek language education	Turkish/not specified	09/08/13
Dimosthenis	1943	Istanbul	M	1949 (Istanbul); 1972 (Greece)	Discrimination	Turkish/Greek and Turkish	06/06/13
Eleni	1968	Imbros (Agrídia)	F	1973	Lack of Greek language education	Turkish/Greek (*1982*) and Turkish	04/06/13
Evangelia[d]	1933	Imbros (Agrídia)	F	1966	Lack of Greek language education	Turkish/Greek (by 1983) and Turkish	12/08/13
Fani	1958	Imbros	F	*1964* (Istanbul); 1971 (Greece)	Discrimination	Turkish/Greek and Turkish	07/06/13
Fokas	*1964*	Imbros (Agrídia)	M	*1964* (Istanbul); 1975 (Greece)	Discrimination	Turkish/not specified	13/08/13

Name	Year	Origin	Sex	Departure (place); arrival	Reason	Language	Interview date
Giorgos	*1965*	Imbros	M	Not specified	Not specified	Not specified	14/08/13
Ilias	1923	Imbros (Glyký)	M	1965	Discrimination	Turkish/Greek and Turkish	21/05/13
Katerina	1939	Imbros (Agrídia)	F	Never left	n/a	Not specified (Turkish)	06/08/13
Kleopas	1941	Imbros (Agios Theódoros)	M	1966 (Central Africa); 1979 (Greece)	Not specified	Turkish/not specified	09/08/13
Kostas	1963	Imbros (Agrídia)	M	1981	Studies in Greece	Turkish/Greek (1987)	07/06/13
Kyriakí[e]	*1960*	Imbros (Agrídia)	F	1966 (Istanbul); 1970 (Greece)	Lack of Greek language education	Turkish/not specified	12/08/13
Leonidas	1937	Imbros (Agios Theódoros)	M	1977 (Ismir)	Discrimination	Turkish/Turkish	08/08/13
Loukas	1967	Istanbul	M	1992	Finished university/work	Turkish/Greek (1999) and Turkish	08/05/13
Markos	1953	Imbros	M	1964 (Istanbul); 1967 (America)	Discrimination	Turkish/American (*1972*)	04/05/13
Miltos	1944	Imbros (Agrídia)	M	1969	Not specified	Turkish/Greek and Turkish	06/08/13
Mimis	1955	Istanbul	M	1981	Not specified	Turkish/not specified	13/08/13
Minos	1933	Imbros (Schoinoúdi)	M	1964 (Istanbul)	Discrimination	Turkish/Turkish	13/08/13
Mirela	1947	Imbros	F	1973	Lack of Greek language education	Turkish/Greek (*1982*) and Turkish	10/05/13
Orestis	1934	Imbros (Agrídia)	M	1948 (Istanbul); 1968 (Greece)	Employment came to an end	Turkish/not specified	06/08/2013
Panagiota	1927	Imbros (Panagia)	F	1980	Discrimination	Turkish/not specified	07/08/13
Pantelis	1959	Imbros (Panagia)	M	1977	Studies in Greece	Turkish/Greek (1988) and not specified	27/05/13
Pavlos	1970	Imbros (Agios Theódoros)	M	1975 (Istanbul); 1987 (Greece)	Lack of Greek language education (1975)/discrimination (1987)	Turkish/Greek and Turkish	29/05/13

(continued)

Table 2 *(continued)*

Pseudonym	D.O.B.	Place of birth	Gender	Date of migration	Reason for leaving	Citizenship (in Turkey/present)	Date of Interview
Petroklos	1919	Imbros (Agios Theódoros)	M	Never left	n/a	Turkish/Turkish	08/08/13
Pyrros	1961	Imbros (Agios Theódoros)	M	*1974*	Not specified	Turkish/Greek (*1982*)	21/05/13
Sakis	1930	Imbros (Schoinoúdi)	M	1946 (Istanbul)	Not specified	Not specified (Turkish)	10/08/13
Savvas	*1960*	Imbros (Agridia)	M	1974	Discrimination/lack of Greek language education	Turkish/Greek (1988)	14/08/13
Sokratis	*1940s*	Imbros	M	1974	Not specified	Turkish/Greek (*1984*) and Turkish	30/05/13
Stamatios	1945	Imbros (Agridia)	M	1963	Studies in Greece	Turkish/not specified	07/08/13
Stelios	1958	Imbros (Schoinoúdi)	M	1970	Deteriorating situation/lack of Greek language education	Turkish/none (Greek pending)	27/05/13
Themis	1944	Imbros (Agridia)	M	1966	Discrimination	Turkish/not specified	11/08/13
Tryfon[b]	1929	Imbros (Agios Theódoros)	M	After 1964	Deteriorating situation	Turkish/Turkish	21/05/13
Vasia[a]	*1930*	Imbros (Agios Theódoros)	F	*1984*	Son taken ill in Greece	Turkish/not specified	08/08/13
Vasilis	1938	Imbros	M	1961 (Germany); 1980 (Greece)	Expropriations of land	Turkish/Greek (*1980s*) and Turkish	12/08/13
Voula[d]	*1955*	Imbros (Agridia)	F	1966	Lack of Greek language education	Turkish/Greek (1983) and Turkish	12/08/13
Zacharias	1957	Imbros	M	1966 (Istanbul); 1977 (Greece)	Lack of Greek language education (1966)/military service (1977)	Turkish/Greek (*1988*)	03/06/13
Zoe	1957	Istanbul	F	1975	Felt oppression from all directions	Not specified	07/06/13

* Dates in *italics* are approximate. [a] Interviewed together. [b] Interviewed together. [c] Interviewed together. [d] Interviewed together.

Table 2 List of interviewees: *Imvriótes* (continued)*

Pseudonym	First return	Current frequency of return
Amarillis[b]	Not specified	Not specified
Antigoni	1990	Seasonal
Antonis	*1989–1999*	Permanent resident
Argyris[a]	*1990s*	Permanent resident
Aris	*1999*	Not specified
Babis	1992	Six months of the year
Christos	1988	Permanent resident (since 2011)
Damon	Immediately	Nine months of the year
Despoina[c]	2002	Six months of the year
Dimitra	*1987*	Six months of the year (or more)
Dimosthenis	Not specified	Seasonal
Eleni	2001	Seasonal
Evangelia[d]	(1972) 2000	Seasonal
Fani	1987	Seasonal
Fokas	1988	Permanent resident
Giorgos	1991	Seasonal
Ilias	Immediately	Seasonal
Katerina	n/a	n/a
Kleopas	*1990*	Six months of the year
Kostas	1989	Seasonal
Kyriaki[c]	After 2002	Seasonal
Leonidas	n/a	Ten months of the year
Loukas	*mid 1990s*	Seasonal
Markos	*1990*	Seasonal
Miltos	1989	Permanent resident
Mimis	2011	Permanent resident
Minos	Immediately (never left Turkey)	Ten months of the year (since 2000)
Mirela	1991	Seasonal (until 2009)
Orestis	1995	Six months of the year
Panagiota	Immediately	Seasonal
Pantelis	1989	Seasonal
Pavlos	1987	Seasonal
Petroklos	n/a	n/a
Pyrros	1993	Not specified
Sakis	1982	Permanent resident
Savvas	1988	Not specified
Sokratis	*2001*	Infrequently, if ever
Stamatios	1989	Six months of the year
Stelios	Never	Never
Themis	(1969, 1973, 1975) 1996	Six months of the year (since 2000)
Tryfon[b]	Not specified	Not specified
Vasia[a]	1990s	Permanent resident
Vasilis	1993	Six months of the year
Voula[d]	(1972) 2000	Seasonal
Zacharias	*1988*	Seasonal
Zoe	Not specified	Not specified

* Dates in *italics* are approximate. [a] Interviewed together. [b] Interviewed together. [c] Interviewed together. [d] Interviewed together.

Table 3 List of interviewees: second generation*

Pseudonym	D.O.B.	Place of birth	Descent	Gender	Frequency of visits to Turkey	Citizenship	Date of Interview
Christina[a]	1985	Greece (Athens)	Imbros (mother)	F	Periodic	Greek	07/06/13
Efthemis	1971	USA	Istanbul (both parents)	M	Not specified	Not specified	10/05/13
Eleni[b]	1991	Greece (Athens)	Imbros (mother)	F	Seasonal	Greek	15/08/13
Eva	*1991*	Greece (Athens)	Imbros (mother) Princes' Islands (father)	F	Seasonal	Greek	13/08/13
Filipos[b]	1993	Greece (Athens)	Imbros (mother)	M	Seasonal	Greek	15/08/13
Kosmas	1986	Greece (Athens)	Istanbul (both parents)	M	Seasonal	Greek and Turkish	04/06/13
Lakis	1987	Greece (Athens)	Imbros (both parents)	M	Seasonal	Greek	31/05/13
Lampros	1986	Greece (Athens)	Istanbul (both parents)	M	Once (at least)	Greek	30/05/13
Lia	1991	Greece (Athens)	Imbros (mother)	F	Seasonal	Greek	13/08/13
Maximos	1999	Greece	Imbros (both parents)	M	Never	Turkish	06/06/13
Militiadis	1986	Greece	Imbros (mother)	M	Seasonal	Greek	06/06/13
Natasha	1987	Greece	Imbros (father)	F	Periodic	Greek	07/06/13
Paris	*1951*	Greece (Athens)	Istanbul (father)	M	Not specified	Greek	01/02/12
Paschalis[a]	1976	Greece	Imbros (both parents)	M	Never	Turkish	07/06/13
Takis[b]	1993	Greece	Imbros (both parents)	M	Seasonal	Greek	15/08/13
Vyron	1985	Greece (Athens)	Istanbul (both parents)	M	Once	Greek	06/06/13
Yiannis	1996	Greece (Thessaloniki)	Imbros (mother)	M	Seasonal	Greek	15/08/13

* Dates in *italics* are approximate. [a] Interviewed together. [b] Interviewed together.

Table 4 Decline in Greek-speaking/Orthodox Christian populations of Istanbul and Imbros

Date	Istanbul	Imbros	Source
1927	100,214 (Orthodox Christians); 91,902 (Greek as mother tongue)[a]	4469 (Orthodox Christians); 7938 (Greek as mother tongue) in Çanakkale province	Turkish census (Alexandris 1992:142; Tsilenus no date)
		6762	(Alexandris 2004:120)
1935	95,956 (Orthodox Christians); 79,920 (Greek as mother tongue)	7133 (Orthodox Christians); 7590 (Greek as mother tongue) in Çanakkale province	Turkish census (Tsilenus no date)
1945	76,844 (Orthodox Christians); 69,780 (Greek as mother tongue)	6962 (Orthodox Christians); 7082 (Greek as mother tongue) in Çanakkale province	Turkish census (Tsilenus no date)
1950	Not applicable	6100 Greeks, 200 Turks	Imvrian Association (Imvrian Association 2002:14)
1955	67,550 (Orthodox Christians); 65,108 (Greek as mother tongue)	6613 (Orthodox Christians); 6733 (Greek as mother tongue) in Çanakkale province	Turkish census (Tsilenus no date)
1960	68,118 (Orthodox Christians); 49,081 (Greek as mother tongue)	4163 (Orthodox Christians); 4203 (Greek as mother tongue) in Çanakkale province	Turkish census (Tsilenus no date)
		5487 Greeks, 289 Turks on Imbros	Imvrian Association (Imvrian Association 2002:14)

(continued)

Table 4 (continued)

Date	Istanbul	Imbros	Source
1965	47,207 (Orthodox Christians); 35,097 (Greek as mother tongue)	5221 (Orthodox Christians); 5258 (Greek as mother tongue) in Çanakkale province	Turkish census (Tsilenus no date)
1970	c.15,000	2622	*Istanbul*: Estimate by Ecumenical Federation of Constantinopolitans (Turan *et al.* 2010:244) *Imbros*: figure given by Greek mayor on Imbros (Alexandris 1980:26–28)
		2571 Greeks, 4020 Turks	Imvrian Association (Imvrian Association 2002:14)
1975	<10,000	Not applicable	(Alexandris 2004:119)
1985	Not applicable	496 Greeks, 7114 Turks	Imvrian Association (Imvrian Association 2002:14)
1990s	c. 2500–5000	c. 330	*Istanbul*: Estimates by expatriate organisations (Helsinki Watch 1992:7, 29; Turan *et al.* 2010:244) *Imbros*: (Alexandris 2004:119–120)
2000s	c. 3000–4000	c. 200	*Istanbul*: Estimates by expatriate organisations (Constantinopolitan Society 2009:7; Turan *et al.* 2010:244) *Imbros*: Turkish census (Babül 2006:50)

[a]Alexandris adds 26,419 Greek citizens to these figures (1992:142).

Glossary

Elladítis (m.)/*Elladítissa* (f.)/*Elladítes* (pl.)   Greek(s) of Greece.

éthnos   Usually translated as 'nation', though might also be translated as 'people' (Just 1989:72–73). It is important to note that the *éthnos* is conceptually distinct from the *krátos* (state).

expatriates/expatriated Greeks of Turkey   Orthodox Christians from Istanbul and Imbros, exempted from the 1923 population exchange between Greece and Turkey, who left Turkey and resettled primarily in Greece.

expellees   Greek citizens expelled from Turkey in 1964.

Greek refugees   Orthodox Christian forcibly removed from Turkey and relocated to Greece as a result of the Convention Concerning the Exchange of Greek and Turkish Populations agreed upon by Greece and Turkey in 1923.

Hellene (m.)/Hellene (f.)/Hellenes (pl.)/Hellenism (noun)/Hellenic (adj.)   Translations of the Greek words *Éllinas* (m.)/*Ellinída* (f.)/*Éllines* (pl.)/*ellinismós* (noun)/*ellinikós* (adj.). Sometimes used by the Greeks of Turkey to refer collectively to all Greeks, and sometimes used specifically to designate the Greeks of Greece, or those in possession of Greek citizenship.

Imvriótis (m.)/*Imvriótissa* (f.)/*Imvriótes* (pl.)/**Imvrian** (adj.)   Greek(s) of Imbros.

omogéneia (noun)/*omogeneís* (adj.)   Literally 'homogeneity' or 'homogenous', these terms are typically used to refer to individuals of Greek descent born or living outside Greece.

native Greeks   Translation of the Greek *dópioi Éllines*, commonly used to distinguish Greeks born in the Greek state from the *omogéneia*, i.e. those of Greek descent born outside Greece (and their descendants). Amongst my interviewees, the term is sometimes used to differentiate Greeks with roots in Greece from those with roots outside Greece (including the Greek refugees and their descendants), and sometimes more generally to refer to all of the Greeks of Greece whom the expatriates encountered when they relocated from Turkey.

Polítis (m.)/*Polítissa* (f.)/*Polítes* (pl.)/**Constantinopolitan** (adj.)   Greek(s) of Istanbul.

Romiós (m.)/*Romiá* (f.)/*Romioí* (pl.)/*romiosýni* (noun)/**Romaic** (adj.)   Sometimes used to refer to all modern Greeks, and sometimes used specifically to designate the Greeks of the Ottoman Empire and/or the Greeks of Turkey.

References

(Items marked * are in the Greek language.)

Alexandris, A. (1980). Imbros and Tenedos: a study of Turkish attitudes toward two ethnic Greek island communities since 1923. *Journal of the Hellenic Diaspora*, 7(1), 5–31.

Alexandris, A. (1992). *The Greek minority of Istanbul and Greek–Turkish relations, 1918–1974*. Athens: Centre for Asia Minor Studies.

Alexandris, A. (2004). Religion or ethnicity: the identity issue of the minorities in Greece and Turkey. In R. Hirschon (Ed.). *Crossing the Aegean: an appraisal of the 1923 compulsory population exchange between Greece and Turkey*. New York: Berghahn Books, 117–132.

Babül, E. (2006). Claiming a place through memories of belonging: politics of recognition on the island of Imbros. *New Perspectives on Turkey*, 34, 47–65.

Constantinopolitan Society. (2009). *The violations of the human rights of the Greek minority in Turkey: atrocities and persecutions 1923–2009*. Athens: Constantinopolitan Society.

Helsinki Watch. (1992). *Denying human rights and ethnic identity: the Greeks of Turkey*. New York; Washington; Los Angeles; London: Human Rights Watch.

Imvrian Association (2002). *The Imvrian question in the Greek Parliament*. Athens: Imvrian Association.*

Just, R. (1989). Triumph of the ethnos. In E. Tonkin, M. McDonald, and M. Chapman (Eds). *History and ethnicity*. London; New York: Routledge, 71–88.

Tsilenus, S. (no date). The Orthodox Christian minority in the official statistics of contemporary Turkey and in urban space. Available at: www.demography-lab.prd.uth.gr/DDAoG/article/cont/ergasies/tsilenis.htm [Accessed on 1 November 2017].*

Turan, Ç., Pekin, M., and Güvenç, S. (2010). *Constantinople/Istanbul, my nostalgia: refugee narratives and the nostalgia of the Romioí of Constantinople/Istanbul*. Istanbul: Lozan Mübadilleri Vakfı. [In Greek and Turkish].

Index

15 August festival *see* festival for the Assumption of the Virgin Mary
300 *see* Spartans: last stand of
9/11 *see* September 11 attacks

Aegean Sea: Greek-Turkish disputes over 139–140, 146, 165, 181
Ágios Theódoros 29, 203–204, 208–209, 212, 214, 216–217
Agrídia 29–30, 198, 203–204, 207, 210, 210–211, *212*, 216, 219, 221
Alexander the Great 52, 165
Algerian War of Independence (1954–1962) 119 *see also* decolonisation
Aliens' Bureau 24, 36, 90, 102–103
Ancient Greece 165, 167; and expatriate identity 65–66, 69, 71, 76–80, 83, 230; in Greek historiography/nationalism 49–51, 63–64, 141
Antigóni 21
Archbishop Iakovos of America 149, 202
Armenian genocide (1915) 99, 153, 165–169, 172, 178–180, 182–187
Armenian National Committee of Greece 183
Armenians 21, 24, 92, 99–100, 165–170, 178–179, 182–189, 234; massacres of 176 *see also* Armenian genocide
Armenian Secret Army for the Liberation of Armenia 165
Asia Minor 165, 167, 184; Greek defeat in 17–18, 64, 135, 140, 145, 178; Greeks of 35, 59, 180, 183
Association of Hellenic Citizens Expelled from Turkey 12, 31–32, 138–139, 166
Atatürk, Mustafa Kemal 19–20, 178, 180

Bademli köyü see Glyký
Bosnian War *see* Yugoslav Wars
Burgazada see Antigóni
Büyükada see Prínkipos
Byzantium 59, 63, 154, 165, 167; claimed as a heritage by the Greeks of Istanbul *31–32*, 67, 69–73, 77–78, 83, 140–142, *143*, 148–151, 155–156, 230–231; in Greek historiography/nationalism 50, 62–64

cadastral survey (on Imbros) 207
Chálki 21, 23, 92
Çınarlı see Panagía Baloméni
Citizen, speak Turkish! campaign 19, 22–23, 174
citizenship 79, 83 *see also* Greek citizenship; Turkish citizenship
clientelism *see* corruption
colonialism 119, 124 *see also* decolonisation
Constantine Palaiologos: commemoration of 141–144, 154, 234–235; dietary habits of 3; last stand of 146–148, 151
Constantinopolitan Society: activism by 103–104, 149–151, 166–167, 170, 176, 184–185, 231; anniversary events organised by 138–147, 153–155; differences in approach compared with other expatriate organisations 32, 151–155; foundation and purpose of 30–31
Constantinopolitan Union 31 *see also* Association of Hellenic Citizens Expelled from Turkey; New Circle of Constantinopolitans
Colonels' Regime (1967–1974) *see* Greek military junta

Convention Concerning the Exchange of Greek and Turkish Populations (1923) *see* Greek-Turkish population exchange
Convention of Establishment, Commerce and Navigation (1930) 19, 23
corruption 107–108
cosmopolitanism 4, 35, 72–74, 83, 103, 105, 230, 236 *see also* cosmopolitan memory
cosmopolitan memory 120–121, 126, 164, 169
Crete 48–49, 54, 99–100
cultural intimacy 9, 54, 233
Cyprus 69, 92–93, 97–98, 127, 136, 176, 181; 1974 conflict on 23, 28, 36, 53, 70, 102, 137–138, 145, 149–151, 155–157, 166–167, 169, 172, 183–184, 186, 231; Greek-Turkish tensions over 20, 22–23, 27, 101, 139–140; independence of 22, 166
'Cyprus is Turkish' Association 20

Davos process 140, 184, 202, 206
decolonisation 121–122, 127
Dereköy see Schoinoúdi
diaspora 4, 118; Armenian/Kurdish 165, 183–184; Greeks of Turkey as 59–62, 73, 83; and return 198, 223
digital media 123, 179, 181
dópioi see native Greeks

Eastern Roman Empire *see* Byzantium
Ecumenical Federation of Constantinopolitans: activism by 157, 170–172, 187, 235; anniversary events organised by 147, 151–155; differences in approach compared with the Constantinopolitan Society 32, 151–155; foundation and purpose of 32
Ecumenical Patriarchate of Constantinople 20, 23, 32, 145, 152, 209
Ecumenical Patriarch Athenagoras I 20, 171
Ecumenical Patriarch Bartholomew I 203
Ecumenical Patriarch Gregory V 135, 147
ethnic cleansing 127, 153, 167, 171, 176, 179
everyday nationhood 45–46, 235
expulsion of Greek citizens from Turkey 7, 22–23, *24*, 31, 104, 141, 145, 149, 171, 179–181 *see also* Association of Hellenic Citizens Expelled from Turkey; Hellenic Union of Istanbul

Fall of Constantinople (1453) 26; commemorated by the Greeks of Istanbul 103, 140–144, 231; palimpsestically linked to the Greek Revolution 144–148, 154–155, 231; palimpsestically linked to the Istanbul Riots 134–135, 148–151, 153–157, 231–232, 234
Federation of Constantinopolitans *see* Ecumenical Federation of Constantinopolitans
festival for the Assumption of the Virgin Mary 79, 198–199, 201, 216–217, 224n3
financial crisis *see* Greek sovereign debt crisis
First World War 26, 180, 188
food 3, 30, 36, 37n9, 63, 230
football *see* sport
forced labour battalions (1941–1942) 19–20, 26, 149, 176, 178
French Revolution 125

genocide 119–120, 166, 168, 176–179, 182 *see also* Armenian genocide; Holocaust
Gezi Park protests (2013) 82, 108
Glyký 29, 204
Great Famine (Ireland) 119
Greek Armed Forces 105, 142
Greek citizenship 18–19, 46, 64–65, 201; applying for (and Greek state's reluctance to issue) 36, 37n10, 61, 102–103, 202, 230; dual Turkish and 61, 67; rejection of 66–67
Greek language 18, 22–23, 26–28, 34, 63, 71, 74, 101, 178, 208–209
Greek military junta 34, 136
Greek refugees 30, 35, 37n8, 48, 59, 72, 91, 105, 135, 145, 149, 166, 201
Greek Revolution (1821) 63, 134–135, 140–141, 181, 230; palimpsestically linked to the Fall of Constantinople 144–148, 154–155, 231
Greek sovereign debt crisis 10, 84n2, 108
Greek-born generation *see* second generation
Greek-Turkish population exchange 7, 17–18, 26, 30, 99, 166, 173–174, 178, 201
Greek-Turkish War (1919–1922) 17, 26, 165, 180, 184

Hamidian Massacres (1894–1896) *see* Armenians: massacres of
harmony narrative 8, 24, 91–92, 100–101

Index

Hatay annexation 167
Heimat 13, 47–48
Hellenic identity 62–64; expatriate expressions of 64–65, 67–81, 103, 220; expatriate rejection of 65–67
Helleno-Romaic dilemma 62–63, 65, 69–70, 80–81, 235
Hellenic Union of Istanbul 19, 22–23, 31
Heybeliada see Chálki
Holocaust: memory of 118–124, 126–128, 149; expatriate analogies with 169–173, 176–178, 186–188
homeland *see patrída see also* Heimat
Homer 76–79, 146
Horton, George 98
Hugo, Victor-Marie 98

Imvrian Association 12–13, 222; activism by 61, 77–78, 80, 87–88, 102–103, 136–138, 164, 166–168, 170, 173–176, 184, 204, 206–207, 232–233; as a social space 75, 77, 217–218; foundation of 33, 201; involvement in New Imbros 200–202, 225n4; involvement in return movement 198, 203–204, 206–210
Imvrian Union of Macedonia-Thrace 202
inclusive particularity 62, 69–80, 83–84, 229–231
Iraq 167
Islam 93–94, 97, 108, 126
Israel 120, 126
Israeli–Palestinian conflict 119, 121
Istanbul Riots (1955) 20–22, 37n1, 92, 104–105, 110, 135, 174, 183–185; and aid given by Muslims to non-Muslims 21–22, 37n5, 92, 95–96, 98–100, 110, 111n2; commemorated by the Greeks of Istanbul 138–140, 153, 166–167, 170, 231; compared to other histories 170–172, 175–178, 182, 187; memories of 9, 23, 94–100, 178, 180–181; palimpsestically linked to the Fall of Constantinople 134–135, 148–151, 153–157, 231–232, 234

janissaries 165
Jews 21, 24, 50, 92, 119–120, 152, 169–172, 175, 177–178, 182, 185–186, 189

Kaleköy see Kástro
Kalymnos 53, 89–90, 134–135
Kástro 29–30, 204, 214

Kemal, Mustafa *see* Atatürk, Mustafa Kemal
Kemalism 93, 184
Kınalıada see Prótos
Kolokotronis, Theodoros 141, 148
Kosovo War *see* Yugoslav Wars
Kristallnacht 126, 153, 170–172, 176–177, 187
Kurdish-Turkish conflict 166, 168–169, 178–179, 181–182, 186
Kurdistan Workers' Party 165, 182
Kurds 107; as antagonists of the Greeks 97, 185; as friends of the Greeks and fellow victims 98–100,165–169, 172, 178, 181–189, 234; settlers on Imbros 28–30, 214

lost homelands 201, 204, 206–207, 232–233
lost *patrídes see* lost homelands

Macedonia 50–52, 54–55, 90
manners 71, 105–107, 109–110, 232
memory activists 129, 179, 185
methodological nationalism 4–6, 118, 235
military service *see* national service
minority schools 3, 18, 20–21, 24–26, 31, 74, 152; closure on Imbros 27–28, 66, 74, 166; reopening on Imbros 204, 208–209; in Western Thrace 173
multiculturalism 73, 216
multidirectional memory 121–122, 125–129, 134, 157, 172–173, 178, 186–187, 189, 235–236

Nagorno-Karabakh 184
National Liberation Front of Kurdistan 184
national service 24–25, 30–31, 36, 202
Nazism 119, 125, 169–173, 176–178, 186–188 *see also* Holocaust
native Greeks 7, 35, 37n8, 52, 64, 72
New Circle of Constantinopolitans 31–32, 138–139, 166
New Imbros 200–202, 206, 225n4, 232

Öcalan, Abdullah 182–183, 186
off-the-peg memories 188–189, 233
Óhi Day 110, 140, 147
Olympian gods 79
open prisons on Imbros 28–29, 174, 202
O Polítis: activism by 101–103, 140, 145–148, 164–170, 172–176, 182–183, 187; foundation of 12

Orthodox Christianity: and expatriate identity 25, 34–35, 67, 70, 80, 83, 230; and Greek identity generally 7, 50, 63, 154; supposed lack of respect in Greece towards 71, 107
Ottoman Empire 17–18, 26, 50–51, 63–66, 72, 77, 111n4, 165, 169, 184 *see also* Fall of Constantinople; Greek refugees; Greek Revolution
Özal, Halil Turgut 184

Palestine 119, 121
palimpsestic memory 124–125, 134
Panagía Baloméni 29, 204, 210
Papandreou, Andreas 206
past presencing 3, 10, 232–235
patriarchate *see* Ecumenical Patriarchate of Constantinople
patrída: compared to Heimat 48–49; in expatriate narratives 60–61, 65, 67, 70–71, 75, 83, 102, 105, 201, 203, 206–207, 212–215, 221; in narratives of second-generation expatriates 218–223 *see also* lost homelands
Persians 135, 137, 147, 165–166, 231
PKK *see* Kurdistan Workers' Party
politics: expatriate disinterest in 25, 34; and partisanship in Greece 108–109
Pontic Greeks 145, 167–168, 176, 180, 183
postmemory 122, 183–184, 198
Princes' Islands 21, 24–25, 30–31, 92, 197
Prínkipos 21
prosthetic memory 122–123, 185, 189
Prótos 21

rape *see* sexual violence
religion *see* Olympian gods; Orthodox Christianity; Islam
renovation of houses (on Imbros) 203–205, 215
residence permits (Greece) *see* Aliens' Bureau
Romaic identity 62–65; expatriate expressions of 65–67, 69–74, 79–83, 229–230; expatriate rejection of 65, 67–69, 230
Romans 63, 66, 68, 78, 154
Rum 63–64, 66, 68, 79 *see also* Romaic identity
Rwandan genocide 119, 177–178

sacrifice of oxen *see* festival for the Assumption of the Virgin Mary
Schoinoúdi 28–29, 202–205, 207, 209, 214, 222
second generation 33, 93, 170, 198–199, 204, 217–224, 230
Second World War 19, 119, 140, 170 *see also* forced labour battalions (1941–1942); Holocaust; wealth tax (1942–1944)
'seeds of the Turks' 35, 59, 71, 229
September 11 attacks 119, 126
Septemvrianá see Istanbul Riots (1955)
sexual violence 21, 96, 103, 174
Smyrna 59, 180, 183
South America: dictatorships in 119, 127, 169
Spain: Franco's rule of 119, 127, 169
Spartans 77–78; last stand of 135–137, 147, 155, 231–232
sport 25, 59
St Bartholomew's Day Massacre (1572) 149, 175–176
strife narrative 8, 24, 101, 146

Tenedos 14n3, 26, 30, 32, 101, 145, 167, 175–176, 206, 218
Tepeköy see Agrídia
Thrace 139, 145, 170, 181, 201–202 *see also* Turks/Muslims of Western Thrace
tourism: on Imbros 27, 202, 208, 212, 215–217, 224, 224n1; and expatriate returnees feeling like tourists 212–214, 219, 221–222
trade unionism 107–108
Treaty of Lausanne (1923) 17–18, 25–26, 137, 166–167, 173, 175, 208
Trojans 78
Turkish Armed Forces 22, 25, 30, 104–105
Turkish citizenship 18, 23, 64–65; dual Greek and 61, 67; losing or renouncing 36, 202, 207, 230; reclaiming 67, 76, 152, 208, 219–220, 222, 230
Turkish identity: tentative expatriate expressions of 67, 76, 81–83
Turkish language 18, 24, 27, 31, 33–34
Turkish music 81
Turks/Muslims of Western Thrace 18, 20, 190n2; compared to the Greeks of Turkey 68–69, 173–176, 178–179, 187

Index 255

Union of Constantinopolitans of Northern Greece 9, 31, 166
United Nations 153, 166
urbanism 27, 35, 72–74, 83, 93, 105, 208, 221

Varlık Vergisi see wealth tax (1942–1944)
Vatandaş türkçe konuş! see Citizen, speak Turkish! campaign
Venizelos, Eleftherios 19
visas: to enter Greece 28, 102; to go to Imbros 200–201
Vlachs 50–51, 54, 74

wealth tax (1942–1944) 19–20, 26, 149, 170, 174, 178, 180
Western Thracian minority *see* Turks/Muslims of Western Thrace
work permits (Greece) *see* Aliens' Bureau
workmanship 107–108

Yenimahalle see Evlámpio
Yugoslav Wars 119–120, 127, 176

Zeytinli köyü see Ágios Theódoros